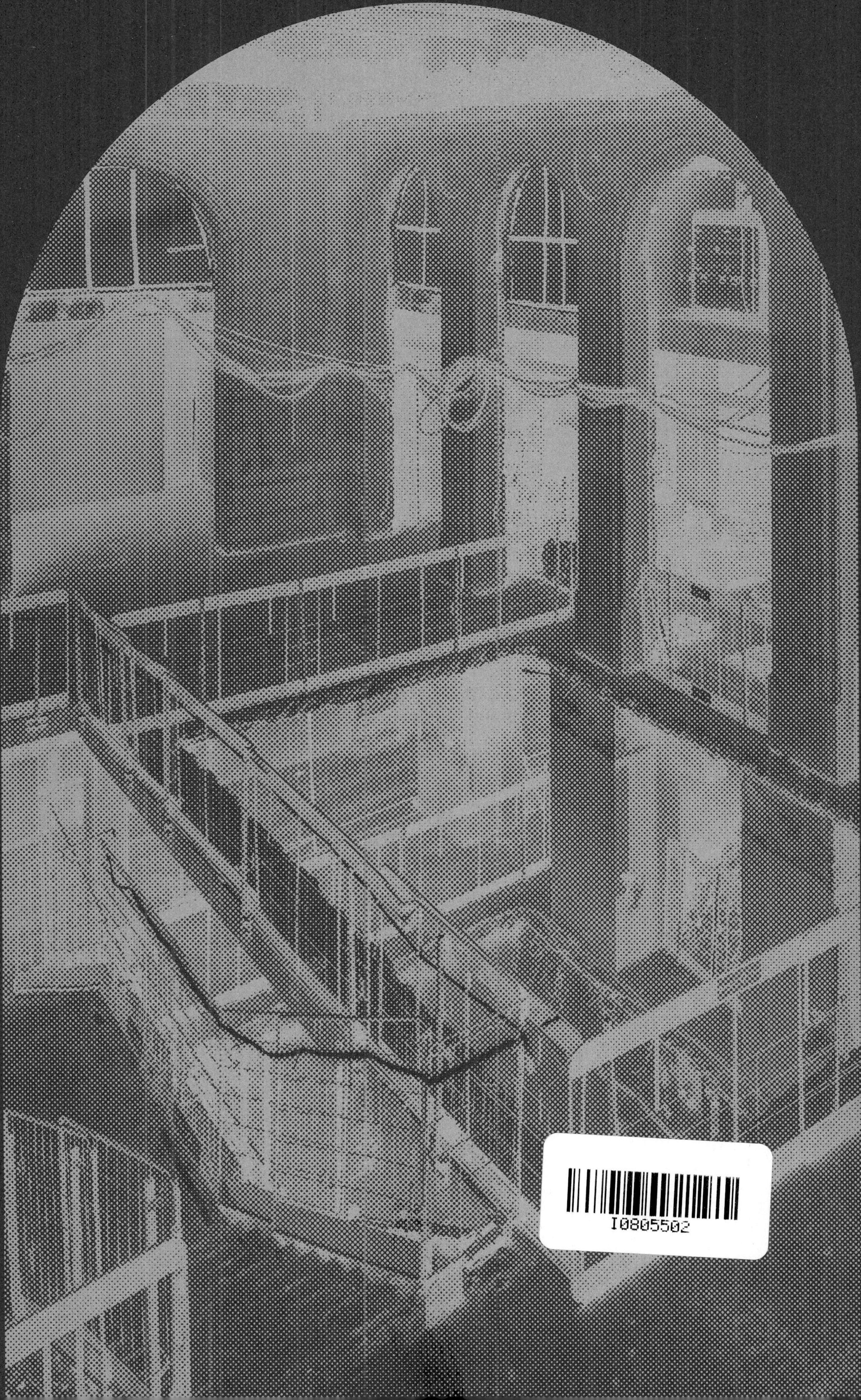

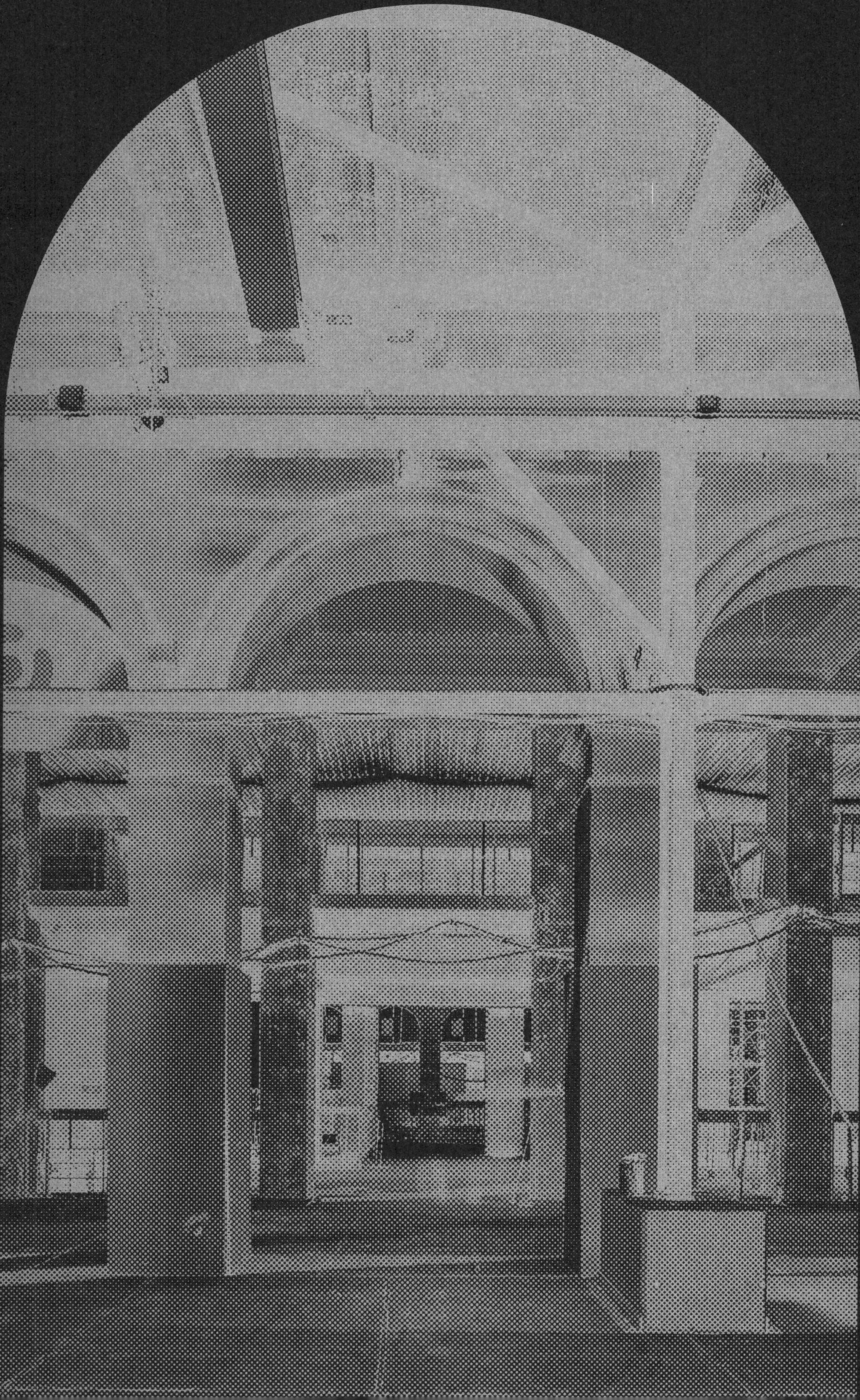

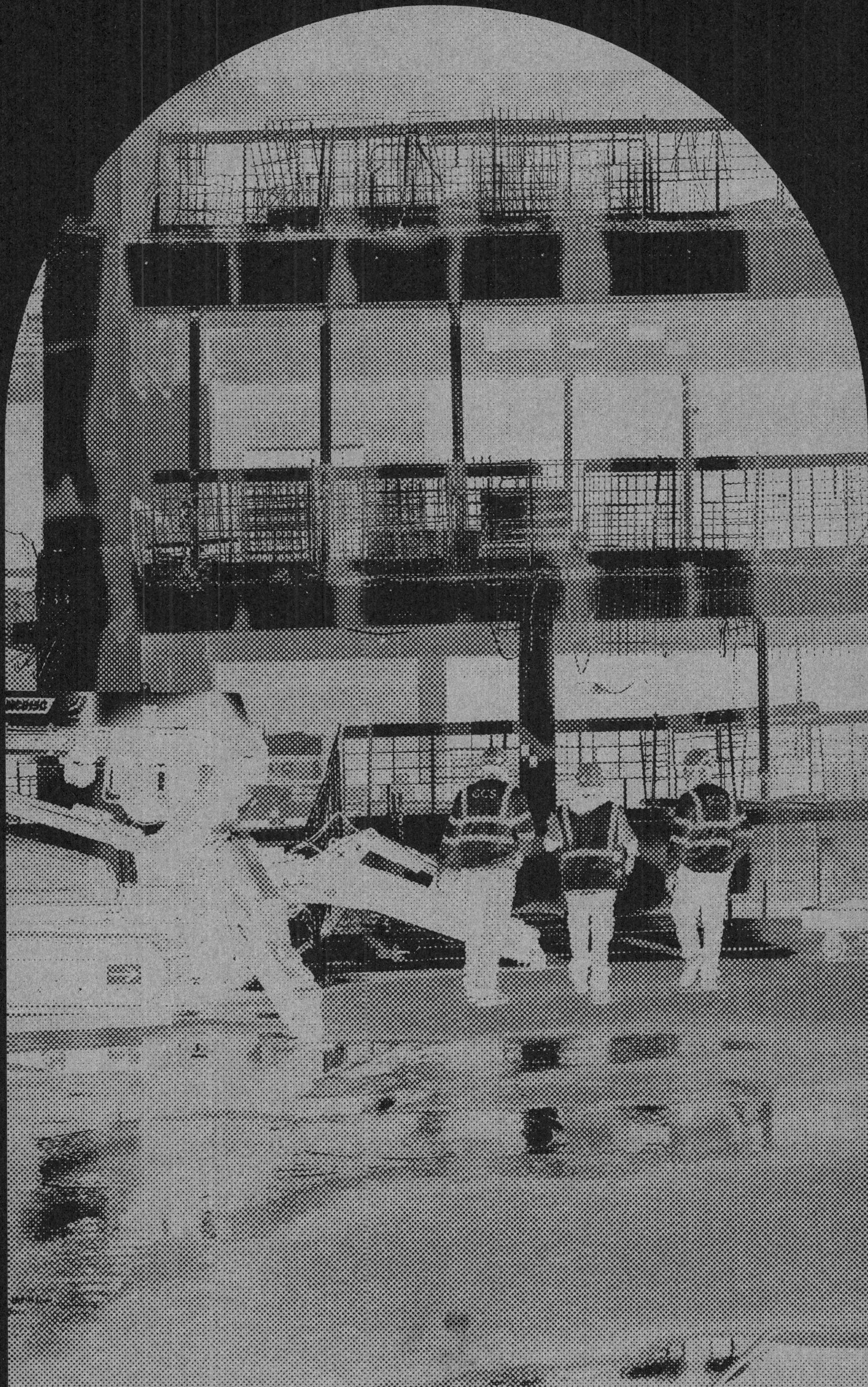

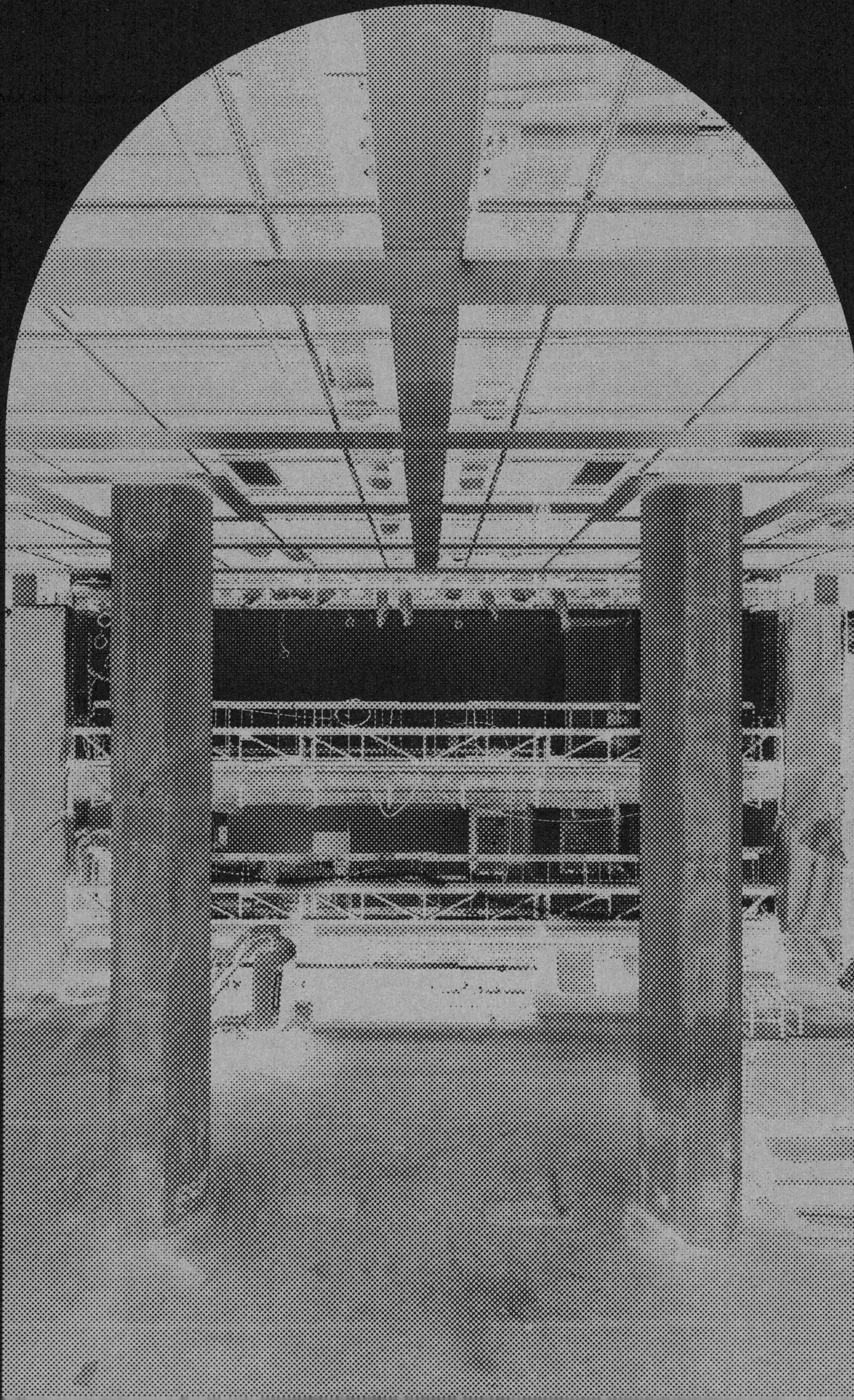

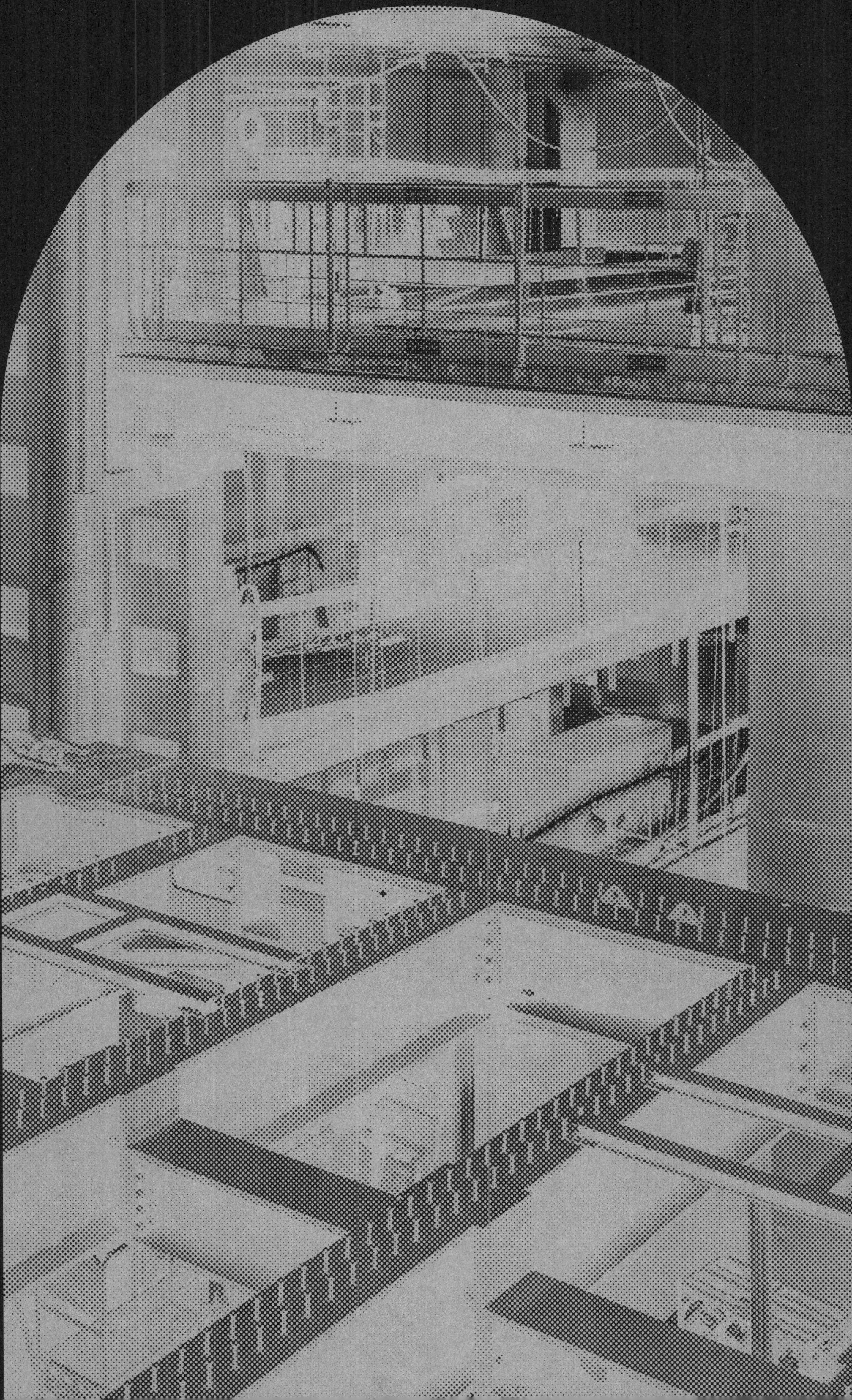

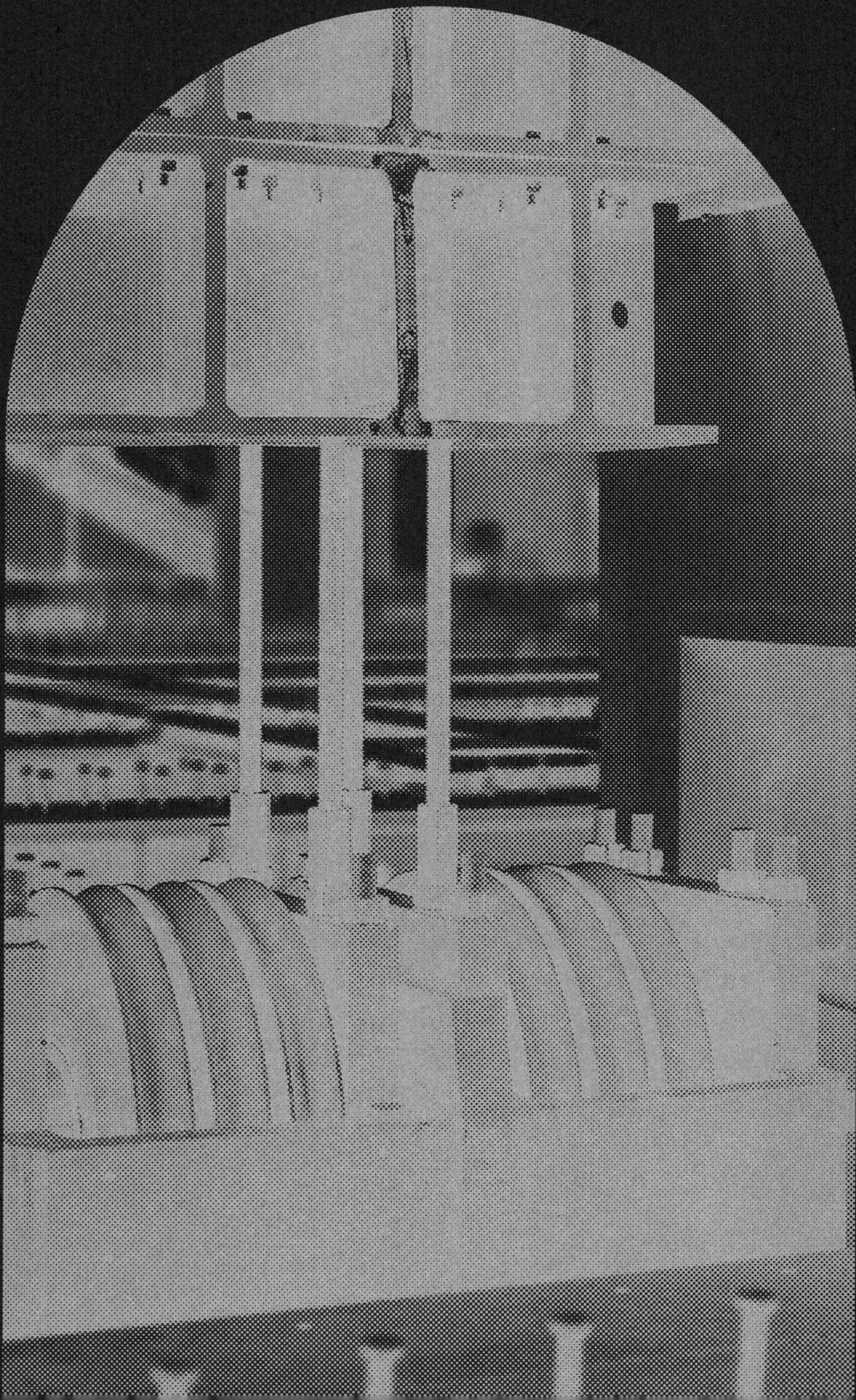

"The Fondation Cartier pour l'art contemporain has found its permanent place in space and time. Never does it forget where it is. Never does it forget when it is. It feels itself a part of Paris, at the heart of the body of Paris. It feels that here it must welcome, with open walls and open roofs, the mutations of living inventions in art that will come, for a time, to confront eternal Paris. From the depths of its foundations—reminders that time is a long time passing, and leaves its mark—the Fondation Cartier in Paris will invite the whole world to explore its inventive, intimate, profound and fleeting exhibitions. Its aim is to provoke a mysterious dialogue with the memories, present and enigmatic, to which the old stones of Paris eternally bear witness."

JEAN NOUVEL

This book was published in conjunction with the opening of the
new venue of the Fondation Cartier pour l'art contemporain in Paris,
2 Place du Palais-Royal, inaugurated in October 2025.

THE FONDATION CARTIER POUR L'ART CONTEMPORAIN BY JEAN NOUVEL

2 PLACE DU PALAIS-ROYAL, PARIS

Fondation Cartier
pour l'art contemporain

FOREWORD

Alain Dominique Perrin

President of the Fondation Cartier
pour l'art contemporain

Chris Dercon

Managing Director

In October 2025, the Fondation Cartier pour l'art contemporain left its premises at 261 Boulevard Raspail and moved to the center of Paris. Its new address, 2 Place du Palais-Royal, opposite the Louvre, is a historic building whose interior volumes underwent a radical redesign by the architect Jean Nouvel. The new spaces expand upon the principles of the Raspail building the architect designed for the Fondation Cartier: made entirely of glass and steel, the transparent structure and its play with immateriality shook up exhibition practices upon opening in 1994. Today Jean Nouvel's new architectural project continues to explore architecture's potential to reshape the esthetics of the museum, doing so this time within a Haussmannian building that dates back to 1855, which previously housed the Grand Hôtel du Louvre (1855–1887), then the Grands Magasins du Louvre (1887–1974), and finally the Louvre des Antiquaires (1978–2019). The governing principle of the spaces is a mechanism that enables a myriad of possible transformations of the interior of the building in service to artistic intention and exhibition design. Behind the fully preserved exterior, we find a dynamic architecture composed of five mobile platforms which allow the creation of an unexpected range of volumes, voids, and spaces, firmly placing the design of the exhibition space at the heart of the institution's artistic program.

The dynamic architecture of the Fondation Cartier is itself inscribed in a history of architecture in which Paris has played a major role. In 1925, the International Exhibition of Modern Decorative and Industrial Arts marked the beginning of an architectural revolution. On this occasion, the modern decorative arts workshops of the booming department stores showcased presentations in which applied art and industrial production techniques converged, establishing them as key players of the architectural innovations of the time. The Studium Louvre pavilion, a shopping mall designed by French architect Albert Laprade for the Grands Magasins du Louvre, was erected alongside the international pavilions on the Esplanade des Invalides and contributed to endowing architecture with a key role in the development of the modern exhibition. Other architectural presentations also embodied this revolution which was soon to unfold, and the conflicting ideologies that would accompany them: Le Corbusier's Pavillon de l'Esprit Nouveau, the *City in Space* structure designed by Frederick J. Kiesler for the Austrian section, and, above all, the Soviet pavilion by Konstantin Melnikov—a pioneering Cubist edifice—heralded the dawn of a mobile and fluid form of architecture. It was also at this same 1925 exhibition that Jean Prouvé was awarded a diploma of honor for his utilitarian, modular furniture. Later, he would join forces with architects Eugène Beaudouin and Marcel Lods, as well as engineer Vladimir Bodiansky, to design the dynamic architecture of the Maison du Peuple in Clichy (1939). With its modular floors and walls, the building was the first attempt at creating a multifunctional space, whose ambition was to offer the greatest flexibility and possibilities to its users.

Another Parisian landmark that aspired to modularity was the Centre Georges Pompidou, whose initial project, designed by Richard Rogers and Renzo Piano in 1971, featured mobile levels. Here, museum architecture was already being conceived in response to the multiplicity of uses it was intended to accommodate, some even unknown at the time. The Centre Georges Pompidou was inspired by Cedric Price's Fun Palace, an educational and cultural complex commissioned in 1960 by theater director Joan Littlewood for London's East End. The site was supposed to host an interactive multidisciplinary program, capable of adapting to the changing social conditions of the day. Although it was never actually built, the Fun Palace had a decisive influence on the architecture of cultural institutions, their imperatives and objectives. In 1994, Cedric Price would write: "The 21st-century 'culture center' will utilize calculated uncertainty and conscious incompleteness to produce a catalyst for invigorating change, whilst always producing 'the harvest of the quiet eye.'"

This pursuit of modular spaces has prominently featured in projects that transformed the history of architecture: Rem Koolhaas's Maison à Bordeaux (1994–1998) and Lafayette Anticipations (Paris, 2012–2018), as well as The Shed (New York, 2015–2019) designed by Diller Scofidio + Renfro. Highly experimental, these last two projects had to comply with the regulations that public buildings must adhere to, as well as the challenges that arise with inventing operative models to program these new types of spaces. Drawing on the lessons learned from these architectural sites, the new spaces designed by Jean Nouvel for the Fondation Cartier are in line with these efforts to design a cultural institution that is both modular and adaptable.

Beyond the dialogue on the evolution of museum spaces and what they should welcome and make possible, Jean Nouvel's architectural project also responds to the historical urban Parisian context in which it is situated. The Grands Magasins du Louvre once played an essential role in the heart of the capital's cultural life. Through his transformation of the site, Jean Nouvel highlights the existing architectural and urban elements that exemplify this historical modernity of the 19th century. The tall picture windows that have been added and which run along the facades make the building transparent and reveal the entirety of the interior from one end to the other, forming a visual system that reinterprets the building's vitrines, which once allowed passersby to gaze at the wide variety of objects on display as they strolled by. The addition of a glass awning, reminiscent of the one that once ran along that same Rue Saint-Honoré and Rue de Marengo, reinforces this unique urban unity and merges the experiences of the street, the historic arcades, and the interior spaces. Similarly, the addition of three glass ceilings, equipped with shutters that vary brightness levels, allows the sky and natural light to feature as an element in the exhibition spaces. The dynamic architecture is further strengthened by the porosity that exists with the exterior, profoundly affecting the visitor's experience of the building, depending on the season or time of day it is visited.

This book delves into Jean Nouvel's architectural project for the Fondation Cartier, explains its technical specificities, and highlights the role it plays in its urban environment, all while putting it in perspective with the history of dynamic architecture and exhibition spaces. In his text entitled "Machine (E)motion," Antoine Picon relates Jean Nouvel's "architectural machine" to the stage devices used in theater. He explores the way in which the platforms serve to introduce new ways of presenting and experiencing works. In "The Unstable Ground of Art," Beatriz Colomina analyzes the dynamic and changing nature of Jean Nouvel's architecture, considering the new spaces of the Fondation Cartier as a "machine for seeing" that revolutionizes ways of exhibiting.

All the architectural elements, whether original, reconstructed, or added, of the Fondation Cartier building now form a unity that anchors the institution in its current and past urban context. These conceptual intentions and the technical aspects of its implementation are detailed in texts authored by Jean Nouvel and the two head architects on the project: Mathieu Forest and Cyril Desroche, from the Ateliers Jean Nouvel.

In a sense, this new space created for the Fondation Cartier represents a culmination of Jean Nouvel's thinking on museum spaces. His vision has been built progressively, through each of the museum projects he has designed over the past fifty years. It began theoretically with the competition for the Centre Georges Pompidou in 1971 and continued with the Institut du Monde Arabe (1987), the Fondation Cartier Boulevard Raspail (1994), the Musée du Quai Branly – Jacques Chirac (2006), and the Louvre Abu Dhabi (2017), architectural projects that can be said to have deconstructed the dominant codes of museological practices. Furthering this, in a text entitled "Between Preservation and Modernization: The Architecture of Jean Nouvel," Béatrice Grenier analyzes how the architect's approach to the Fondation Cartier building on the Place du Palais-Royal is part of a broader reflection on the relationship between architecture and the city. By studying a panorama of cultural sites and museums designed by Jean Nouvel, in France and abroad, she examines the way in which he transcends the ontological limitations of architecture by designing buildings that are no longer autonomous entities but rather extensions of the urban landscape.

The new spaces of the Fondation Cartier testify to the collaboration between Jean Nouvel and the Fondation Cartier—notably with Alain Dominique Perrin, Marie-Claude Beaud, Hervé Chandès, and Chris Dercon—which spans almost forty years. Beyond the building on the Boulevard Raspail and the one located on the Place du Palais-Royal, Jean Nouvel designed multiple projects that reflect the institution's evolution. While these spaces never actually saw the light of day, they have contributed to his theories about museum spaces. In 1986, he first imagined a glass and steel building integrated into the landscape of the Montcel Estate in Jouy-en-Josas, near Versailles, where the Fondation Cartier had been located since 1984. In 2009, as part of the urban development project for the Île Seguin, an island on the Seine river in the west suburbs of Paris, he sketched plans for a concrete and glass structure to house its exhibitions. Finally, in 2018, Jean Nouvel designed an extension for the Boulevard Raspail site on the neighboring grounds of the Saint-Vincent-de-Paul Hospital, which had been abandoned for several years.

The Fondation Cartier has always placed the practice of architecture at the heart of its programming, considering it to be a vector for interdisciplinary dialogue. Today, at 2 Place du Palais-Royal, the institution materializes a vision of architecture which enables a merging of disciplines, visual art, performance, theater, science, and new technologies. Merging with public space, past and future coexist in a building that is at once an extension of the urban landscape, a reflection of its history, and the perfect application of a dynamic architecture at the service of a cultural institution.

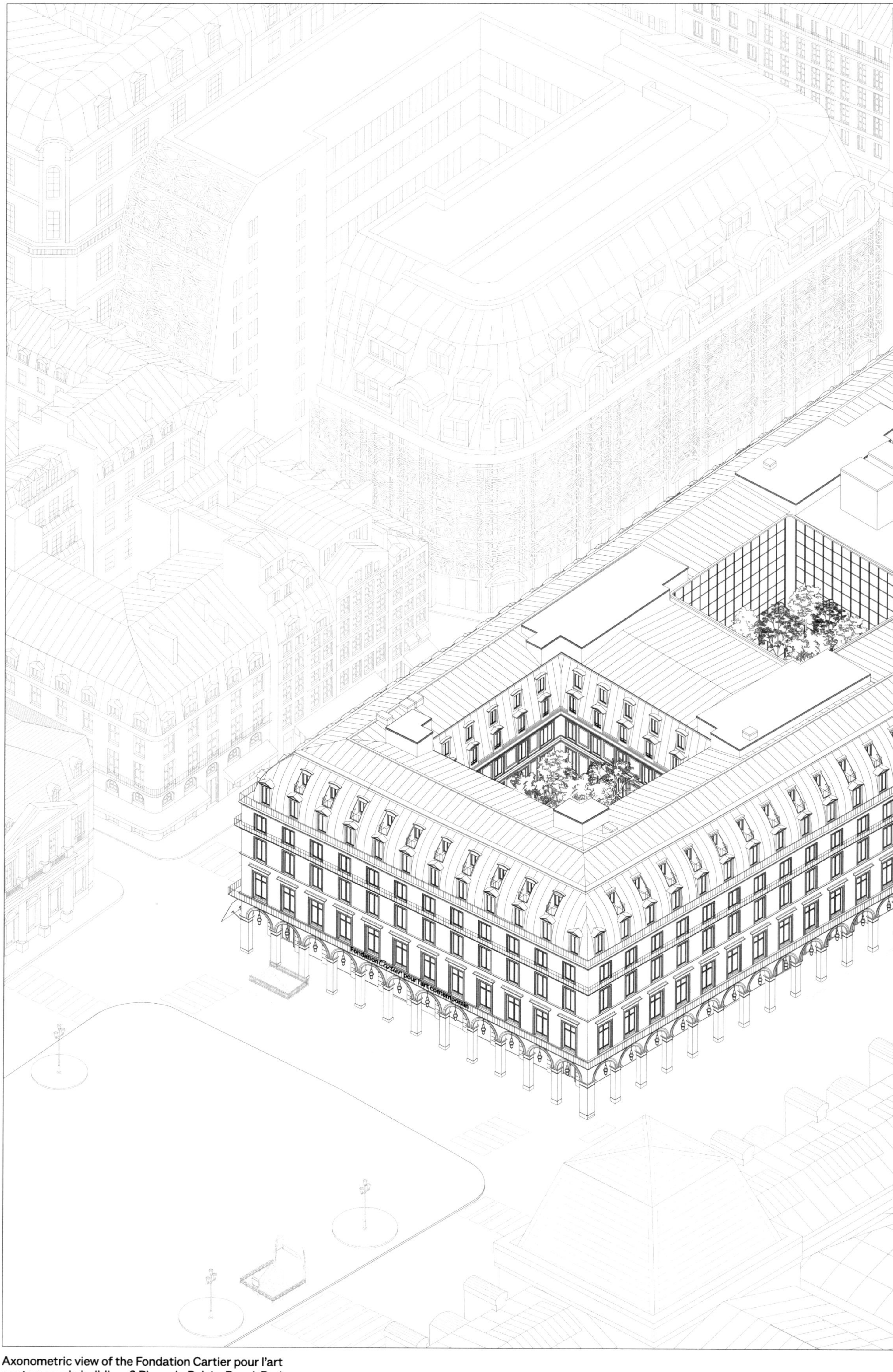

Axonometric view of the Fondation Cartier pour l'art
contemporain building, 2 Place du Palais-Royal, Paris

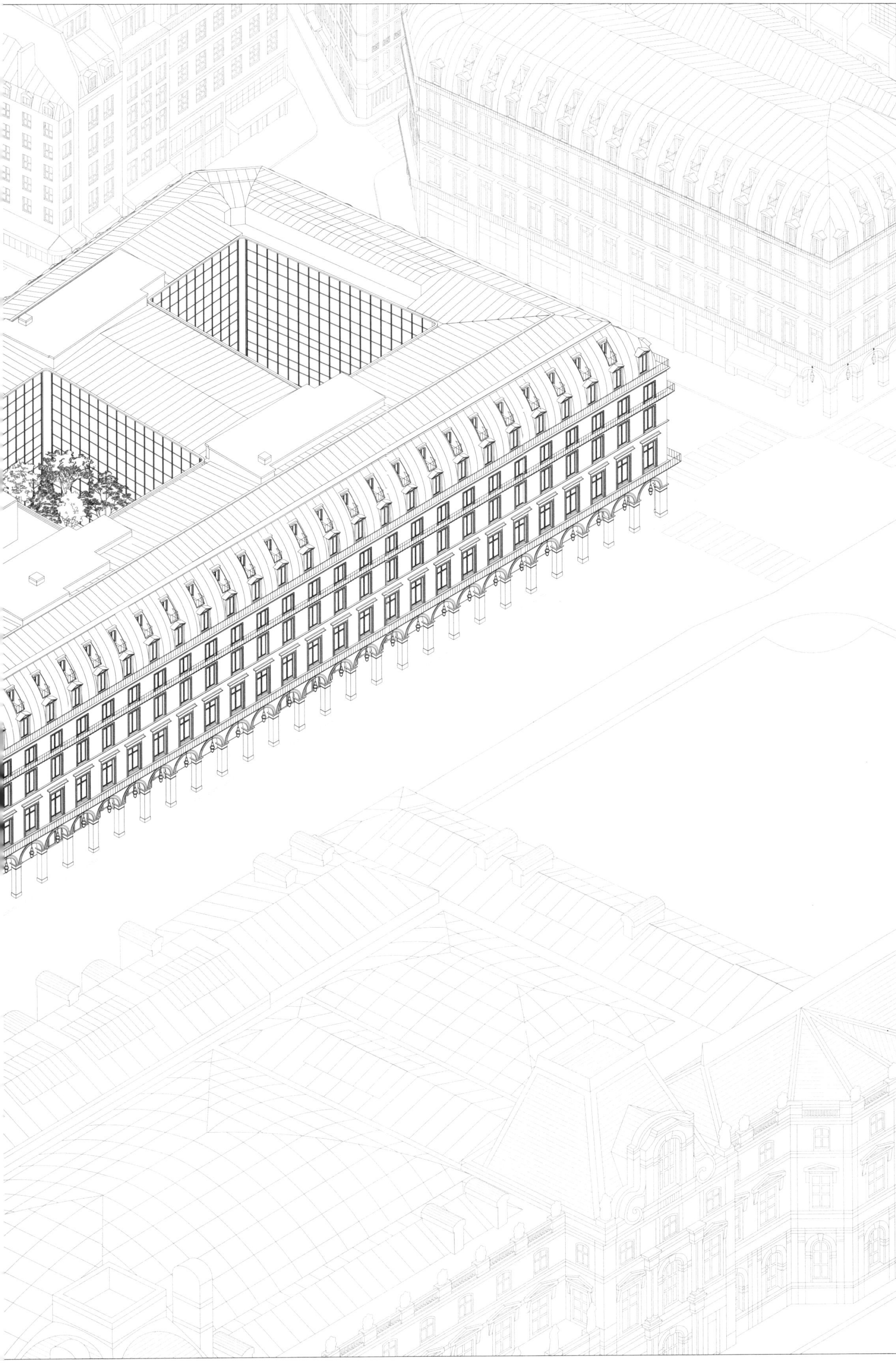

A PLACE FOR THE UNEXPECTED

Jean Nouvel

I have always imagined the Fondation Cartier pour l'art contemporain as a haven, a welcoming sanctuary where everyone is invited to discover the art of today. Not just another neutral gallery, but a dynamic space of uninhibited inspiration, a grand workshop that adapts to artists' works and ideas. The building's mission is to redefine spaces and introduce new ways to exhibit that harmonize with history, while also unveiling that history's essence. Repurposing the building at 2 Place du Palais-Royal in this way meant making it more open and generous toward Paris, but also more representative of the city. By nurturing the emergence of new art forms here, the Fondation Cartier doubly enriches the space: it welcomes history into the heart of the Fondation Cartier and instils creation in the heart of the city.

The Fondation Cartier is not simply its new building—it is a neighborhood within the neighborhood of the Palais-Royal, where its identity must be expressed in an exceptional way. Perhaps it could be the final element in this urban composition, among the strategic, administrative, cultural, and political landmarks surrounding Place du Palais-Royal. These buildings, shaped by different eras, have accumulated layers of history—creating, enriching, and contrasting with one another. At street level, the fully glazed facade along Rue de Rivoli and Rue Saint-Honoré allows the gaze to traverse the space from one street to another, blurring the boundaries between interior and exterior. This transparency of the side facades reinforces a sense of belonging to the streets and history of Paris, in the same way that the overhead glass roofs, planted with trees, create a suspended grove through whose canopy the eye perceives the light and shadows that change with time and the exhibitions, and the sun's rays that blend with the motifs created by the hues of nature and the colors of the sky. This sense of boundless space is also felt from Place du Palais-Royal: the interior of the Haussmannian block, open along its full length, provides a 150-meter view as far as Rue de Marengo. The focus of the architectural approach was to unveil the void—its depth, its height, its presence. It must be understood that contemporary architecture is increasingly moving in this direction. The concept is no longer about constructing *a space* but of building *inside space* itself. This void becomes the place for expression—the promise of endless possibilities.

Moving into a place so impressive—on account of its location and history—entails an act of invention, but not necessarily something manifested in steel or stone. Rather, what takes root is a different way of doing things—a way of thinking that prioritizes artists' greatest possible freedom of expression. A place like this requires boldness, a fearless creativity that artists might not exhibit in other institutional settings. Like the Greeks, I have always believed that a museum is the perfect place to generate ideas, to discuss them, to be present, to be elsewhere, to be inside, to be outside, to be in the city... My goal is to offer this possibility in each of my projects of this kind. Architecture is a testament to its era. The most important aspect is the change in perspective—the ability to reveal what is directly linked to history.

The architectural design of the Fondation Cartier building on Boulevard Raspail was undoubtedly initially elusive: the significance of the "almost nothing," the way the architectural elements blended seamlessly without asserting themselves, the changing light that altered with the seasons, responding to budding leaves, to rain... It was a building of presence.

At the Palais-Royal, this continuous interplay of variations unfolds inside. In this architectural space, which retains only the characteristic facade and a few structural elements from the 19th century, one feels as if enveloped by the airy yet expansive framework of an industrial cathedral. It emanates a strong presence and power through its five steel platforms, with their evident mobility, which contrast starkly with the building's Haussmannian exterior. It's a little like a gigantic theater, where massive floors can be raised—a concealed dynamic. The space's true innovation lies in its adaptability, accommodating all possible altimetries, all the varying intensities of light, even to the point of complete darkness, depending on the degree of closure of the glass roofs and side facades.

It is probable that the Fondation Cartier will be the institution offering the greatest versatility in its spaces, the most ways to exhibit, and the widest range of perspectives. The strength of its platforms allows for the display of extremely heavy works and entirely new means of exposition. The aim is to achieve what would be impossible elsewhere, and to reinvent the very manner of exhibition. It is an approach that sets the stage for uniquely distinctive exhibitions, fashioned by the imaginations of artists, curators, and scenographers. It is a space of limitless possibilities, where environments can be towering, deep, or the most compressed possible. Depending on the configuration chosen, these geometrically variable spaces will be continuously reinvented and explored with each project. This very adaptation is what should leave a lasting impression—the fact that this evolving space, visible from Rue de Rivoli and Rue Saint-Honoré, never ceases to surprise.

It is vital to keep pace with the spirit of our time, to be fully immersed in the art of the moment. This can only happen if this haven grants artists complete freedom to express their works, and if the floors, walkways, and ceilings are similarly unrestricted. The space is a foundation for invention—for the inspired, and, naturally, for artists as true inventors. Each empty space becomes an opportunity for expression. Every surface—floors, walls, columns, and glass roofs—serves to provoke thought. Every opening frames a view, inviting exploration from every perspective. Every material, every color, every unexpected detail is there to inspire the artists, to challenge them, to spur them toward transformation if that is what they want. Everything has been conceived to foster and provoke invention, to evoke emotion. The Fondation Cartier will be a place for the unexpected, drawing us into the magnetic attraction of 21st-century Paris. Its purpose is to disorient, to offer a fresh perspective on the place of art in the city's life—in its streets, its squares... A living, thriving art scene, in the very heart of Paris.

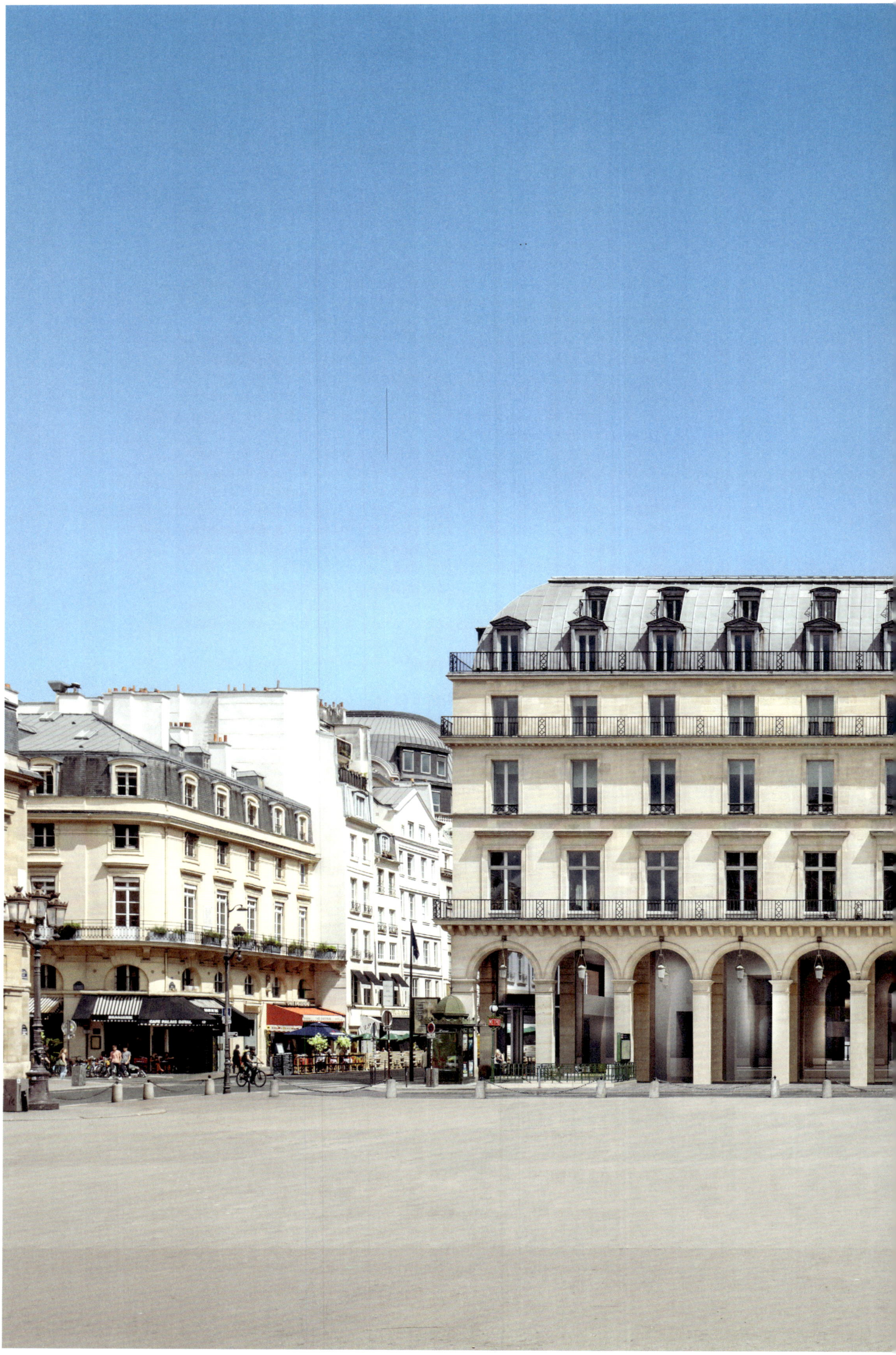

The Fondation Cartier pour l'art contemporain building
seen from Place du Palais-Royal, Paris

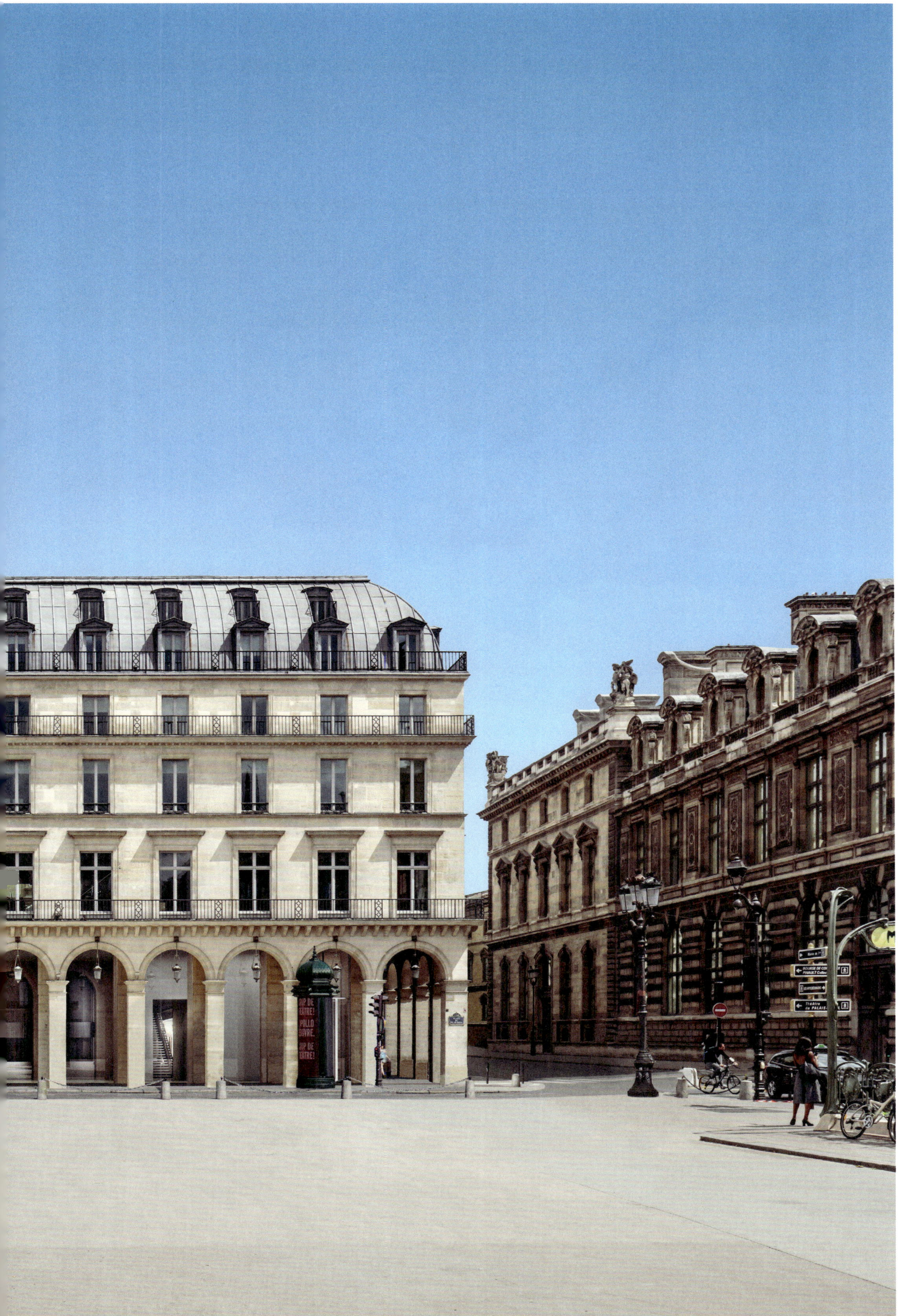

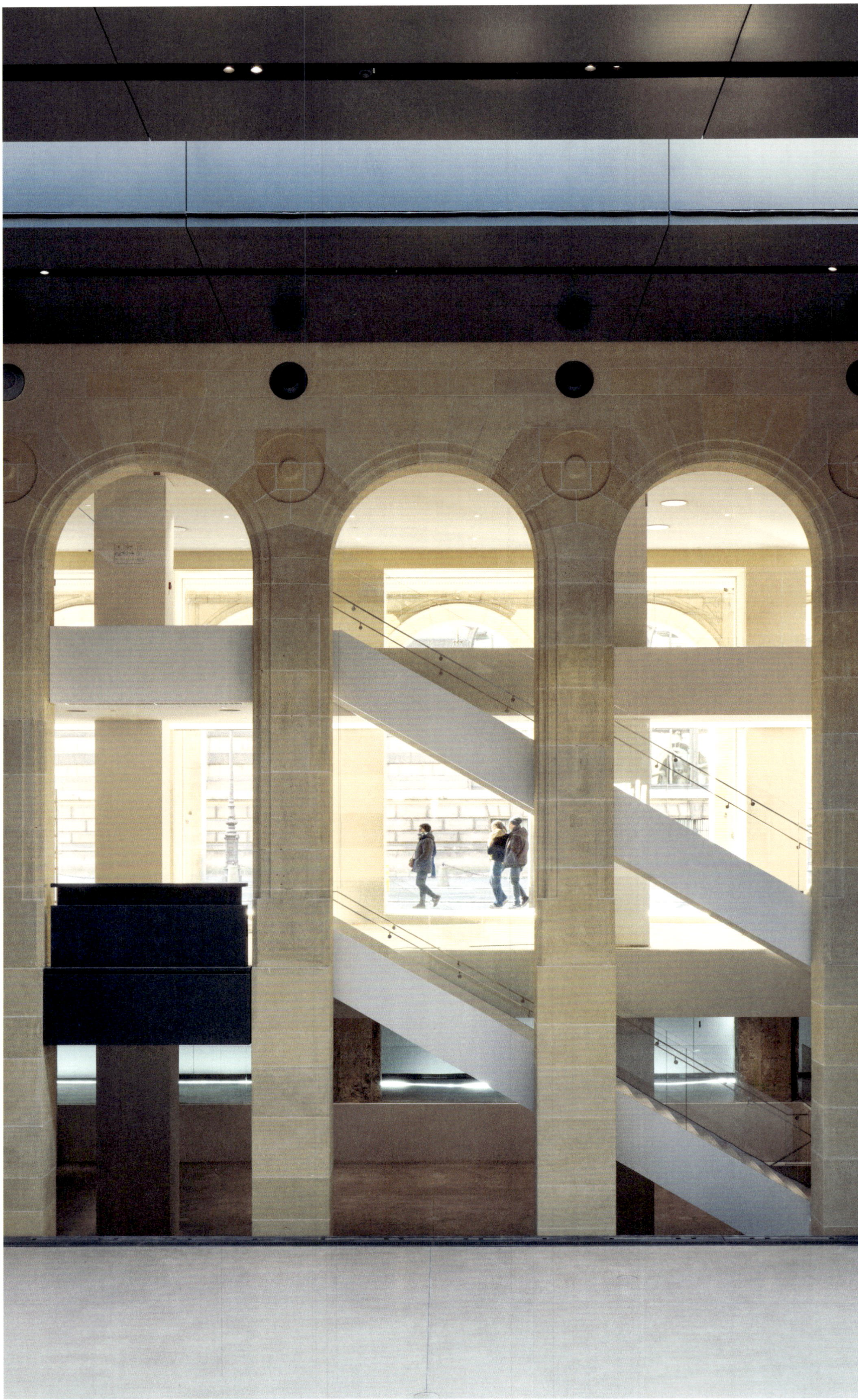

Interior spaces of the Fondation Cartier building

THE UNSTABLE GROUND OF ART

Beatriz Colomina

Architectural Historian and Theorist

"Today we go to the [Grands Magasins du] Louvre as we would to a museum, an exhibition," wrote the journalist and playwright Alfred d'Aunay in 1880. "We enjoy these superb immensities. We come for pleasure, to see beautiful things, to admire the masterpieces of our opulent factories, to explore all the seductive fantasies, the adorable caprices of the industry of elegance."[1] A century and a half later, the Fondation Cartier pour l'art contemporain opens its new exhibition spaces, designed by Jean Nouvel, in that very department store building, occupying the whole block from the Place du Palais-Royal to the Rue de Marengo, from the Rue de Rivoli to the Rue Saint-Honoré.

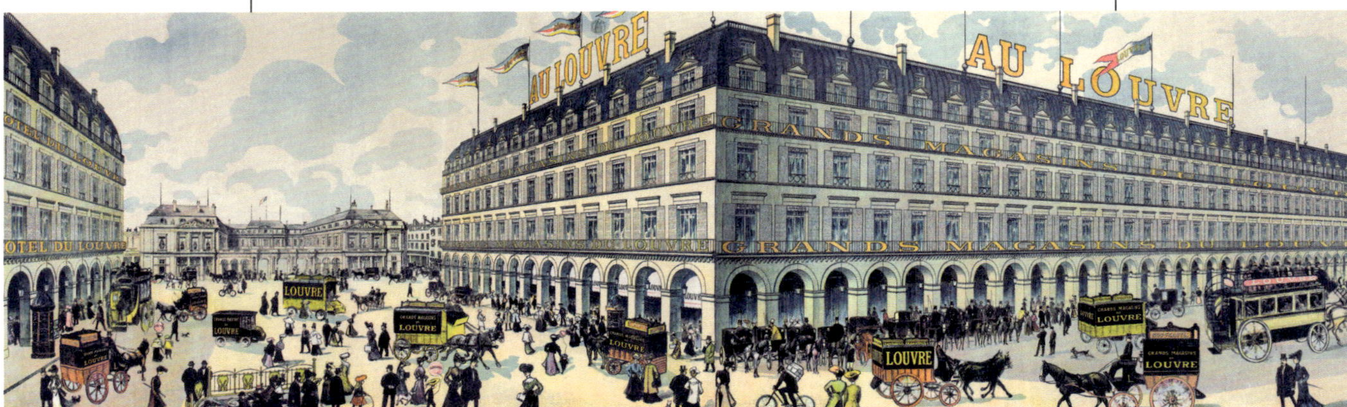

Grands Magasins du Louvre, Paris, c. 1907 (lithograph by Eugène Verneau)

The Spectacle of Modernity

The vast Haussmannian building opened in 1855 as the first luxury hotel in Paris, Le Grand Hôtel du Louvre, commissioned by Napoleon III to accommodate visitors to the Exposition Universelle that year[2]. A newspaper report on the opening of the hotel said of the unprecedented crowds arriving in Paris via the new train networks of France and Europe, and from all other continents: "a moving population floats incessantly on the surface of the sedentary one. It is no longer houses that are needed to house it, but cities within cities," describing the Grand Hôtel du Louvre as new "travel phalanstery."[3] In other words, a self-sufficient utopian enclave, a kind of paradise.

The design team of four architects, led by Alfred Armand, who had built several railway stations in and around Paris for the hotel's entrepreneurs, Émile and Isaac Pereire, used an iron frame structure and glass roofs over the three courtyards.[4] The building was

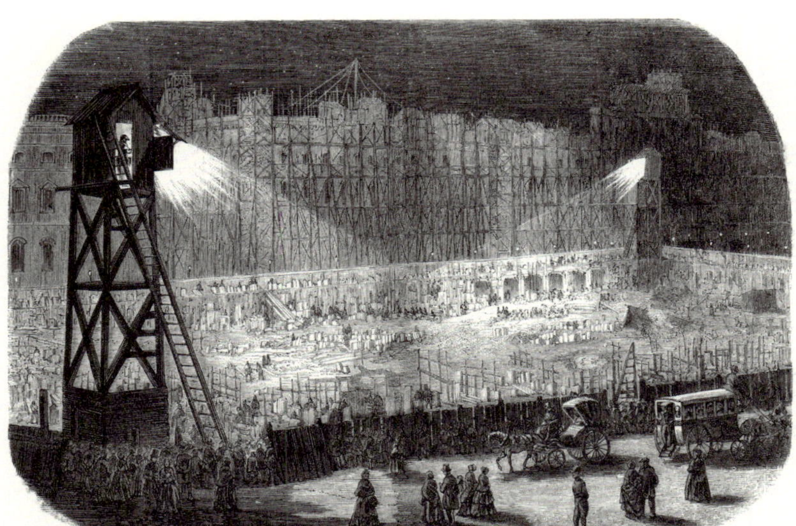

Construction of Rue de Rivoli at night, lighted by electricity, 1854 (lithograph by Jules Gaildrau)

lined with arcades along the Rue de Rivoli and the Rue Saint-Honoré. Like an ocean liner in the heart of the city, the 153-meter-long building with over 1,200 rooms—from sumptuous suites on the first two floors to smaller bedrooms on the upper floors, from storerooms to vast halls, from stables to hairdressing salons—was indeed a miniature city, with a staff of 1,250 satisfying its cosmopolitan visitors' every need, 24 hours a day. It was relentlessly modern, a vast machine, with heating, gas lighting, electric bells, a post and telegraph office, the latest English toilets, plumbing, and novel ven-

1 — *"On se plaît dans ces superbes immensités. On y vient par plaisir, pour voir de belles choses, pour admirer les chefs-d'œuvre de nos opulentes fabriques, pour connaître toutes les séduisantes fantaisies, tous les aimables caprices de l'industrie élégante."* Alfred d'Aunay, *Le Louvre. Grand Hôtel et Grands Magasins* (Paris: Firmin-Didot and Cie, 1880), pp. 27–28 [translated by Phoebe Green].

2 — See Bernard Marrey, *Les Grands Magasins, des origines à 1939* (1979) (Saint-André-de-Roquepertuis: Le Linteau, 2018), p. 85.

3 — Paul de Saint-Victor, "L'Hôtel du Louvre," in *La Presse*, October 15, 1855, unpaged.

4 — Alfred Armand (1805–1888) had worked with Émile and Isaac Pereire throughout the 1830s and 1840s, since they first began their railroad business. He built, among others, the Versailles (1836 and 1839), Saint-Lazare (1841–1842, and 1851–1853) and Saint-Germain-en-Laye (1845) railway stations.

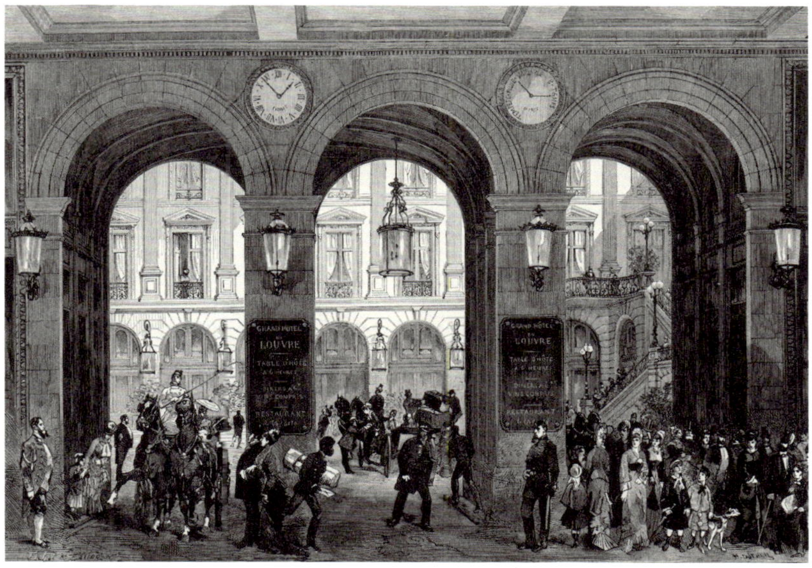

Entrance to the Grand Hôtel du Louvre from Rue de Rivoli, peristyle and *cour d'honneur*, 1880 (drawing by Charles Fichot and Edmond Morin, engraving by Hippolyte Constant Dutheil)

tilation techniques. Even the breakneck speed of its construction had been modern. As Walter Benjamin noted, electric lighting was used on the building site to double the number of labor hours.[5] An unprecedented 3,000 workers were employed on the site, working day and night in a spectacle covered in the press.

A marvel of mechanization, speed, and spectacle, then, shaped by a new way of looking linked to a new concept of exhibition. Not only was the Exposition Universelle of 1855 presenting the commodities of 28 countries to an audience of five million, but the visitors themselves were on display. The Grand Hôtel provided multiple theatrical opportunities for its inhabitants to see and be seen: from arrival by carriage in the *cour d'honneur* with its frosted glass roof, observed from all sides, to the grand operatic staircases, the great dining room, the billiard room, and the reading room, which doubled as an exhibition venue. Many of the spaces in the building were filled with artworks by noted painters and sculptors, a number of whom were also exhibited in the neighboring Louvre museum—so art was encountered at all hours between sleeping, eating, drinking, reading, and dancing—but the real display, the new art, was commerce itself, which was becoming a kind of spectacle.

5 — "For the first time, the entrepreneurs used electric light on the site in order to double the day's labor." Georges d'Avenel, *Le Mécanisme de la vie moderne*, part 1, in "Les Grands Magasins," in *Revue des deux mondes* (July 15, 1894), p. 340, quoted by Walter Benjamin in *The Arcades Project* (Cambridge and London: Belknap Press of Harvard University Press, 2002), p. 167.

Cour d'honneur of the Grand Hôtel du Louvre, c. 1870–1879 (lithograph by Charles Rivière)

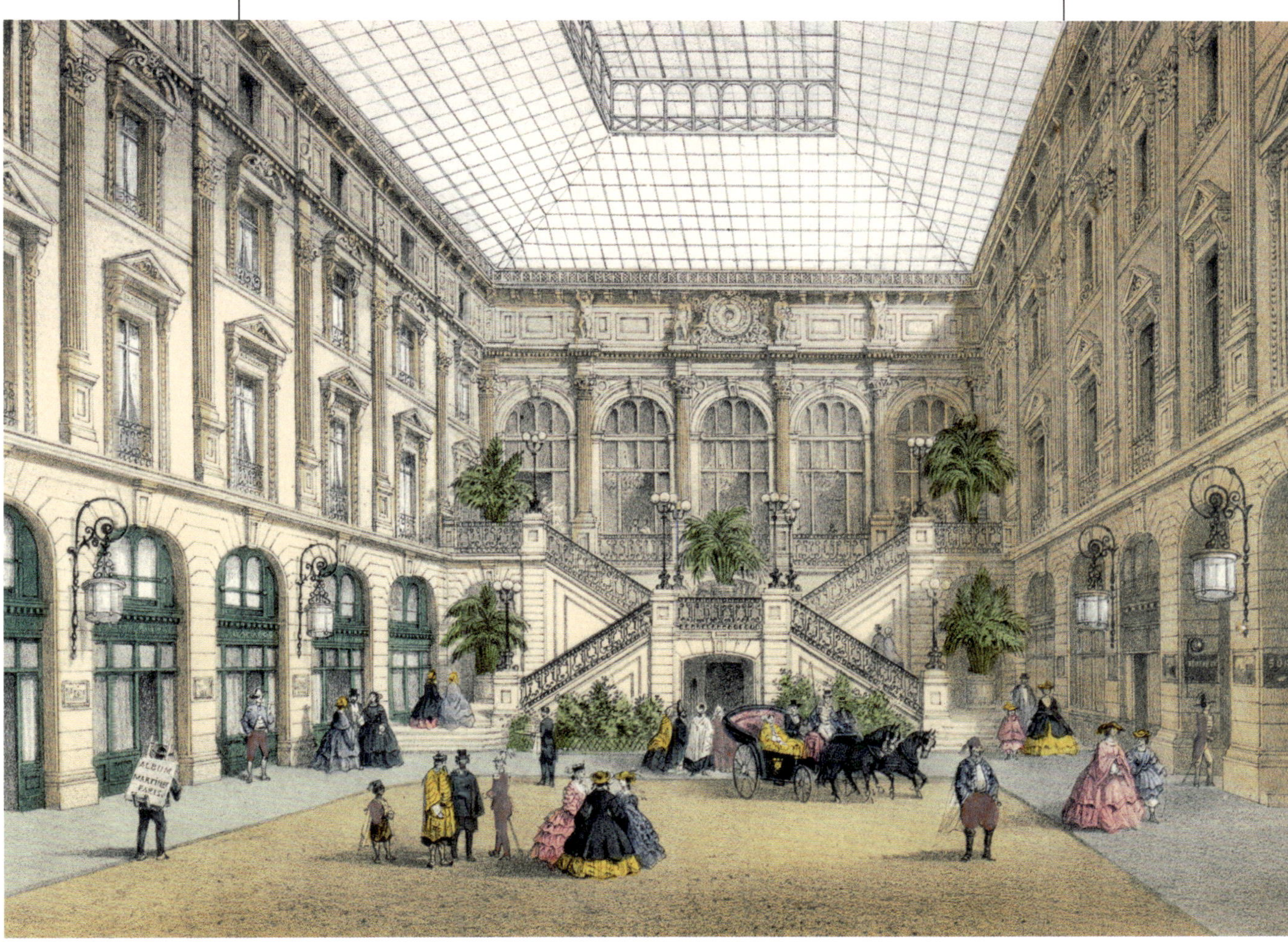

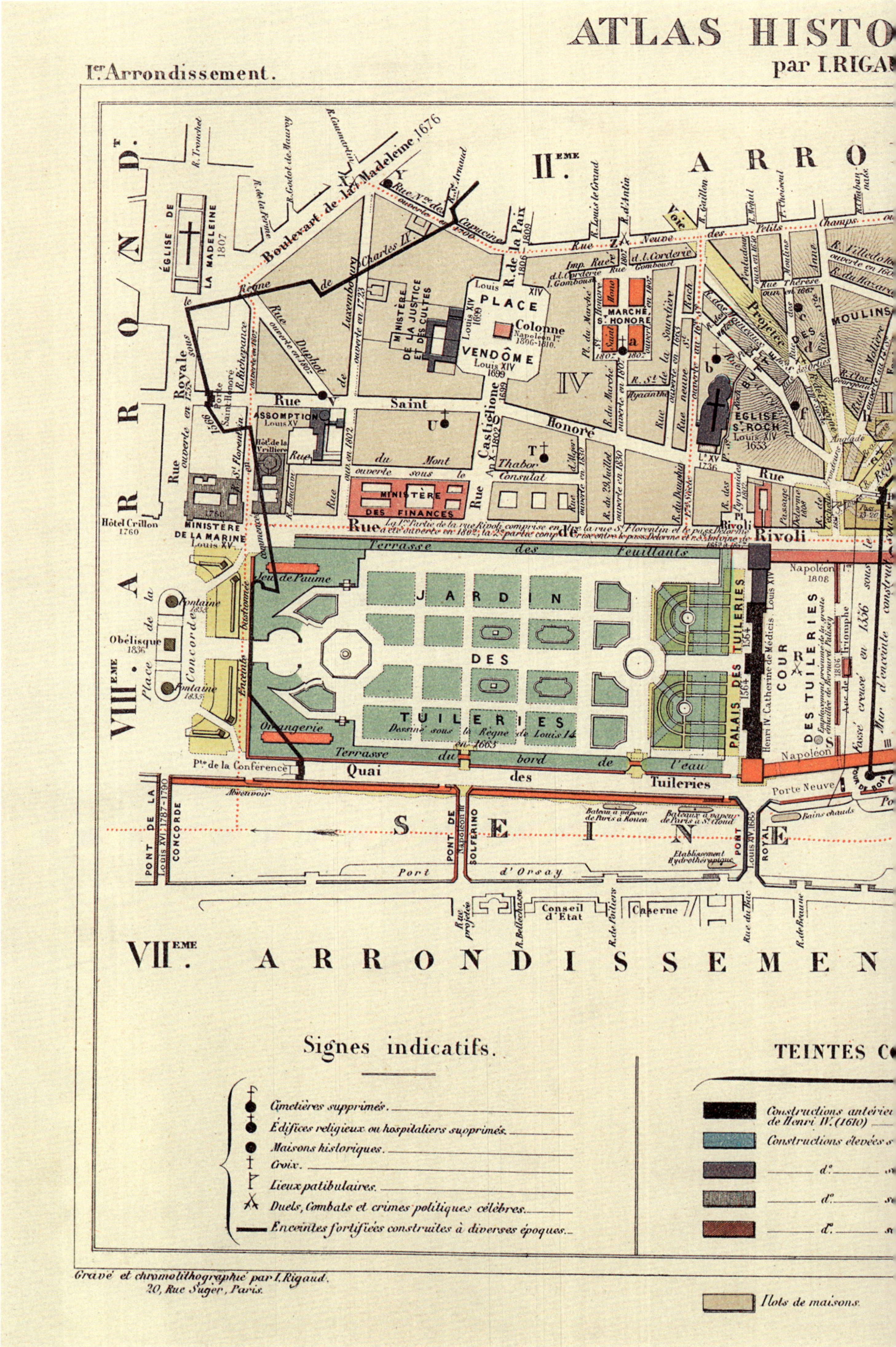

Plate from the *Atlas historique de Paris* by Isaac Rigaud, c. 1860

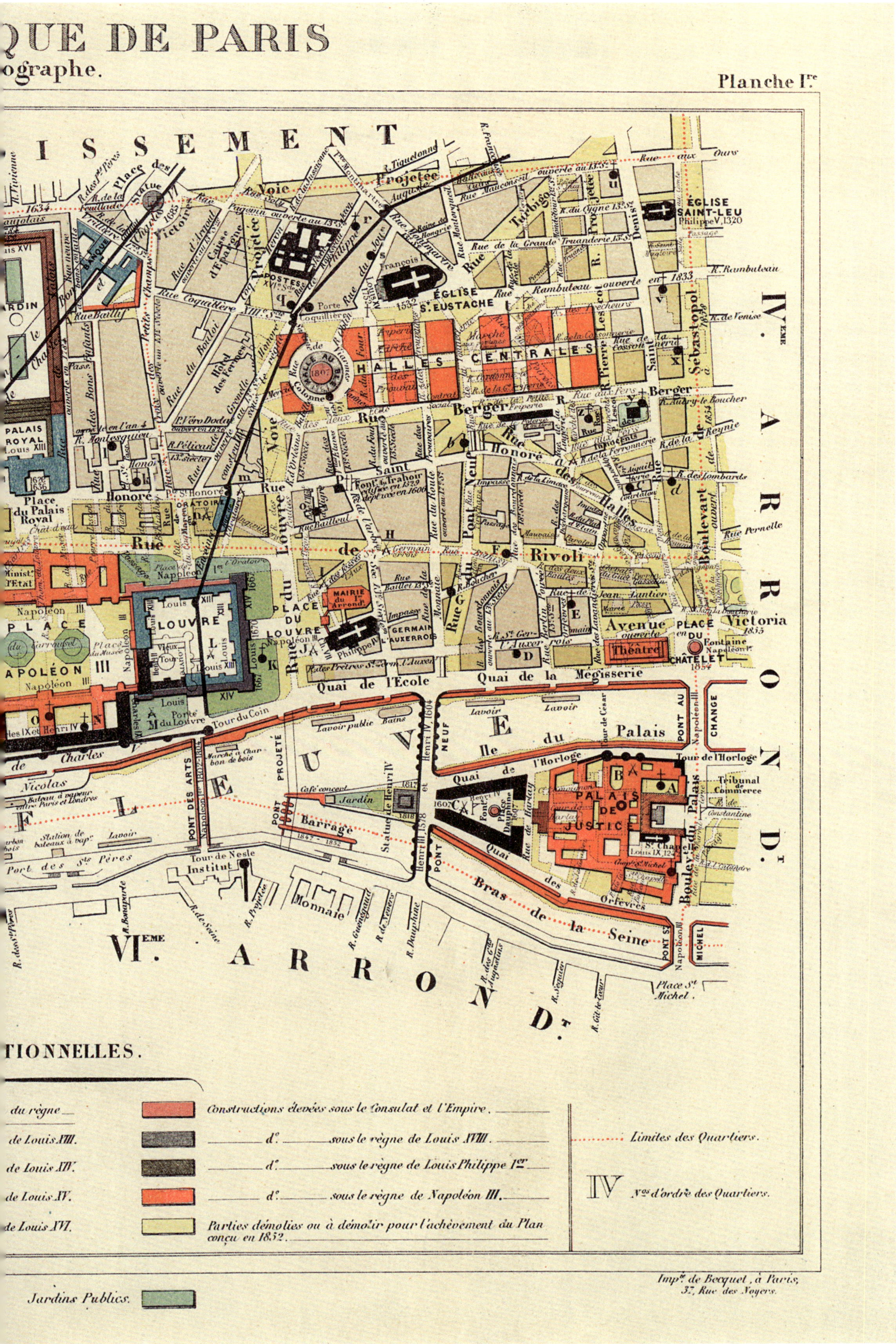
QUE DE PARIS
ographe.
Planche Ire
ISSEMENT
IV.EME ARROND.T
VI.EME ARROND.T
EGLISE SAINT-LEU
Philippe V, 1320
EGLISE S.T EUSTACHE
HALLES CENTRALES
Halle au Blé
Rue Rambuteau
Rue de Rivoli
Rue S.t Honoré
Boulevart de Sebastopol
PALAIS ROYAL
Place du Palais Royal
LOUVRE
PLACE DU LOUVRE
MAIRIE du 1er Arrond.t
GERMAIN L'AUXERROIS
PLACE NAPOLÉON III
Quai de l'Ecole
Quai de la Mégisserie
PLACE DU CHATELET
Théatre
Avenue Victoria 1855
Ile du Palais
PALAIS DE JUSTICE
Tour de l'Horloge
Tribunal de Commerce
PONT NEUF
PONT DES ARTS
PONT AU CHANGE
PONT S.T MICHEL
Bras de la Seine
Quai des Orfèvres
Quai de l'Horloge
Tour de Nesle
Institut
Monnaie
Place S.t Michel
Barrage
Jardin
Statue de Henri IV
Tour du Coin
TIONNELLES.
du règne
de Louis XIII.
de Louis XIV.
de Louis XV.
de Louis XVI.
Jardins Publics.
Constructions élevées sous le Consulat et l'Empire.
d.o sous le règne de Louis XVIII.
d.o sous le règne de Louis Philippe 1er.
d.o sous le règne de Napoléon III.
Parties démolies ou à démolir pour l'achèvement du Plan conçu en 1852.
Limites des Quartiers.
IV N.os d'ordre des Quartiers.
Impr. de Becquet, à Paris, 37, Rue des Noyers.

Everything, including the visitors, was turned into a commodity—always on display, like a new form of goods seen with new eyes. The Grand Hôtel set up for the Exposition Universelle was first and foremost an exhibition, a symptom of an optical shift. In his *Passagen-Werk*, a vast and unfinished study project, Benjamin noted that between the years 1850 and 1890 exhibitions took the place of museums.[6] The hotel was not just across the street from the Louvre museum but represented its successor, a new form of exhibition tied to the idea of international commerce.

From the beginning, the hotel building hosted an unprecedented density of shopping. More than forty luxury stores leased shops under the arcades in the Rue de Rivoli, across the street from the Louvre, and on the other sides of the building.[7] A long stretch of the remaining spaces was occupied by *Au Louvre: Magasin de Nouveautés*, a proto-department store that demolished the divisions between shop spaces to form a continuous gallery, like an internal street exposed to the streets outside through new expanses of glass, replacing all the existing doorways with grand entrances at the corners.[8] The hotel itself had around fifty of its own specialized boutiques. Over time, Au Louvre swallowed more and more shop spaces and kept growing inside the hotel, taking over even the most luxurious suites on the first floor. Eventually most of the building was dedicated to shopping, becoming the *Grands Magasins du Louvre* in 1863 and promoting itself as "the largest store in the world,"[9] with a 700-room hotel still part of the building. The building was repeatedly redesigned to accommodate the constant expansion of shopping, which reached a spectacular 3.76 km of gallery length in 1879.[10] The Cour du Palais-Royal and Cour Marengo were turned into exhibition halls and visited like a museum, or the last trace of what the museum had been. In 1887 the hotel was finally moved across the Palais-Royal to make even more room for shopping.

6 — "In the years 1850–1890, exhibitions take the place of museums," Benjamin, *The Arcades Project*, p. 407.

7 — "Originally, there were six shops on the Rue de Rivoli, 23 on the Rue Saint-Honoré, 12 on the Rue de Marengo and one on the Marengo/Saint-Honoré cutaway." [translated by PG.] In Cabinet Recherches & Études Appliquées, *Centre d'affaires Le Louvre / Louvre des Antiquaires : étude historique et architecturale* (rapport) (Société Foncière Lyonnaise: February 2008), p. 9.

8 — "Most of the Paris arcades come into being in the decade and a half after 1822. The first condition for their emergence is the boom in the textile trade. *Magasins de nouveautés*, the first establishments to keep large stocks of merchandise on the premises, make their appearance. They are the forerunners of department stores." Benjamin, *The Arcades Project*, p. 3. *Au Louvre* already occupied all of Rue de Marengo and some of Rue de Rivoli and Rue Saint-Honoré when it opened in July 1855. After expansion work, it extended almost to Place du Palais-Royal, referring to its enlarged premises as "*immenses magasins.*" Advertising insert in *Le Petit Courrier de Bar-sur-Seine*, October 5, 1855, unpaged.

9 — *Au Louvre* had already adopted the slogan *"Les plus vastes du monde"* in October 1855, as if announcing the goal long before it was achieved. Advertisement for the opening of the expanded *Au Louvre*, *Journal du Cher*, October 18, 1855, unpaged.

10 — G. Clerc, "Les Nouvelles Galeries des Grands Magasins du Louvre," *Le Monde Illustré* supplement, October 4, 1879, p. 228.

Hall Marengo of the Grands Magasins du Louvre, 1880 (drawing by Charles Fichot, engraving by Charles Maurand)

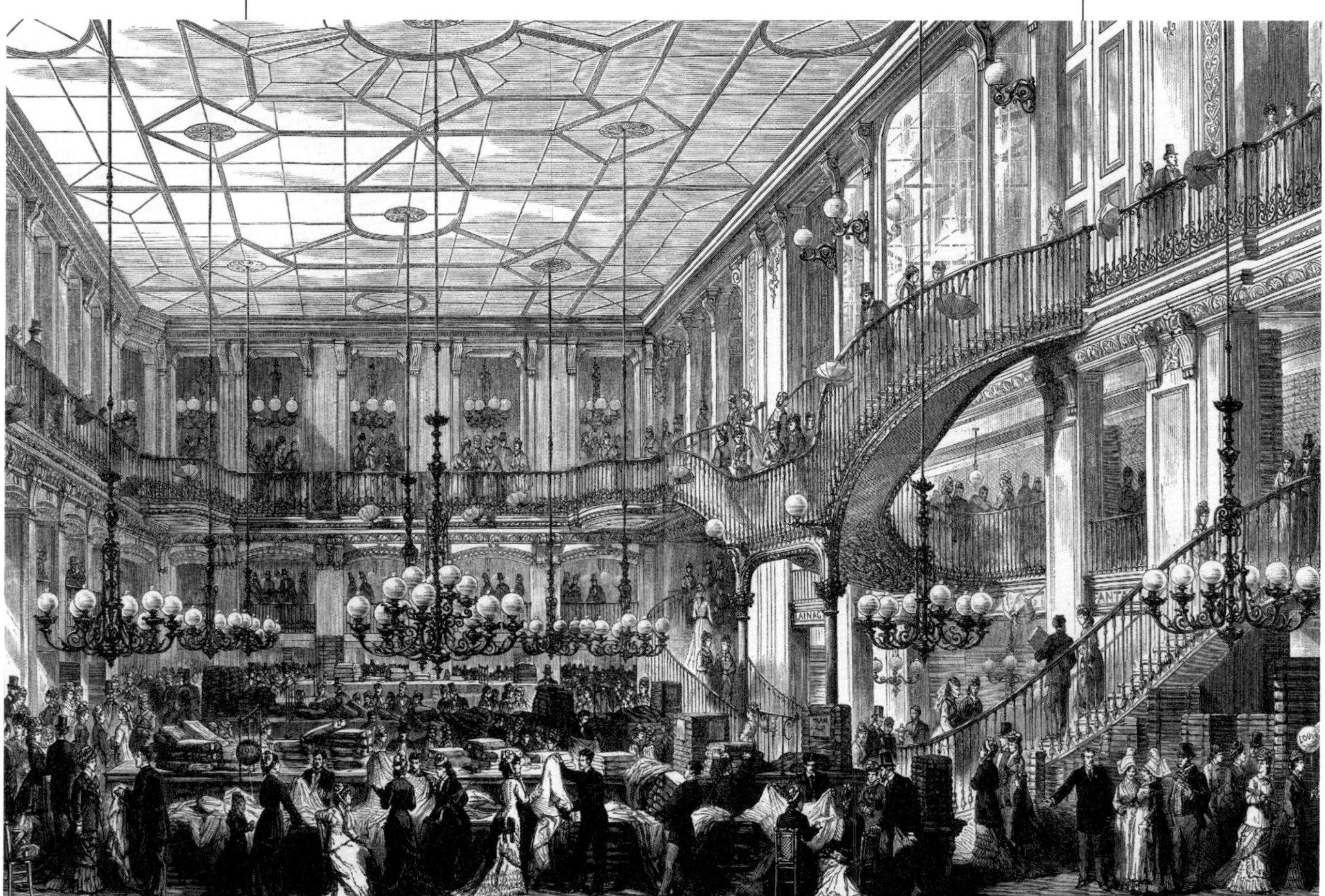

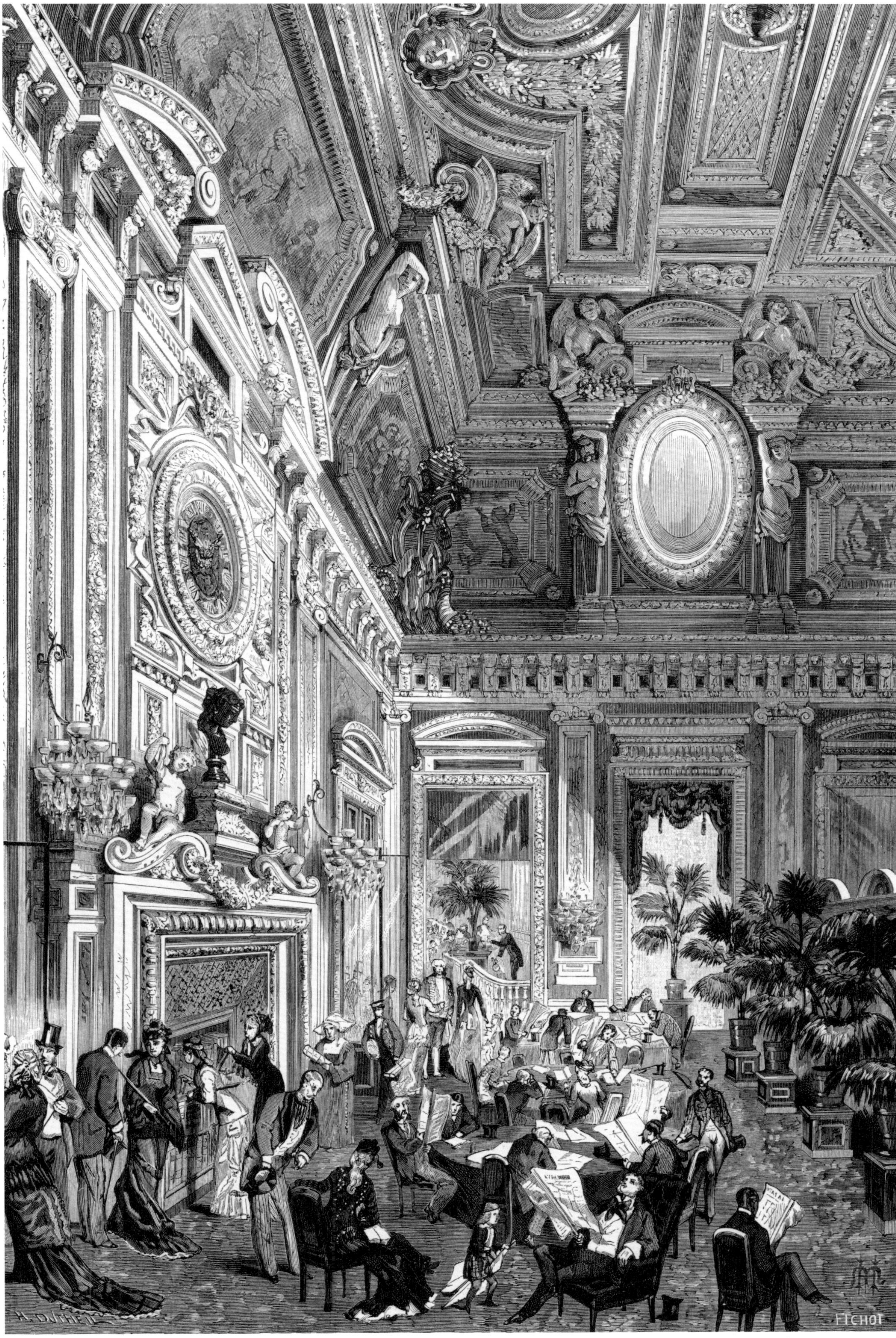

Reading room of the Grands Magasins du Louvre, 1880
(drawing by Charles Fichot, engraving by Hippolyte
Constant Dutheil)

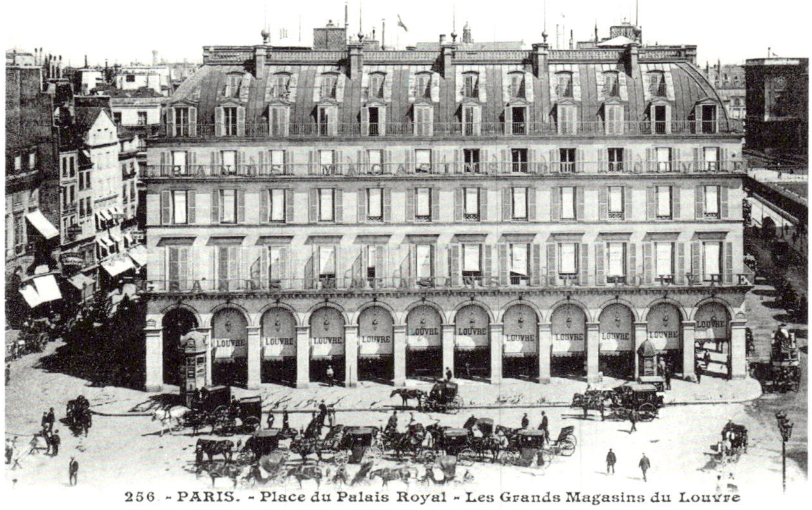

Grands Magasins du Louvre, Place du Palais-Royal, c. 1900 (photographic postcard)

Hall des soieries (fabric department) of the Grands Magasins du Louvre, 1929 (photograph by François Harand)

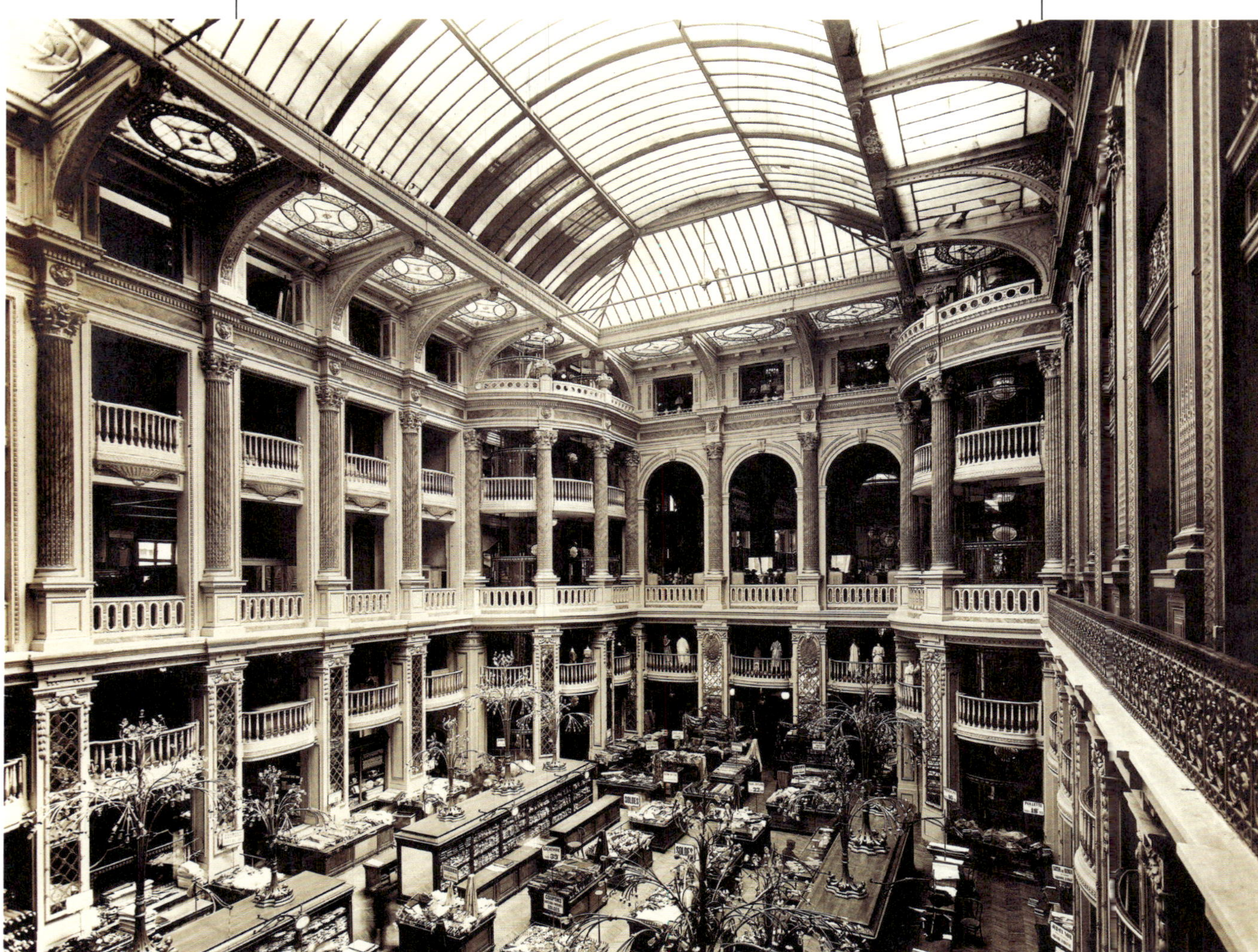

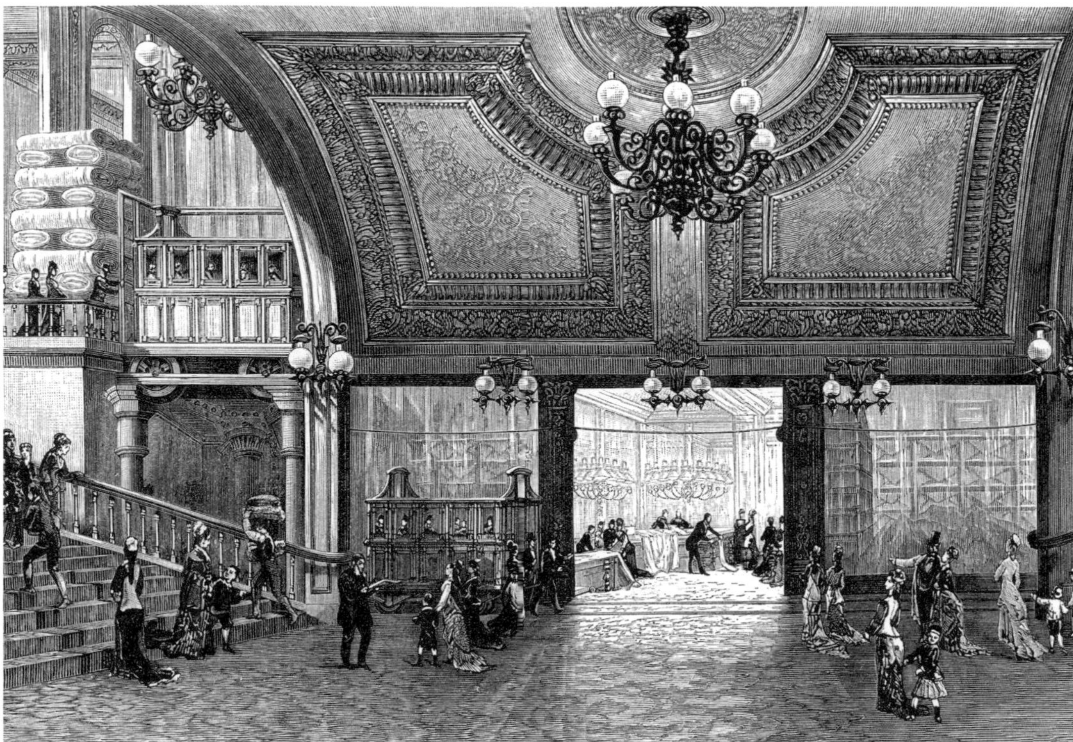

Underground tramway allowing customers to go from one hall of the Grands Magasins du Louvre to another; in the background, the "*salon de lumière,*" where fabrics could be examined under artificial light, 1880 (engraving by Charles Maurand)

The department store had taken over from the Grand Hotel as the space of spectacle. Charles Baudelaire called shopping the "religious intoxication of great cities," announcing that "department stores are temples consecrated to this intoxication."[11] Benjamin pointed to the emergence of the department store as representing a shift in the status of art and the institutions devoted to its display. It was not just that the department store was a new kind of museum, the museum itself was understood as a kind of department store:

> There are relations between department stores
> and museums and here the bazaar provides a link.
> The amassing of artworks in the museum brings them
> into communication with commodities.[12]

It was the culmination of a very long polemical debate on museums. Already, in 1796, the architectural theorist and arm-chair archeologist Quatremère de Quincy opposed, in his *Letters to Miranda*, the looting of artworks from Italy in order to bring them to the Louvre museum, where he claimed that deprived of their context the artworks were seen as "jewels or diamonds that we enjoy merely for their monetary value."[13]

For Benjamin, the shopping arcades were the very paradigm of modernity, understood as a simultaneously optical, psychological, economic and technological condition. Modernity itself was a technology of vision. The Great Exhibitions mechanized vision itself. Machines were both on display and ways of seeing. In the Universal Exhibition of 1889 in Paris, the Galerie des Machines featured two huge electric moving platforms that transported up to 200 visitors a time from one end of the 400-meter-long building to the other, allowing them to see all the other machines from above ground. These mobile platforms had been used to construct the building and were now both on display and a way of seeing the display. It was a kind of theater in which the visitors and the machines were the performers. Likewise, the double-decker Otis passenger elevators in the Eiffel Tower during the 1889 exhibition put the whole city on display and were themselves highlights of the exhibition. Not by chance, the first passenger elevator had been theatrically displayed by Elisha Otis as a single platform suspend-

"TODAY WE GO TO THE [GRANDS MAGASINS DU] LOUVRE AS WE WOULD TO A MUSEUM, AN EXHIBITION," WROTE THE JOURNALIST AND PLAYWRIGHT ALFRED D'AUNAY IN 1880.

11 — Charles Baudelaire, "Fusées" (1867), quoted by Benjamin, *The Arcades Project*, p. 61.

12 — Benjamin, *The Arcades Project*, p. 415.

13 — Antoine Quatremère de Quincy, *Letters to Miranda and Canova on the Abduction of Antiquities from Rome and Athens* (Los Angeles: Getty Research Institute, 2012), pp. 93–123. Quoted in Martin Gaier, "The Art of Civilization: Museum Enemies in the Nineteenth Century in the History of Museology," in Eva-Maria Troelenberg and Melania Savino (ed.), *Images of the Art Museum. Connecting Gaze and Discourse in the History of Museology* (Berlin/Boston: Walter de Gruyter GmbH, 2017), p. 37, and in Yve-Alain Bois, "Foreword," in Julian Rose, *Building Culture: Sixteen Architects on How Museums Are Shaping the Future of Art, Architecture, and Public Space* (New York: Princeton Architectural Press, 2024), p. 10.

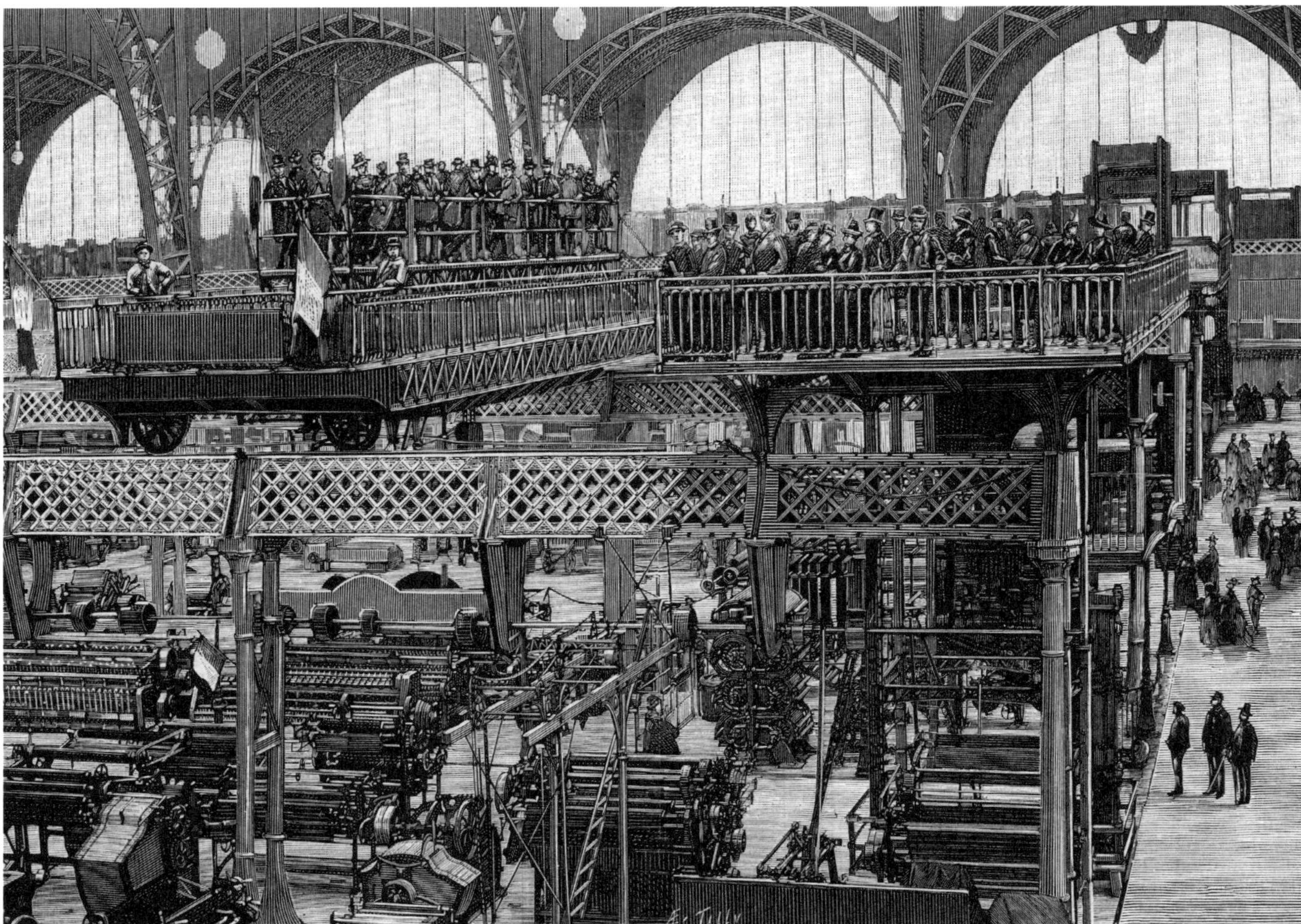

Electric moving platforms of the Galerie des Machines, Universal Exhibition, Paris, 1889 (engraving by Auguste Tilly)

ed high above the visitors in the 1853 World's Fair exhibition in New York. In a sense, the whole point of visiting these great 19th-century exhibitions was to feel the ground move.

In this new world, the idea of a stable ground was theatrically displaced by moving platforms and constantly changing new angles of view, drawing on the millennial tradition of theaters creating alternative worlds with elaborate machinery raising or lowering stage platforms. In Charles Garnier's Paris Opera house, built between 1861 and 1875 and commissioned by Napoleon III, a vast system of pulleys and counterweights enabled multiple platforms to move up and down so that elaborate fantasy worlds miraculously appeared, transformed, and disappeared. Yet in the new optical regime of modernity, theater was not an alternative world of fantasy but the everyday world itself—the world of what Benjamin called the "phantasmagoria of capitalist culture" which "attains its most radiant unfolding" in the world exhibitions.[14]

JEAN NOUVEL'S ARCHITECTURAL GESTURE CHANNELS THE HISTORY OF THE BUILDING, RETURNING TO THE MOMENT WHEN EVERYDAY LIFE WAS FIRST MECHANIZED, AND NEW WAYS OF VIEWING WERE INITIATED—THE MOMENT IN MODERN LIFE WHEN THE FLOOR WAS ALWAYS MOVING.

The Grands Magasins du Louvre absorbed the moving world around it. It had steam-powered elevators theatrically positioned in the building that were given a whole page in *Le Monde illustré* as a spectacle in their own right.[15] A unique tram car took clients along the perimeter of the enormous building, plunging them down into the underground level through a tunnel before bringing them up at the other end of the building. Every child that visited the building wanted to go on the ride. The basement was an underground city which included its own railroad system with one kilometer of iron tracks, two fire stations, a post office, a printing press atelier, and countless workshops.

14 — Benjamin, *The Arcades Project*, p. 8.

15 — G. Clerc, "Les Nouvelles Galeries des Grands Magasins du Louvre," *Le Monde Illustré* supplement, October 4, 1879, p. 227.

Platform Fever

The new spaces of the Fondation Cartier reclaim this mechanical legacy, preserving the envelope of the original building and inserting five enormous independently moving platforms that take their measure from the courtyards of the original building, as if using their voids to reanimate the building. The stable unchanged exterior structure now hosts a vertiginous instability. The mobile platforms are, not by chance, made by a company expert in the moving stages of theaters. They represent a dramatic and radical transformation of traditional spaces for the exhibition of art.

Perhaps the platforms could be seen as an echo of the moving floors without walls in Richard Rogers and Renzo Piano's initial competition project for the Centre Georges Pompidou (1971), which was itself an echo of the mobile structures in Cedric Price's Fun Palace project (1964), developed in 1960 with the theatrical director Joan Littlewood as a kind of theater without walls—an enormous theater containing nothing but stage machinery. Yet there is nothing of the 1960s' spirit here. Nouvel's project resonates, rather, with one of Price's main inspirations, the 1936-1939 Maison du Peuple in Clichy, designed by the architects Marcel Lods and Eugène Beaudouin in collaboration with Jean Prouvé and the engineer Vladimir Bodianksy, in which the whole floor, walls, and ceiling can move independently or even disappear altogether to create vastly different spaces. The structure likewise occupies a whole city block. It too is not so much a building as a way of dissolving a traditional building from inside—a machine for transforming space and social relationships. Something of the Maison du Peuple lives on in the new Fondation Cartier space, in its vast mechanisms, endless possible reorganizations of space, and even the idea of balustrades that automatically appear when the floor moves away. Above all, these non-buildings are not predictable. They have many possible futures. Their mechanisms challenge the visitor to see, think, and act differently.

For the new Fondation Cartier space, Jean Nouvel reaches back even further, to the age of the big machines that so inspired modernist architects like Le Corbusier and architectural historians like Sigfried Giedion—the massive turbines powering electrical mobility and the suspended moving platforms of bridges like the Marseille *pont transbordeur* of 1905, which Giedion

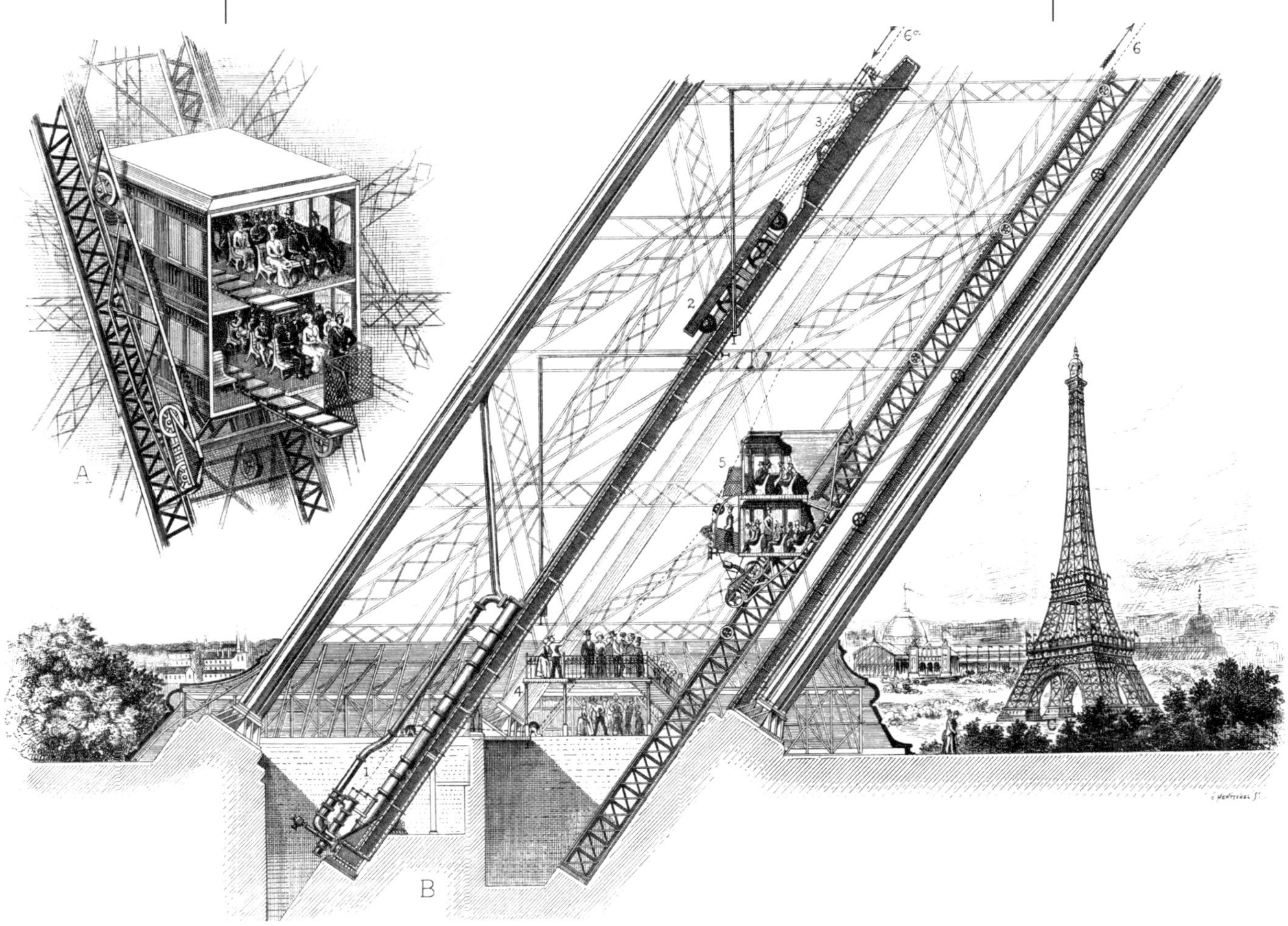

Details of the operation of the Otis elevators in the Eiffel Tower, Universal Exhibition, Paris, 1889 (engraving by Carl Hentschel)

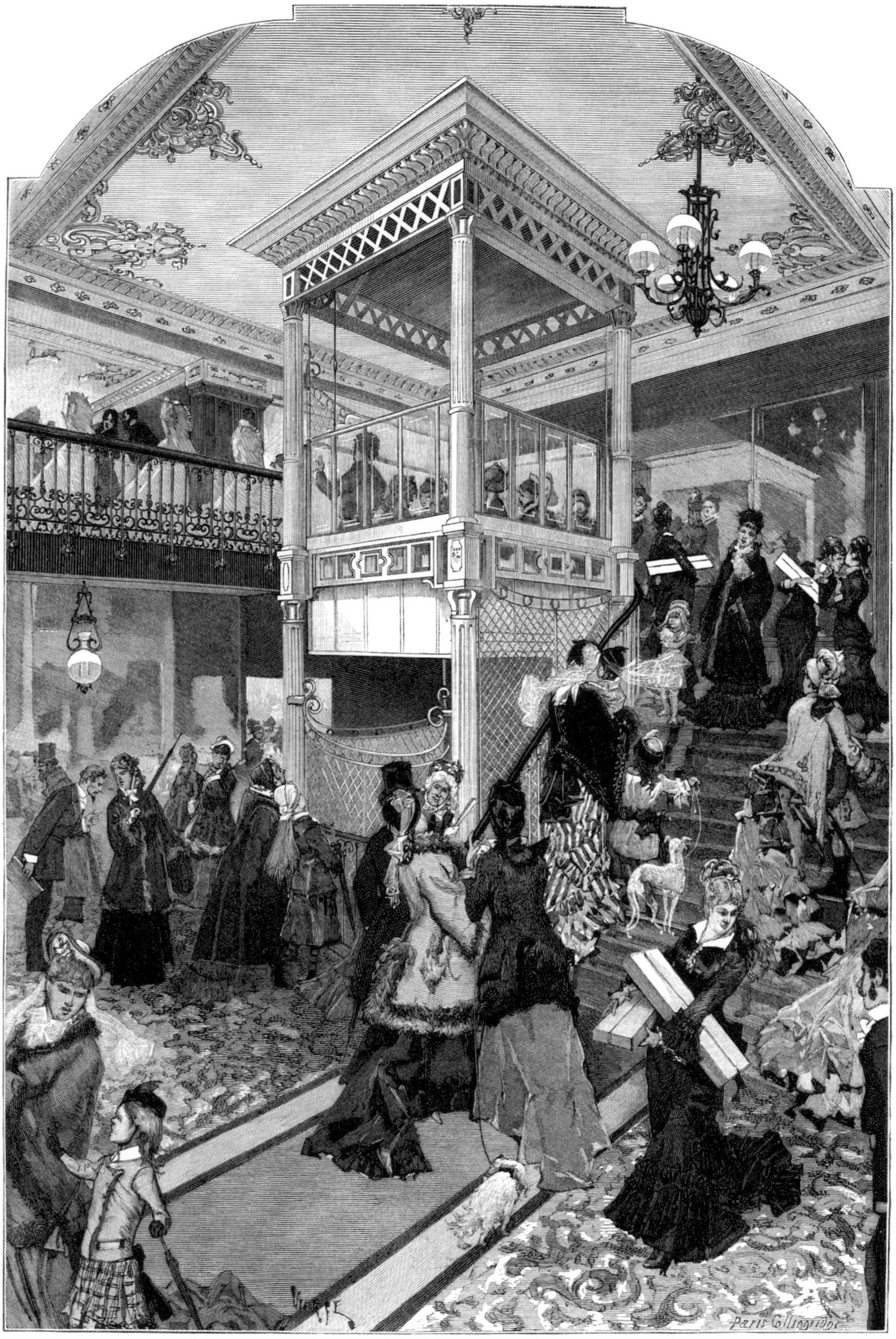

Engraving published in *Le Monde Illustré* supplement, October 4, 1879, featuring one of the elevators of the Grands Magasins du Louvre (drawing by Daniel Vierge, engraving by Arthur Collingridge de Tourcey)

symptomatically used as the cover image of his first book on modern architecture: *Bauen in Frankreich*, *Bauen in Eisen*, *Bauen in Eisenbeton* of 1928. For Giedion, the massive perforated metal structure of the bridge that moves the ground by sending a horizontal platform 240 meters across the water "blurs" the limits of architecture. It "engenders floating relations and interpenetrations," the very symptom of modernity in which "everything is based on mobility."[16]

Jean Nouvel's architectural gesture channels the history of the building, returning to the moment when everyday life was first mechanized, and new ways of viewing were initiated—the moment in modern life when the floor was always moving. Everything was displayed from multiple changing angles. Viewers viewed in multiple ways, and they themselves were being viewed. There was no shared solid ground, only ever-changing interrelationships. The optical logic of shopping dissolved the stability of buildings and of social relationships. This shift in architecture coincided with the arrival of new forms of wealth and taste. It was as if monumental architecture needed to be dissolved to admit not only new kinds of vision

16 — The original cover was designed by László Moholy-Nagy, using photographs taken by Giedion himself. Sigfried Giedion, *Building in France*, *Building in Iron*, *Building in Ferroconcrete*, English translation of 1928 book (Santa Monica: The Getty Center For The History Of Art, 1995), pp. 90 and 147 (caption of images of the bridge).

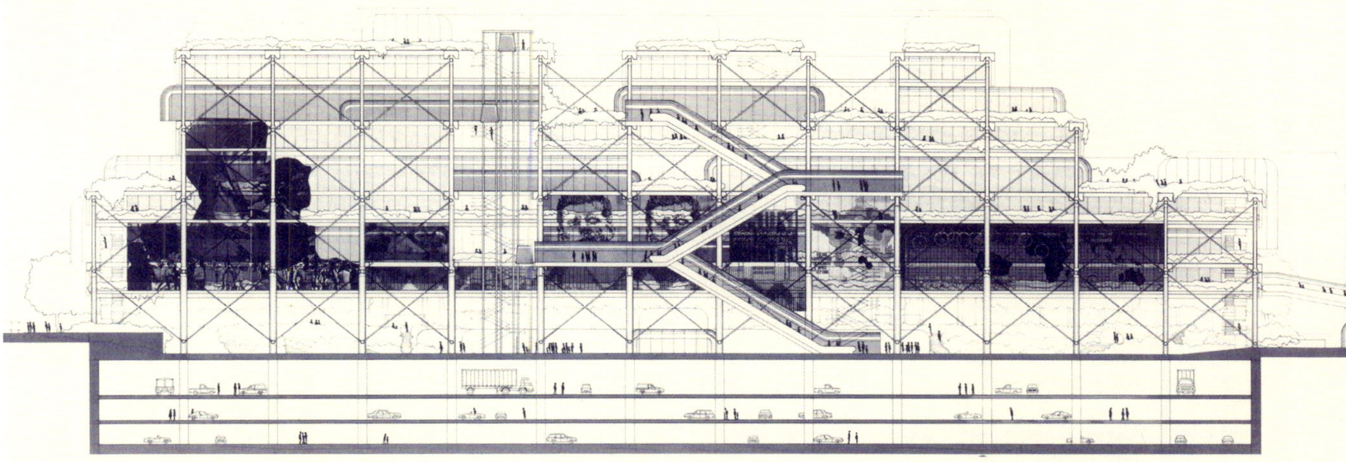

but new kinds of citizens. The shop window blurred the distinction between inside and outside, encouraging an aspiration for social mobility through the purchase of objects. The interior was denser than the street, an internal crowd encountering a multitude of objects, seemingly from every corner of the planet, curated by the store and allowing the visitors to curate themselves.

Renzo Piano and Richard Rogers, longitudinal section of the initial project for the Centre Georges Pompidou, 1971

Cedric Price, interior perspective of the Fun Palace, c. 1960–1964

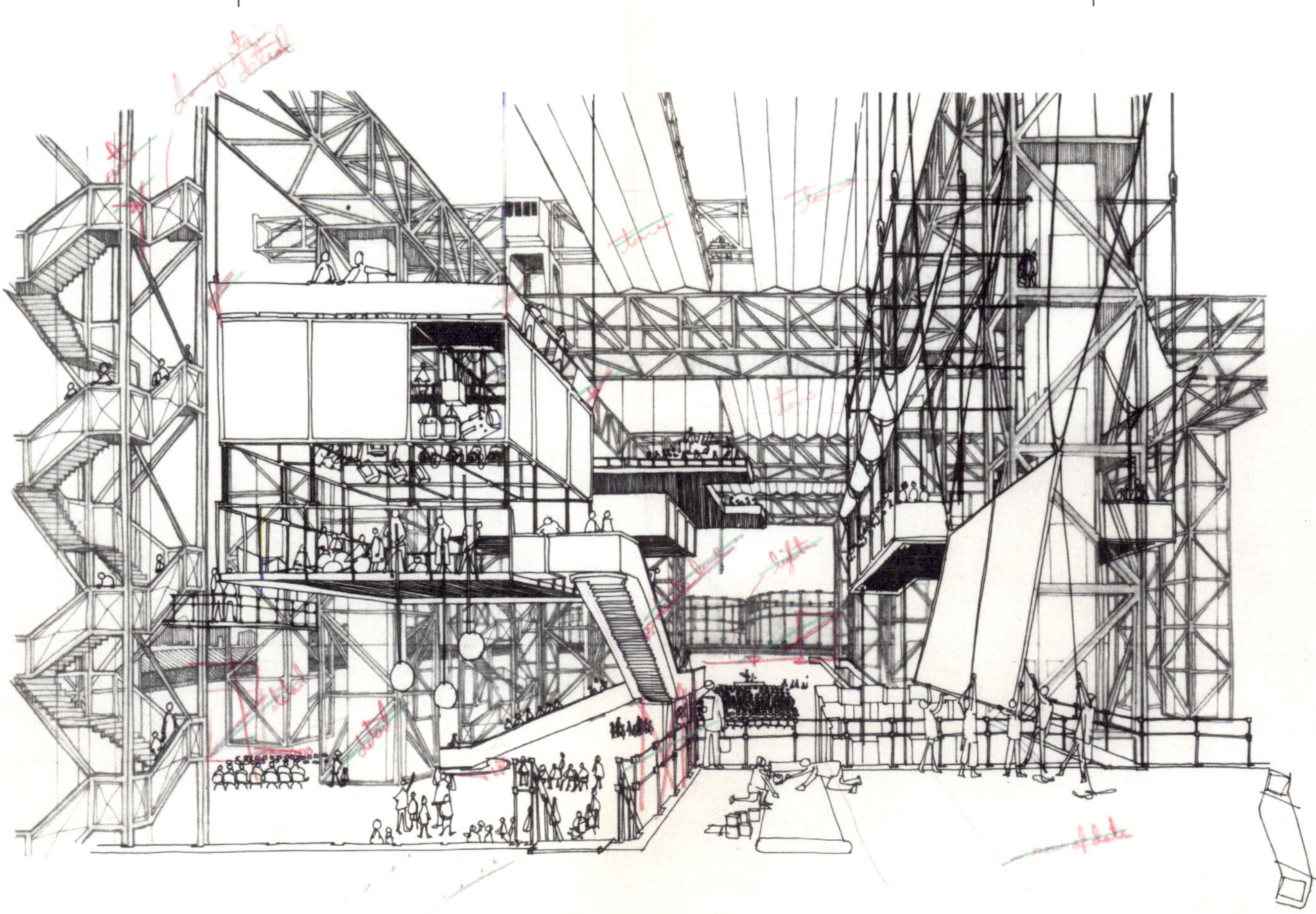

Reinventing Art

The new space that Jean Nouvel has designed for the Fondation Cartier forces art to live outside the safety of museums. There are no gallery walls and what is displayed can be seen from the streets through the arcade picture windows that once showed goods in the stores. The new space is part of the streetscape; a form of streetscape itself. It offers new possibilities for what it means to exhibit art, not just to the audience in the building, but to the passersby in the street, who can see through the whole building from the Rue de Rivoli to the Rue Saint-Honoré. In fact, standing on the Rue de Rivoli, passersby can simultaneously see sculptures in the Louvre museum, provocatively positioned near the glass windows as if to tempt them, and glimpse fragments of works of art or performances in the Fondation Cartier, all while being themselves observed from all sides. Conversely, the visitors inside the building never completely leave the street. The monumental building is perforated by multiple gazes that cut through the city. In a sense, it is not an interior but a continuation of the exterior, an animation of the street level. Art in the space once reserved for goods. Art as goods. Art lovers as inventive shoppers. Not simply passively receiving what is offered but shaping it through their desires, curiosities, expertise and interactions. The mobile floors put both art and viewers in motion, calling for new kinds of interaction, new kinds of art and curation.

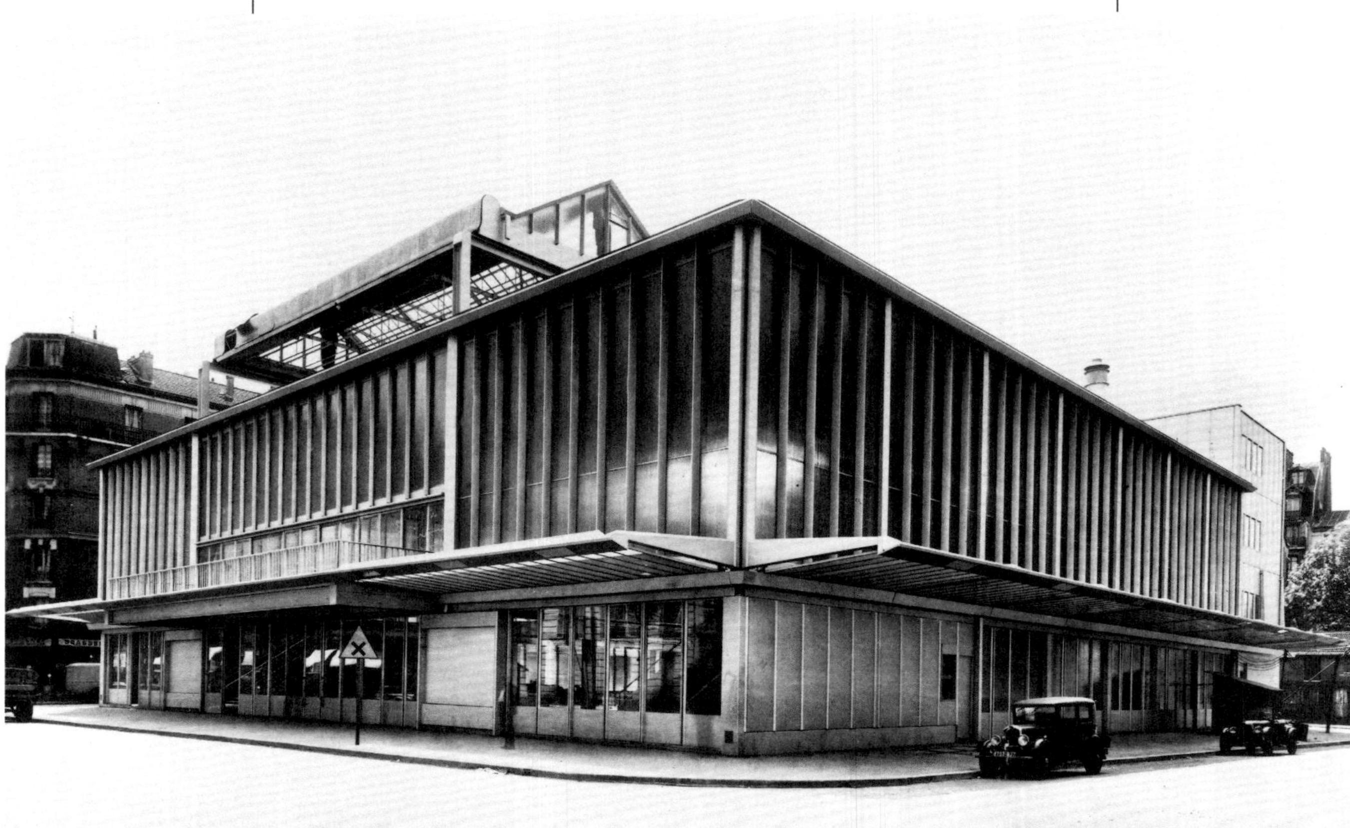

Eugène Beaudouin and Marcel Lods (architects), Vladimir Bodiansky (engineer), and Jean Prouvé (constructor), Maison du Peuple de Clichy, 1939

Curators are no longer in a safe bubble. The usual gallery protocols are of no use in this alternative optical machine. Curators must invent rather than simply presenting artworks, "shifting the system of the act of showing," in Nouvel's words.[17] Artists too are handed an enormous challenge, a power usually reserved to architects. Space becomes part of their work. The ability to adjust the platforms to different levels will inevitably engage their architectural capacities, provoking new ways of occupying space, new kinds of work, new angles, new sensations. When the floor moves, nothing about art can be taken for granted. It may also force artists into new and productive collaborations. Art can become something else, should be something else. As Nouvel put it, "what is invented is not automatically seen in the steel or stone. The space is marked by a different way of doing: a way of conceiving how artists can have maximum power of expression."[18] The Fondation Cartier has never been a "container" for art that existed somewhere else, but rather an institution that creates content, commissioning numerous works for its spaces, often conceived or produced for specific sites, whether Jouy-en-

17 — "Here, it is possible to do what cannot be done elsewhere, by shifting the system of the act of showing." Jean Nouvel quoted in *Voir venir, venir voir: Fondation Cartier, 40 years pour l'art contemporain*, press kit, Fondation Cartier pour l'art contemporain, Paris, 2024, p. 3.

18 — J. Nouvel, *Voir venir, venir voir: Fondation Cartier, 40 years pour l'art contemporain.*

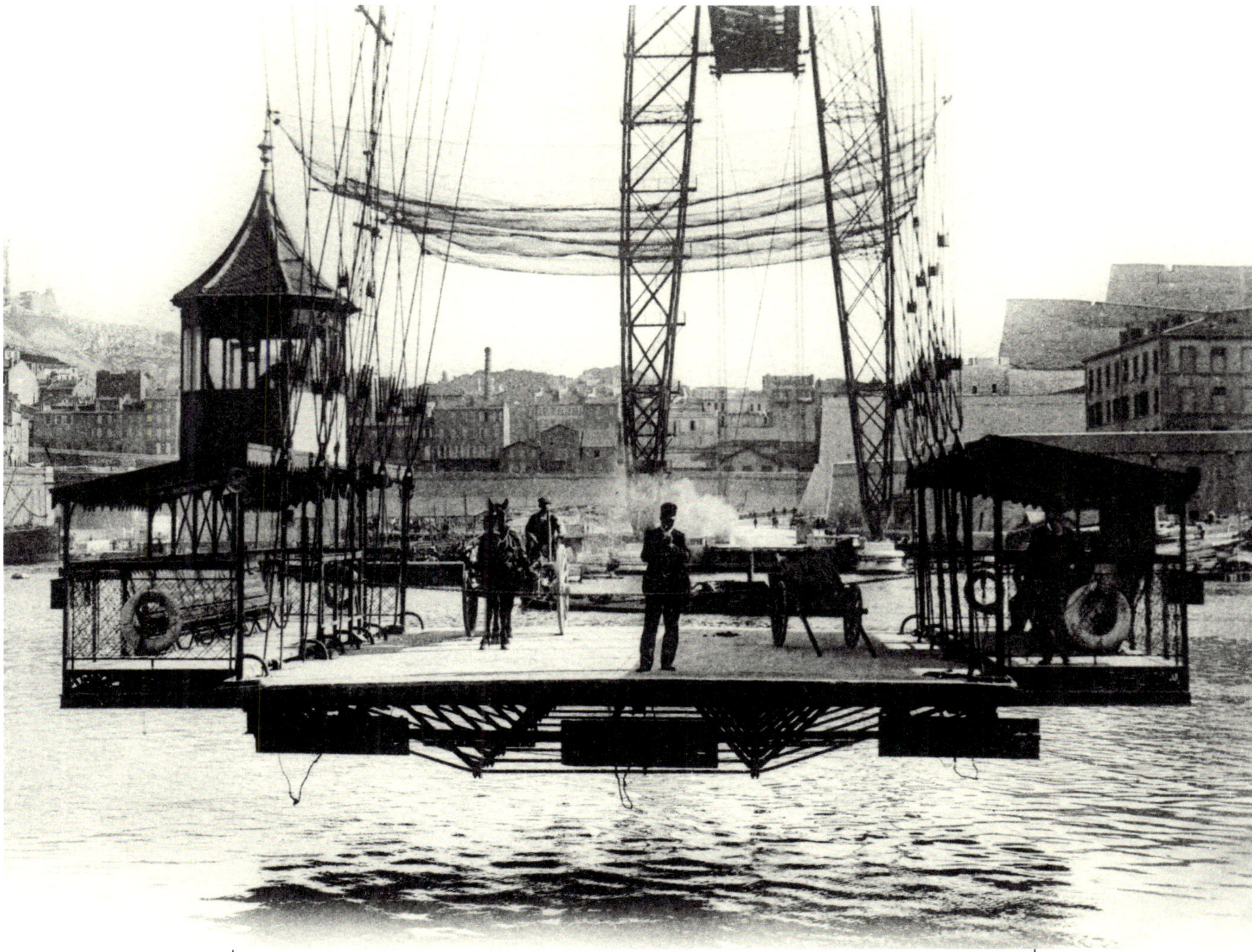

Ferdinand Arnodin, moving platform of the Marseille *pont transbordeur*, 1905 (photographic postcard, c. 1919)

Josas, the first site of the Fondation, near Versailles (1984–1994), or the Nouvel building on the Boulevard Raspail (1994–2025). The Fondation engaged artists and architects in exhibition design and asked artists to rework their pieces when showing them in a different space. Nothing in the Collection of the Fondation Cartier exists outside a particular space. In that sense, the Collection is already infused with architecture.

The building on the Boulevard Raspail, a huge glass vitrine without walls, open to the garden and street, was initially considered by curators, artists and critics as a challenging place for works of art. But art accommodated itself to the building, with its transparency, its reflections, its lack of walls, its blurring of inside and outside. Installations were positioned in front of, within, and behind the two layers of glass. They were seen equally and simultaneously from the garden where the building sits, from the street, and from the interior. Works adjusted themselves to this hyper-exposure. The works in the Collection of the Fondation Cartier wear the imprint of the buildings for which they were conceived. The question for this new building is: What kind of work will it make possible that wouldn't have happened in another context? What kind of curatorial strategies will emerge? What kind of active viewership? Good architecture asks questions, multiplies questions, challenges stabilities.

THE NEW SPACE THAT JEAN NOUVEL HAS DESIGNED FOR THE FONDATION CARTIER FORCES ART TO LIVE OUTSIDE THE SAFETY OF MUSEUMS.

In an age in which more and more artists engage with architecture, the new spaces seem an open invitation. Artists, curators, and visitors all become a new kind of architect engaging space. The mobile platforms trigger the possibility in the imagination that the space, the works, and the experience can and will change, or have just changed. Perhaps the space is different in the morning than it is in the afternoon. One is never sure if a platform has moved. The visible mechanism for shifting the floor means the idea of movement is always there, even if all the platforms were lined up at the same height and remained there for months. A platform can move to a place where it could display work but not be accessed by visitors; it can go up so close to the ceiling that visitors would have to crouch to discover works specially created for this kind of unprecedented space, triggering memories of the film *Being John Malkovich* (1999) or the ever-shrinking room in Edgar Allan Poe's "The Pit and the Pendulum" (1842). And it is not just the floors that move. Other machines shift panels to adjust or block the light from the glass ceilings above. The mechanisms reject the stability of conventional museums and galleries to present different landscapes and incubate a multiplicity of imagined landscapes as each visitor mentally moves the platforms. A dream space, then, magnified by the surrealism of looking up through the glass skylights to see trees, to be, as it were, in the space of the roots, yet another destabilizing effect.

What is remarkable about this return to the 19th-century revolution of mechanization that transformed viewing itself and the status of art, is that it is happening now, when the restless mobility of digital platforms is again transforming vision, everyday life, shopping, exhibition, and art. The return to the mechanical is polemical in a moment when everyday life has become a form of self-curation, department stores are collapsing, and physical stores—from luxury goods to Apple—are adopting strategies from the art world. It is as if the age of digital and dematerialized commerce provoked its paradoxical opposite, the desire for a sensual encounter—an experience.

TO VISIT THE BUILDING IS TO SEE THE WORKS ON DISPLAY, BUT EQUALLY THE MECHANISM OF DISPLAY AS A MOBILE WORK OF ART.

The Viennese architect and artist Friedrich J. Kiesler comes to mind. His *Contemporary Art Applied to the Store and its Display* (1930) rejected any simple distinction between art and commerce, exploring ways of displaying art in shop windows and merchandise as art—even predicting the idea of displacing the museum with a TELEMUSEUM device visible from the street or at home.[19] Kiesler celebrated shop windows as "loudspeakers" interfacing interior and exterior, drawing on his recent experience doing a series of windows for the Saks Fifth Avenue department store in New York. He noted that it was department stores, not museums, that introduced modernism to the American public. Such stores needed to be understood as centers of culture and social life. Their display systems were "elevated floors" orchestrated by "the principle of flux[20]" against anything static.

The mobile platforms of the new Fondation Cartier space resonate with Kiesler's multiple theatrical stage mechanisms, such as the *City in Space* exhibited in the 1925 *Exposition des Arts décoratifs in Paris*—a series of suspended "platforms"—and the "floating" ramps of his spiraling Endless Theater, exhibited in New York in 1926. In each case, there is a confusion between actors and audiences, an instability of the floor, and an absence of walls. Mobility itself transforms the viewer and the viewed. Mobility even produces the viewer. In an unpublished text about shop windows, Kiesler speaks of a mobile metal system that lures and transforms the gaze, pulling subject and object into a new kind of intimacy:

> Which is the most provocative: the curiosity to look into a neighbor's window or the window which lures us to look in? Let us consider, for the sake of speed, that both curiosity and the desire to lure have been born at the same time. Of unknown parents. Now you have a purchaser and merchandise. So close and yet so far apart. Why is their union so constrained? Some transparent but insurmountable wall separates the two. ... Build the whole window thus. Sliding sheet material. Horizontally sliding, vertically crossing. Stops at any level. Forward. Backward. Someone is going to come to it sooner or later. ... Always the same, always dif-

19 — Friedrich J. Kiesler, *Contemporary Art Applied to the Store and its Display* (New York: Brentano's, 1930).

20 — F. Kiesler, *Contemporary Art Applied to the Store and its Display*, pp. 105 and 14.

ferent. Modern. A companionate linking between the two—the merchandise and the purchaser.[21]

In a sense, the whole space of the Fondation Cartier is a new kind of immense inhabitable shop window, whose moving metal platforms transform viewer and viewed as they dissolve static architecture. In the words of Kiesler's "Manifesto of Tensionism" of 1925, the year he designed a polemical department store as a single 21-story high glass-encased corkscrew floor wrapped around an elevator core: "We will have NO MORE WALLS... No walls, no foundations.... ELASTICITY OF BUILDING ADEQUATE TO THE ELASTICITY OF LIVING."[22]

21 — F. Kiesler, "Merchandise That Puts You on the Spot. Some Notes on Show Windows," undated typescript, c. 1930, Kiesler Estate Archives, Vienna, Frederick Kiesler Foundation, unpaged.

22 — F. Kiesler, *Contemporary Art Applied to the Store and its Display*, pp. 48–49.

Jean Nouvel, longitudinal section of the building of the Fondation Cartier, 261 Boulevard Raspail, Paris, 1991

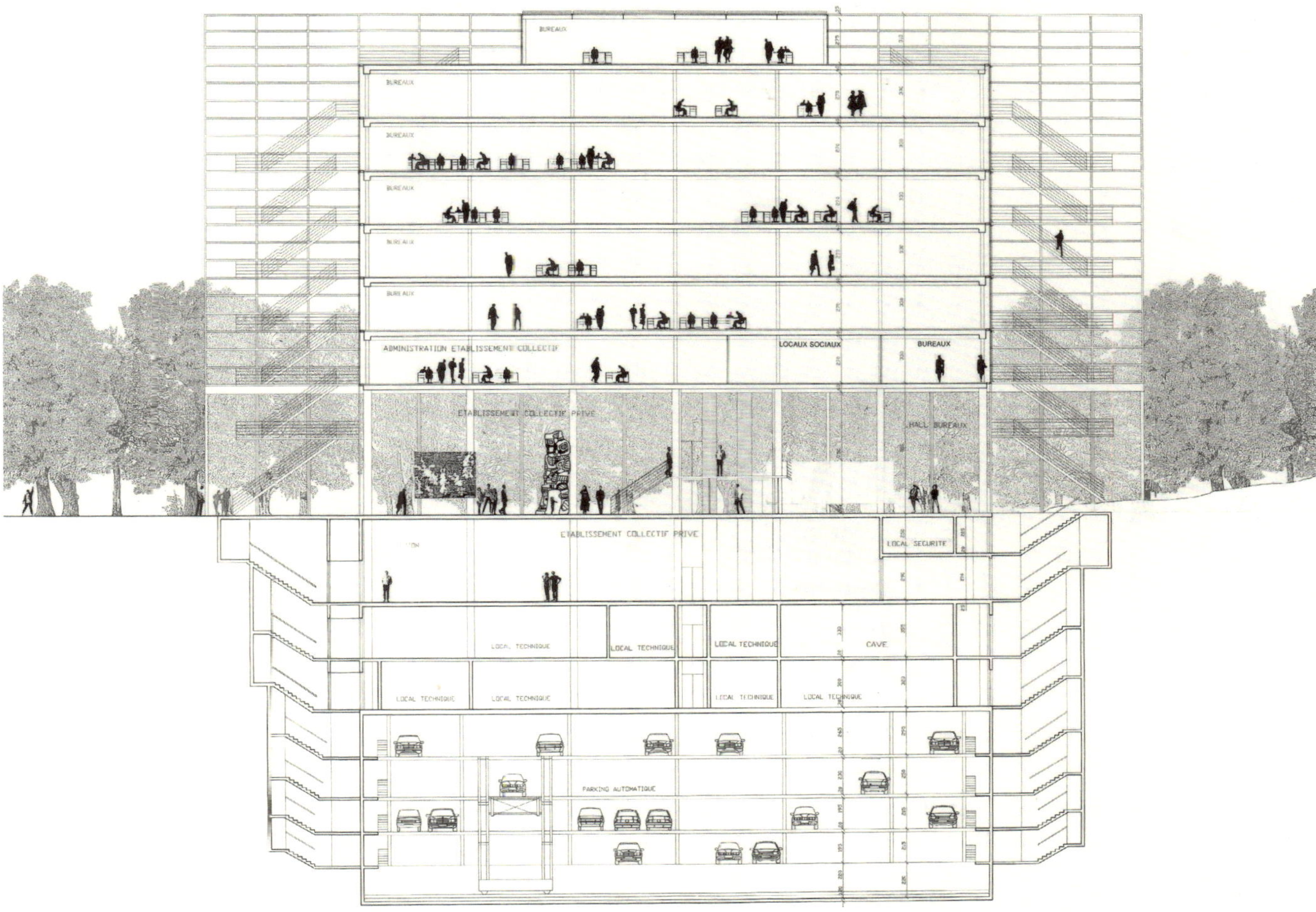

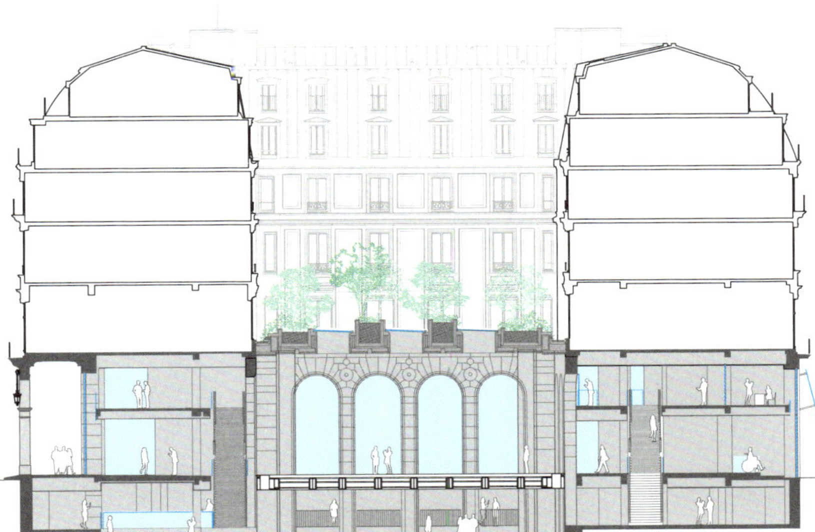

Jean Nouvel, cross-section of the Fondation Cartier building, 2 Place du Palais-Royal, Paris, 2025

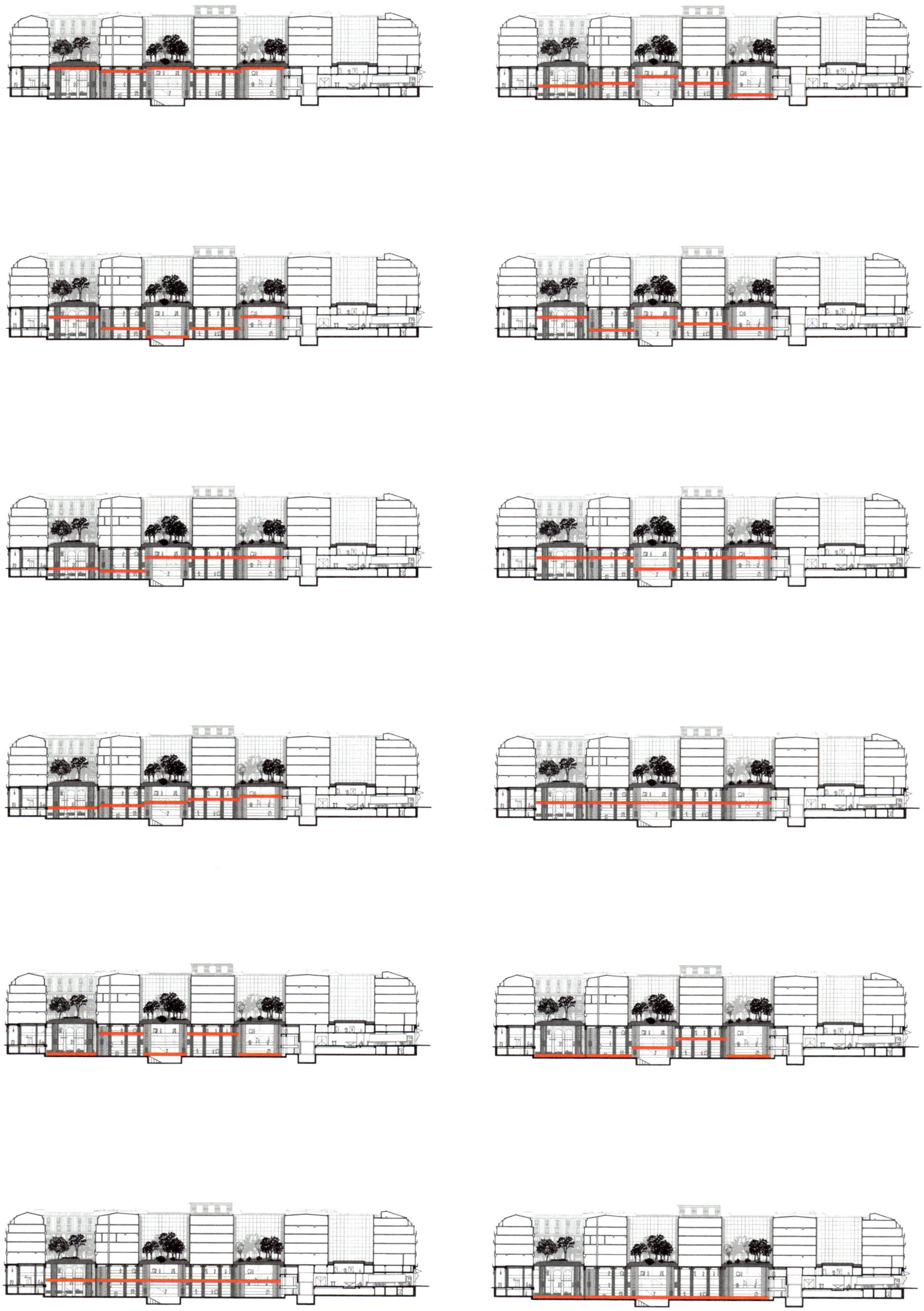

Jean Nouvel, longitudinal sections
of the Fondation Cartier building,
2 Place du Palais-Royal, Paris: examples
of configurations of the five mobile
platforms, 2025

In the new elastic space of the Fondation Cartier, the empty heart of the biggest department store in the world becomes the site of a kind of analog staging of the instability of digital life, and thereby a work of art in its own right that, like all the other works in the Collection, responds to its own site. To visit the building is to see the works on display, but equally the mechanism of display as a mobile work of art. And yet the place is not just for showing art. It is a space to encounter others in its streetscape and thereby encounter yourself. If this is a theater, a mobile stage, the visitors are the actors, and everything is a performance. This immense mechanism is an invitation to act.

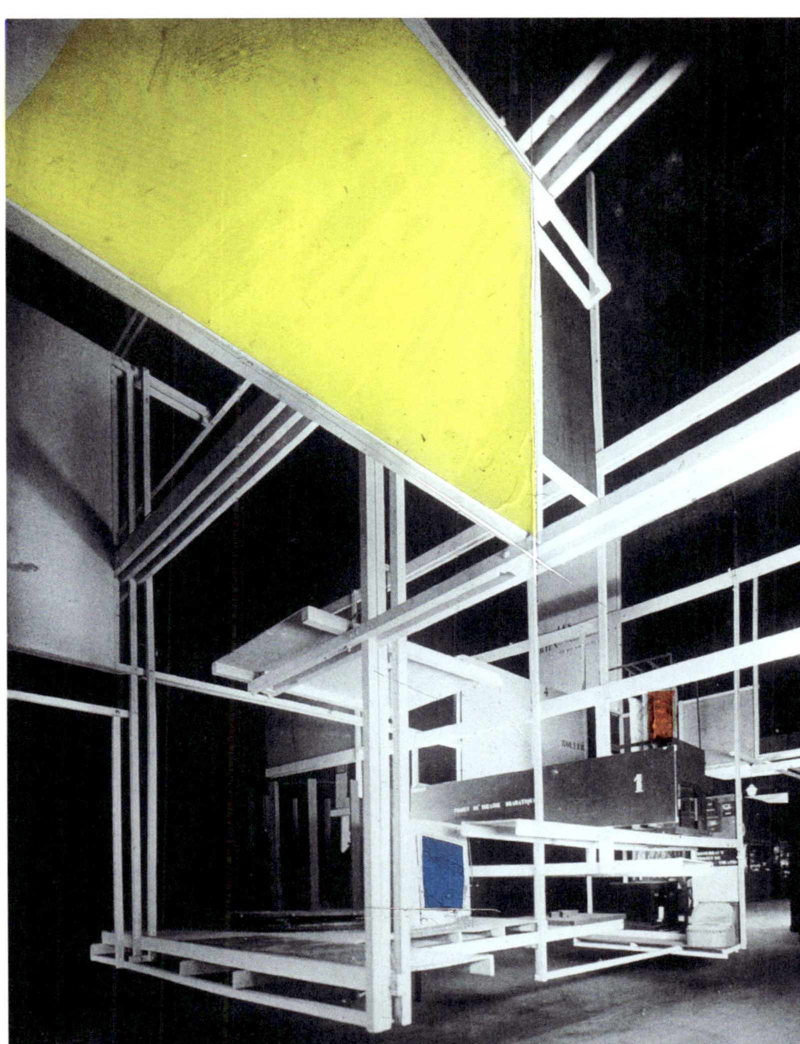

Friedrich J. Kiesler, *City in Space*, International Exhibition of Modern Decorative and Industrial Arts, Paris, 1925

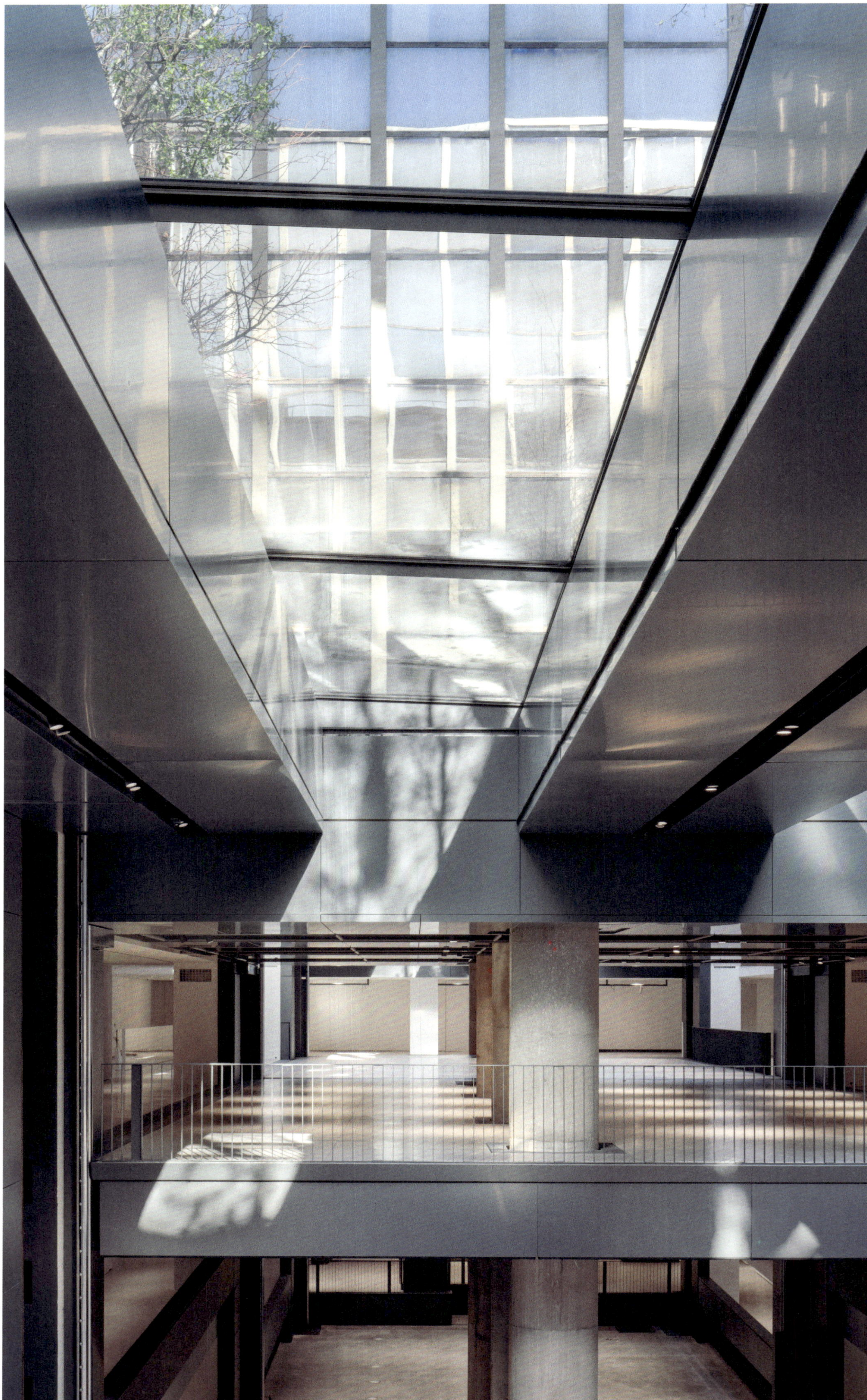

One of the skylights of the Fondation Cartier building
seen from the third platform

Photographs by

DANICA O. KUS

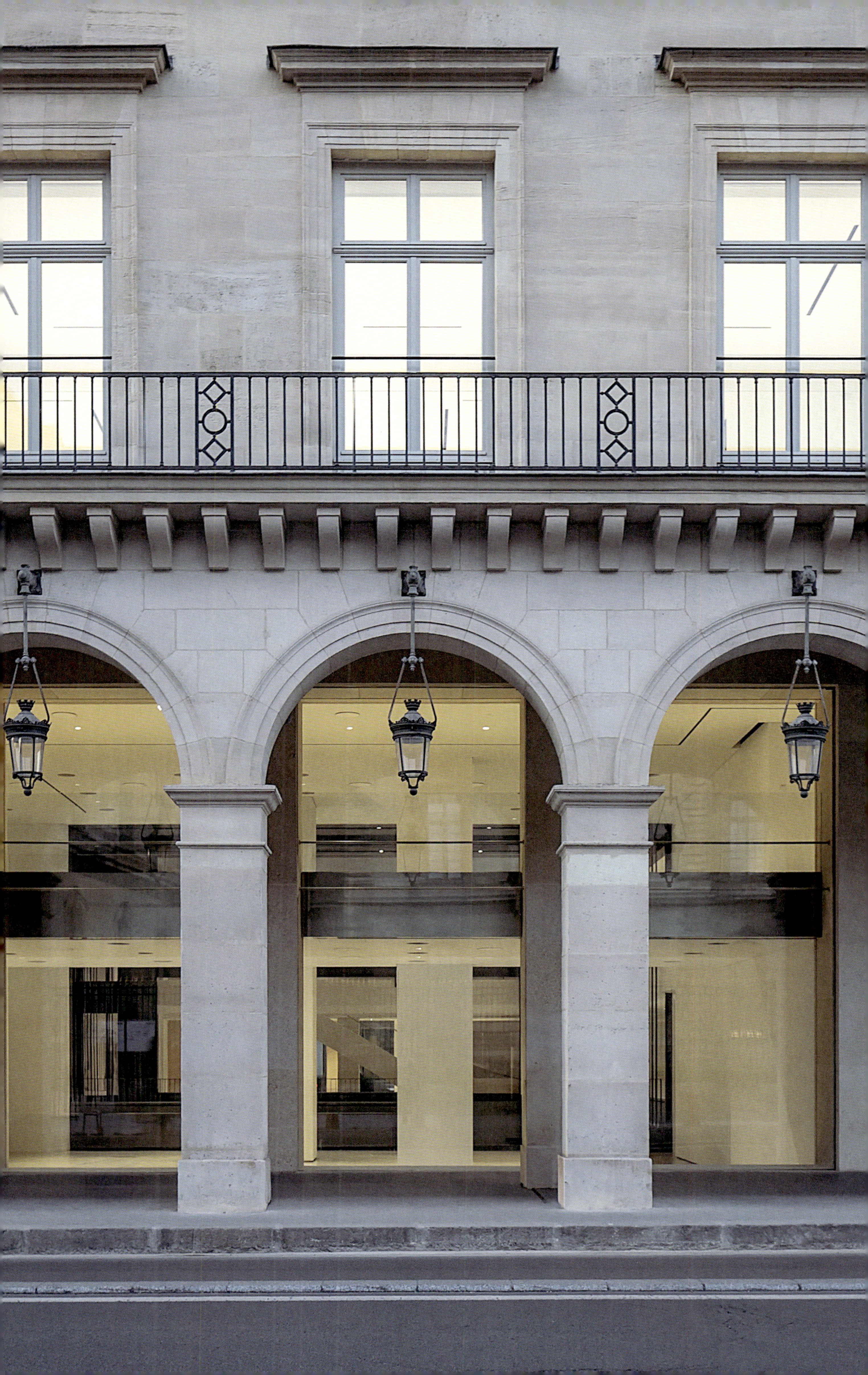

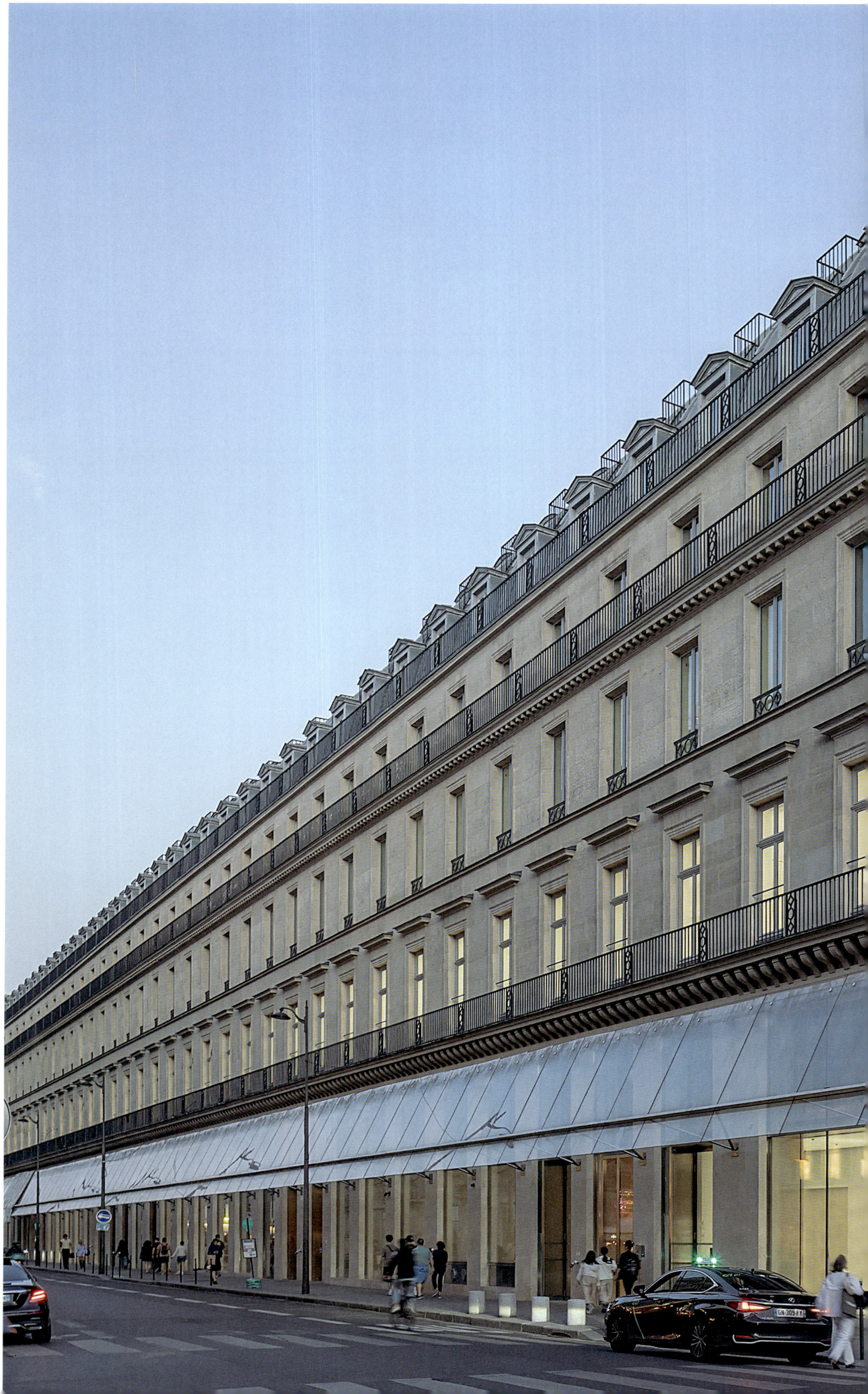

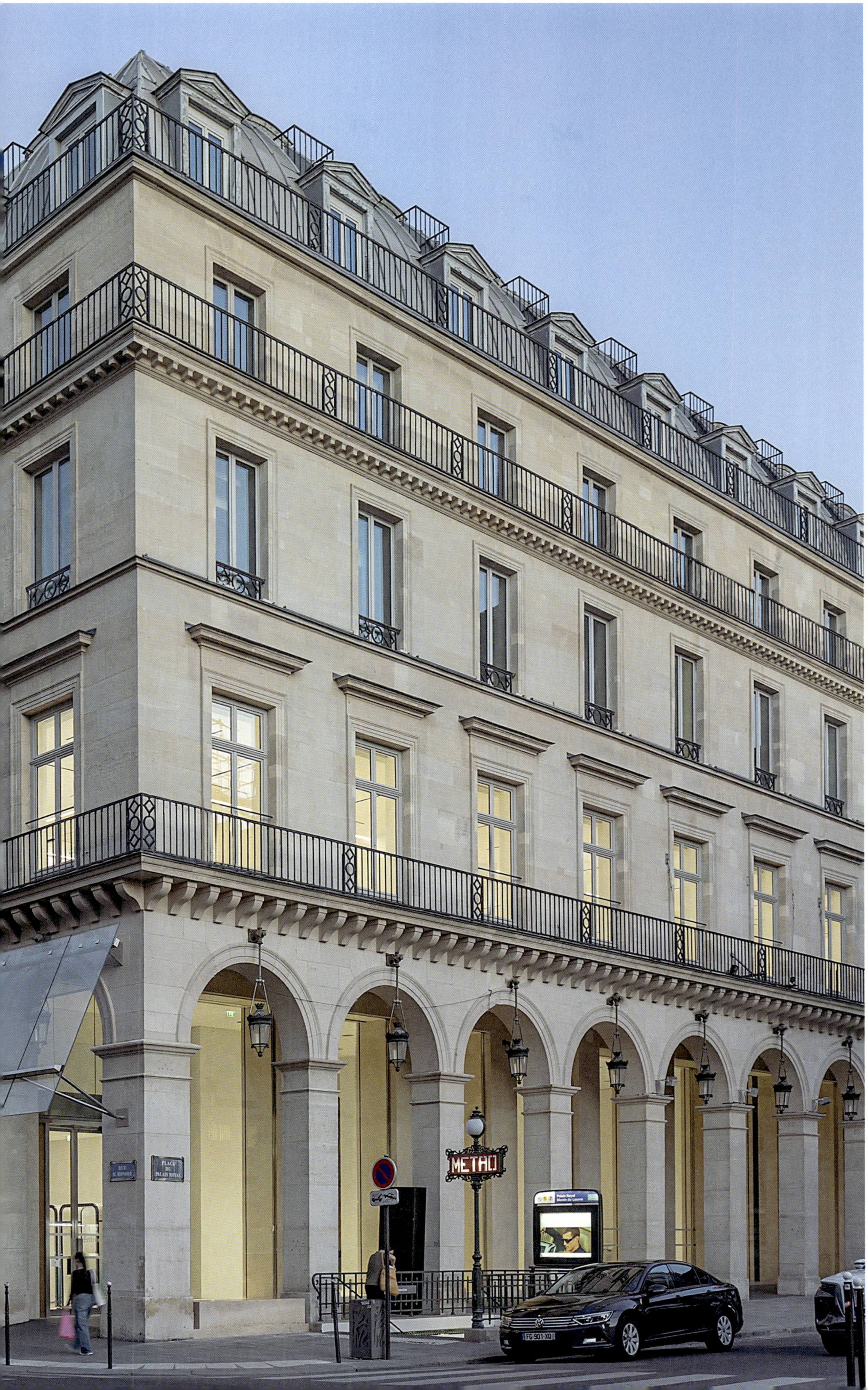
RUE S. HONORÉ
PLACE DU PALAIS ROYAL
METRO
Palais Royal
Musée du Louvre

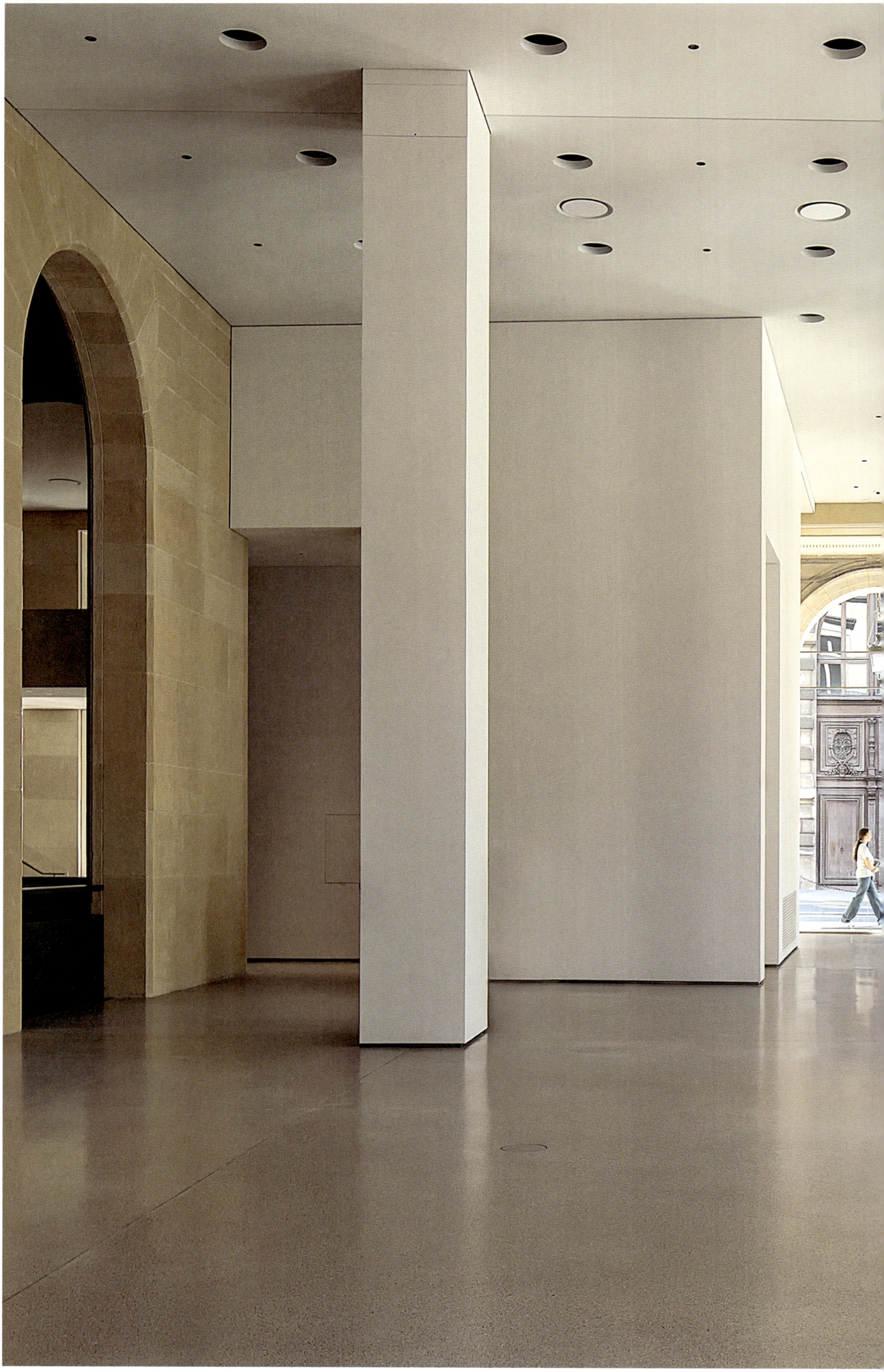

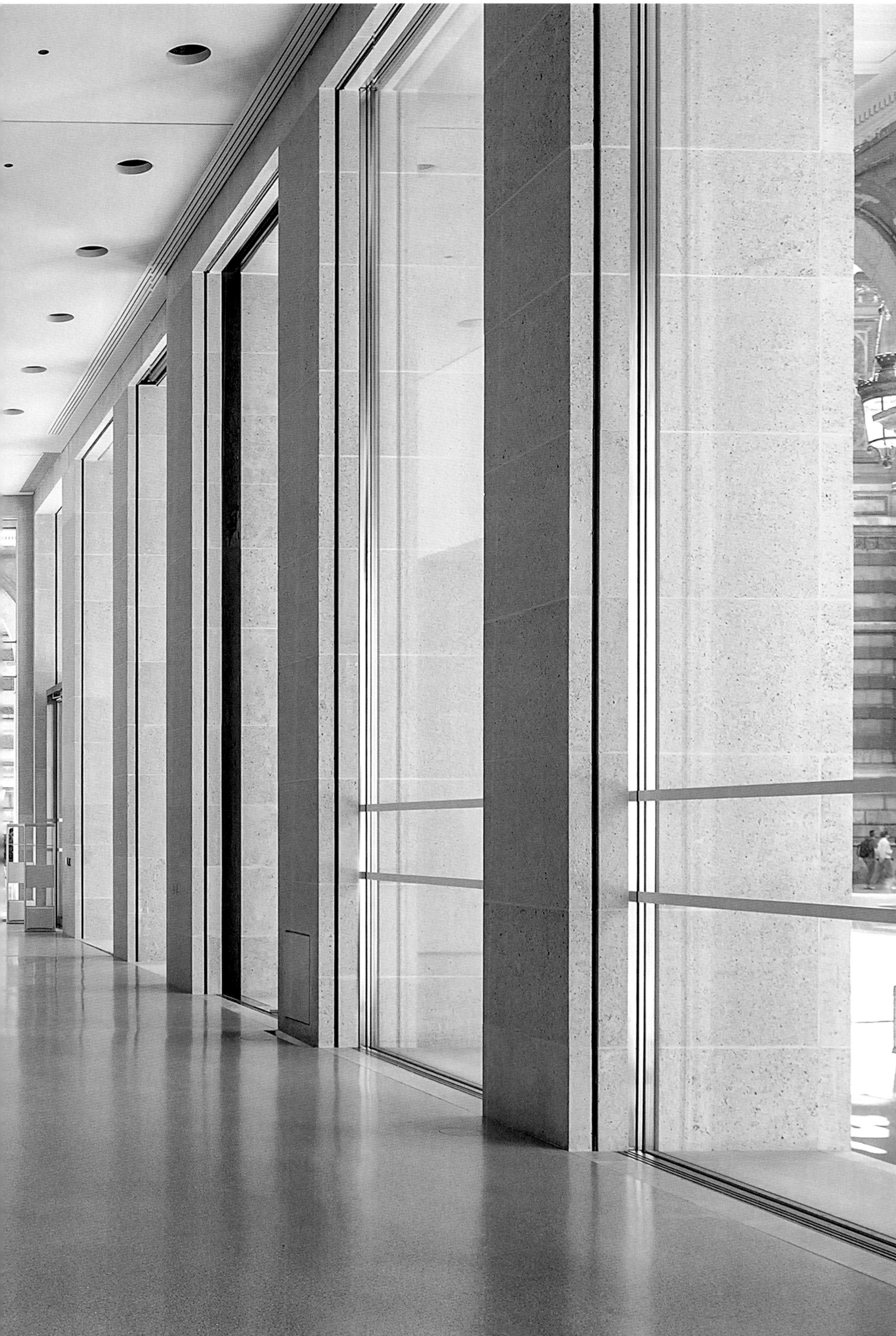

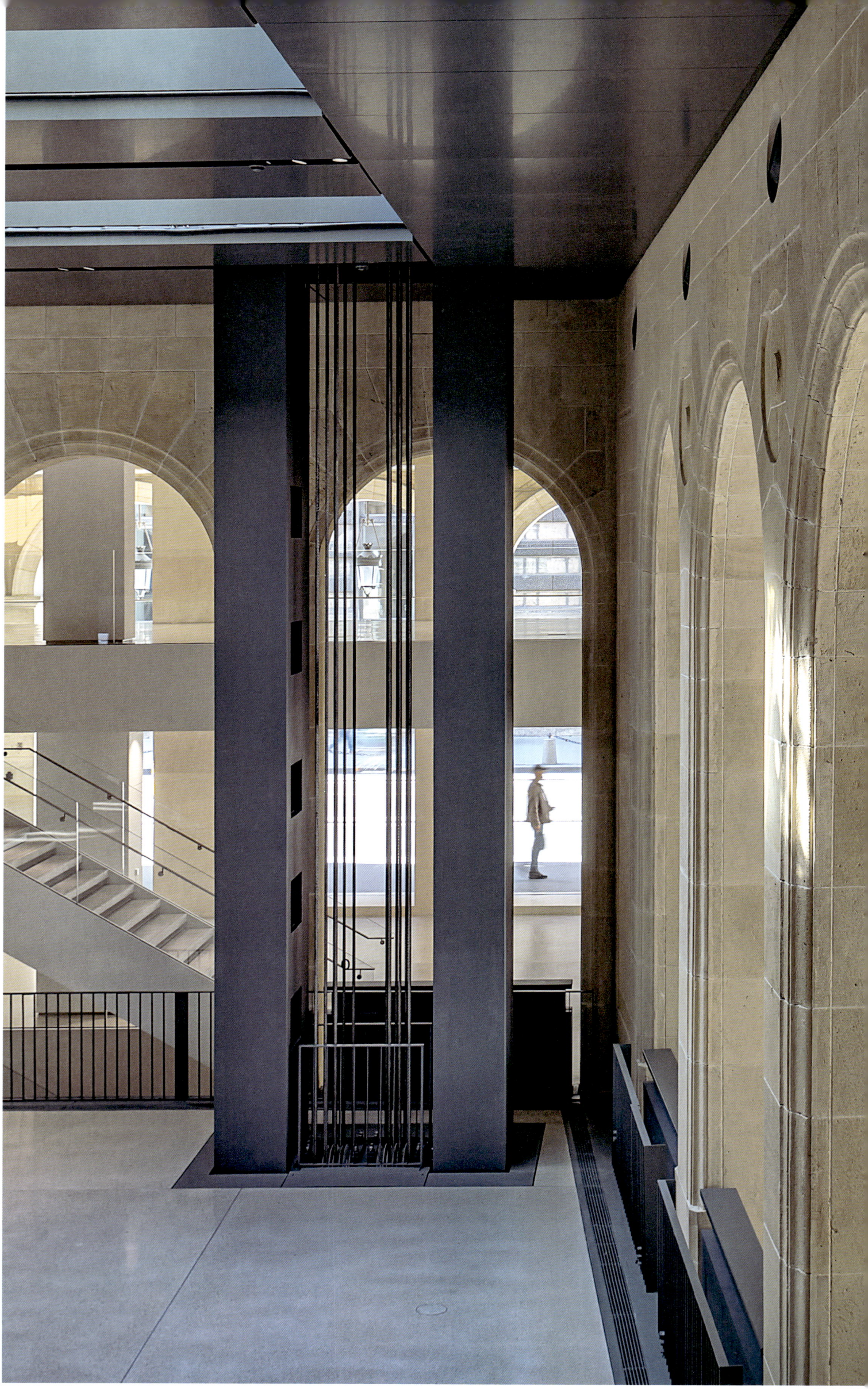

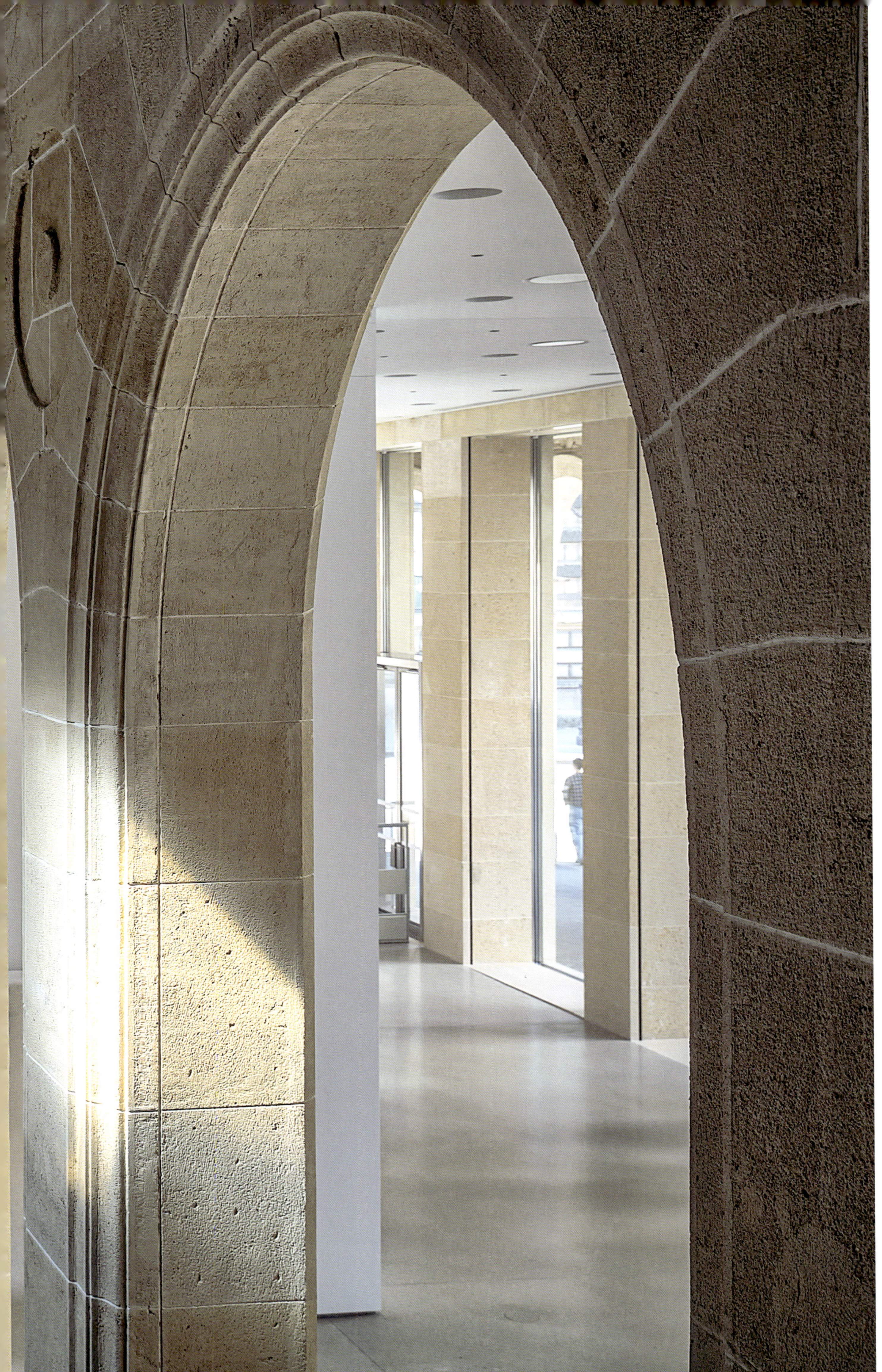

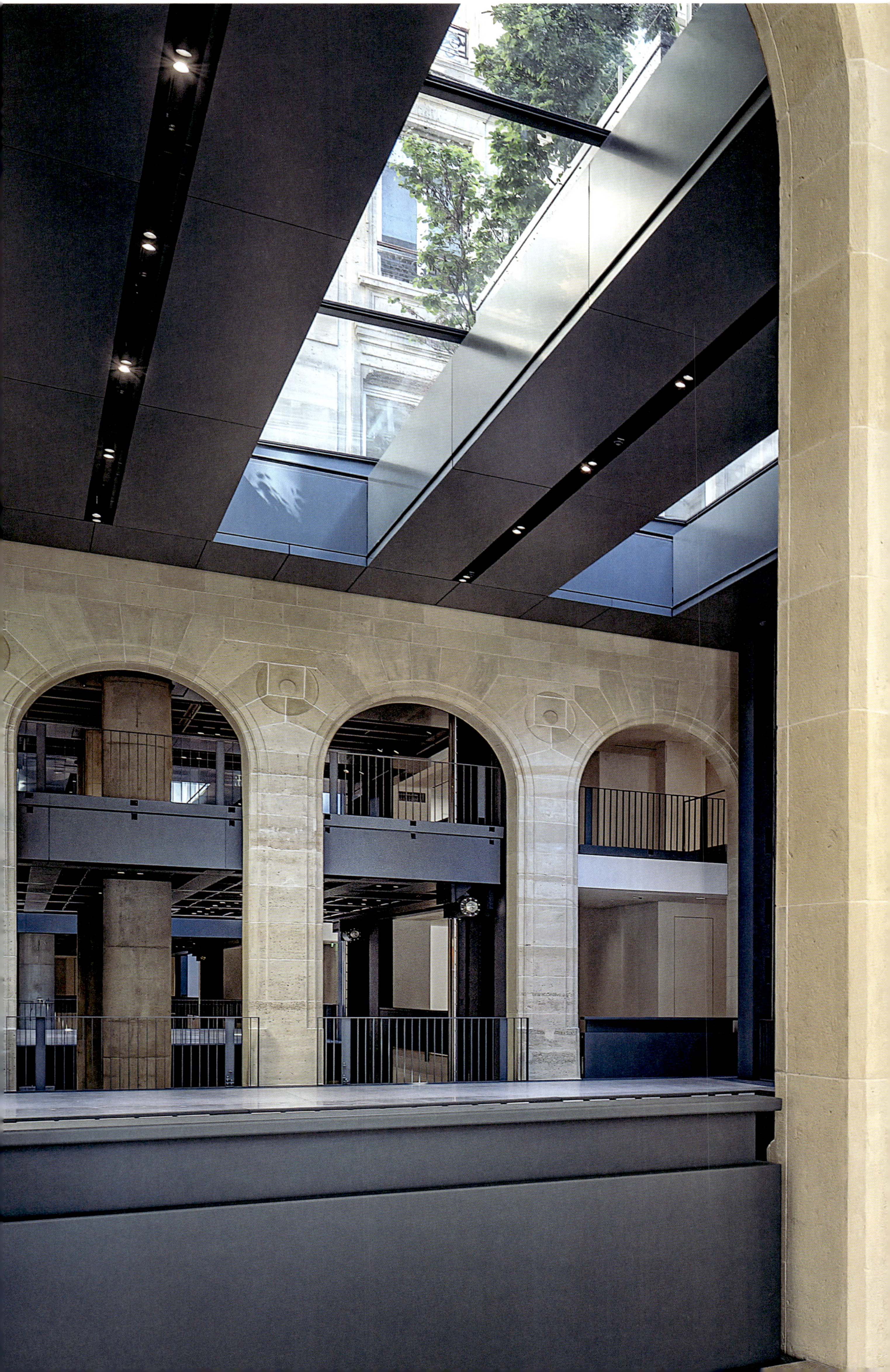

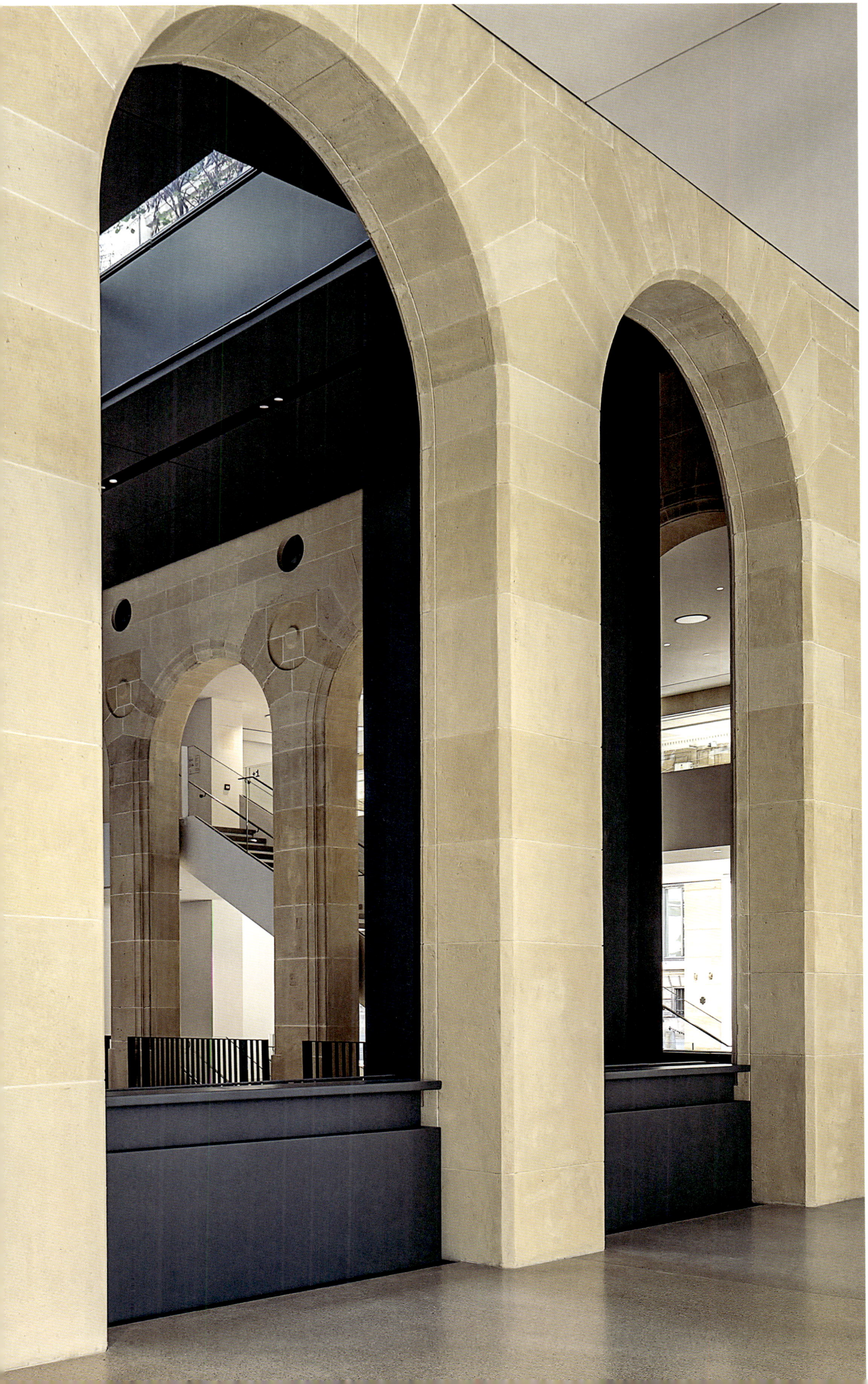

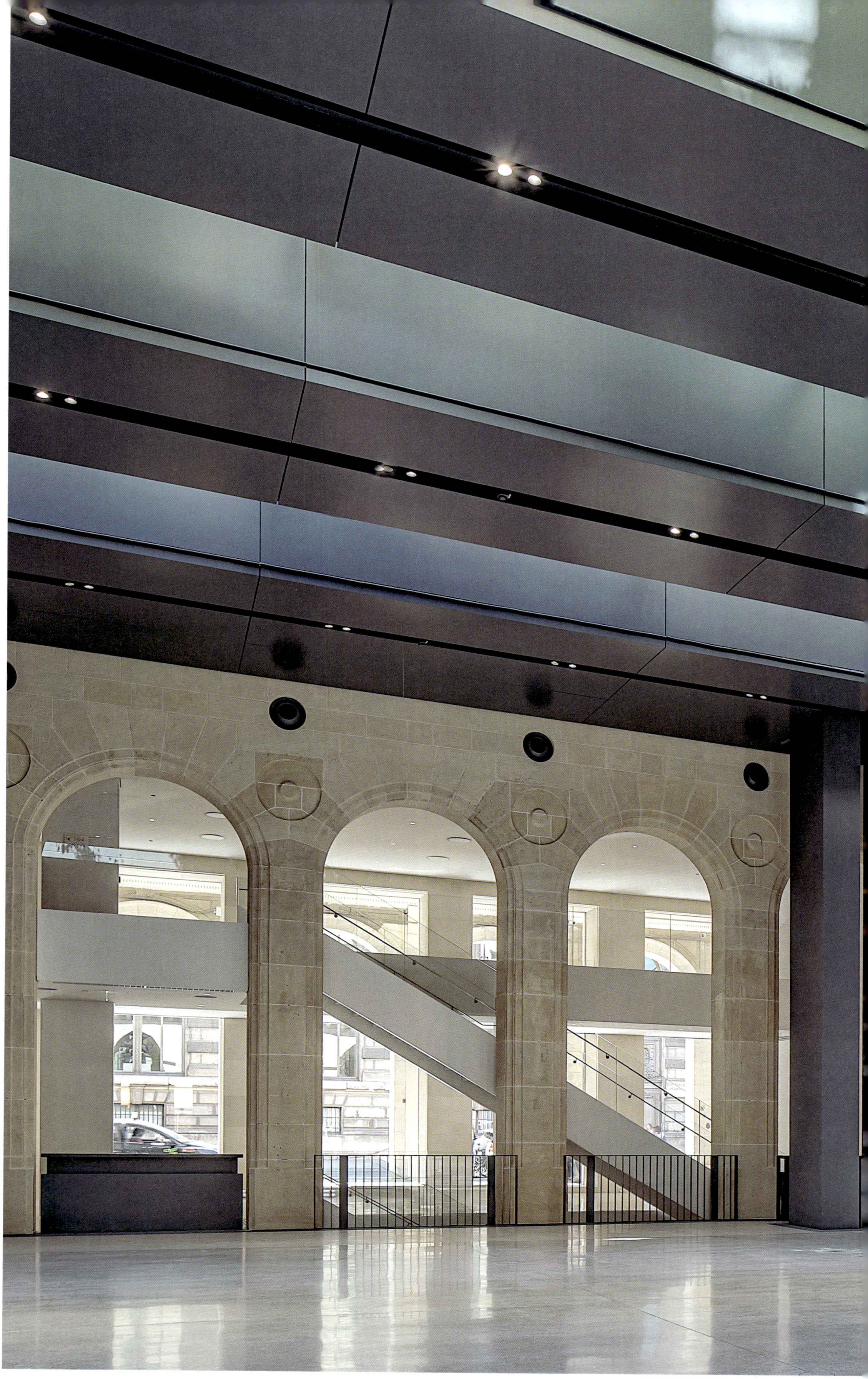

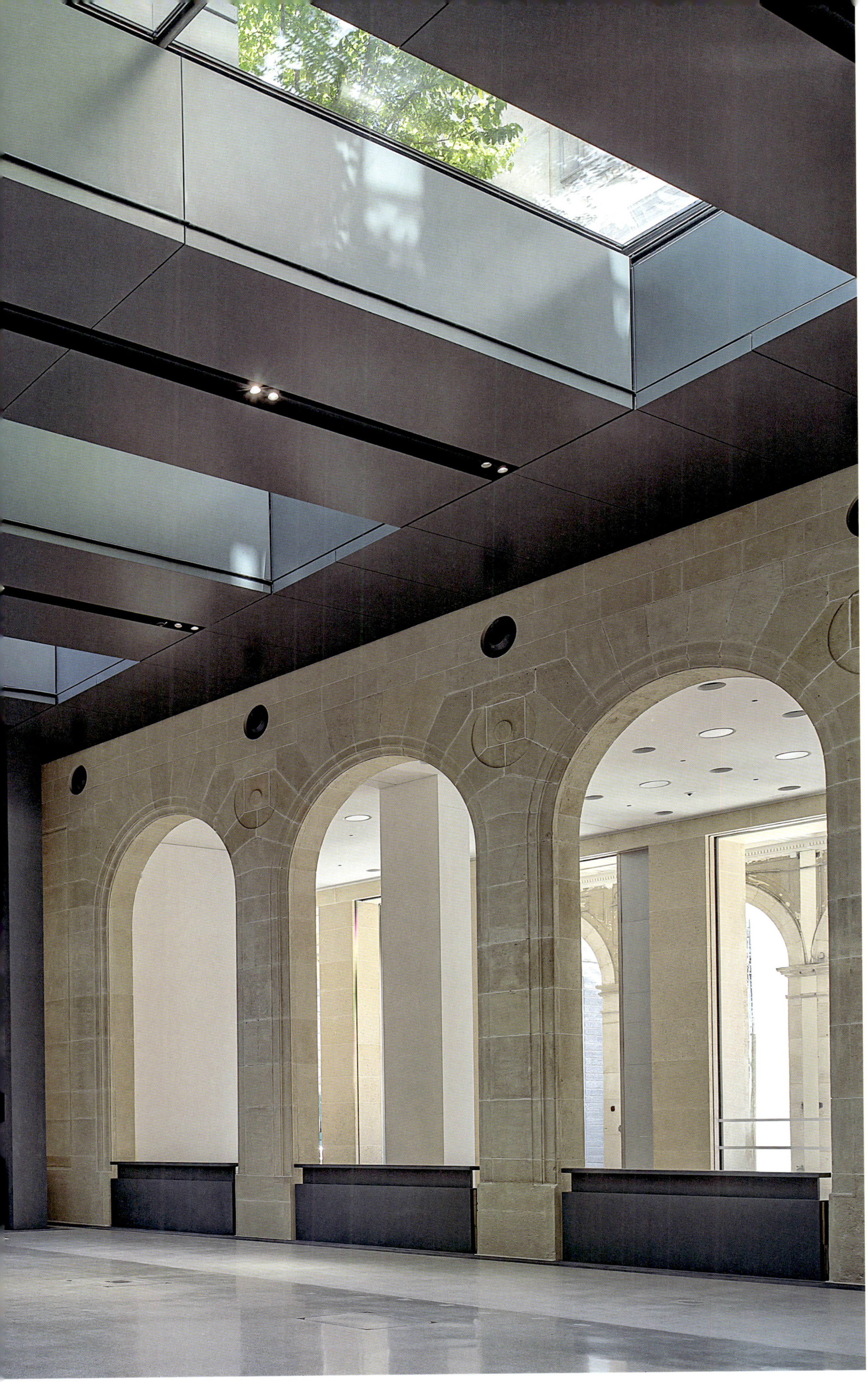

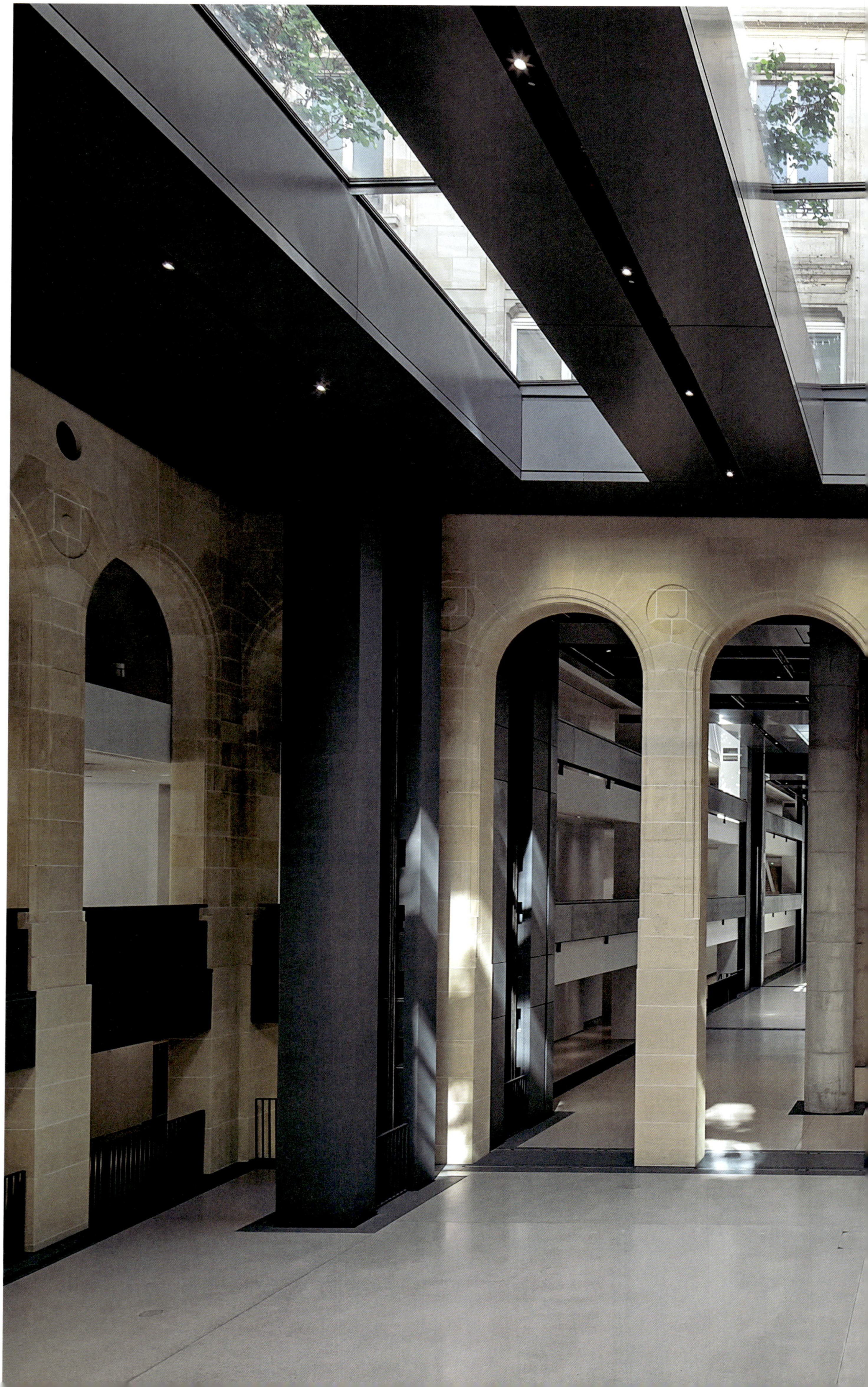

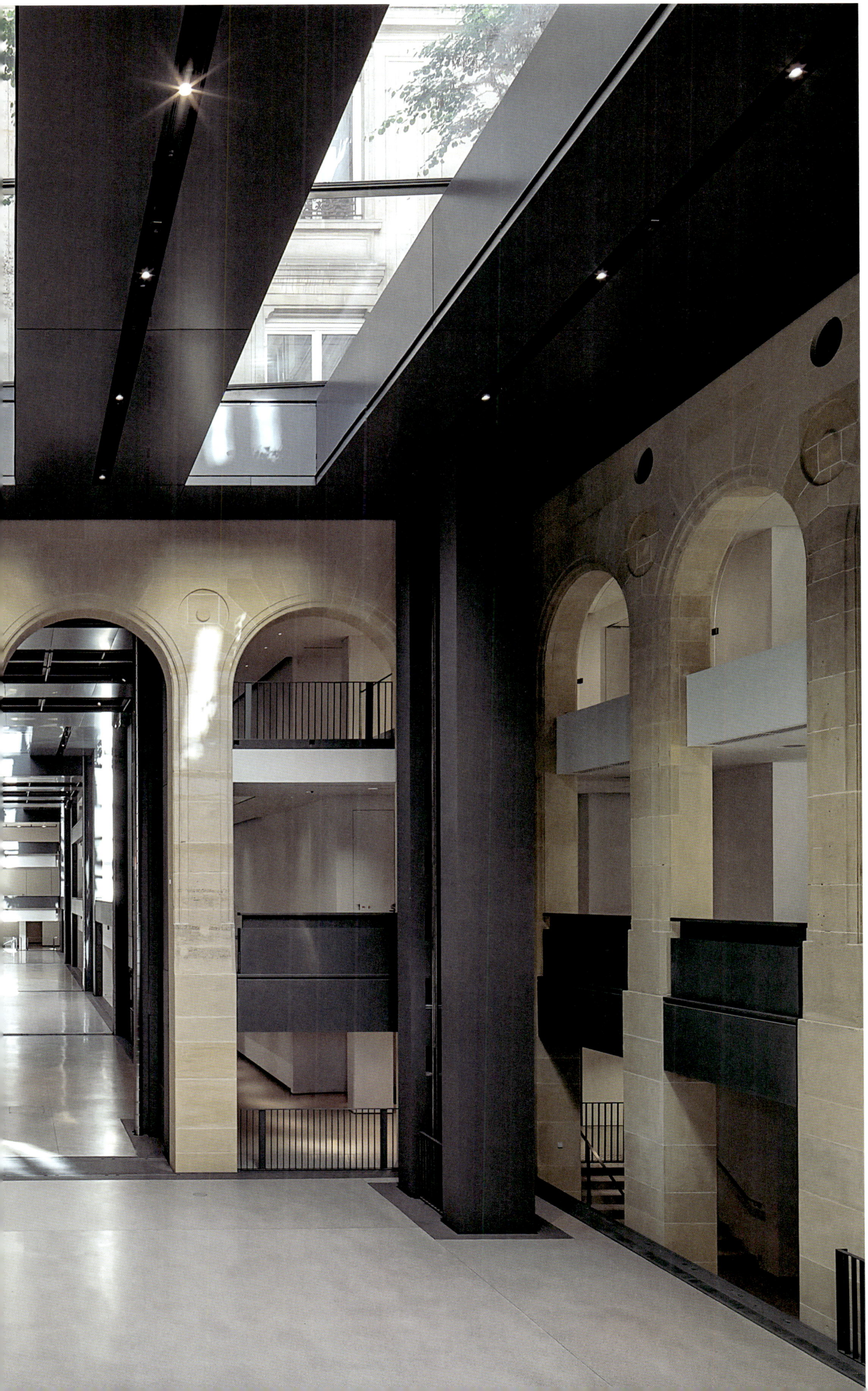

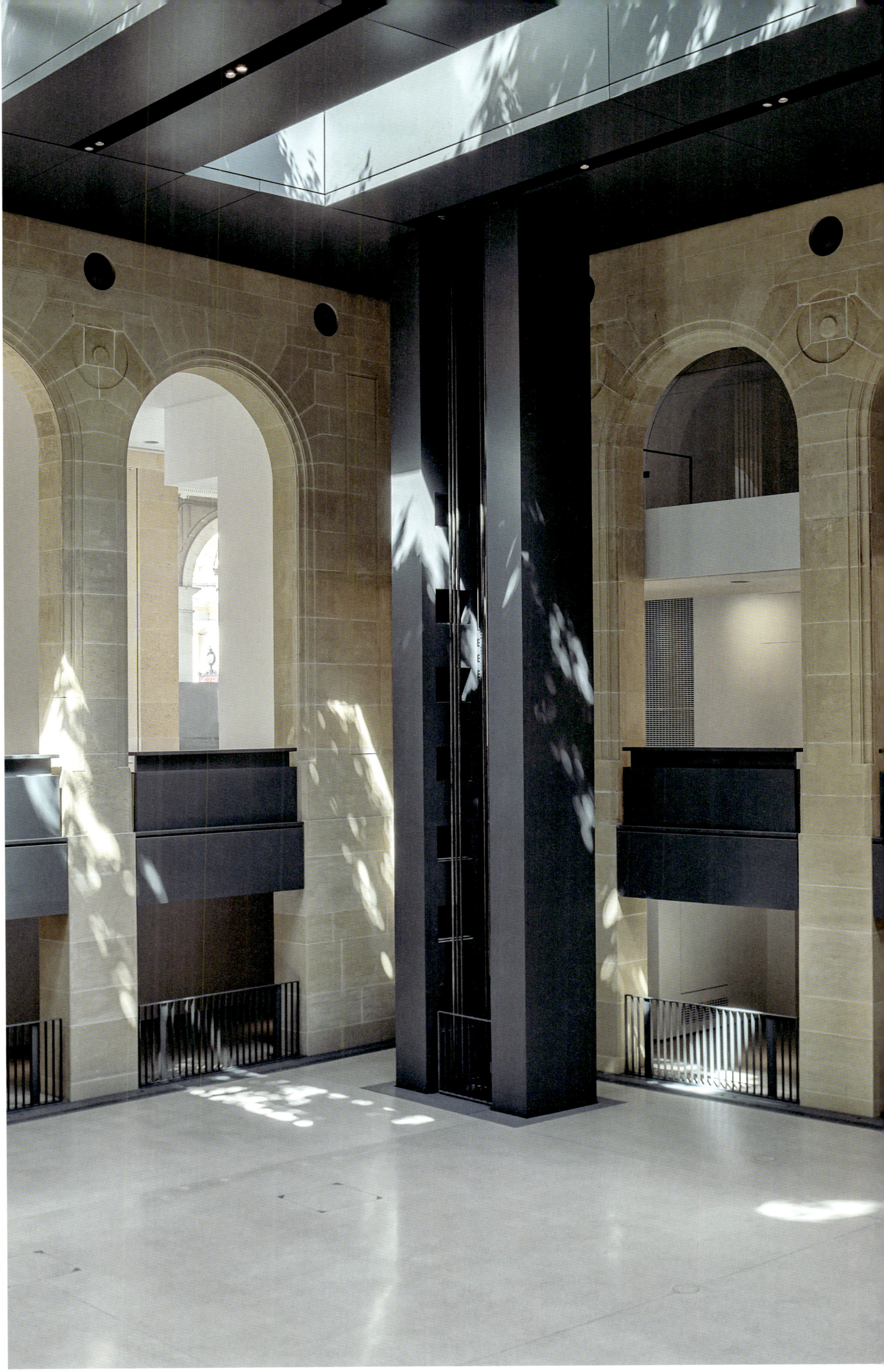

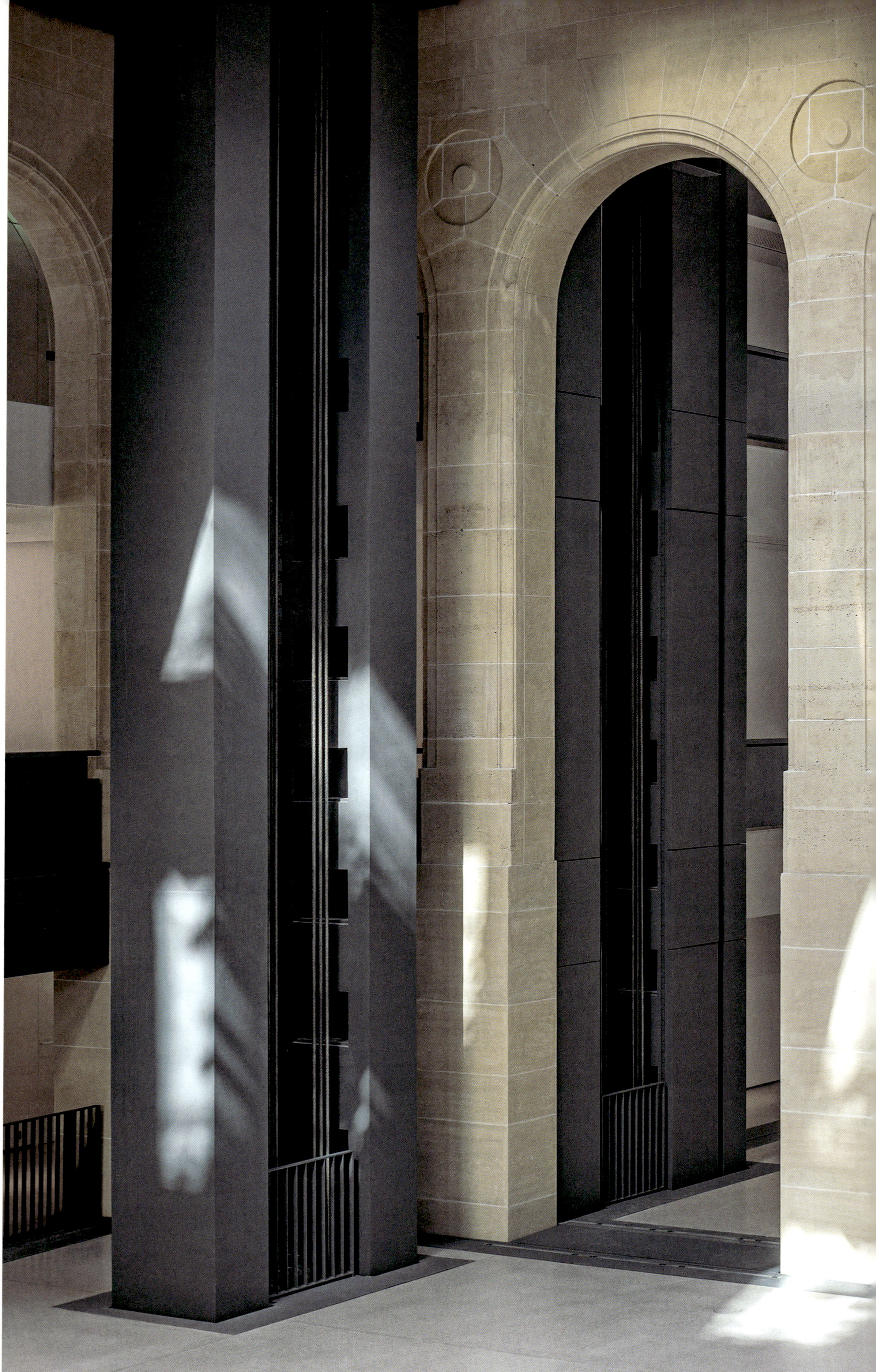

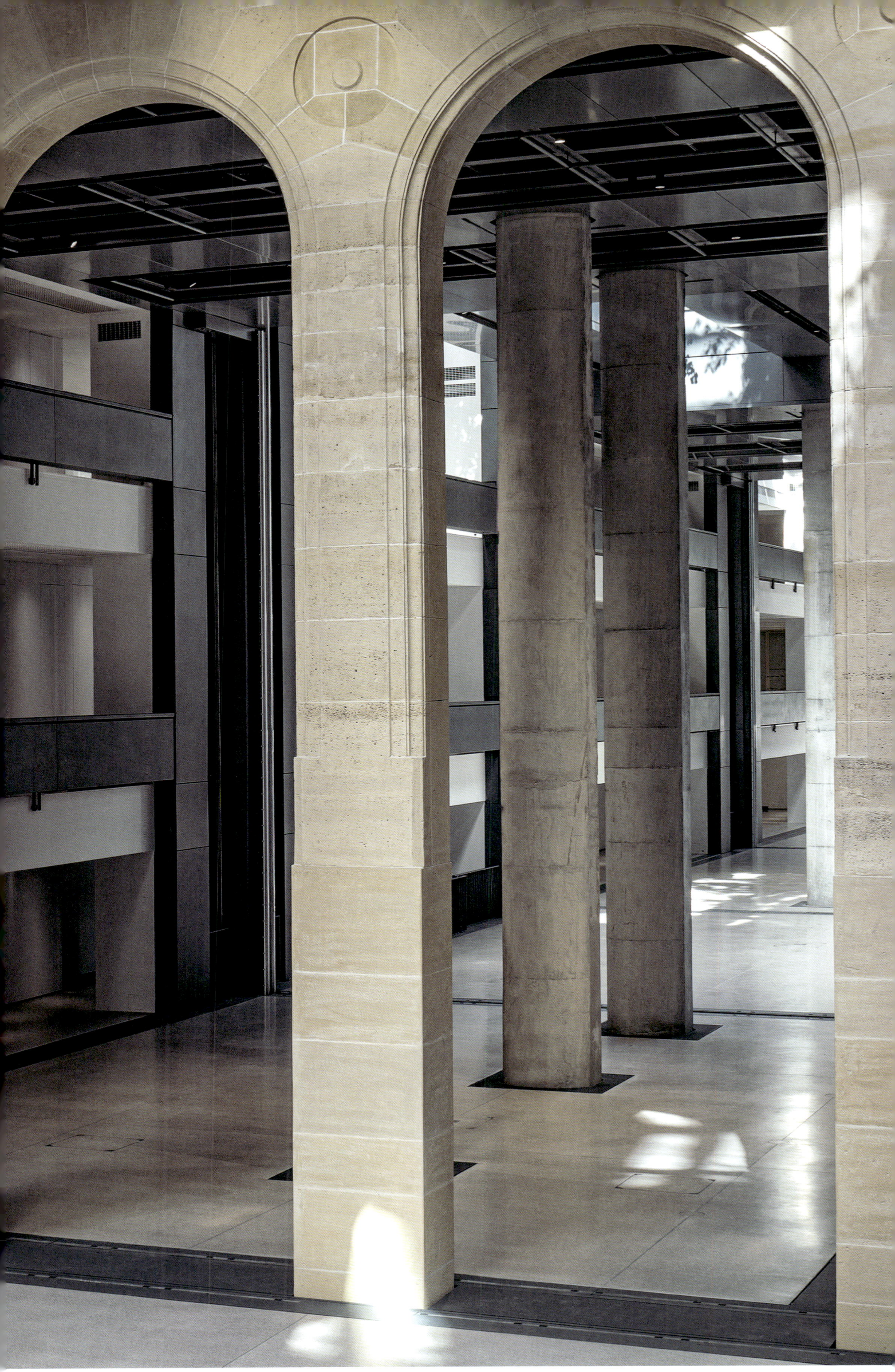

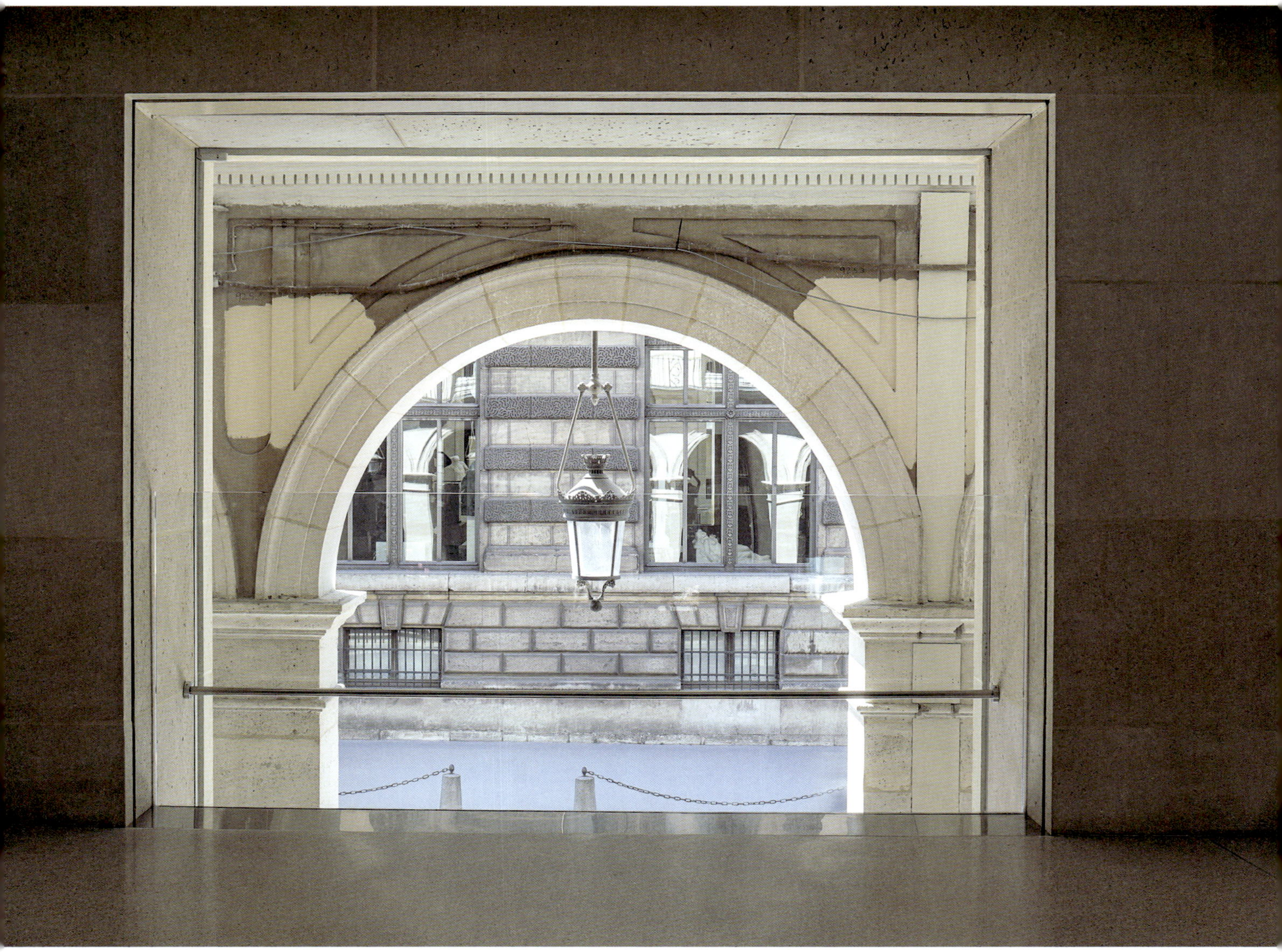

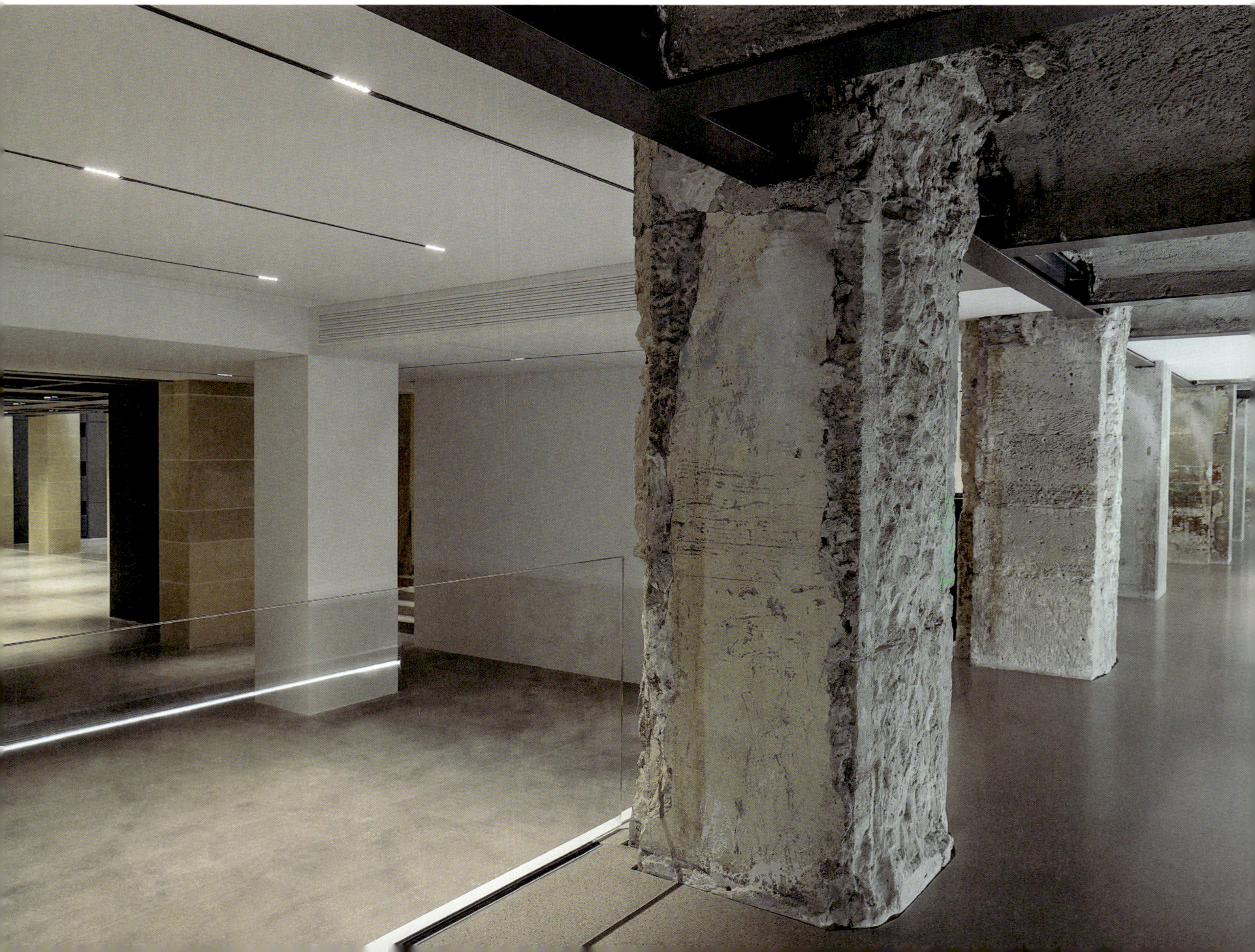

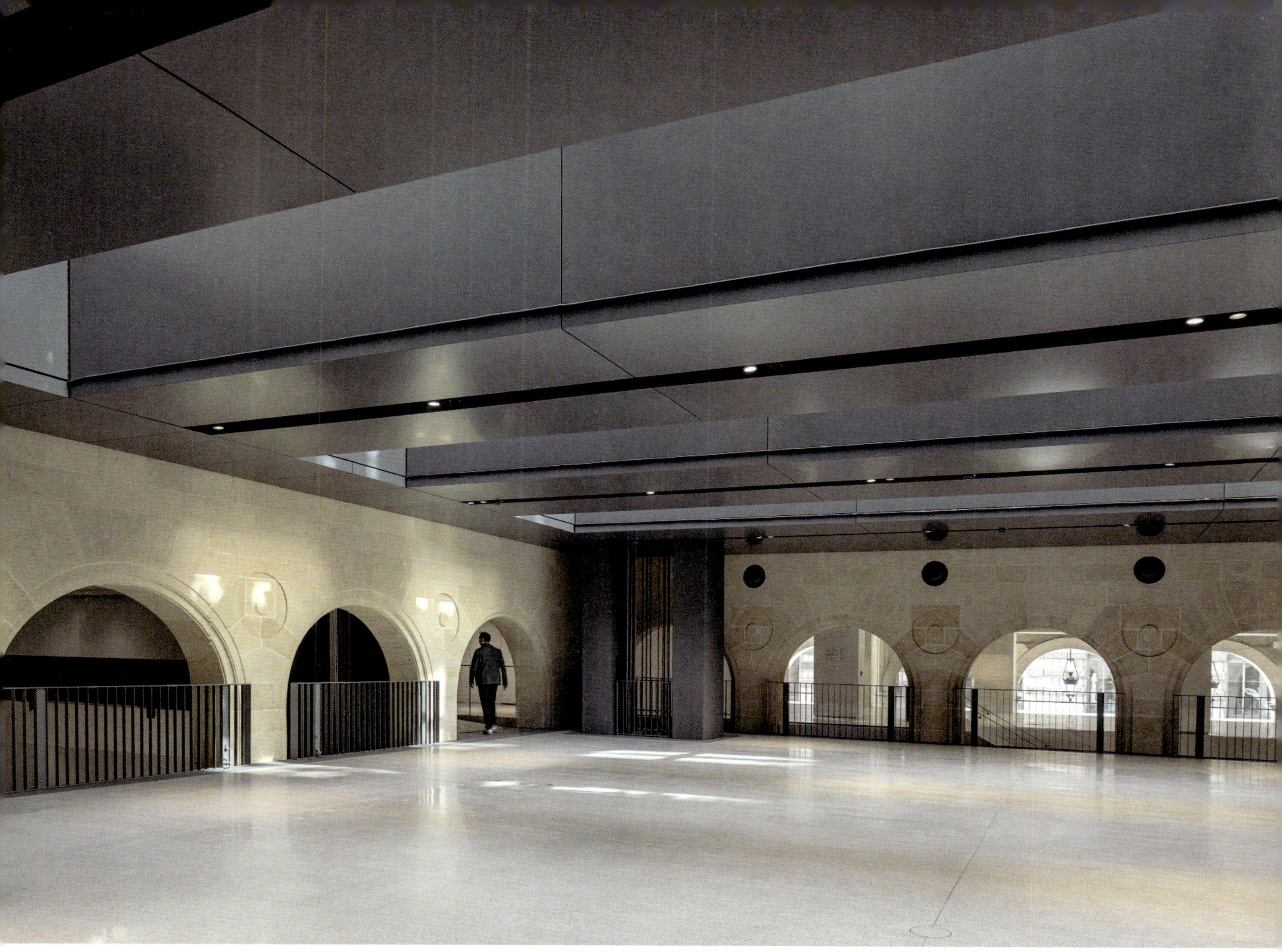

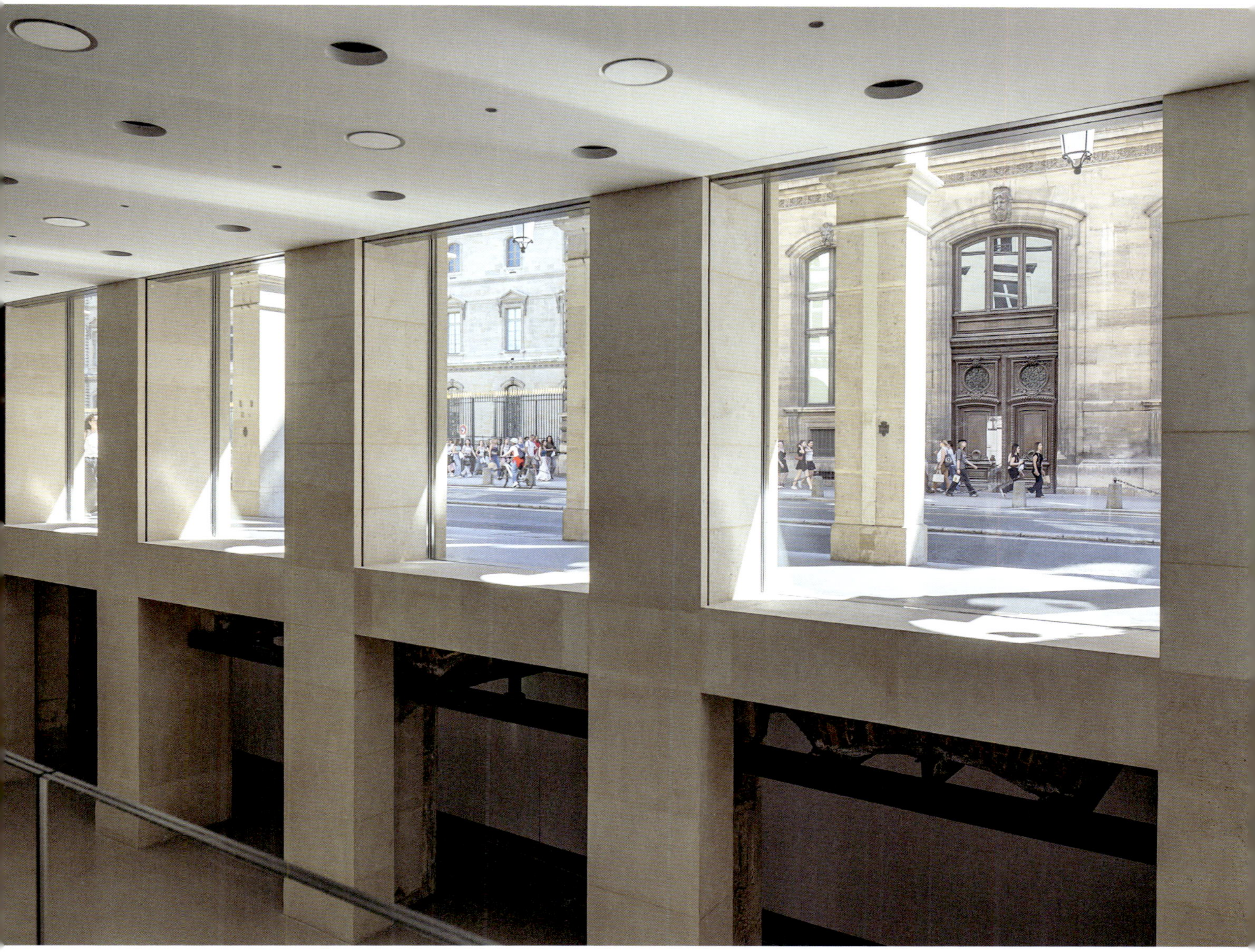

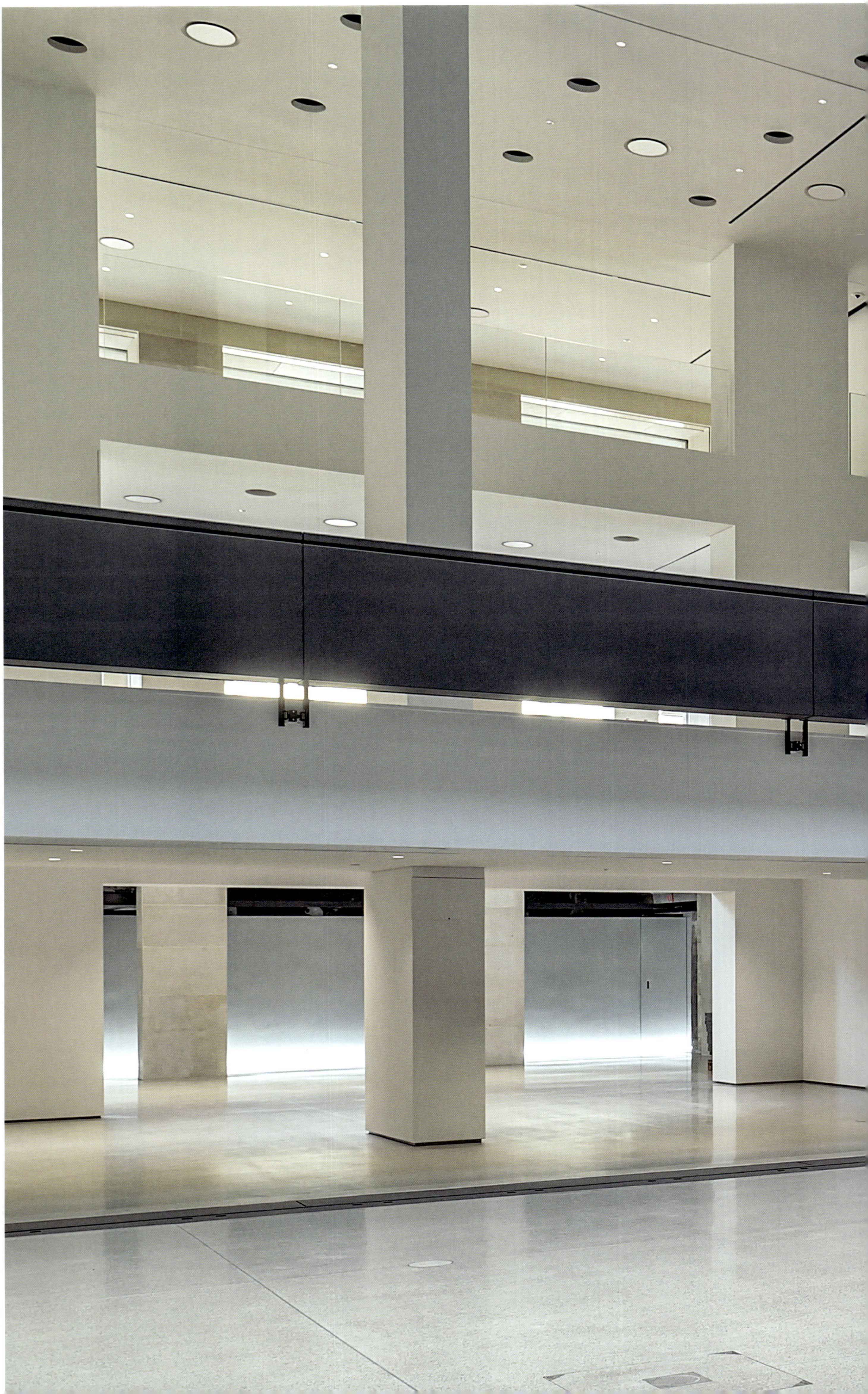

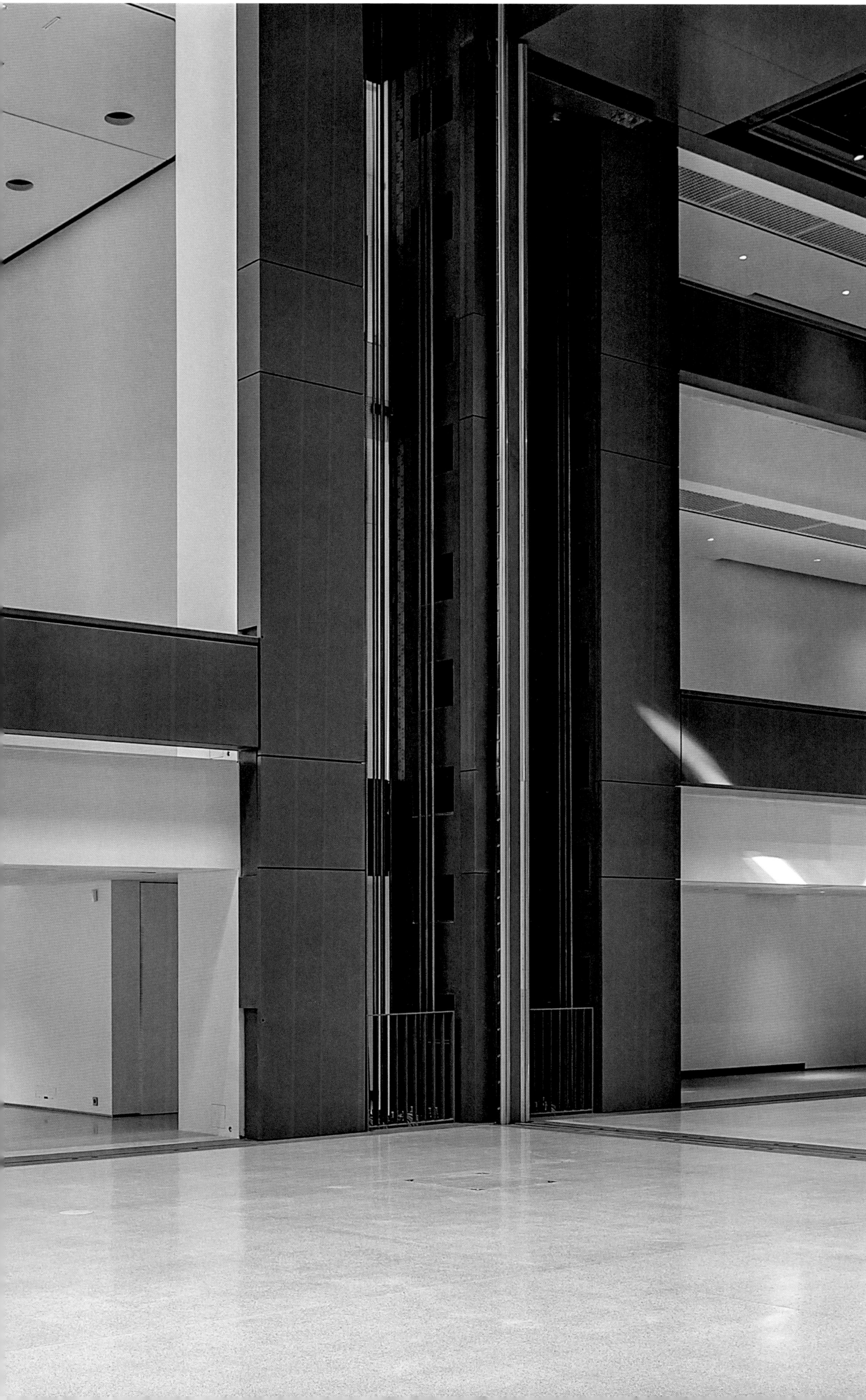

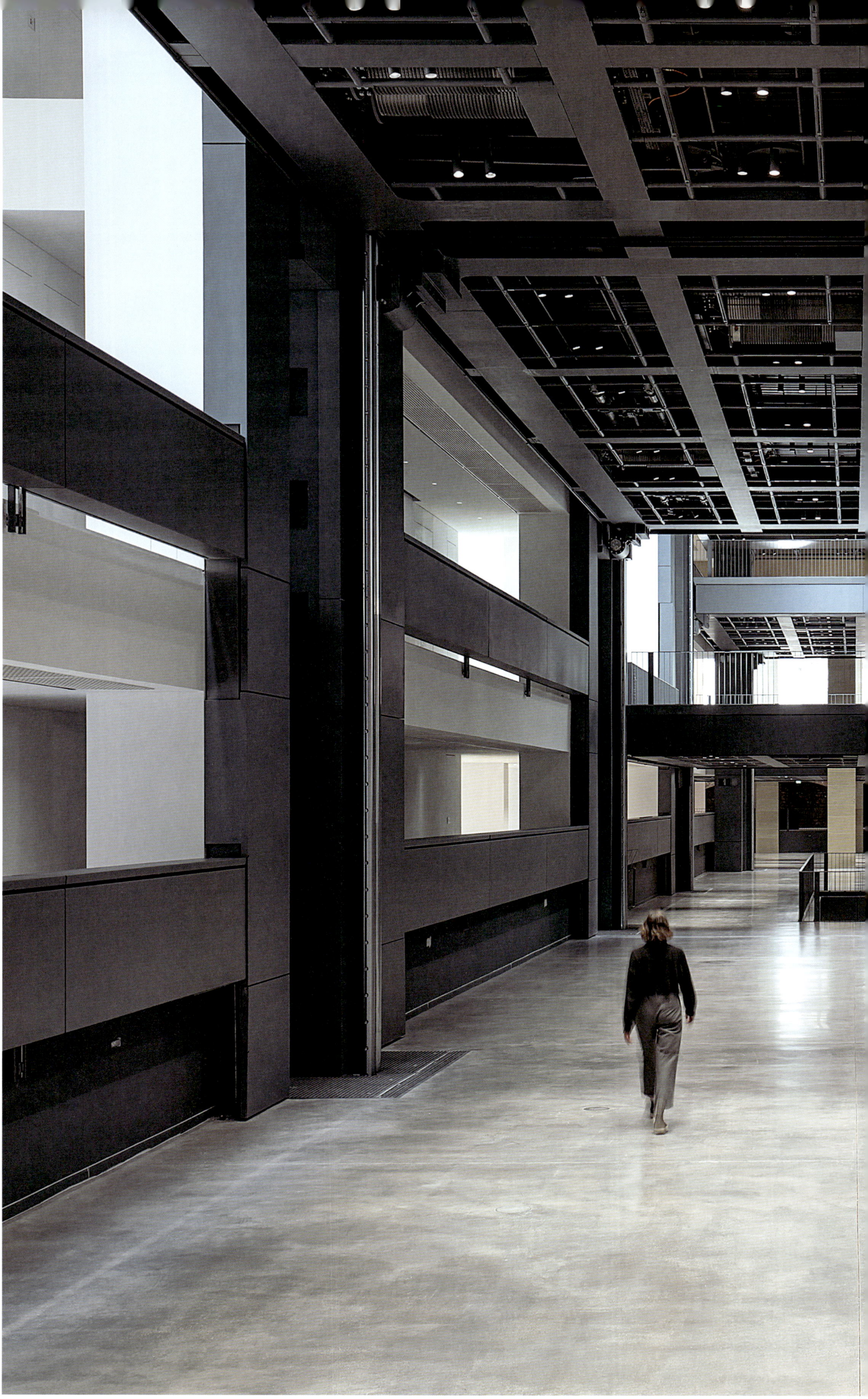

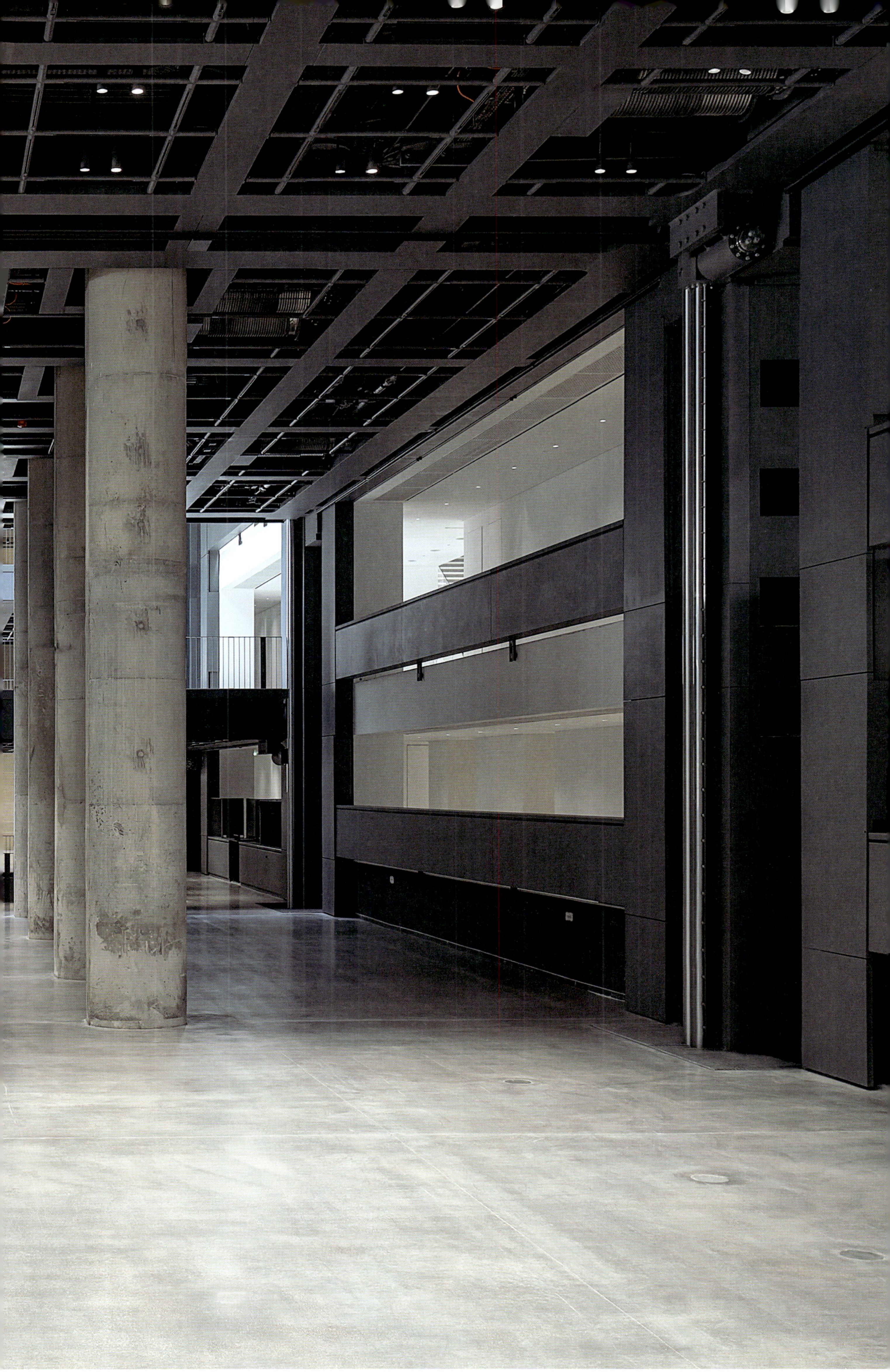

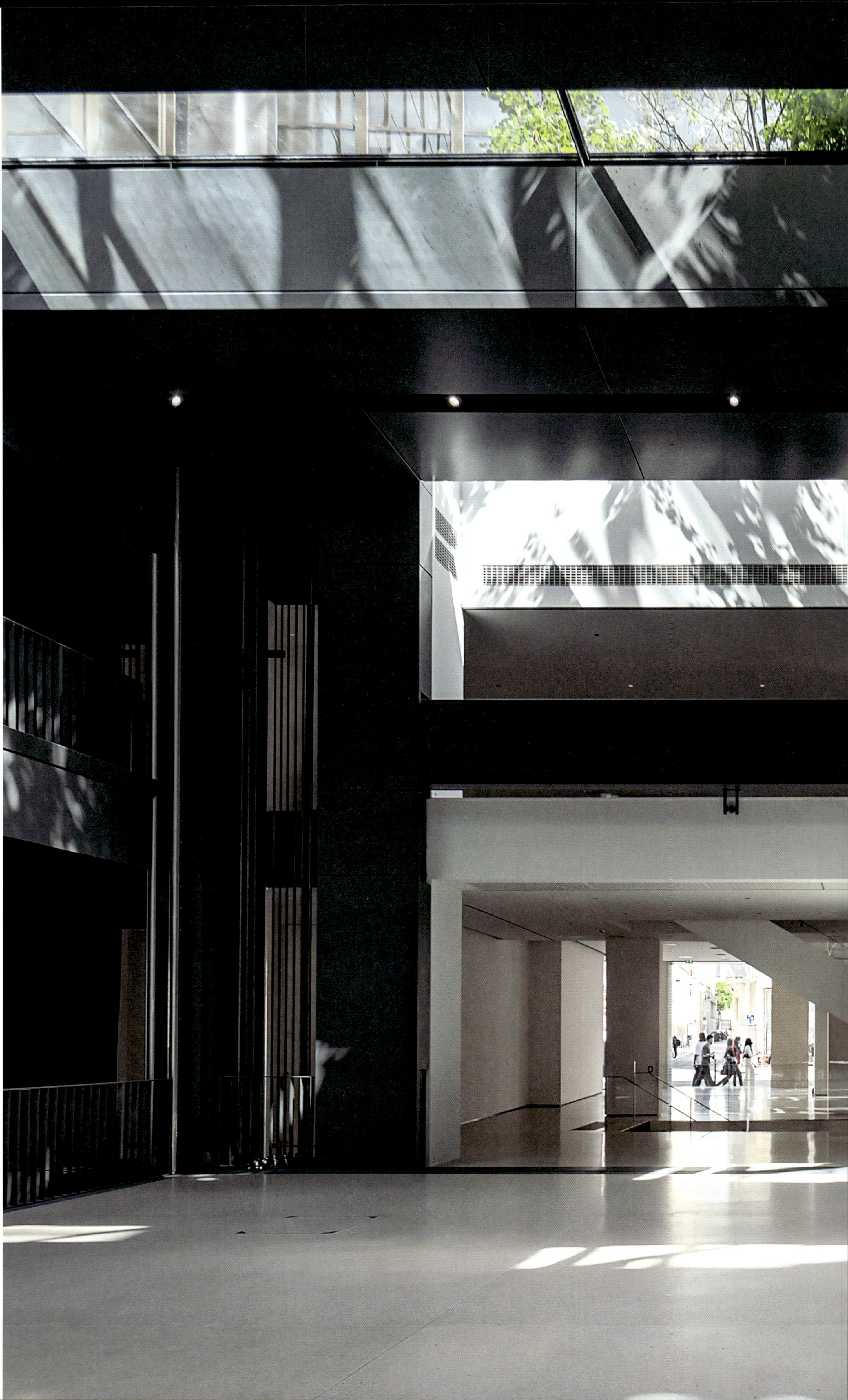

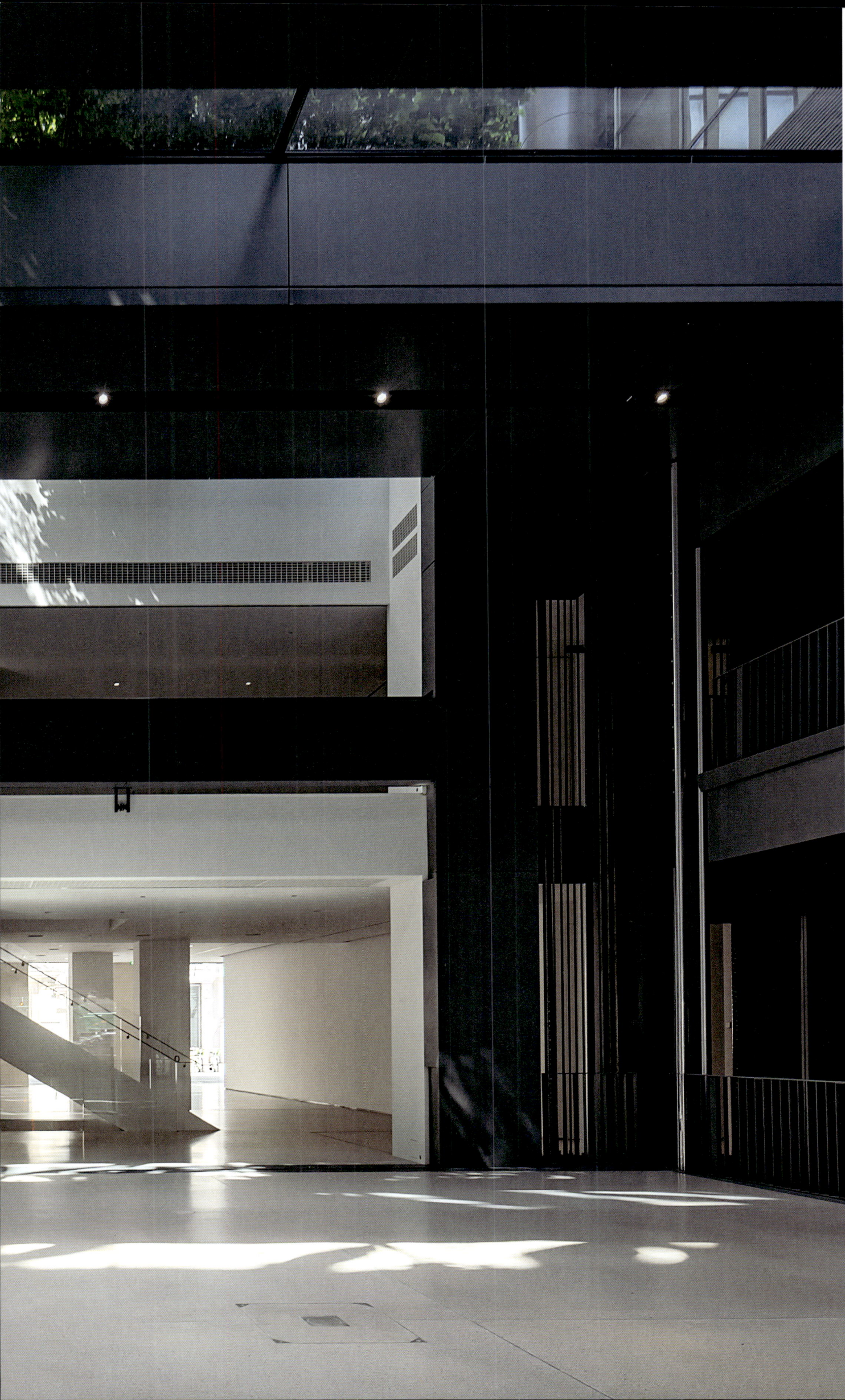

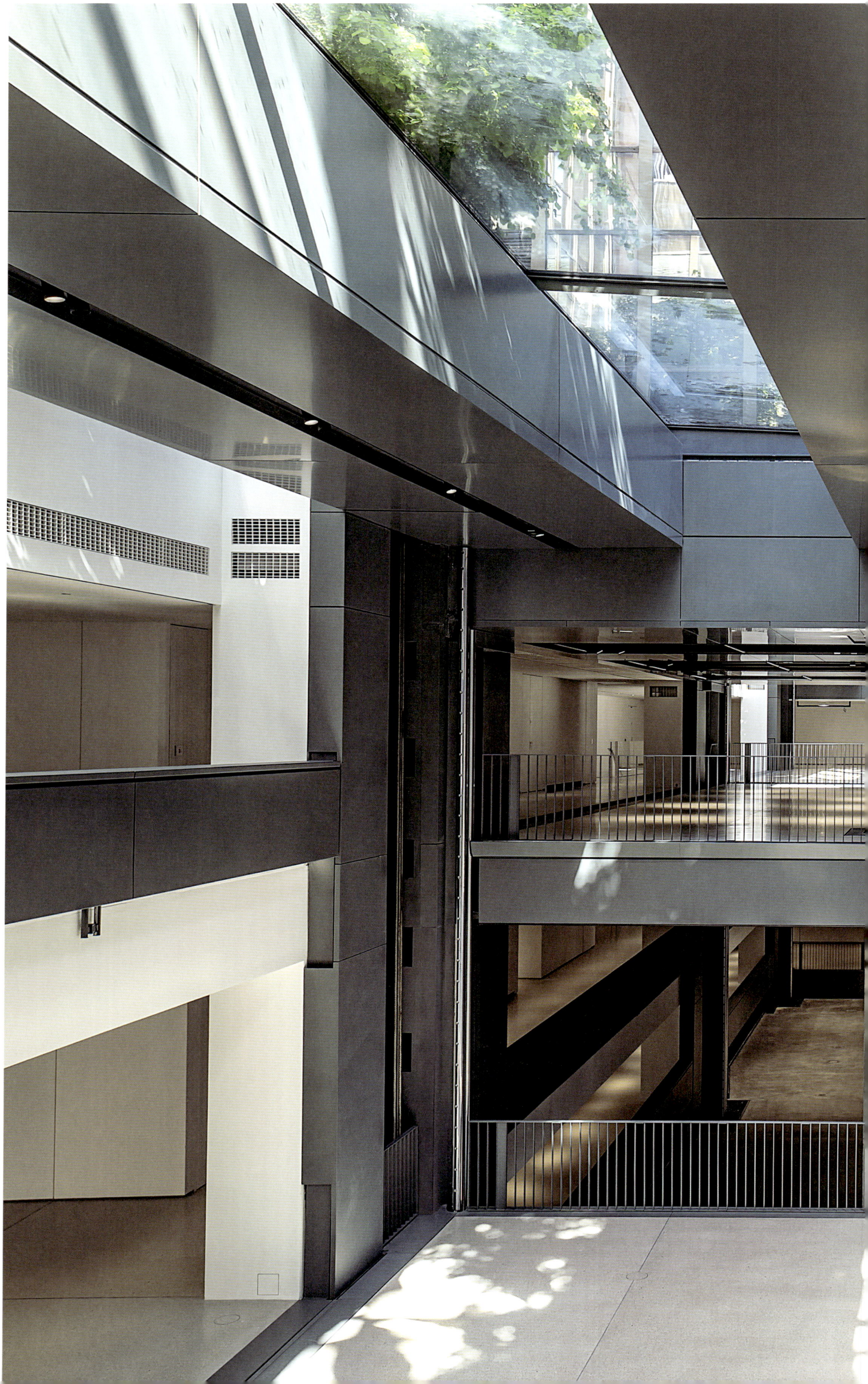

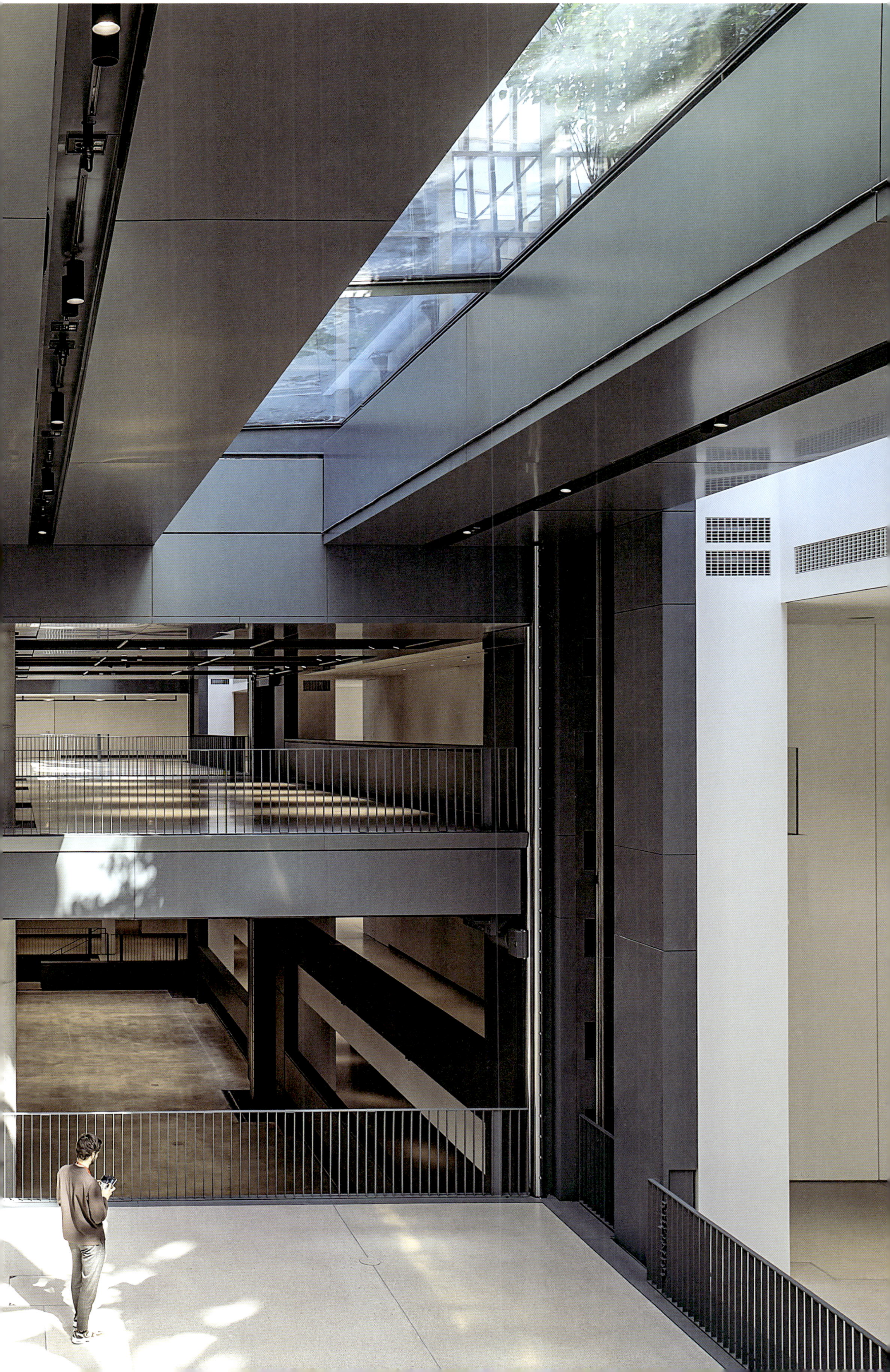

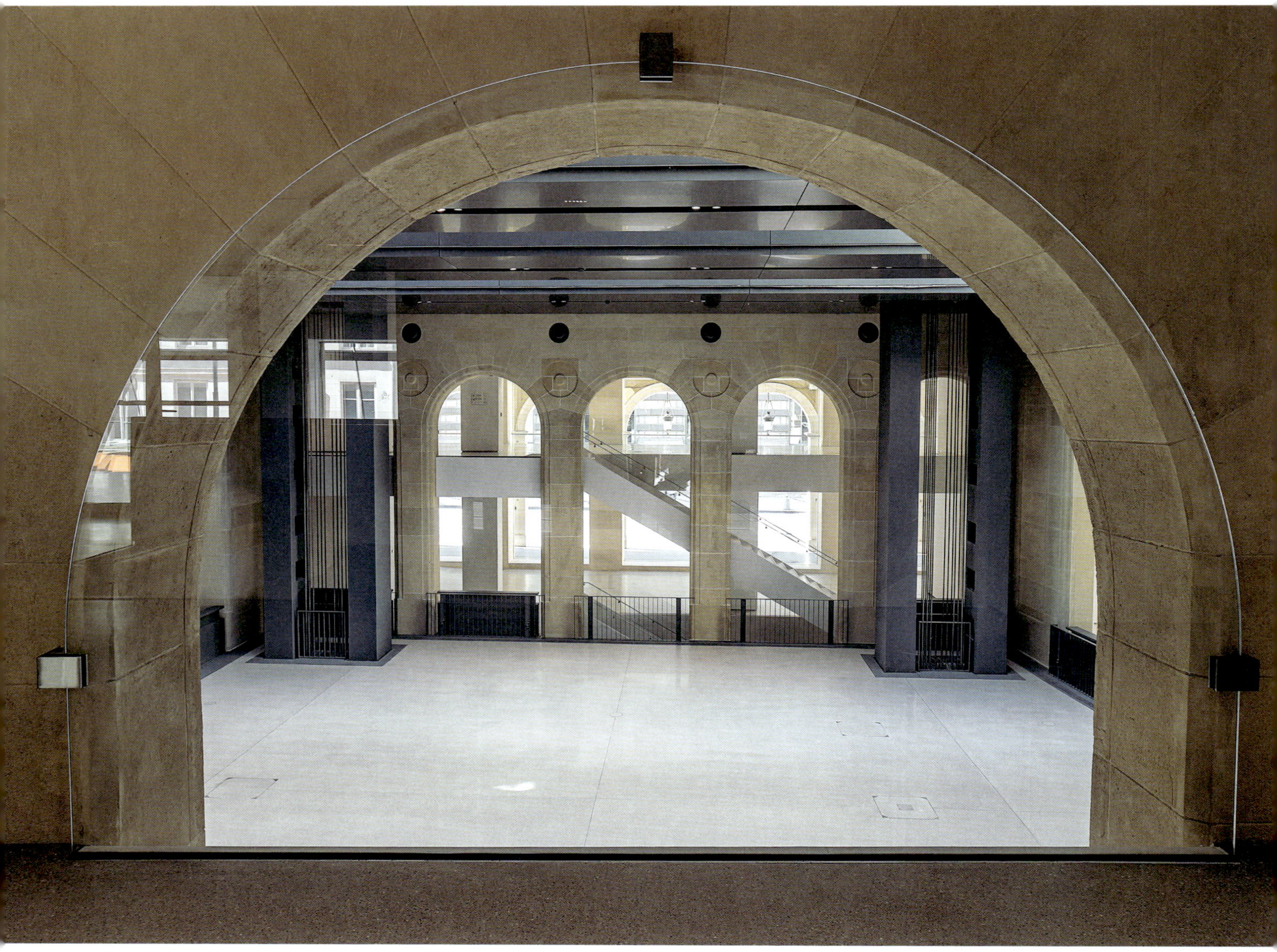

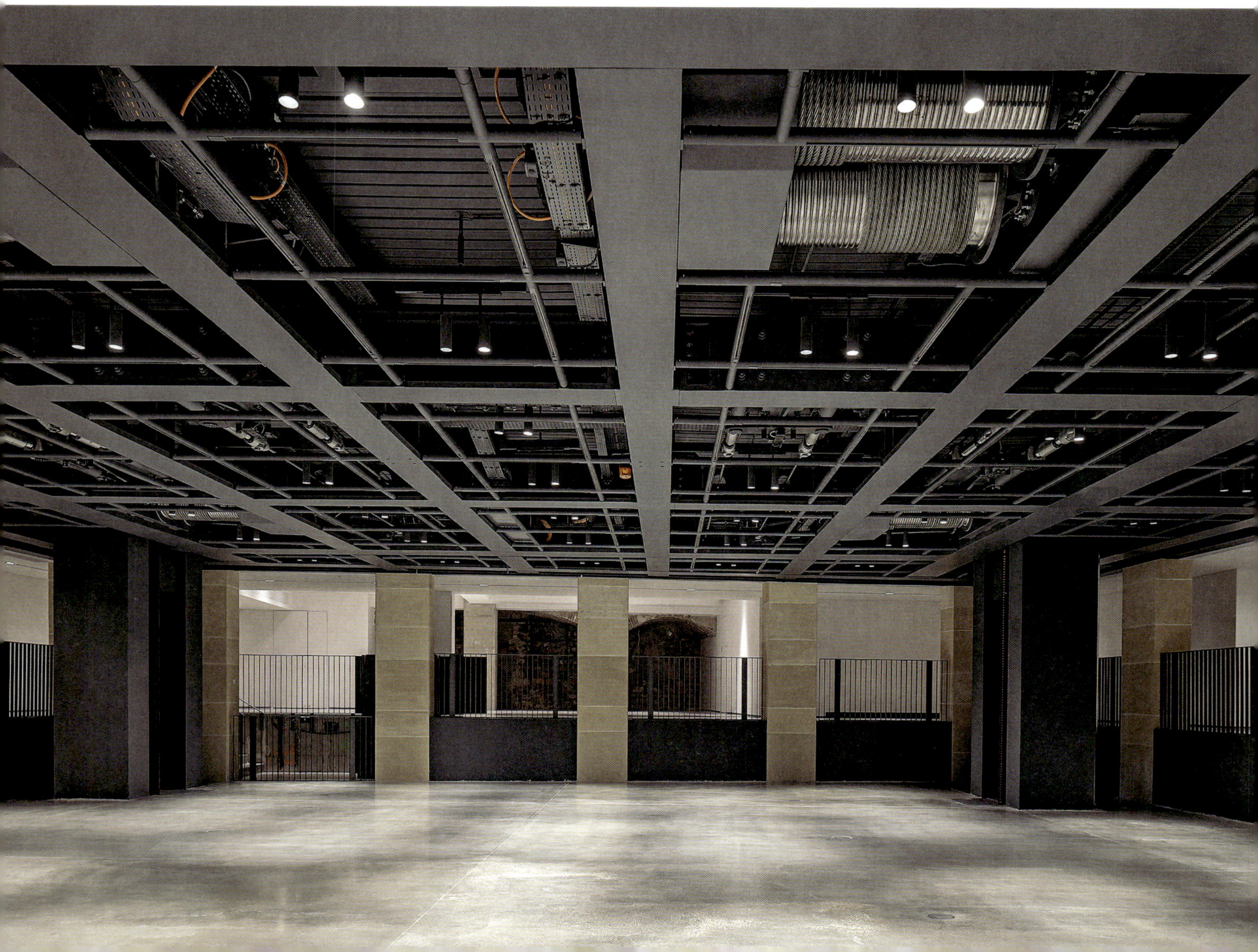

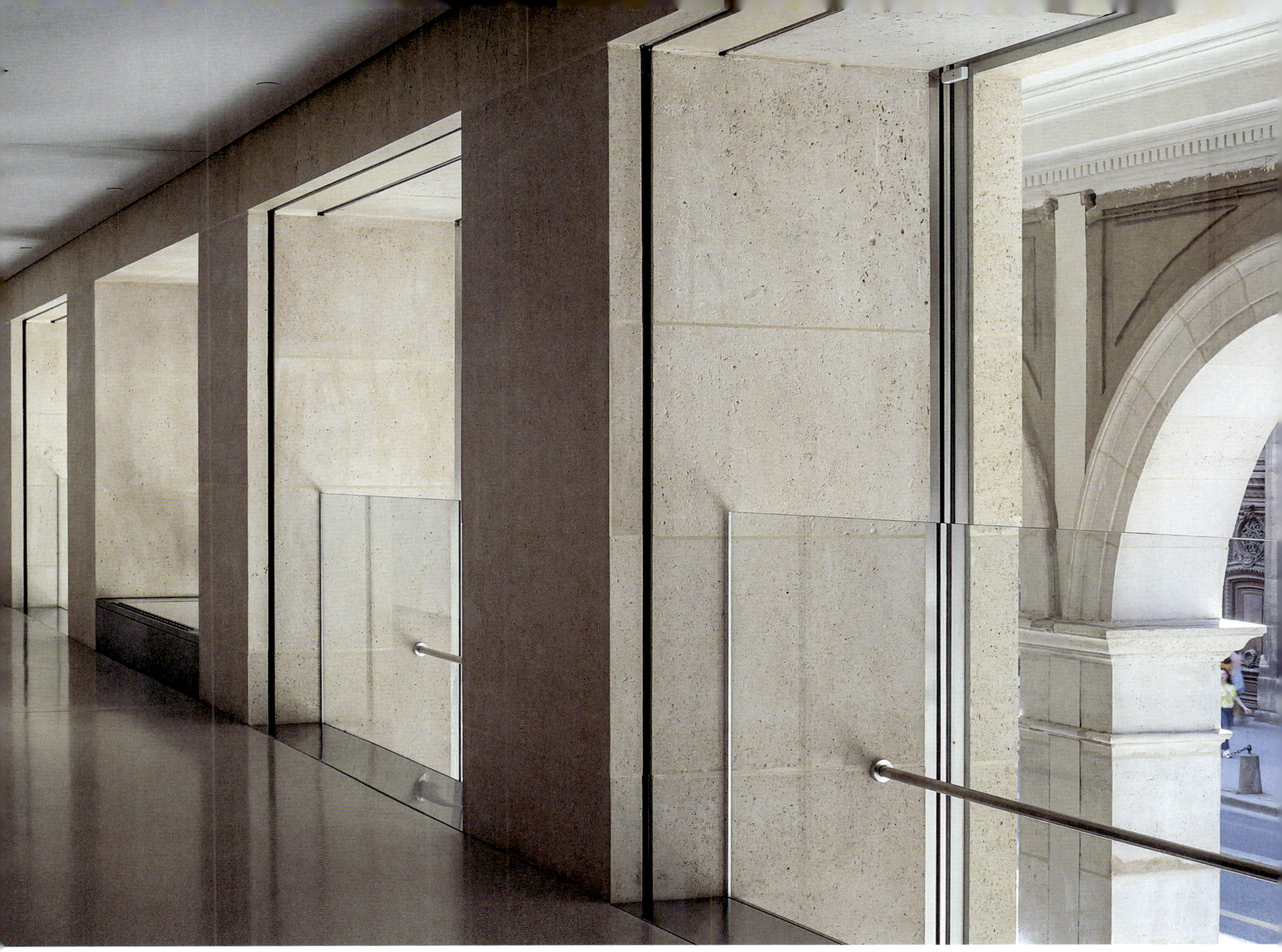

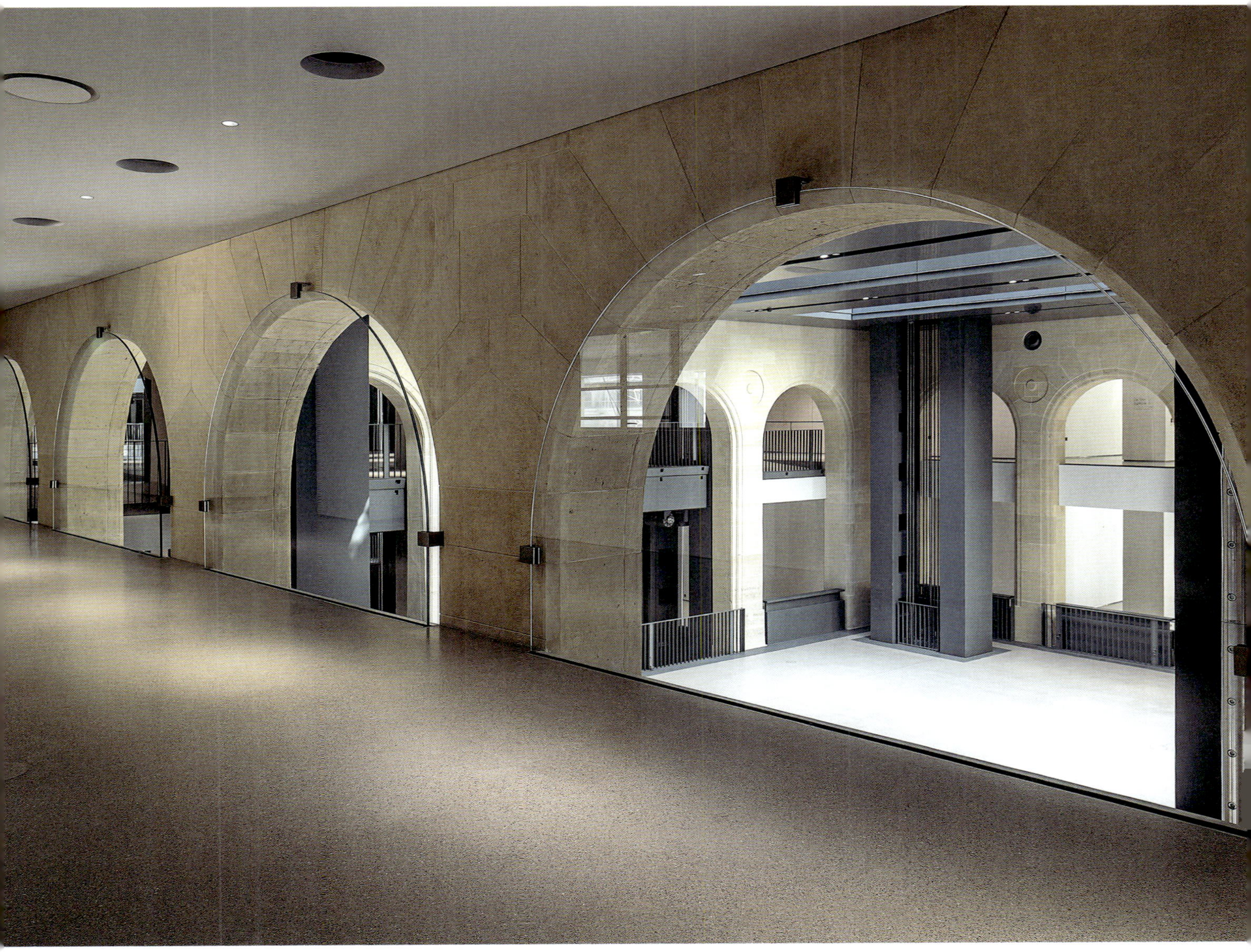

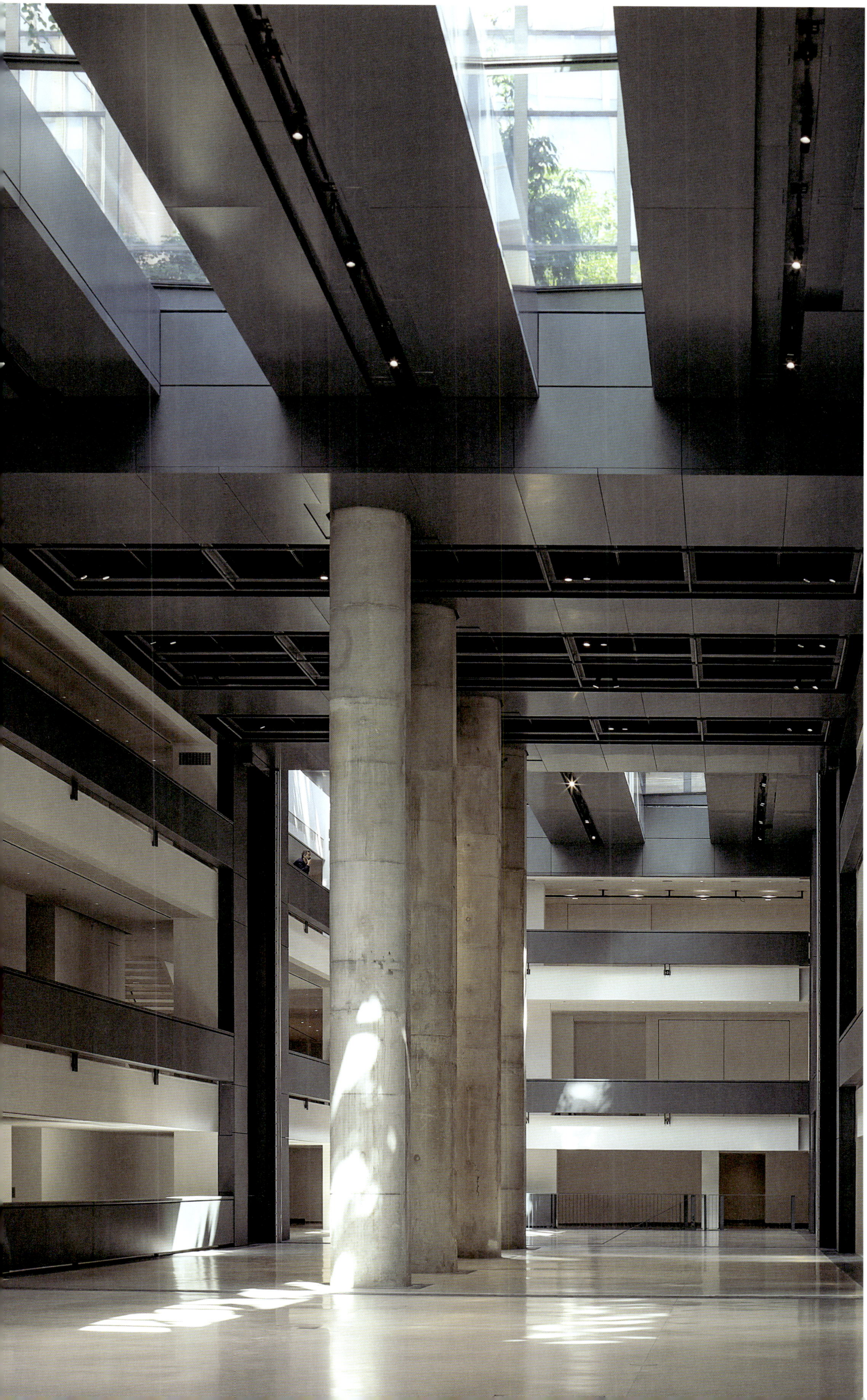

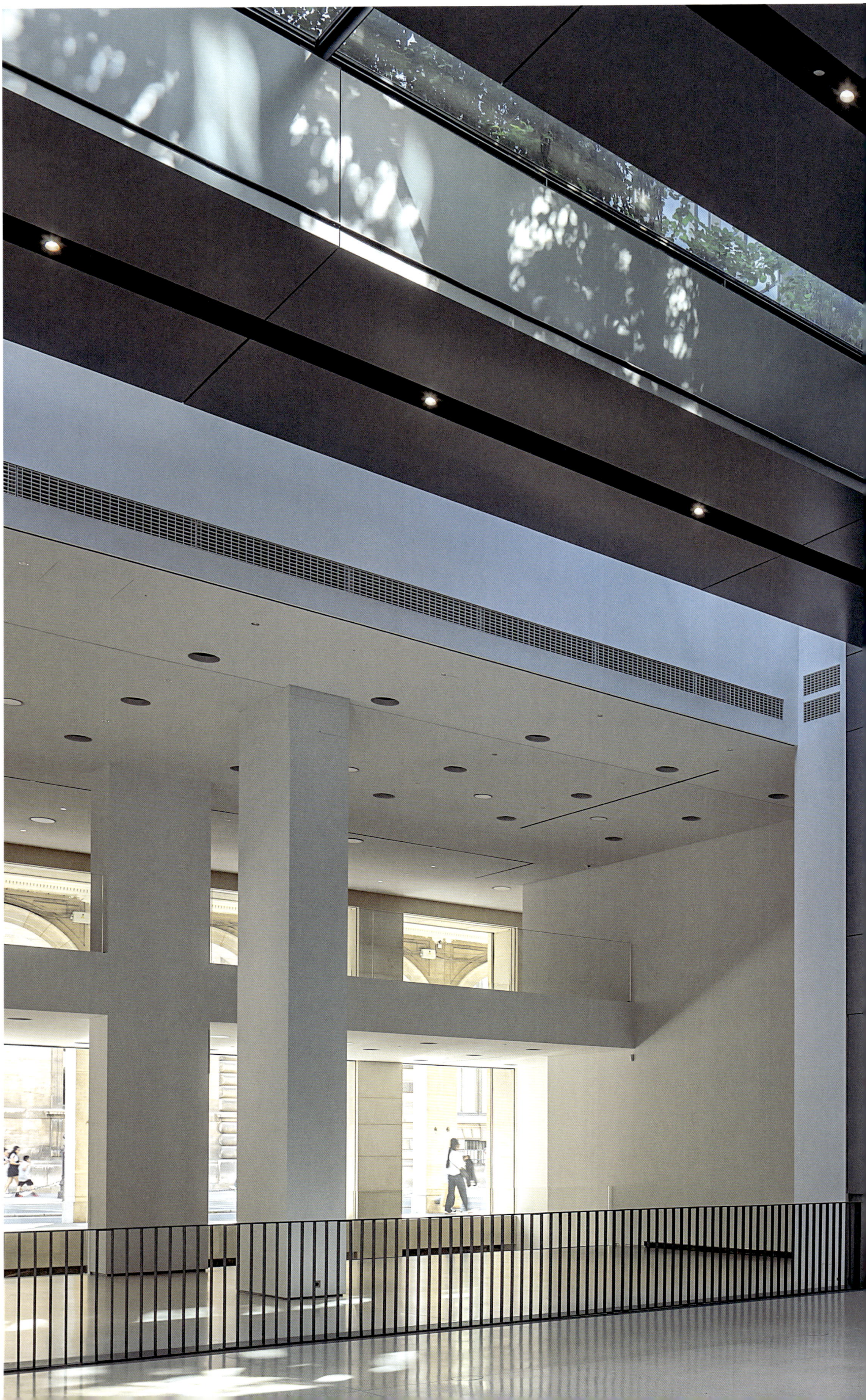

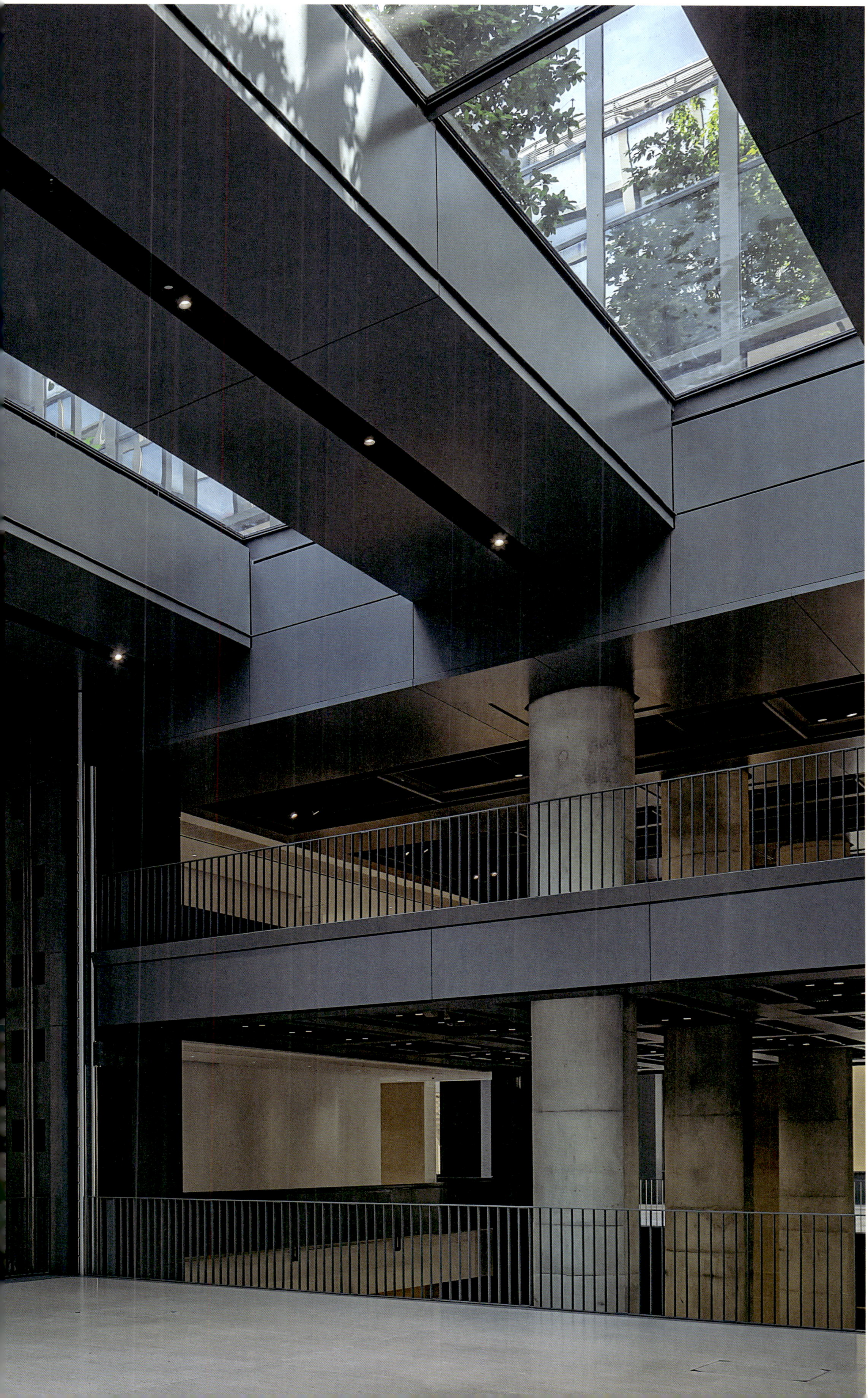

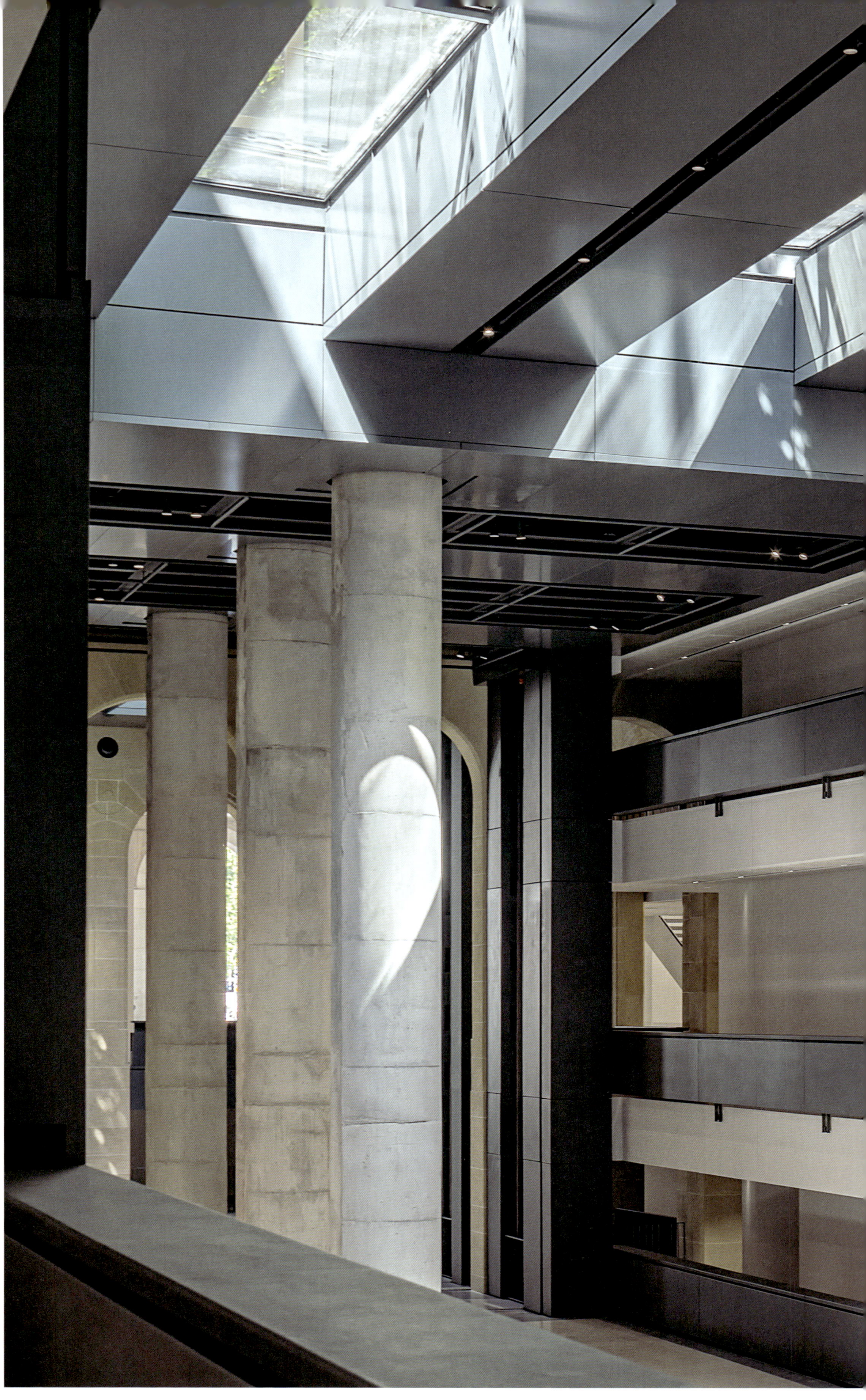

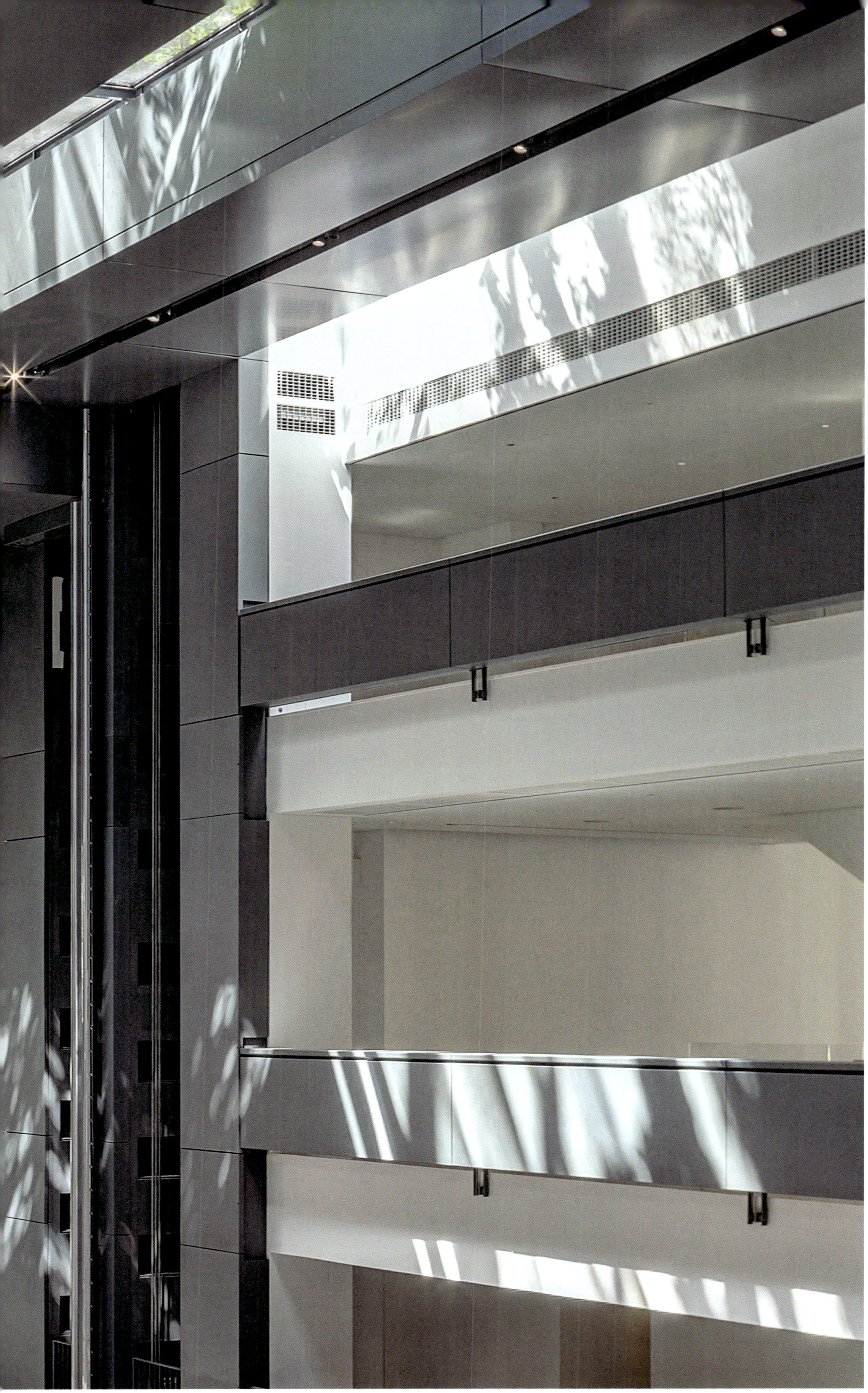

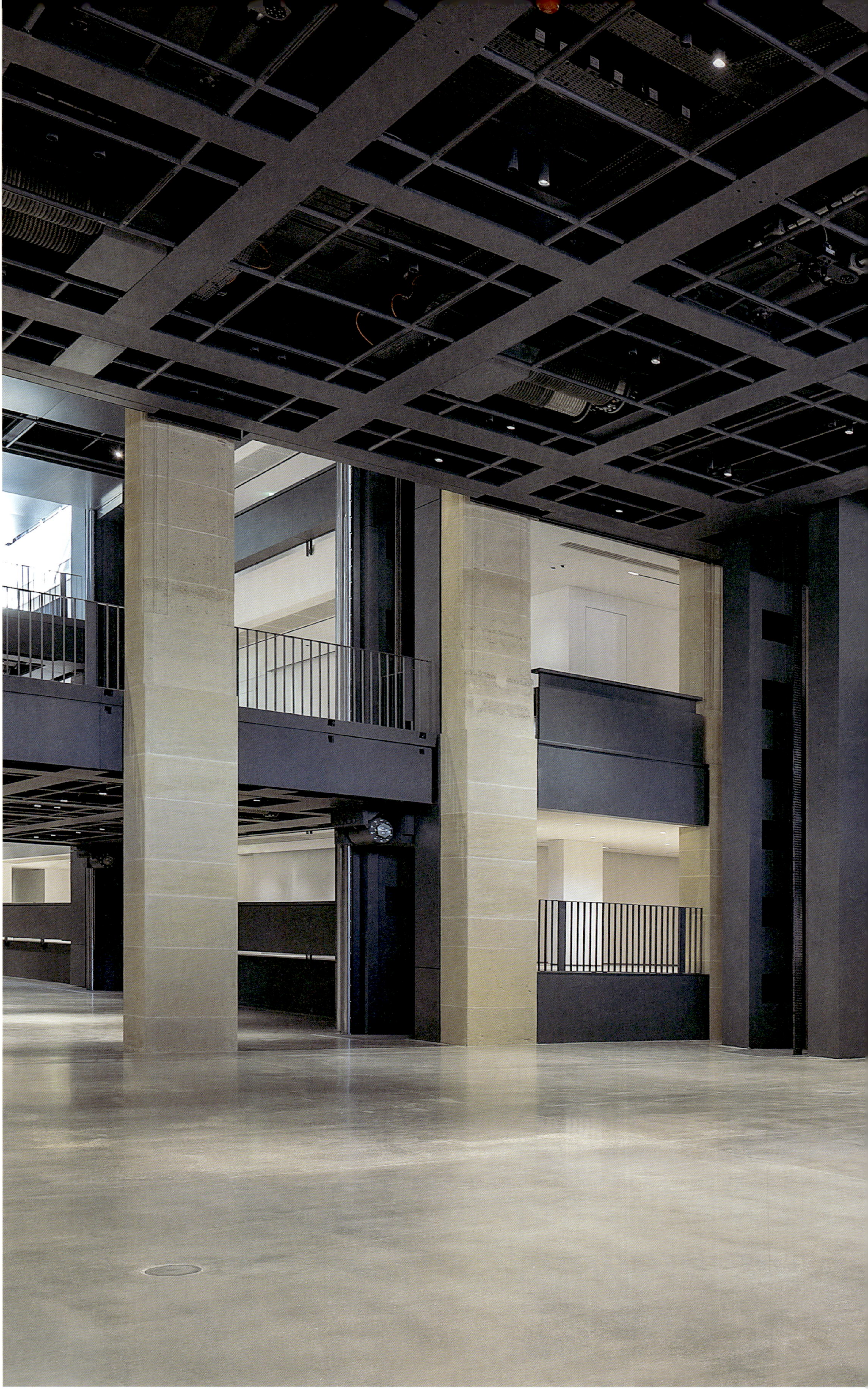

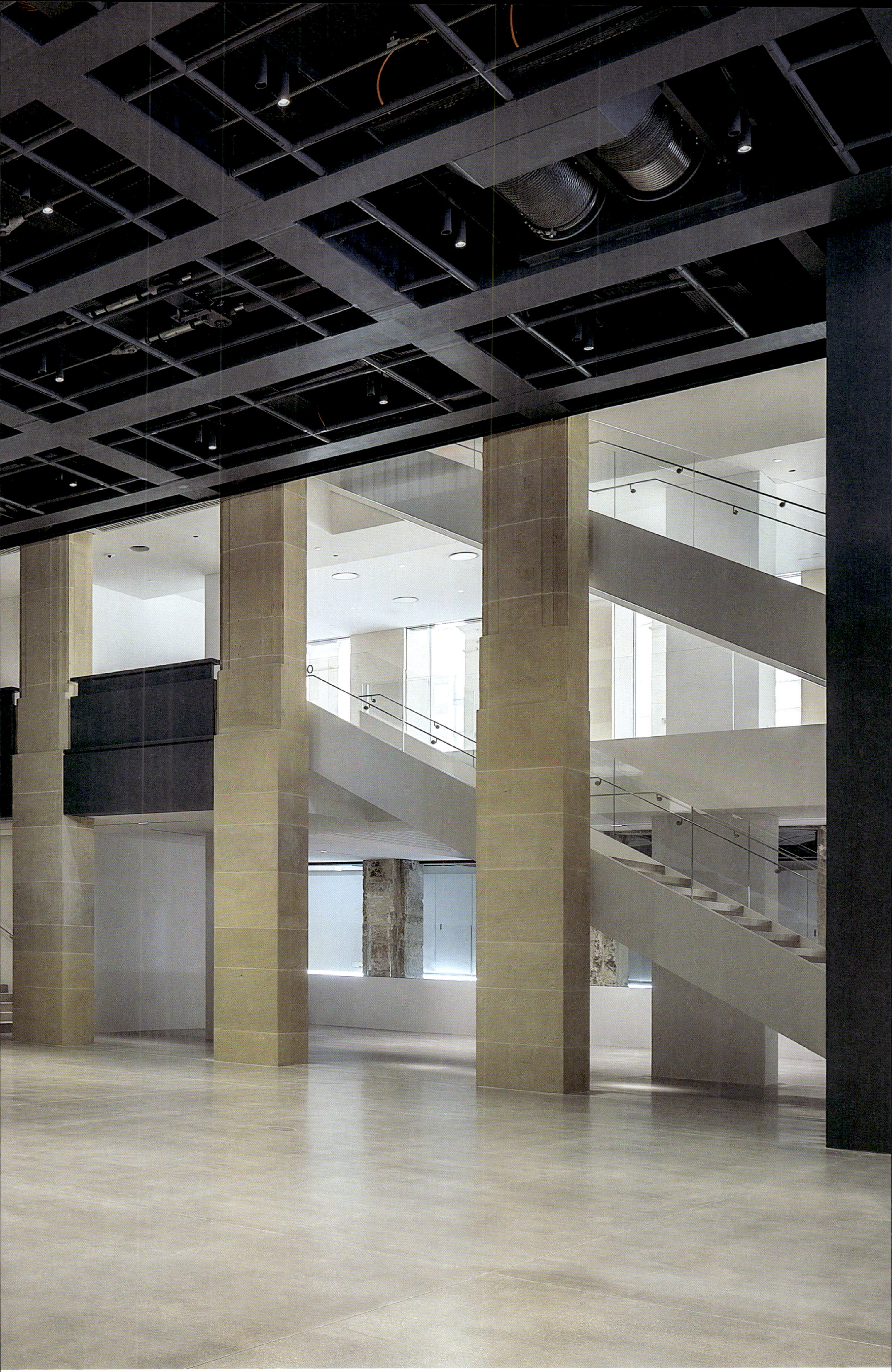

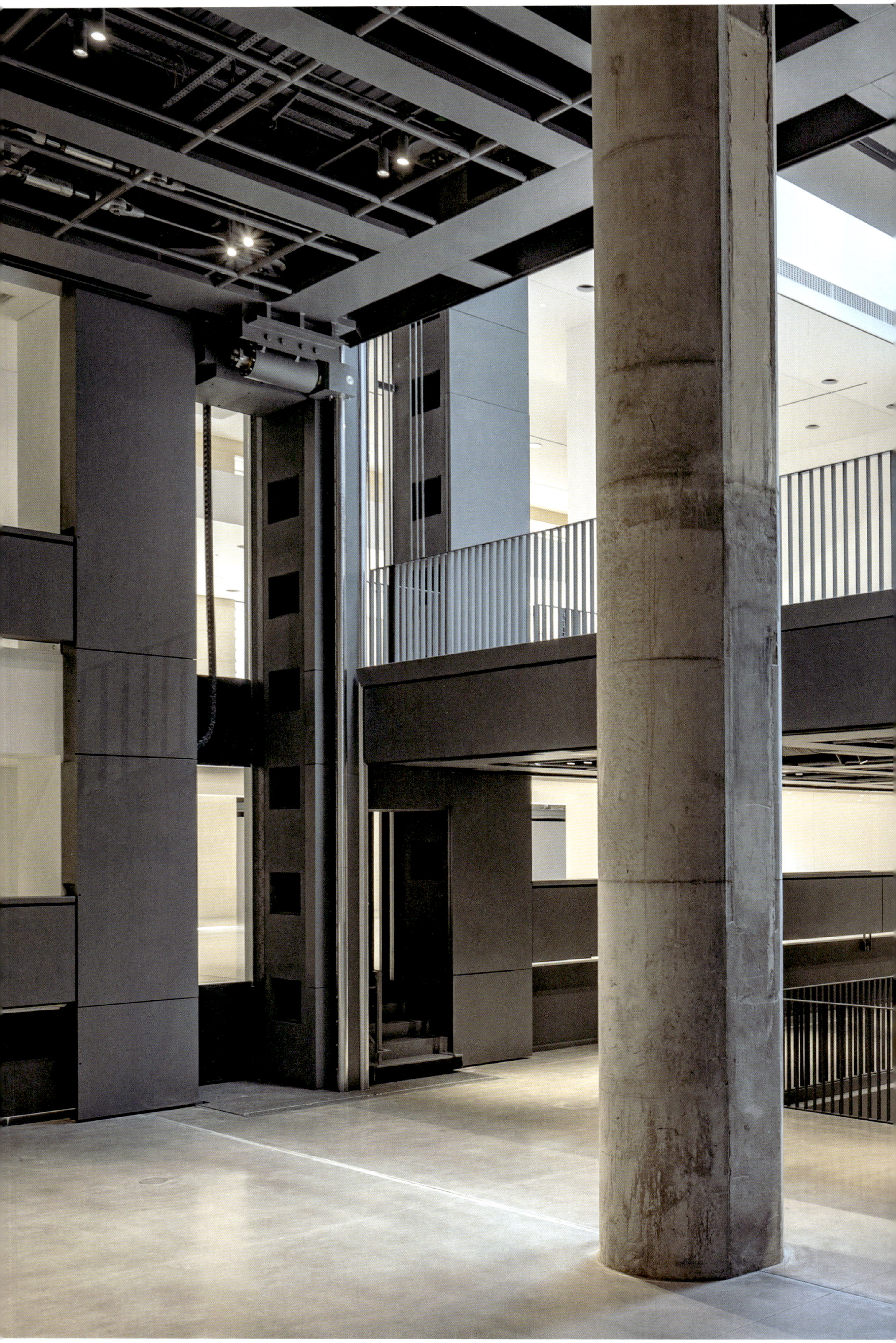

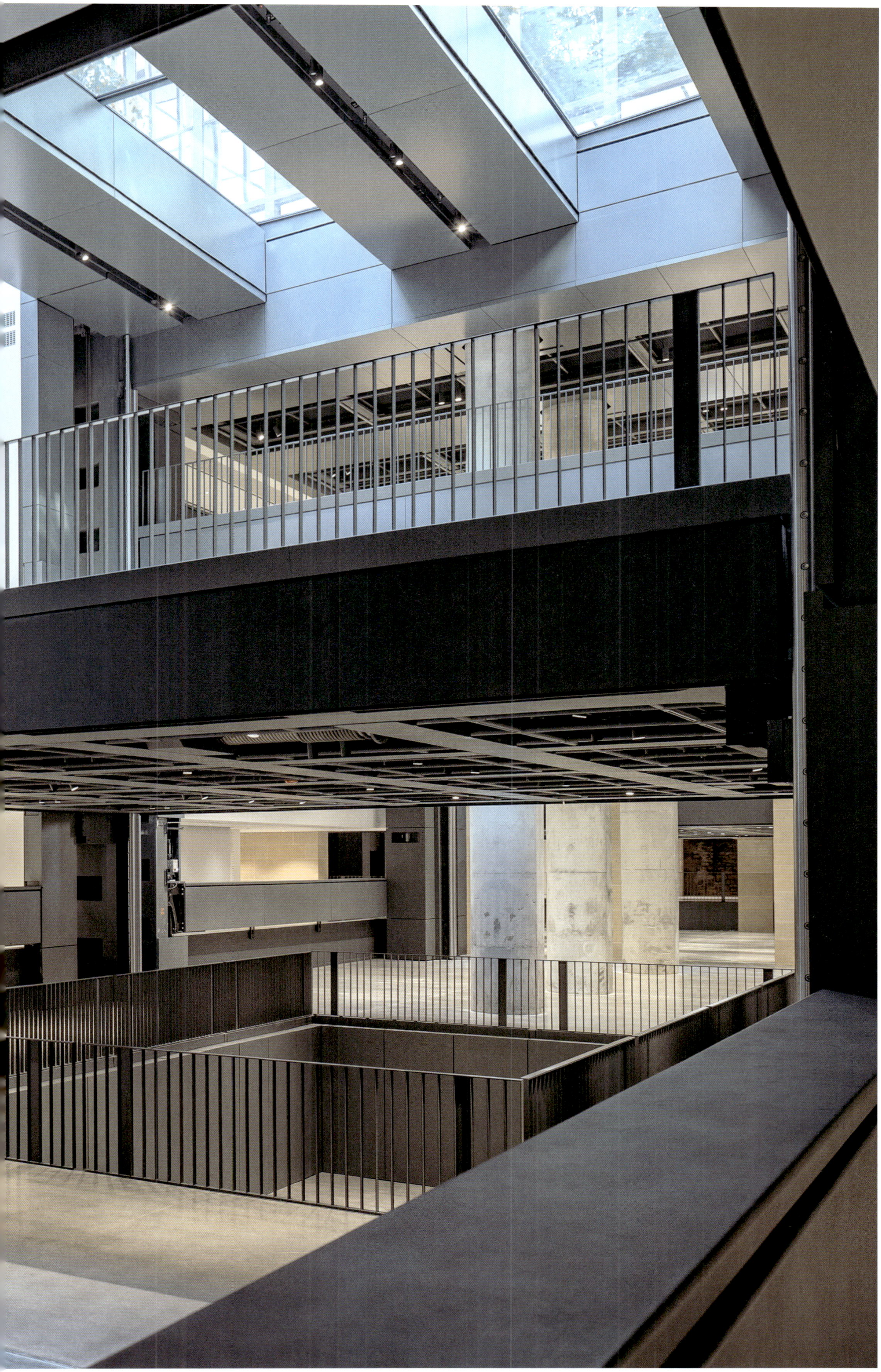

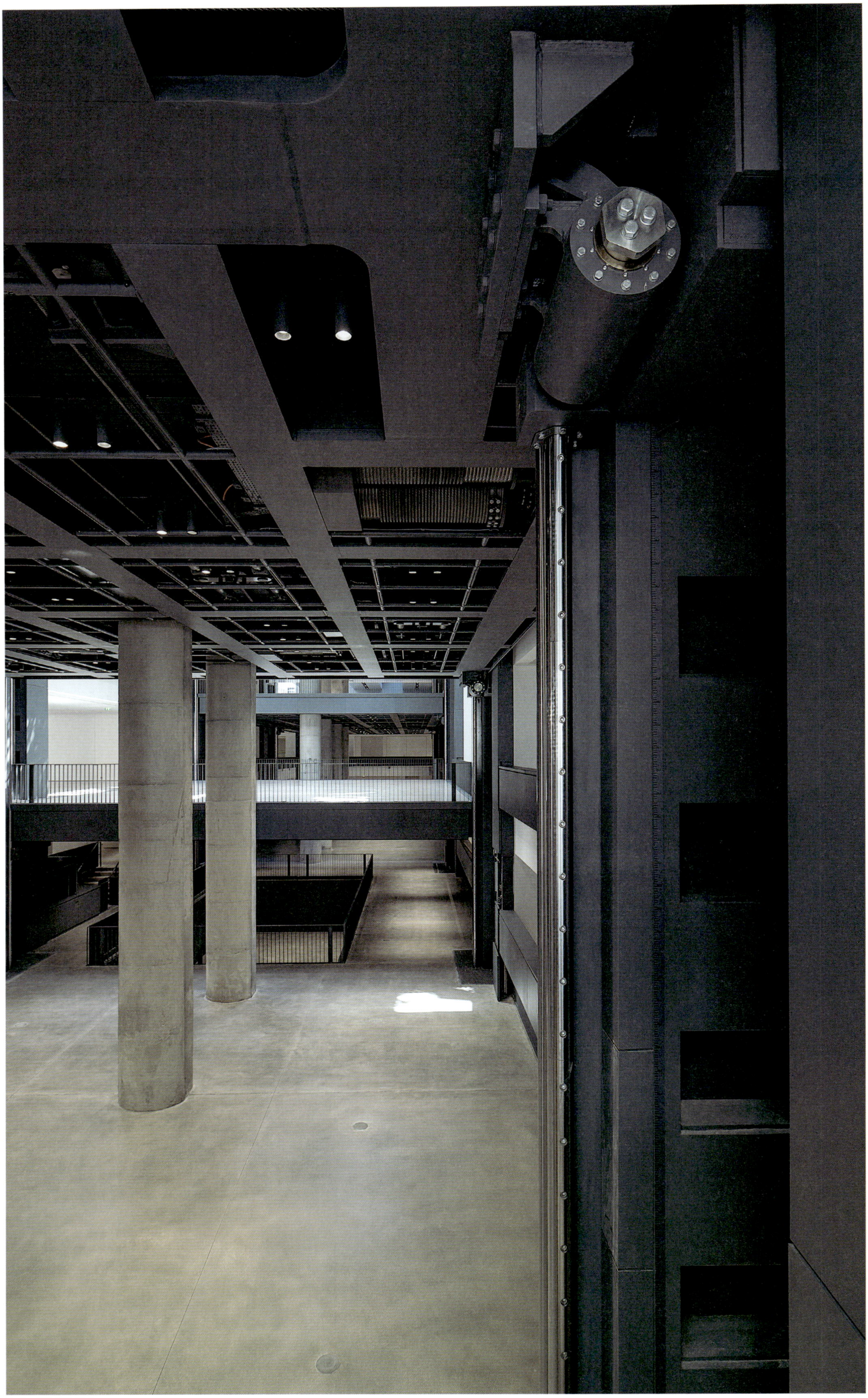

Interior spaces of the Fondation Cartier building

MACHINE (E)MOTION

Antoine Picon

Architectural Historian

Wonderment in Architecture

With such creations as the Opéra de Lyon (1993), the Louvre Abu Dhabi (2017), the Torre Agbar in Barcelona (2005), and the National Museum of Qatar (2019), Jean Nouvel has designed many spectacular buildings during his career. However, the wonderment produced by the spaces he has designed for the Fondation Cartier pour l'art contemporain, opened in October 2025, is even greater. Located at 2 Place du Palais-Royal in the heart of Paris, they fill the basement, ground floor, and first floor of the building formerly occupied by the Louvre des Antiquaires, which earlier succeeded the Hôtel and Grands Magasins du Louvre.[1] There is something arresting about the apparent simplicity of the building's conversion, which respects the footprint of a city block constructed during the Haussmann era, but also hollows it out, allowing the gaze to play over this huge space, 153 meters long and 58 meters wide, designed to hold exhibitions covering 6,500 m², with five mobile platforms—its only visual interruption throughout both its length and height. Visitors exploring the building will find their minds buzzing with images. With its staircases and walkways, its imposing machinery and shadowy recesses, the interior is not unlike some 17th- or 18th-century stage apparatus designed to produce spectacular effects through audacious perspectives and chiaroscuro. The vast interior also suggests the bowels of an aircraft carrier, its platforms like the elevators that carry planes up to the flight deck. But such allusions ultimately carry little weight in light of the striking impact made by Jean Nouvel's architectural project. For although it speaks immediately to its visitors, their surprise leaves them momentarily speechless.

THIS IMMENSE SPACE IS SUGGESTIVE OF A SHIP, AN AIRCRAFT CARRIER OR A LINER.

In this building so close to the Louvre, what seems all of a piece is undergirded by oppositions that, as they are gradually perceived, bring the architect's choices into high relief. The first is a paradoxical relationship with movement. This immense space is suggestive of a ship, an aircraft carrier or a liner, but, rather than sailing, the vessel is anchored right in the center of the city. Nonetheless, its immobility is offset by the flexibility enabled by the vertical movement of the platforms, which can each occupy eleven different positions and thus offer a multitude of combinations. Such modularity calls to

1 — Originally constructed to welcome visitors to the 1855 Exposition Universelle, the building designed by architect Alfred Armand initially comprised a prestigious hotel and a few boutiques. New commercial spaces were regularly opened, and in 1887, the entire building was turned into a department store. Following extensive structural work, in 1978 it became a center for antique shops. After a decline in commercial activity, the Louvre des Antiquaires closed its doors in 2019.

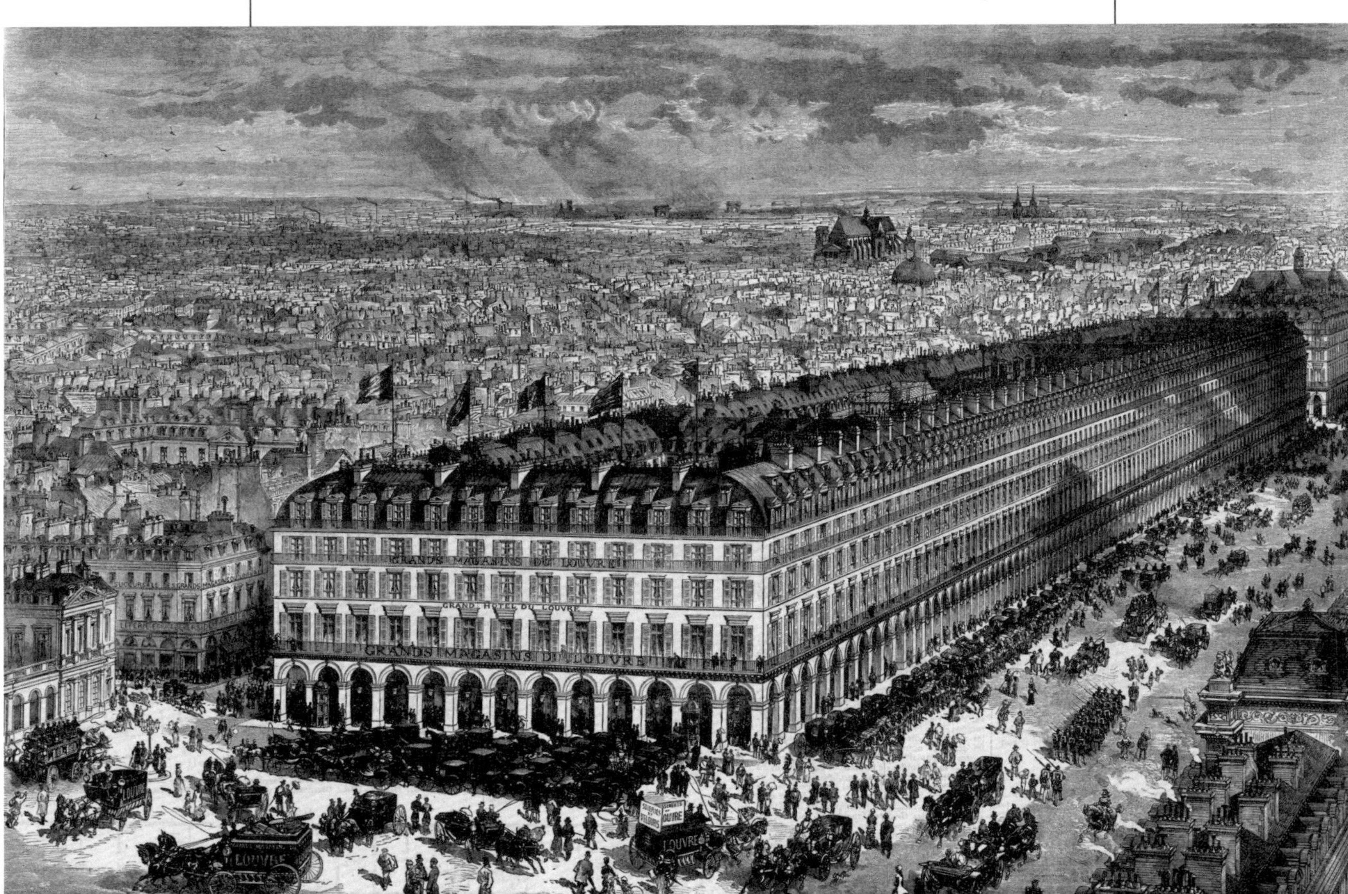

Grands Magasins du Louvre, 1877 (drawing by Charles Fichot and Edmond Morin, engraving by Charles Maurand)

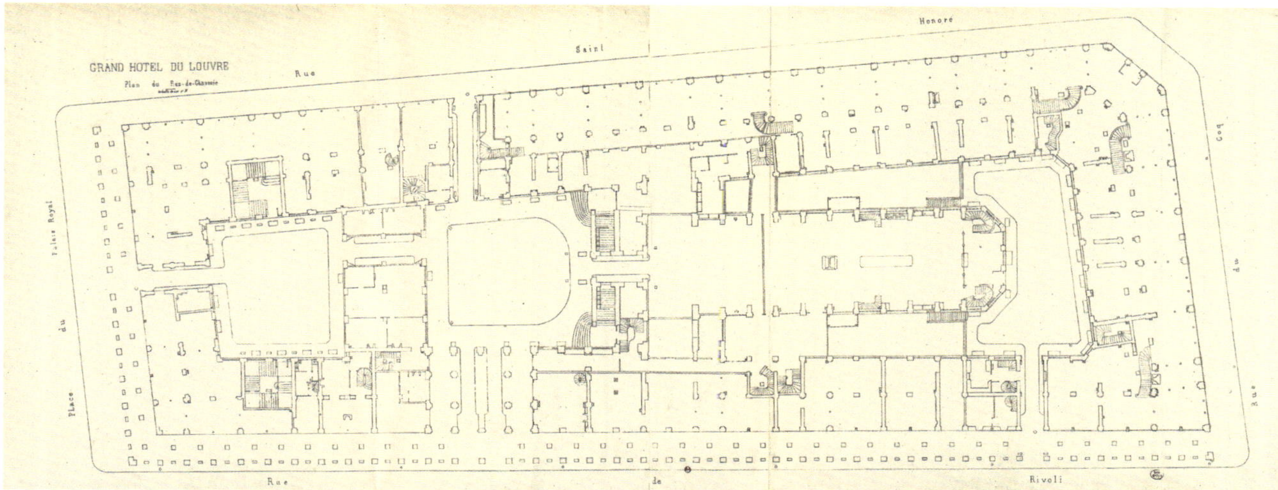

Ground floor plan of the Grand Hôtel du Louvre, c. 1854 (architect: Alfred Armand in collaboration with Charles Rohault de Fleury, Jules Pellechet, and Jacques Ignace Hittorff)

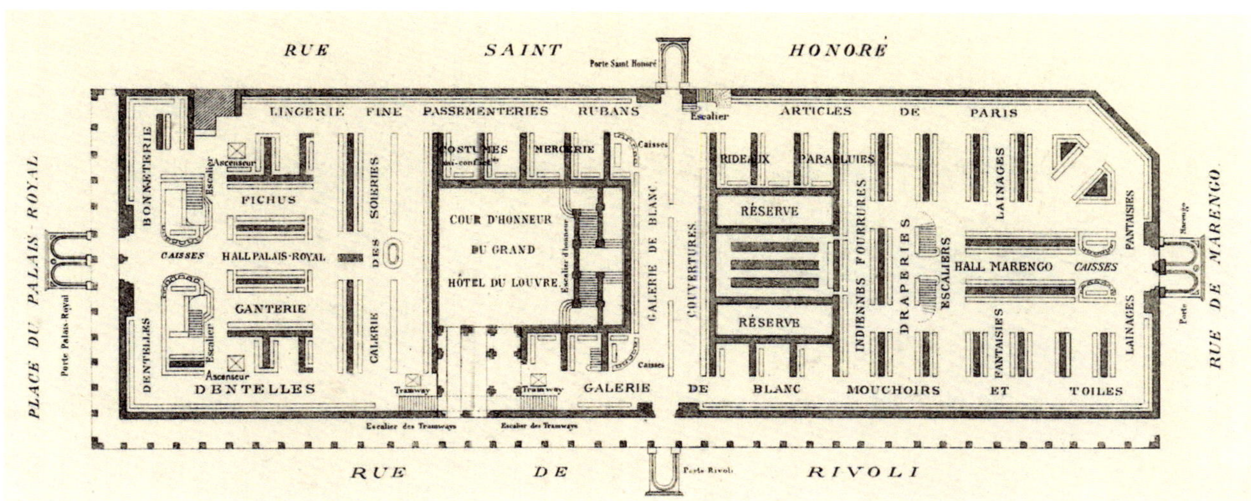

Ground floor plan of the Grands Magasins du Louvre, 1877

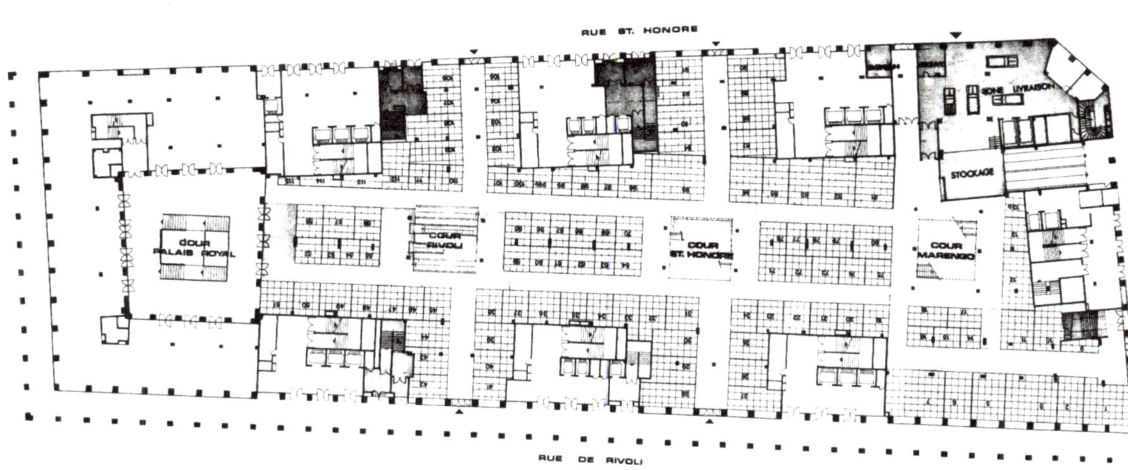

Ground floor plan of the Louvre des Antiquaires, 1978

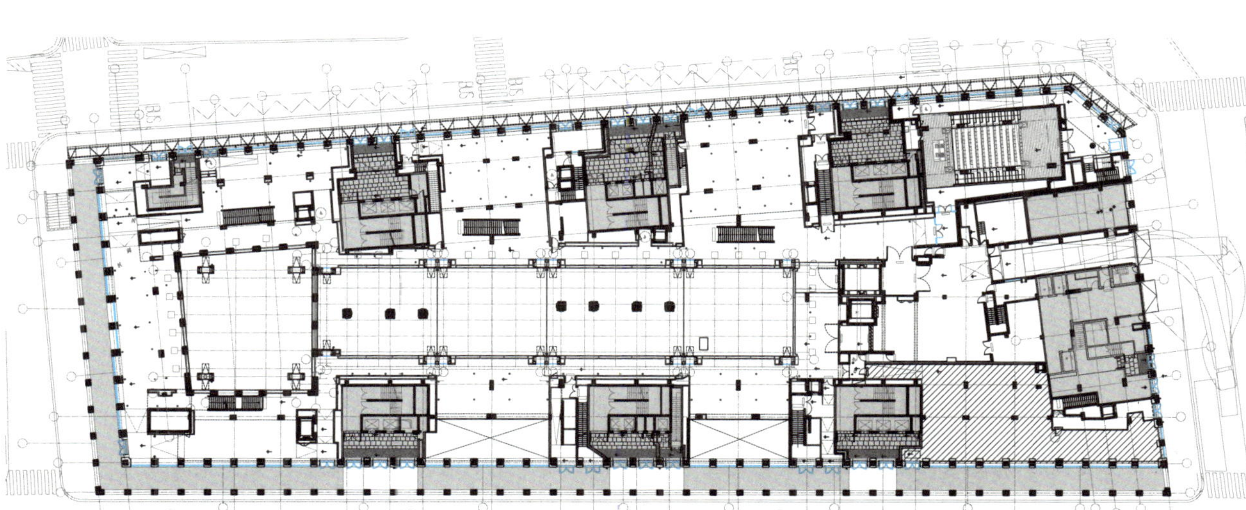

Ground floor plan of the Fondation Cartier by Jean Nouvel, 2025

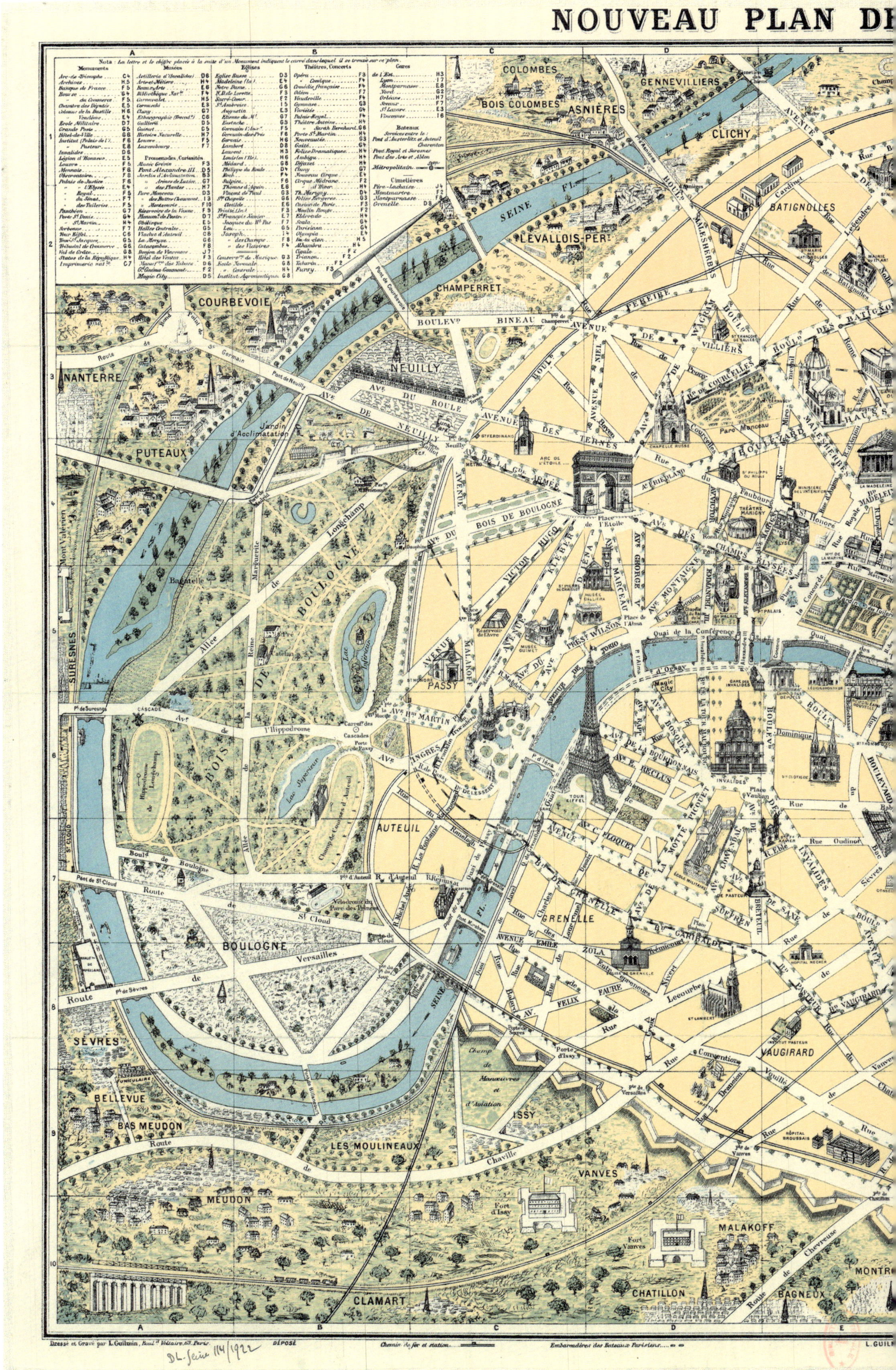

Nouveau plan de Paris monumental, c. 1890
(map by L. Guilmin)

ARIS MONUMENTAL.

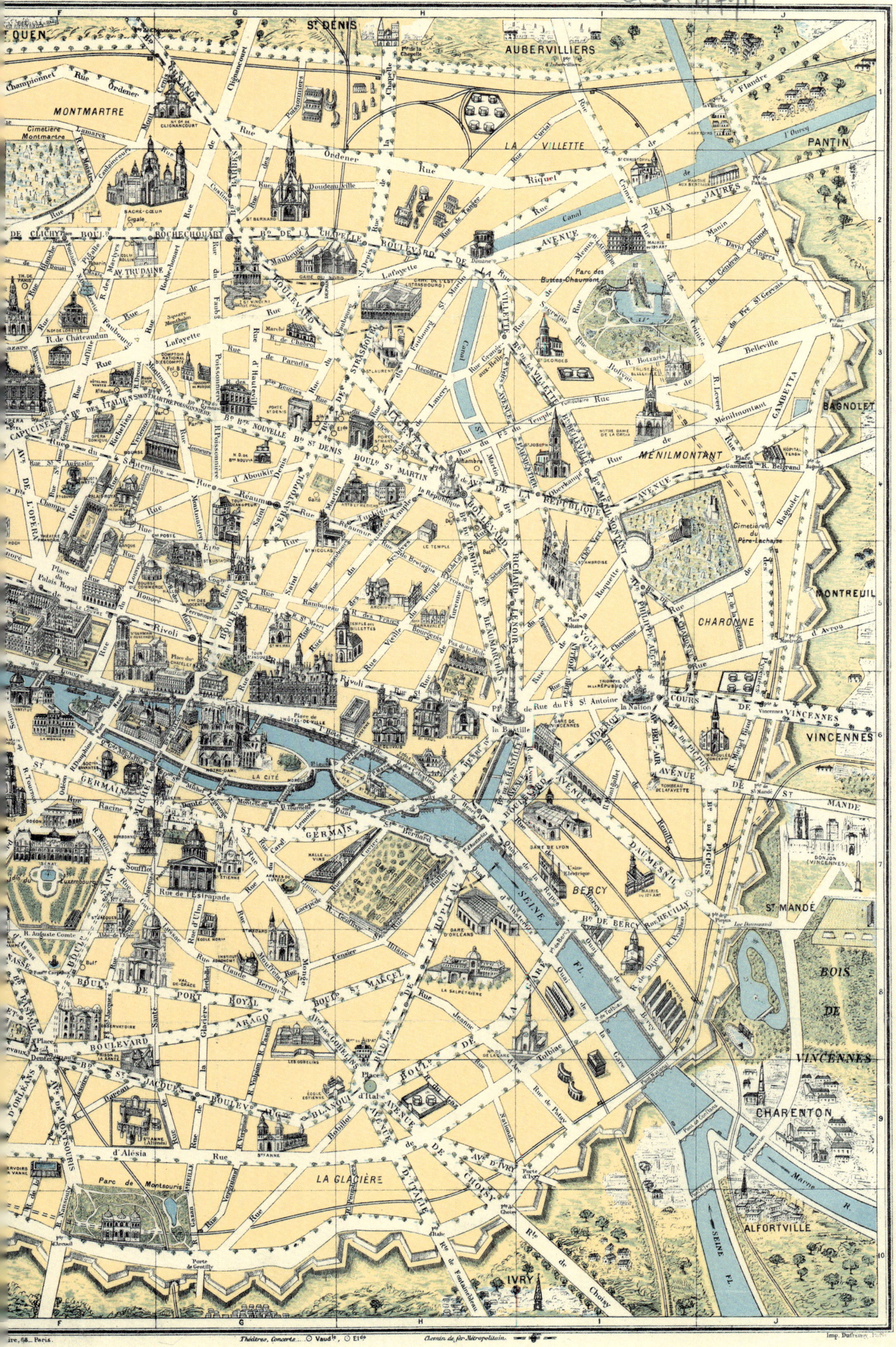

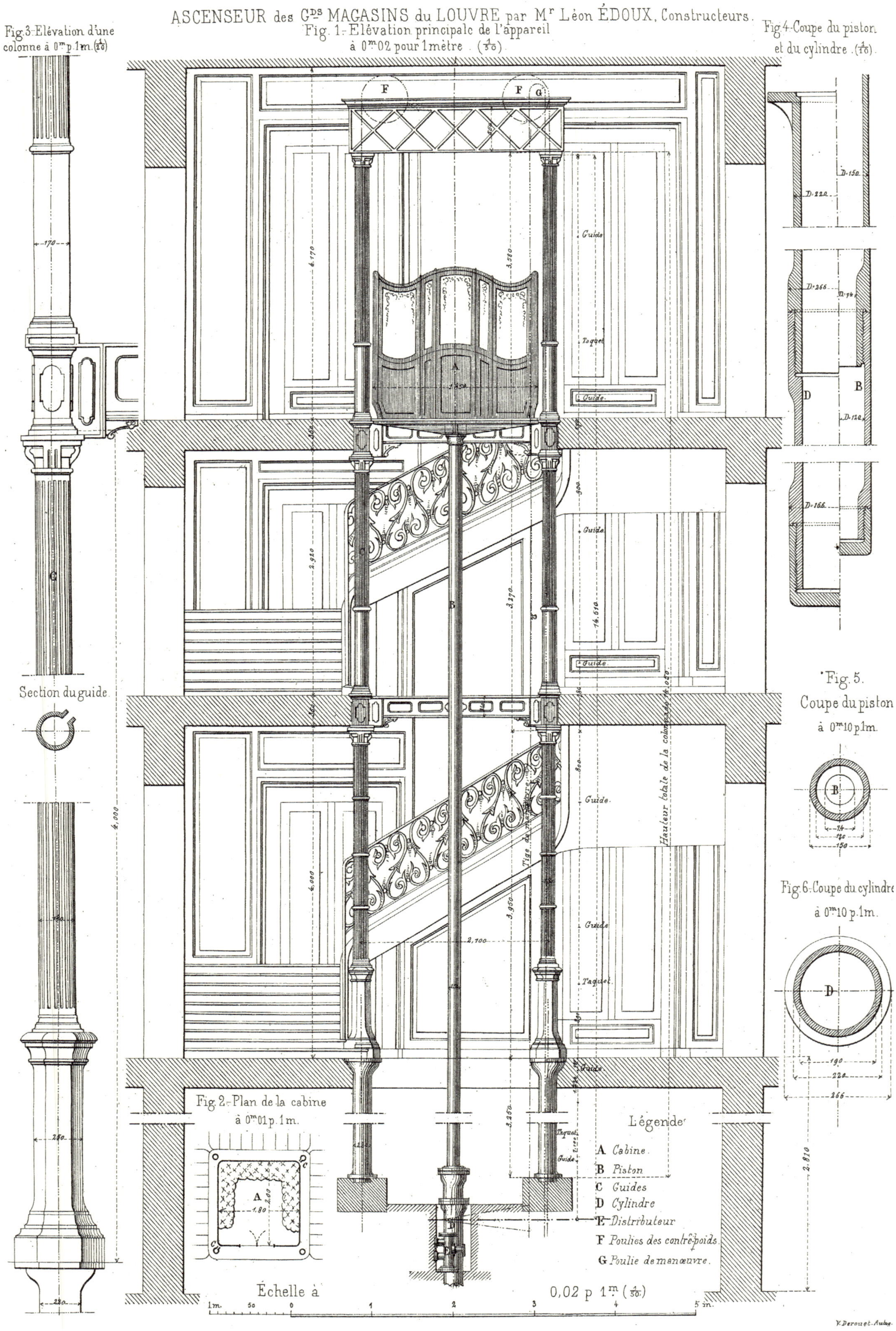

Detail of the operation of one of the elevators of the Grands Magasins du Louvre, designed by Félix Léon Édoux, 1877

mind the versatility aspired to in the 1960s and 1970s by projects like Cedric Price's Fun Palace and the first version of the Centre Pompidou by Renzo Piano and Richard Rogers, which were meant to be almost completely convertible. So—from immobility to movement. However, the arches and columns supporting the upper floors of the block occupied by the Fondation Cartier and the apparent fixity of the platforms that only move between two exhibition height settings complicate the situation. These elements tell a more static story, one firmly anchored in a traditional approach to monumentality. In this respect, the stone arches around the first platform encountered by the visitor play a determining role. Their simplicity makes them look almost neoclassical and the image they convey is above all one of reassuring stability. Immobility and movement: when all is said and done, these contradictory characteristics of the space and its materials are difficult to separate.

A yet more tangible opposition resides in the contrast between the minimalism of the general conception and the complexity of

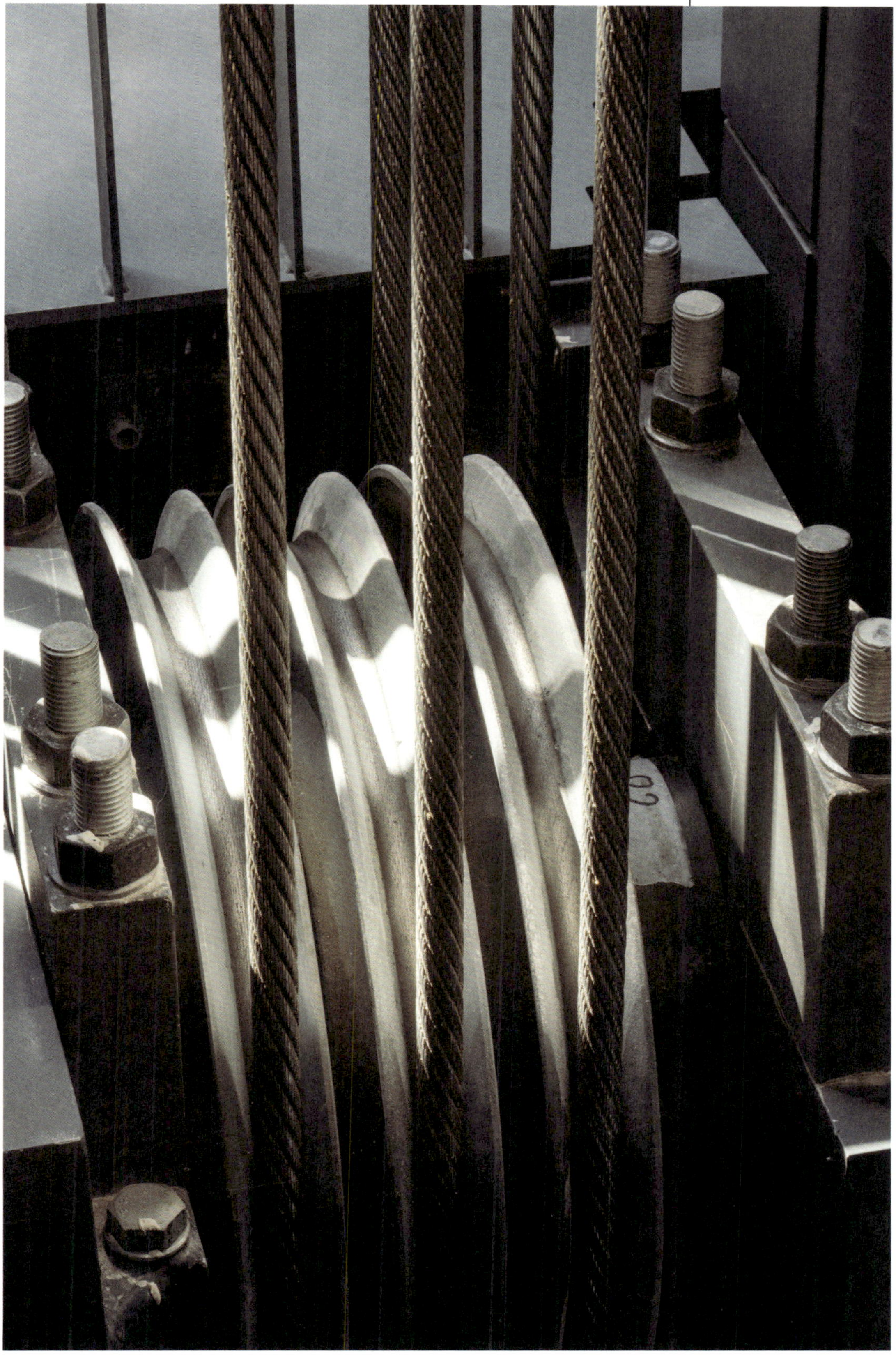

Pulley of one of the platforms of the Fondation Cartier building

the technical means used in its realization. The architectural project appears hybrid: part building, part machine. An impressive display of cables, pulleys, and motors enables the platforms to move. Systems using electric linear actuators allow the platforms to be locked at different heights, while articulated cable carriers supply the power and control networks for the components the platforms carry. Horizontal shutters modulate the light entering from the block's internal courtyards. Technology is apparent everywhere, but in a form that suggests the early days of the machinist era, taking a mechanical and electrical rather than digital form, though a command-and-control system guides the platforms' movements, keeping them secure at every stage. This machinery evokes the novels of Jules Verne or representations of industry in early- to mid-20th-century films, as opposed to the Hollywood science fiction of today.

Jean Nouvel's purpose in using technology is not to appear high-tech or to present the image of an avant-garde architect using the latest developments. It is instead one element in a search to create effects that are both palpable and poetic. This disavowal of the most recent technological advances and reference to a kind of generic machinist era invest the project with a certain modernity, yet also a strange timelessness that is almost archaic. Considered in this light, the mobile platforms are like large sacrificial stones or altars that accommodate works of art as though they were offerings. Although cinematic in character, the technical vision deployed by Jean Nouvel tends towards the universal with its combination of simplicity and complexity, contemporaneity and detachment from actuality.

FOR JEAN NOUVEL, THE PURPOSE OF TECHNOLOGY IS TO SERVE A PROJECT MORE POETIC THAN TECHNICAL. IT SEEKS TO TELL A STORY.

One of the most remarkable aspects of the Fondation Cartier's new venue is how it succeeds in blending into the city, embracing its morphology and history, despite being composed of elements that at first sight are little suited to integration. What possible relationship could there be between the platforms, the machinery that drives them, and an urban environment marked by the proximity of the Louvre and the Palais-Royal? The answer exists on several levels, beginning with the visual continuity between the interior and exterior, which Jean Nouvel has reinstated by restoring the windows on all four of the building's facades. This has allowed the Fondation Cartier's spaces to be both radically distinct from the public space and in close relation with the street. By unifying perception of the structure, allowing the eye to see right through it, the building rekindles the logic that prevailed at the time of its construction, that of a vast urban block occupied by a hotel and department store of generous volumes, which were lost when the interior was divided up during the conversion of the 1970s.[2] Today, it has finally assumed its full identity in relation to the Place du Palais-Royal, a space both mineral and monumental, which the project's platforms seem to emulate.

There is no contextuality without happy coincidence. Historians of the city of Paris will not fail to note that Jean Nouvel's project is set close to the site of the Salle des Machines, one of Europe's largest theaters during the 17th century.[3] The name of the theater, which occupied much of the north wing of the Tuileries Palace, derived from its sophisticated machinery, designed by the Italian architect Gaspare Vigarani and used to create extraordinary effects that were regarded as magic by the audiences of the period. With the spectacle offered by its mobile platforms, might the Fondation Cartier building be a new Salle des Machines, a theater devoted to presenting works of art rather than plays?

2 — During the extensive work undertaken following the permanent closure of the Grands Magasins du Louvre in 1974, the internal structure of the building was almost entirely demolished. Of the four inner courtyards, only the one located on the side of the Place du Palais-Royal survived this conversion before the Louvre des Antiquaires was opened in 1978.

3 — Also called the Théâtre des Tuileries, the Salle des Machines was a theater in the Tuileries Palace that could seat 4,000 people. Commissioned by Louis XIV and opened in 1662, it was destroyed in 1871 during the Paris Commune.

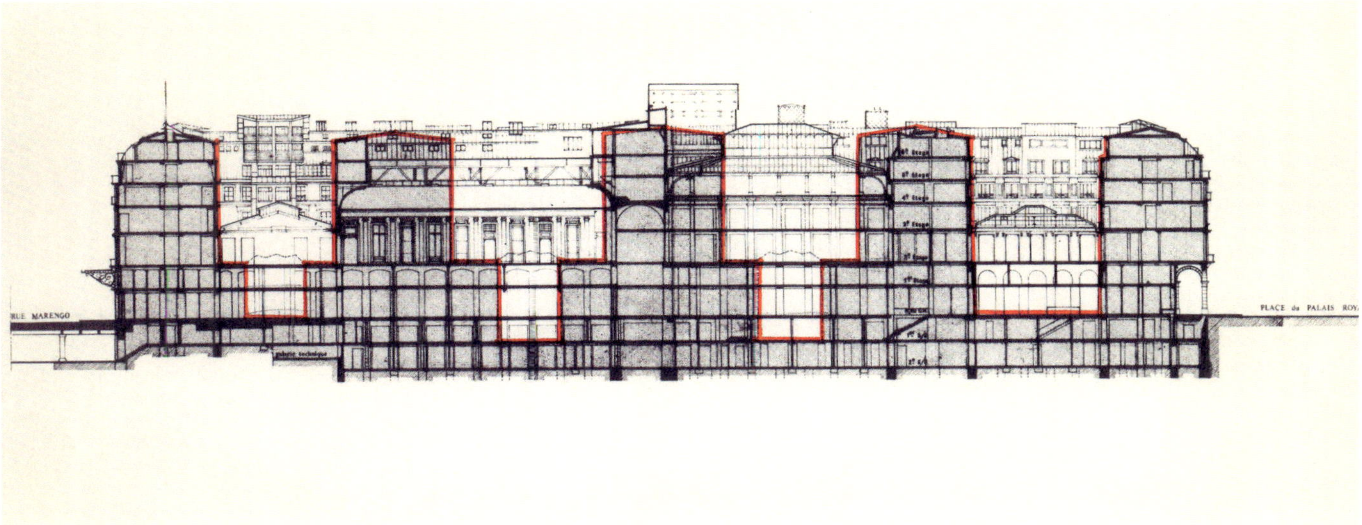

Longitudinal section of the building showing the volume reductions planned for the Louvre des Antiquaires, 1974

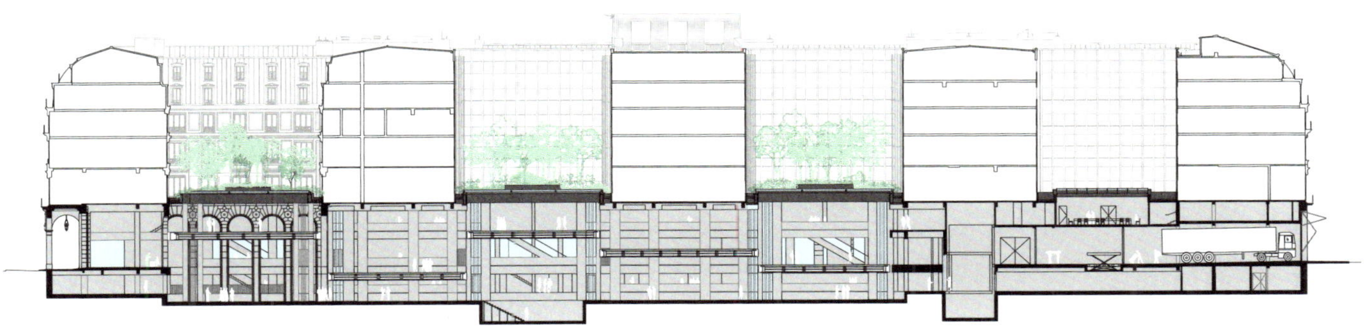

Longitudinal section of the Fondation Cartier building by Jean Nouvel, 2025

Theaters and Machines

The union of the terms “theater” and “machine” can be understood in two distinct ways. The first, when speaking of a *théâtre de machines*, refers to a type of technical treatise first published during the Renaissance, presenting all kinds of mechanical inventions for use in both the applied arts and entertainment. One of the first such instances was issued in 1578, the inventor Jacques Besson’s *Théâtre des instruments mathématiques et mécaniques*. The collection of machines published by the engineer Agostino Ramelli in 1588 was also a foundational work in this tradition, as was the book *Les Raisons des forces mouvantes, avec diverses machines tant utiles que plaisantes*[4] written by the hydraulic engineer Salomon de Caus, published in 1615. Forerunners of the comprehensive descriptions of the arts and crafts of the 18th and 19th centuries, these richly illustrated treatises highlighted not just the diversity of mechanical devices, but also their ingenuity, to be reflected back on the author who brought them together in a single volume.[5] In spite of its formidable machinery, can the Fondation Cartier building be considered in the same light as these treatises? It does not offer a didactic assessment of a set of machines, as does a *théâtre de machines*. Above all, it does not endeavor to impress the viewer with the inventiveness of its creator. Once again, for Jean Nouvel, the purpose of technology is to serve a project more poetic than technical. It seeks to tell a story. “Architecture is there to create emotion,” the architect is apt to declare.[6] Technology participates fully in this quest.

The Salle des Machines in the Tuileries belonged to a different tradition, that of the *théâtre à machines*, which developed in the 18th century.[7] The term used to describe these theaters stems from the importance accorded to the chiefly acoustic, mechanical, and hydraulic apparatuses used to create spectacular stage effects: thunder, lightning, or the crashing of a raging sea, rapid changes of stage scenery, and characters who seemed to emerge from the ground or issue from the clouds. Originating in Italy, these devices spread throughout Europe, to the great delight of audiences. Their

4 — *Theatrum instrumentorum et machinarum Jacobi Bessoni Delphinatis, mathematici ingeniosissimi* (Lyon: B. Vincent, Lyon, 1578); *Le diverse et artificiose machine del capitano Agostino Ramelli* (Paris: A. Ramelli, 1588); and Salomon de Caus, *Les Raisons des forces mouvantes, avec diverses machines tant utiles que plaisantes* (Frankfurt: J. Norton, 1615).

5 — Luisa Dolza, Hélène Vérin, “Figurer la mécanique : l’énigme des théâtres de machines de la Renaissance,” in *Revue d’Histoire Moderne et Contemporaine* (April-June 2004), nos. 51-2.

6 — Alfred Escot, “Jean Nouvel : ‘L’architecture est là pour émouvoir’,” in *Grazia* (26 September 2023), www.grazia.fr/culture/arts-architecture/jean-nouvel-larchitecture-est-la-pour-emouvoir-149946.html.

7 — Hélène Visentin, “Le Théâtre à machines : succès majeur pour un genre mineur,” in *Littératures classiques*, no. 51 (Summer 2004), “Le Théâtre au XVIIe siècle : pratiques du mineur” and Véronique Dominguez, “Les Machines du théâtre français : de la technique à l’illusion,” in Fabienne Pomel (ed.), *Engins et machines. L’imaginaire mécanique dans les textes médiévaux* (Rennes: Presses Universitaires de Rennes, 2015).

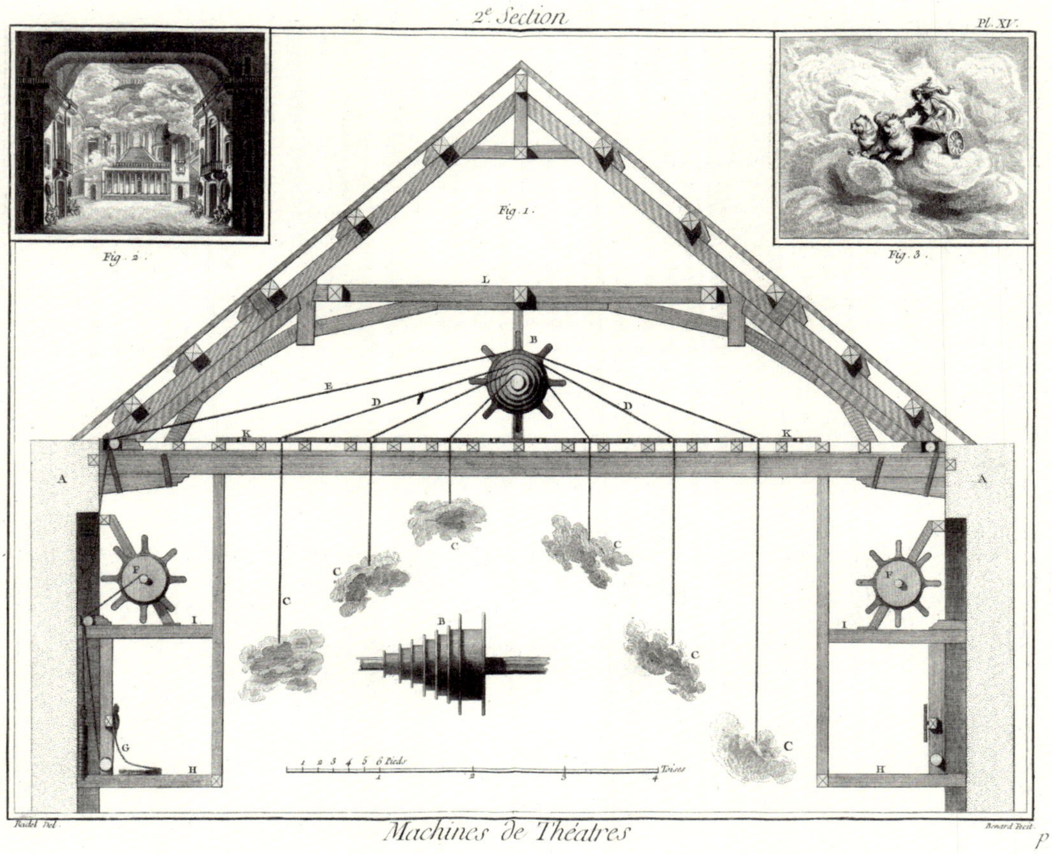

"Theatrical machinery": clouds, plate from the *Encyclopédie* of Diderot and d'Alembert, tome X, 1772 (engraving by Jacques Renaud Benard)

popularity dimmed at the end of the Baroque period owing to the disturbingly hybrid nature of the spectacle-plays they facilitated. Purists wondered: should theater not be founded exclusively on the text and the actors' performance? Opera, however, with its appetite for the extraordinary, continued to make use of such machines.

Although the Fondation Cartier building may not be a *théâtre de machines*, it is not entirely unrelated to the *théâtres à machines*, minus their Baroque pomp and the exuberant nature of their operations. There are no storms or tempests, no rapid movements of the platforms to astound us, but instead the suggestion of a plot, its development inseparable from the imposing machinery that transforms the space and creates visual short-circuits between near and far. Certain configurations allow the visitor's gaze to flit from one platform and exhibition to another. The general ambience in this shadowy, technological space prompts many questions of a theatrical nature. Where are we? In the auditorium, on the stage, or in the stage's vast and inseparable backstage area? Are we part of the audience, or are we involved in the performance? Is it possible that the machines, platforms, and works of art don't really need visitors for them to burst into life, that they are self-sufficient, like so many great "bachelor" devices, to use the term coined by the Surrealists Marcel Duchamp and Michel Carrouges?[8] Around the middle of the 18th century, the theater in the Tuileries staged a series of performances described at the time as "decorative and silent." Composed by the Franco-Italian architect and set designer Giovanni Niccolò Servandoni, who also designed the theatrical facade of Saint-Sulpice in Paris, these performances were for the most part based on the use of machines and scenery: there were no actors—or at most very few—on the stage, and expression was communicated through pantomime rather than speech.[9] A parallel might be suggested between such theatrical devices and the way in which the Fondation Cartier building, composed of different planes at different heights and animated by objects, could be thought to function as a landscape.

MIGHT THE FONDATION CARTIER BUILDING BE A NEW SALLE DES MACHINES, A THEATER DEVOTED TO PRESENTING WORKS OF ART RATHER THAN PLAYS?

8 — Michel Carrouges, *Les Machines célibataires*, (Paris: Arcanes, 1954).

9 — Michèle Sajous D'Oria, *Servandoni maître des machines* (Paris: Classiques Garnier, 2022).

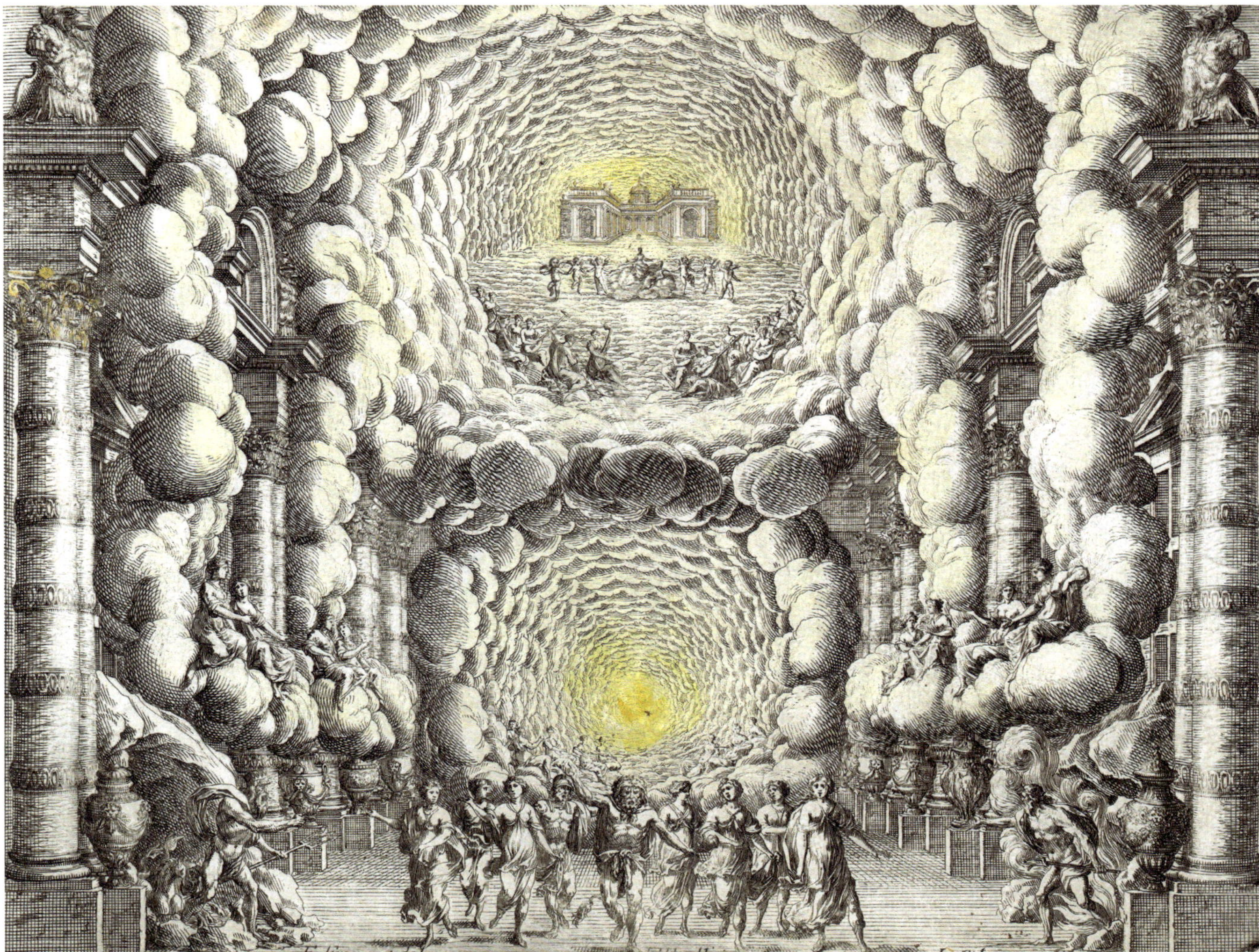

Theatrical scenery design by Giacomo Torelli for the ballet *The Wedding of Thetis and Peleus*, 1654 (drawing by François Francart, engraving by Israël Silvestre)

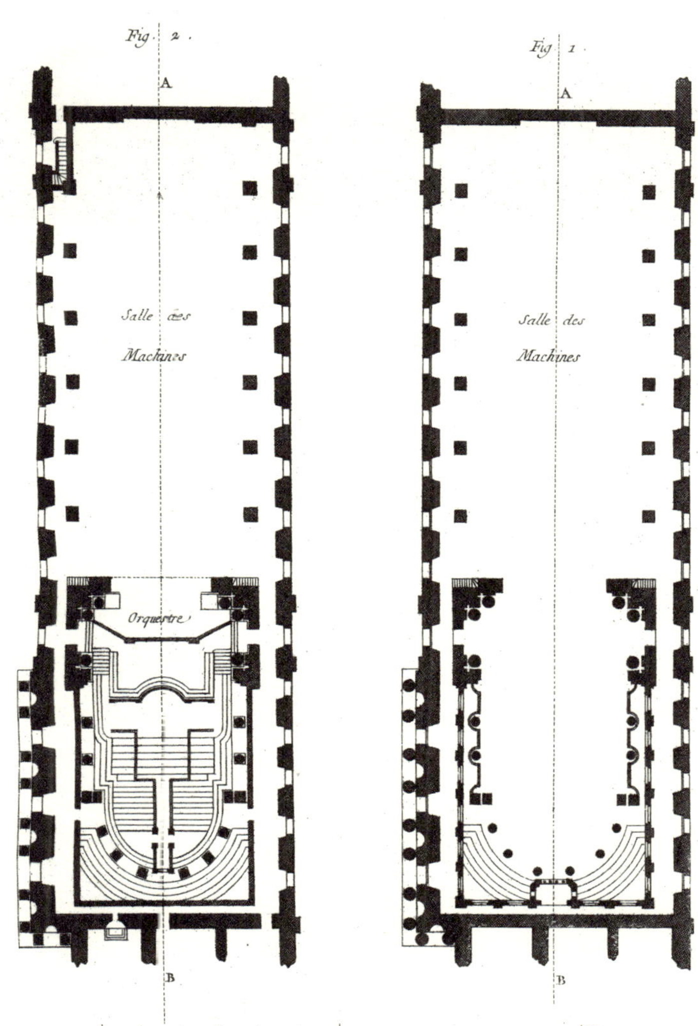

"Theatrical hall": the Salle des Machines of the Tuileries, plate from the *Encyclopédie* of Diderot and d'Alembert, tome X, 1772 (engraving by Jacques Renaud Benard)

While it raises many questions, the solution formulated by Jean Nouvel suggests new ways of presenting works of art. The space in most museums and foundations is divided up into closed areas, usually painted white, like a series of boxes created to accommodate the works. The Fondation Cartier's visual openness allows very

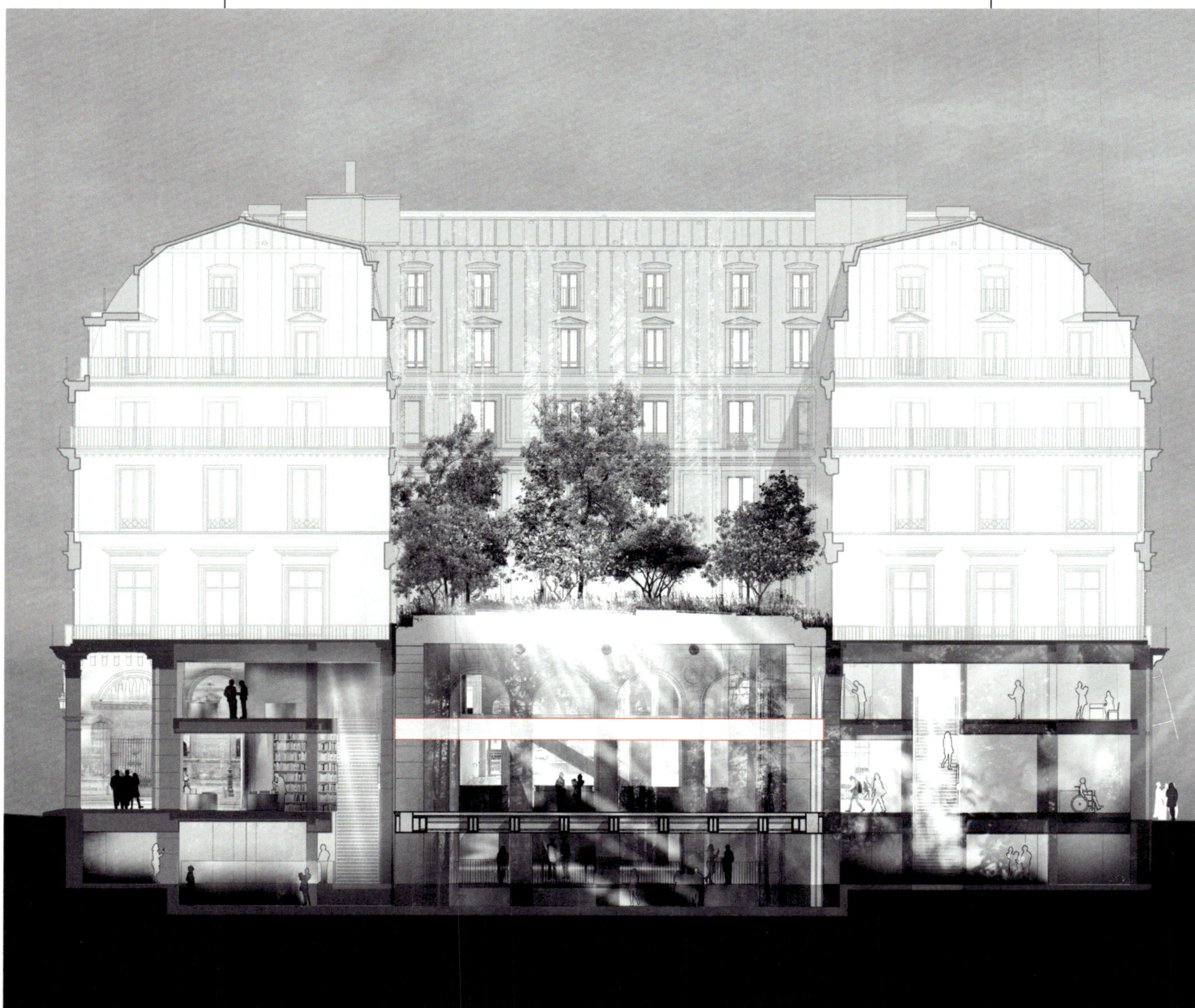

Cross-section
of the Fondation Cartier
building, 2025

different exhibitions to liaise with one another, stimulating new dialogues. One is reminded of the permanent gallery at the Louvre-Lens, where the eye can rove from Greco-Roman antiquities to medieval art or to paintings and sculptures from the 18th and 19th centuries, offering inspiring comparisons. Jean Nouvel's conception takes this fortuitousness even further by playing on the relative heights of the platforms and creating a distance between viewer and exhibition that allows the eye to partially grasp their content. His theater is truly three-dimensional, transforming the space into a landscape of objects and collections.

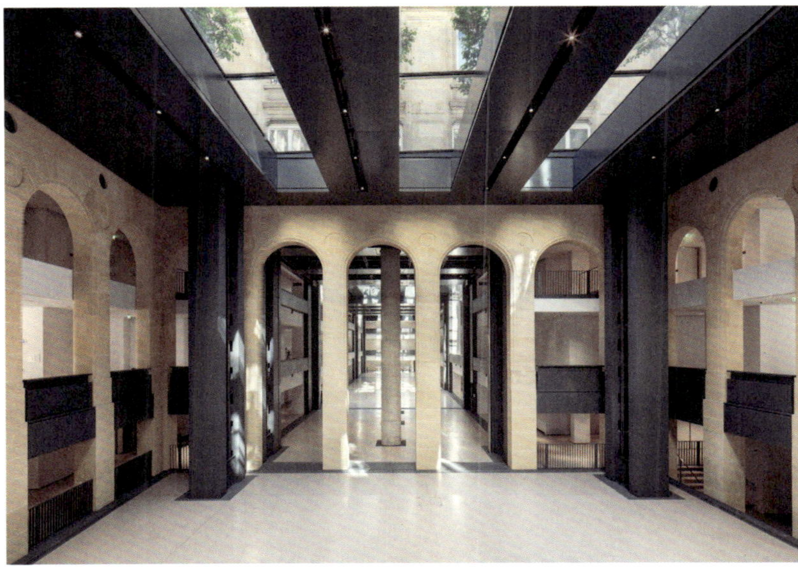

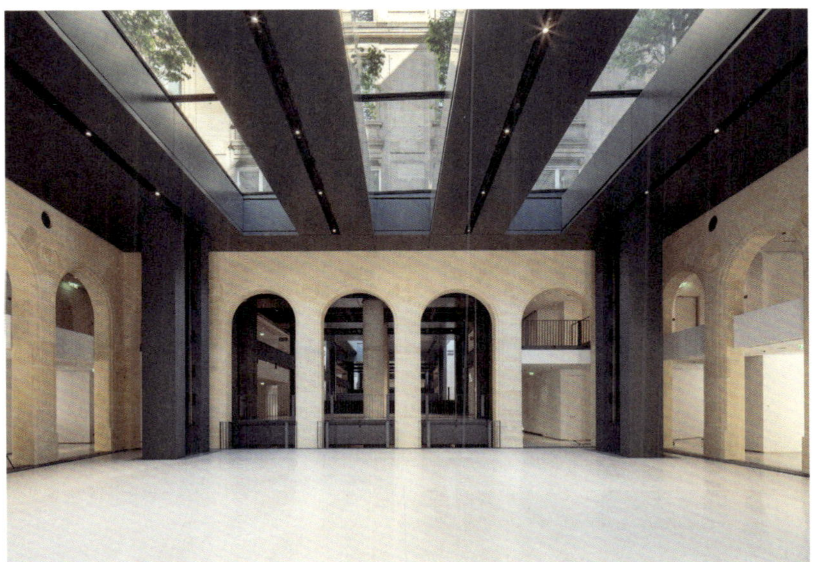

Interior spaces of the Fondation Cartier building

Expanding the Architectural Field

The Fondation Cartier's new spaces bear a resemblance to several of Jean Nouvel's previous projects, in the cultural domain in particular: art centers, museums, theaters. When faced with a challenge of this sort, the architect likes to incorporate effects created by the contrast between transparency and chiaroscuro, with surroundings in which technology is used to enhance a contextual contemporaneity. Contrasts of this nature can be seen, for example, in the Lucerne Culture and Congress Center (2000) and the Palais de Justice in Nantes (2000). Nouvel's work is also characterized by colors that range from browns and blacks typical of nightclubs to the red of opera boxes. This type of red is to be found in the Fondation Cartier's auditorium.

But the striking character of the Fondation Cartier's new spaces also lies in the impression it gives that Jean Nouvel is exploring the limits of architecture in the traditional sense of the term, as though he were extending them. This exploration takes different directions. To begin with, the giant mobile platforms and the machinery powering them suggest there is something infrastructural about his project. It places in full view a supporting activity—the term "infrastructure" refers exactly to this type of activity—that underpins the search for form that ordinarily typifies the architectural discipline.[10] In so doing, Jean Nouvel seems to be proposing other ways to occupy the space, and in an innovative manner. We have a clearer understanding of why this *théâtre à machines* questions the meaning of the human presence with its suggestion that it could, if required, function without it. Naturally, this is only a hypothesis, one that is immediately contradicted by the function of the exhibition spaces, but it prompts us to rethink the museum visit as such, and to give it back the status of an encounter or event. Considered from this perspective, the Fondation Cartier building may well be reviving the ambitions of one of Jean Nouvel's intellectual guides, the architect Claude Parent, whose oblique living spaces questioned the

10 — Ashley Carse, "Keyword: Infrastructure: How a Humble French Engineering Term Shaped the Modern World," in Penny Harvey, Casper Bruun Jensen, and Atsuro Morita (eds.), *Infrastructure and Social Complexity: A Companion* (Abingdon, New York: Routledge, 2017); Konstantinos Chatzis, "Introduction générale. Le nouveau monde des infrastructures," in Konstantinos Chatzis, Gilles Jeannot, Valérie November, and Pascal Ughetto (eds.), *Les Métamorphoses des infrastructures, entre béton et numérique* (Brussels: Peter Lang, 2017).

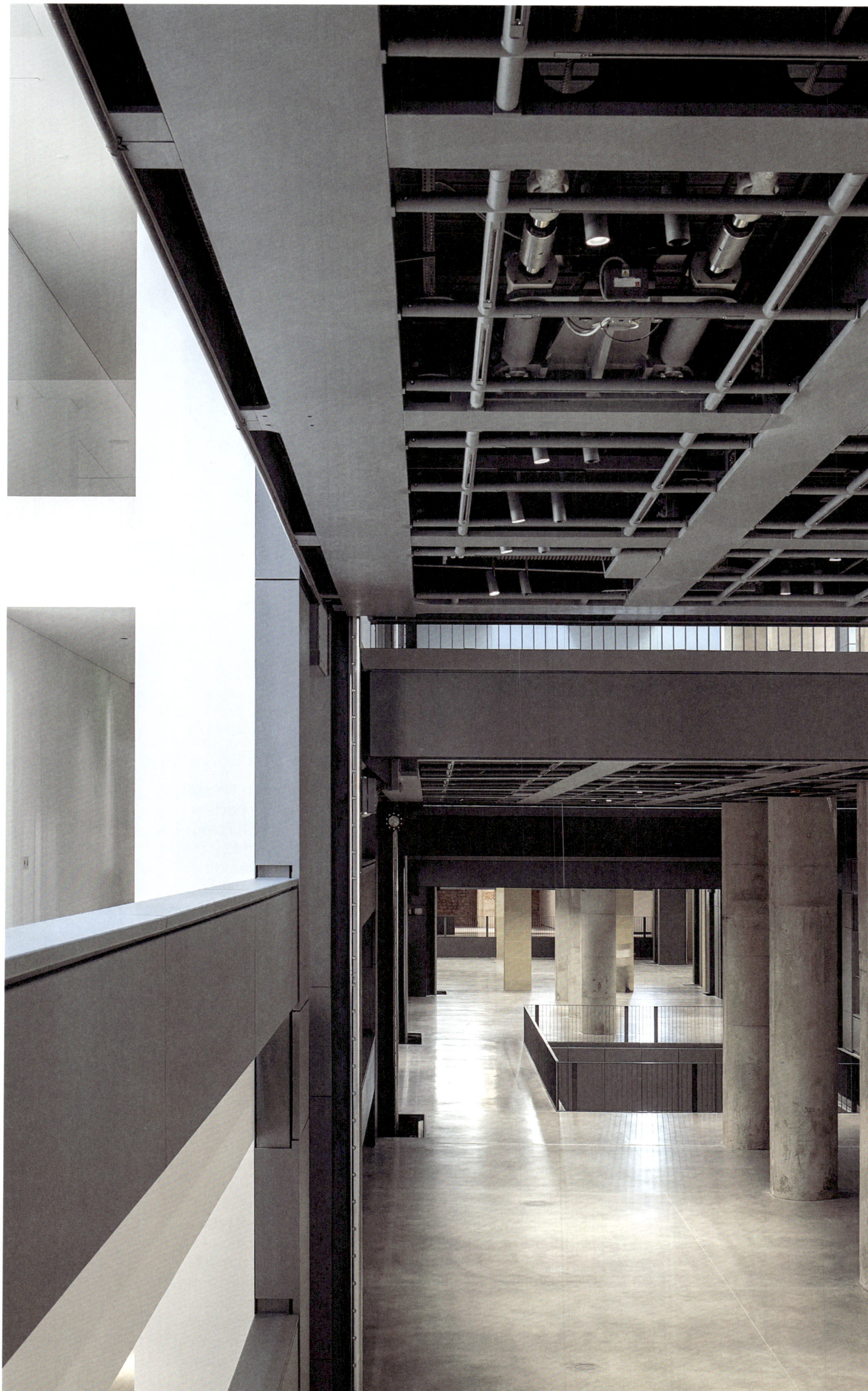

Interior spaces of the Fondation Cartier building

notion of habitation.[11] There are no obliques in Jean Nouvel's work; instead, there is the desire to reconsider what it means to "dwell poetically," to quote Friedrich Hölderlin's famous expression, also used by Martin Heidegger, i.e. creatively, in contact with works of art and live performances, the presence of which is emphasized in a machine-building or an infrastructure-building designed entirely for their benefit.[12]

THE STRIKING CHARACTER OF THE FONDATION CARTIER'S NEW SPACES ALSO LIES IN THE IMPRESSION IT GIVES THAT JEAN NOUVEL IS EXPLORING THE LIMITS OF ARCHITECTURE IN THE TRADITIONAL SENSE OF THE TERM, AS THOUGH HE WERE EXTENDING THEM.

This might seem a long stretch from the traditional definition of a work of architecture, but by maintaining respect for the symmetries of the existing building and the importance ascribed to the staircases and walkways that lead to the platforms at different heights, the project embraces aspects that at times evoke an earlier architectural practice. It comprises, in particular, certain principles, such as axiality, fundamental to the notion of composition that long prevailed in the teaching and practice of architecture. However, that is of little consequence; the crux of the matter lies elsewhere, in a work that is more closely related to the telling of a story, the development of situations, the writing of a scenario, than to a classic architectural composition or its equally composed "deconstruction," as attempted by architects like Peter Eisenman or Rem Koolhaas during the 1980s.[13]

So, on what level does this building exist? The simplicity of the general concept resides in the sphere of infrastructure—that which

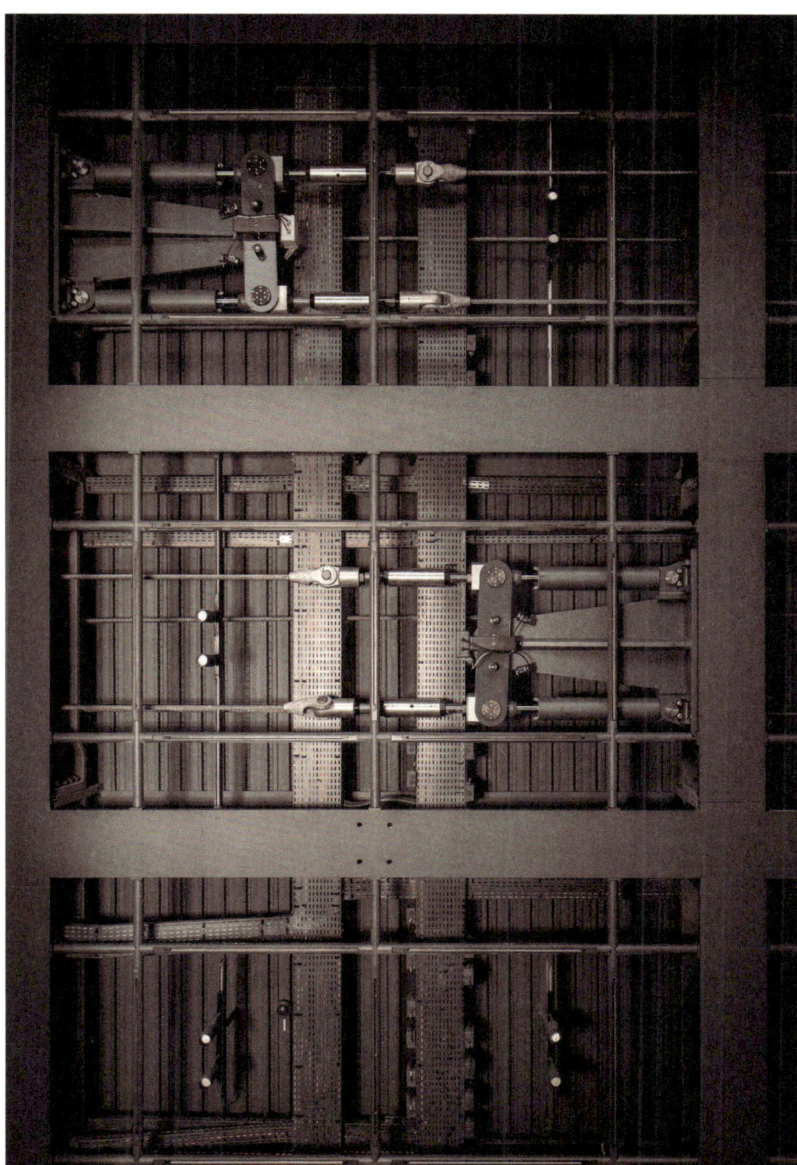

Detail of the underside of one of the five platforms of the Fondation Cartier building

11 — Claude Parent, *L'Œuvre construite, l'œuvre graphique* (Paris, Orléans: Cité de l'Architecture et du Patrimoine, Éditions HYX, 2010).

12 — Martin Heidegger, "... Poetically Man Dwells ...," 1951, in *Poetry, Language, Thought*, trans. Albert Hofstadter (New York: Harper & Row, 1971).

13 — On this, see Jacques Lucan, *Composition, non-composition. Architecture et théories, XIXe-XXe siècles* (Lausanne: Presses polytechniques et universitaires romandes, 2009).

responds to needs, that which serves—rather than in the desire to create an architectural landmark. Most infrastructural works survive only for the time that they are used, even though disused Roman aqueducts still survive today. We are reminded of Hannah Arendt's famous distinction in *The Human Condition* between products of labor, which are doomed to obsolescence, and products of work, which are designed to endure, to consolidate and to furnish the human world.[14] For many architects, technical objects, devices, infrastructures, and machines have long belonged to this first category. Thus, Auguste Perret differentiated between the locomotive, doomed to obsolescence, and Greek temples, capable of enduring the centuries.[15] Of course, entire sweeps of modern and contemporary architecture have been directly inspired by the machine aesthetic, such as the Centre Georges Pompidou by Renzo Piano and Richard Rogers (Paris) and the headquarters of the HSBC by Norman Foster (Hong Kong). Jean Nouvel goes much further with the Fondation Cartier building, having created a gigantic piece of working décor, a 21st-century *théâtre à machines* that redefines the concept of the exhibition space.

Certain renunciations allow contrasts to be reversed. While maintaining a distance from the conventional understanding of architecture, the Fondation Cartier's new space is an architectural achievement that outshines many monuments. It acts by immersing visitors in a unique atmosphere and offering them a different relationship to the objects on display and the exhibitions it hosts. Returning one last time to the metaphor of the theater, this architectural feat may be compared to a stage designed to receive actors of all kinds. Its role is to suggest that the scenarios that play out there have meaning and are rich in consequences.[16] Jean Nouvel's project adopts this strategy. It is not monumental in the traditional sense. It does not fetishize technology, but employs it to serve an original and poetic vision. It offers an experience that enriches the visitor, and in so doing pertains to that endurance that alone allows the human world to exist.

14 — Hannah Arendt, *The Human Condition* (Chicago: University of Chicago Press, 1958).

15 — Quoted by Roberto Gargiani in *Auguste Perret. Teorie e opere* (Milan: Electa, 1993).

16 — This theme has been developed further in Antoine Picon, *The Materiality of Architecture* (Minneapolis: The University of Minnesota Press, 2020).

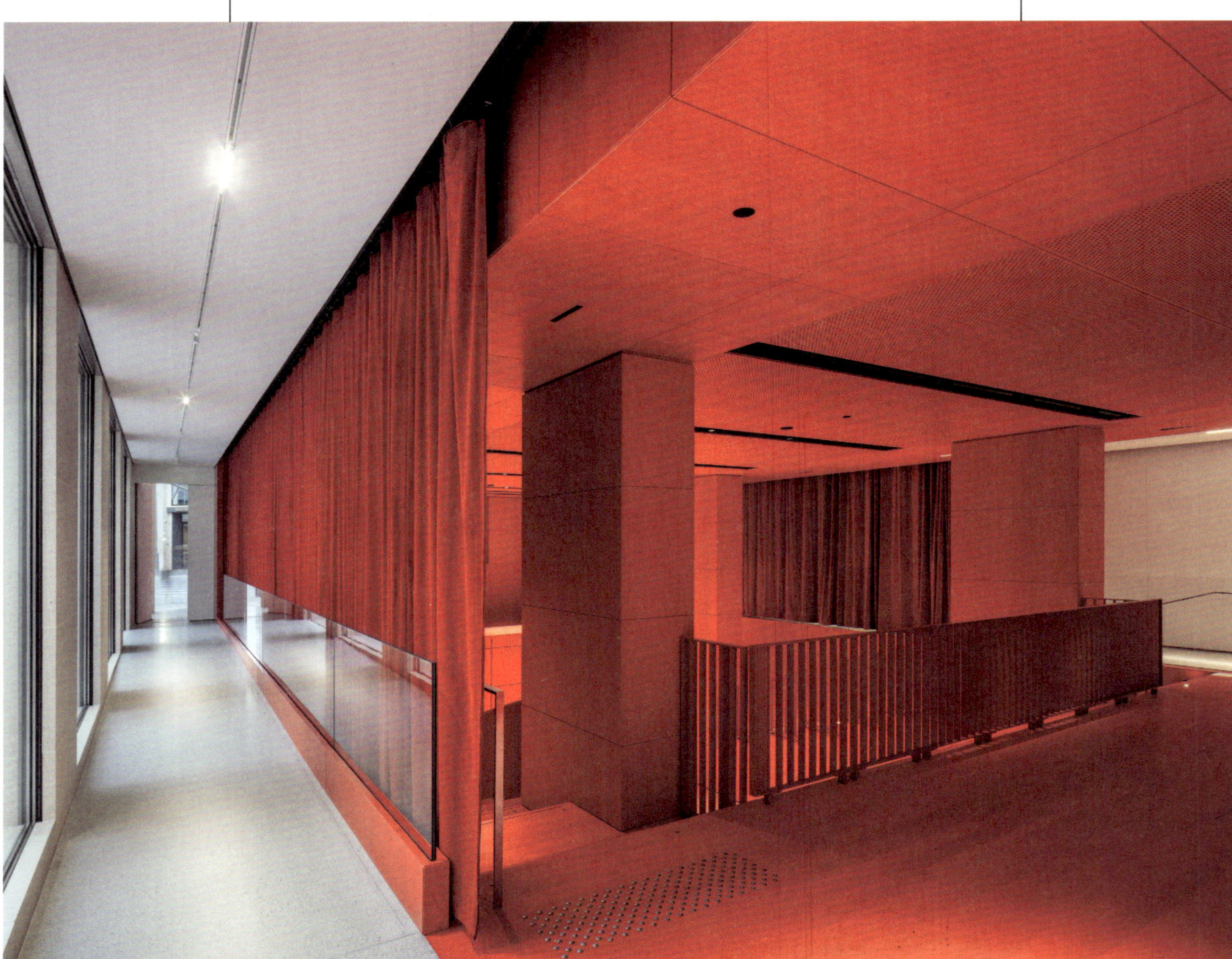

Auditorium of the Fondation Cartier (studio Marie-Claude Beaud)

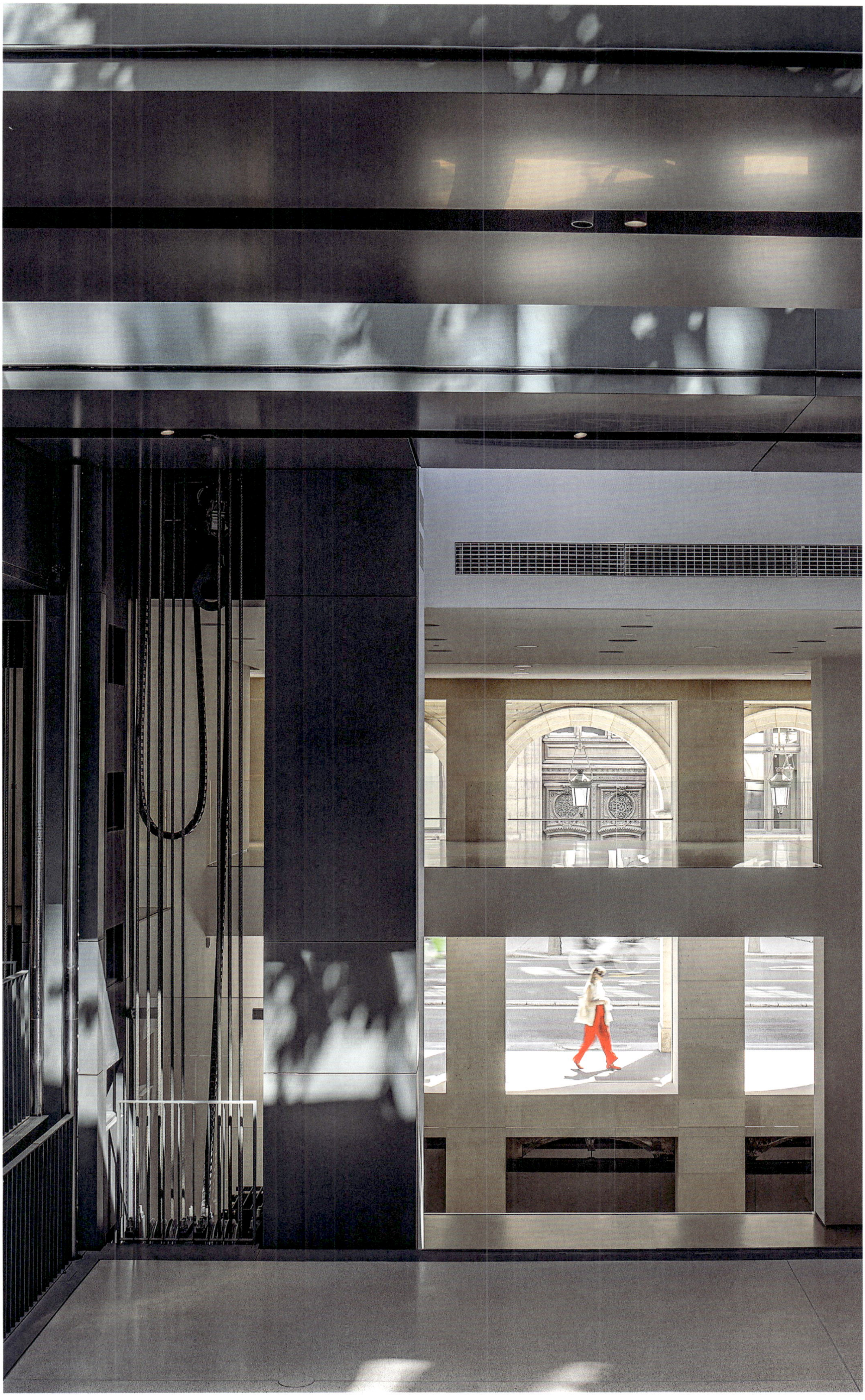

Interior spaces of the Fondation Cartier building

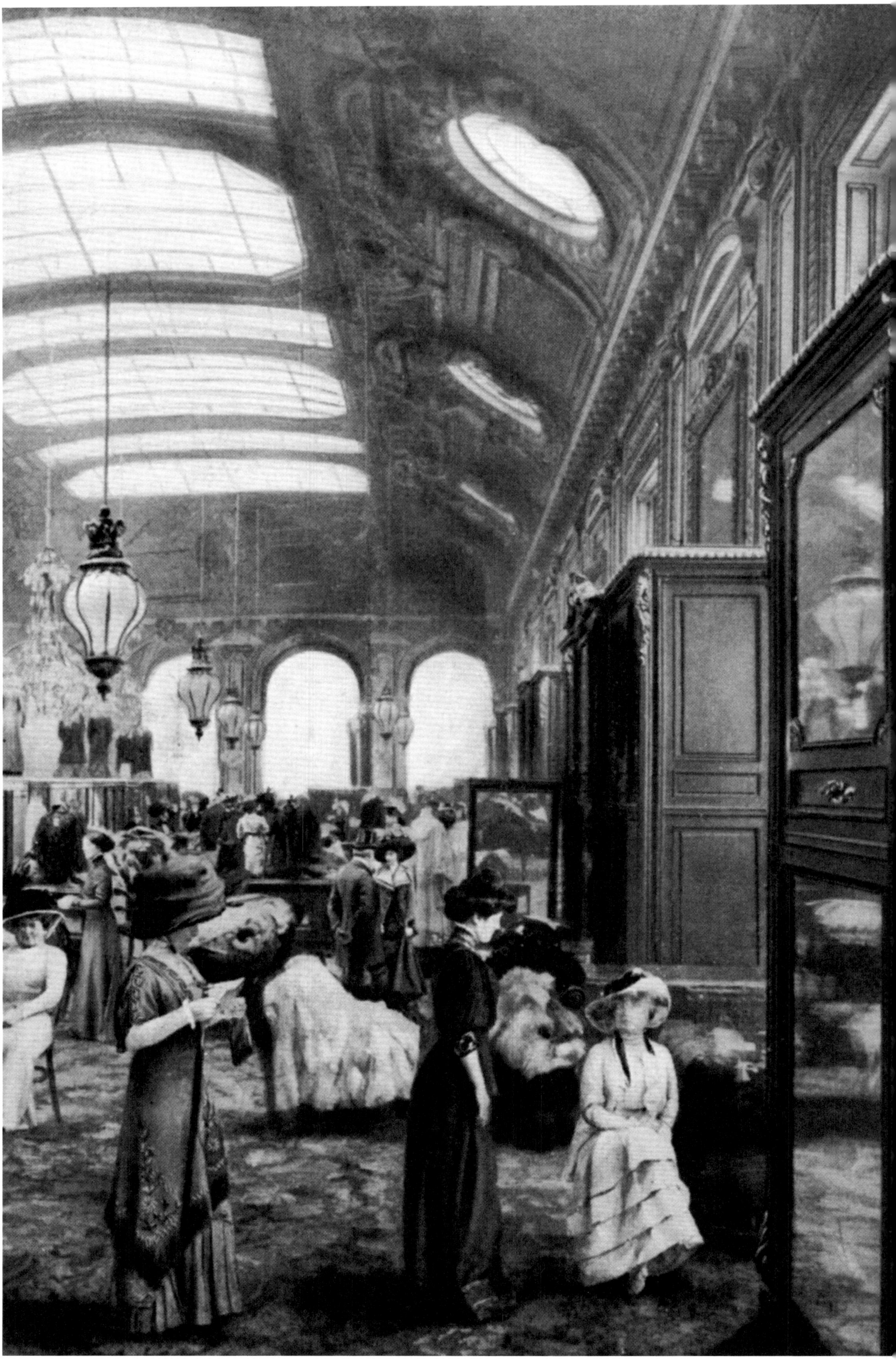

Galerie des manteaux (coat department) of the Grands Magasins du Louvre, c. 1910 (photograph by A. Ehrmann)

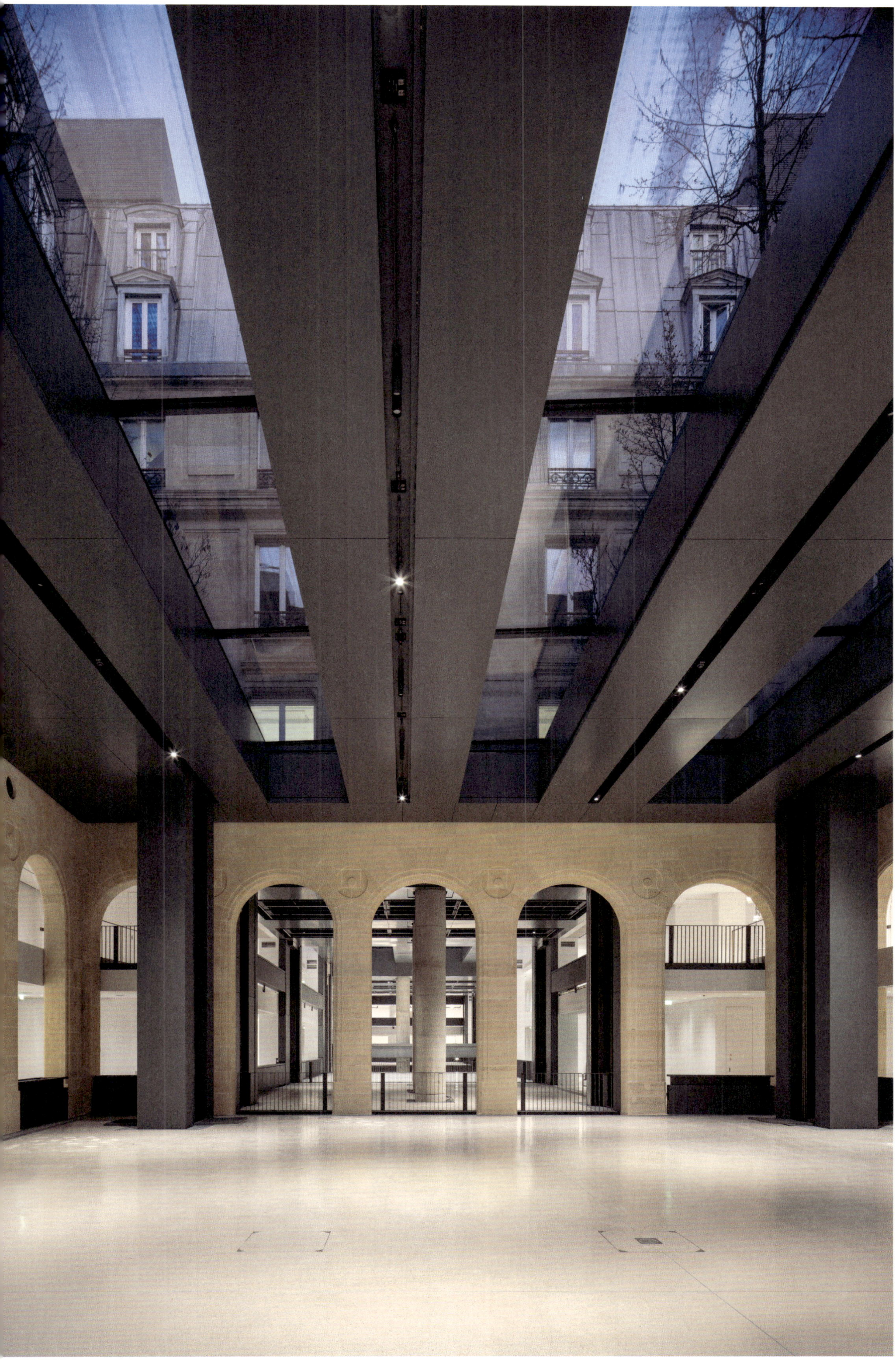

One of the skylights of the Fondation Cartier building
seen from the first platform

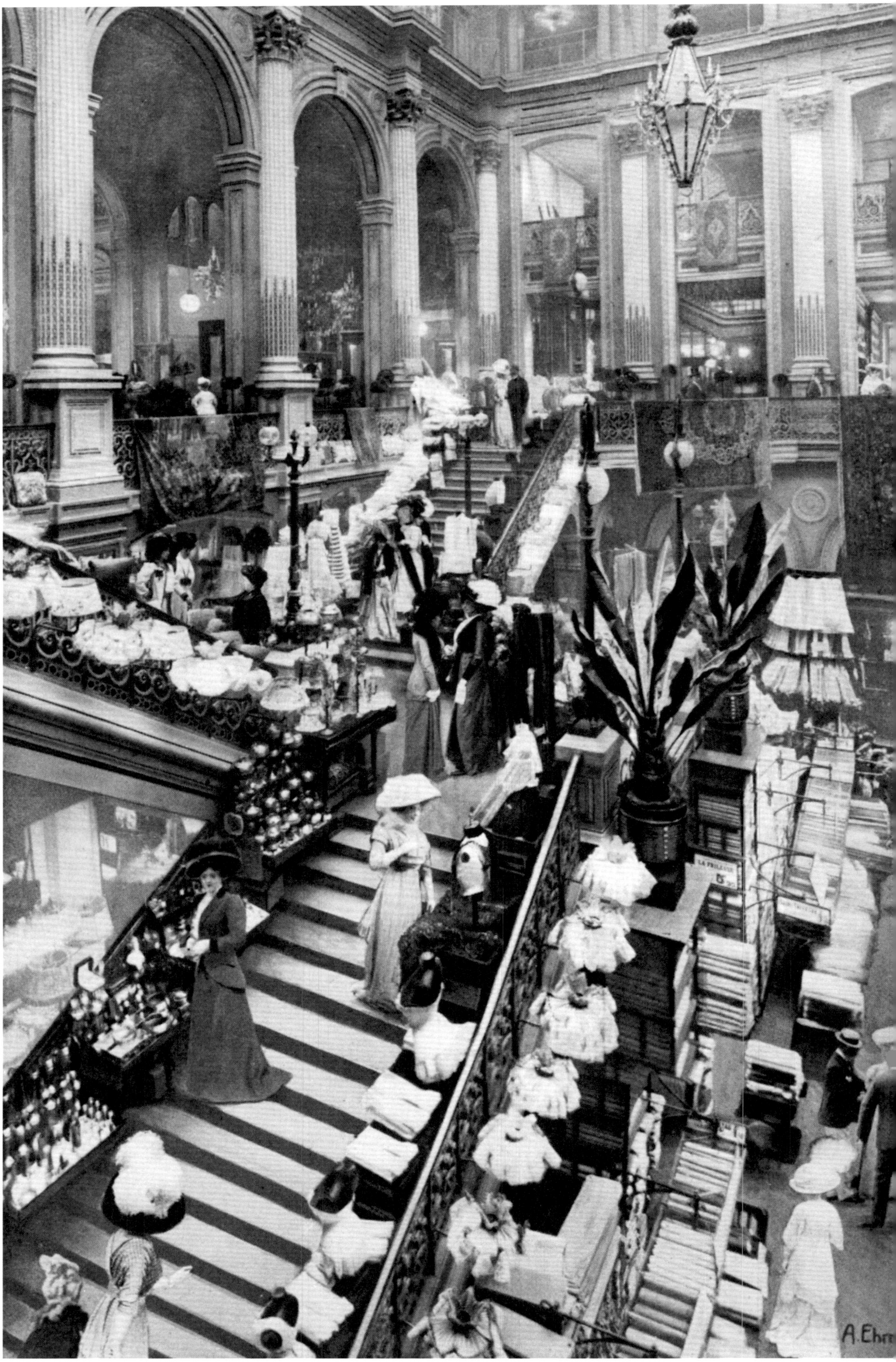

Main staircase of the Grands Magasins du Louvre, c. 1910
(photograph by A. Ehrmann)

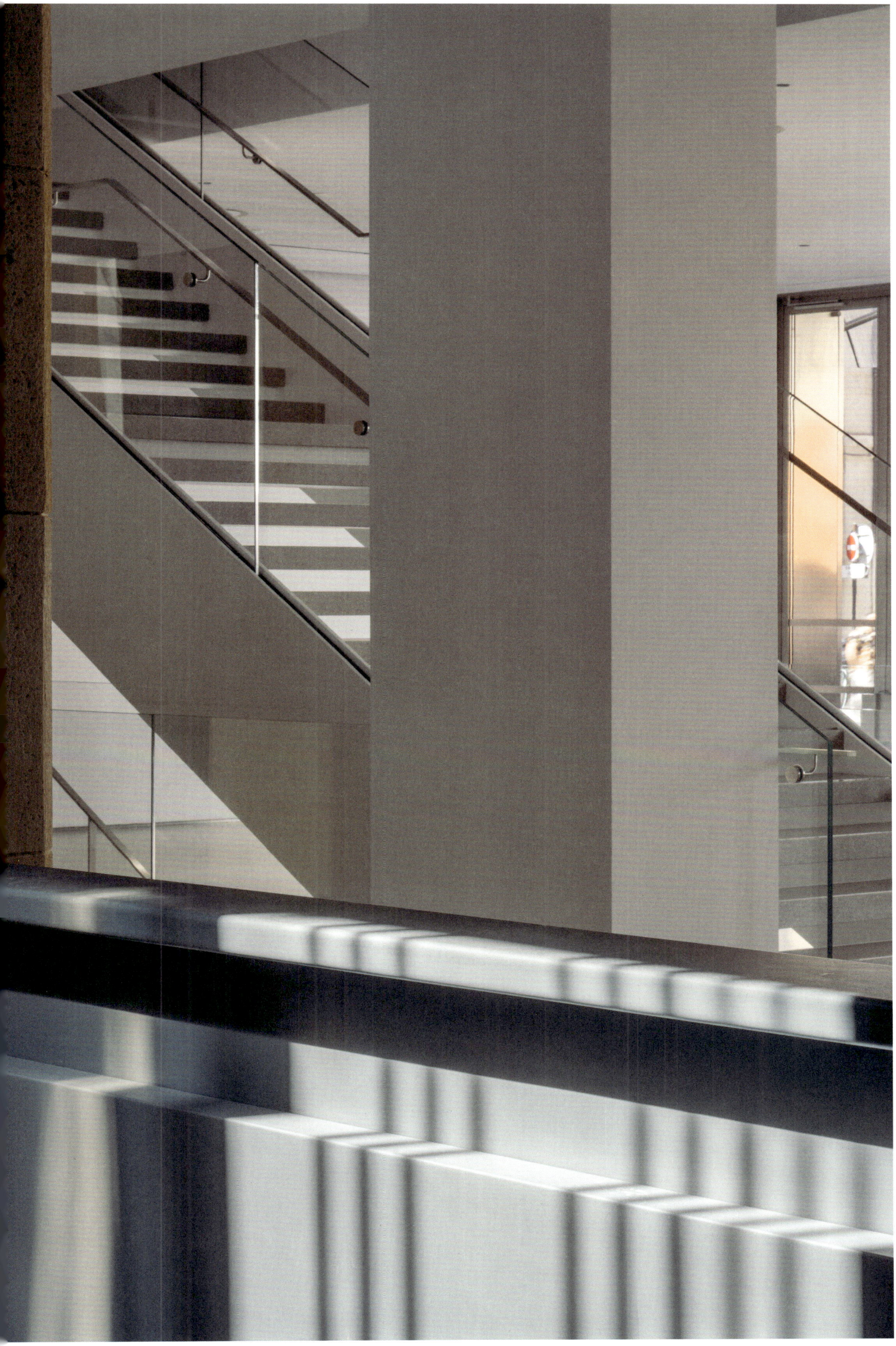

Interior spaces of the Fondation Cartier building

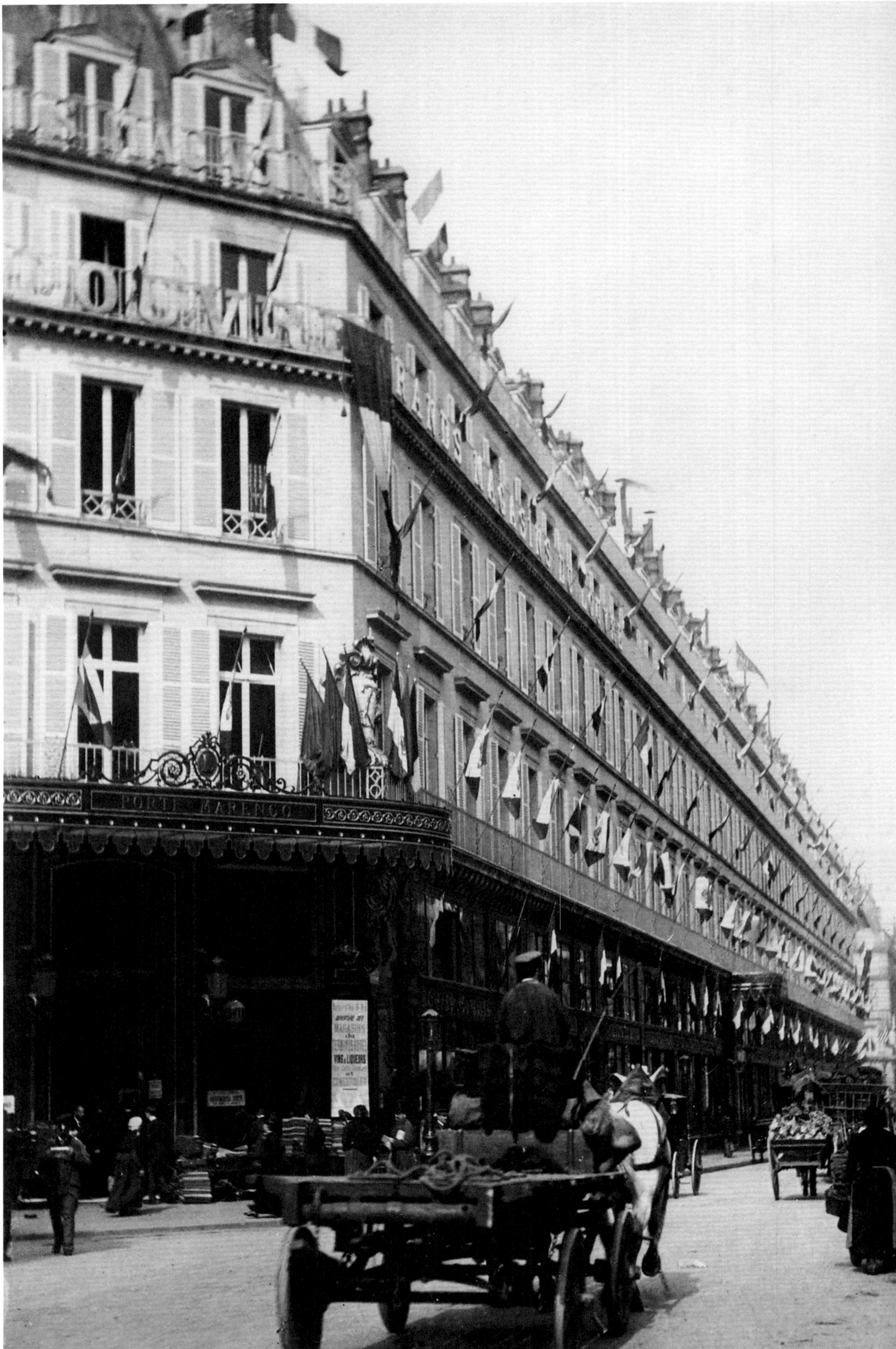

Canopy of the building in 1888 and in 2025

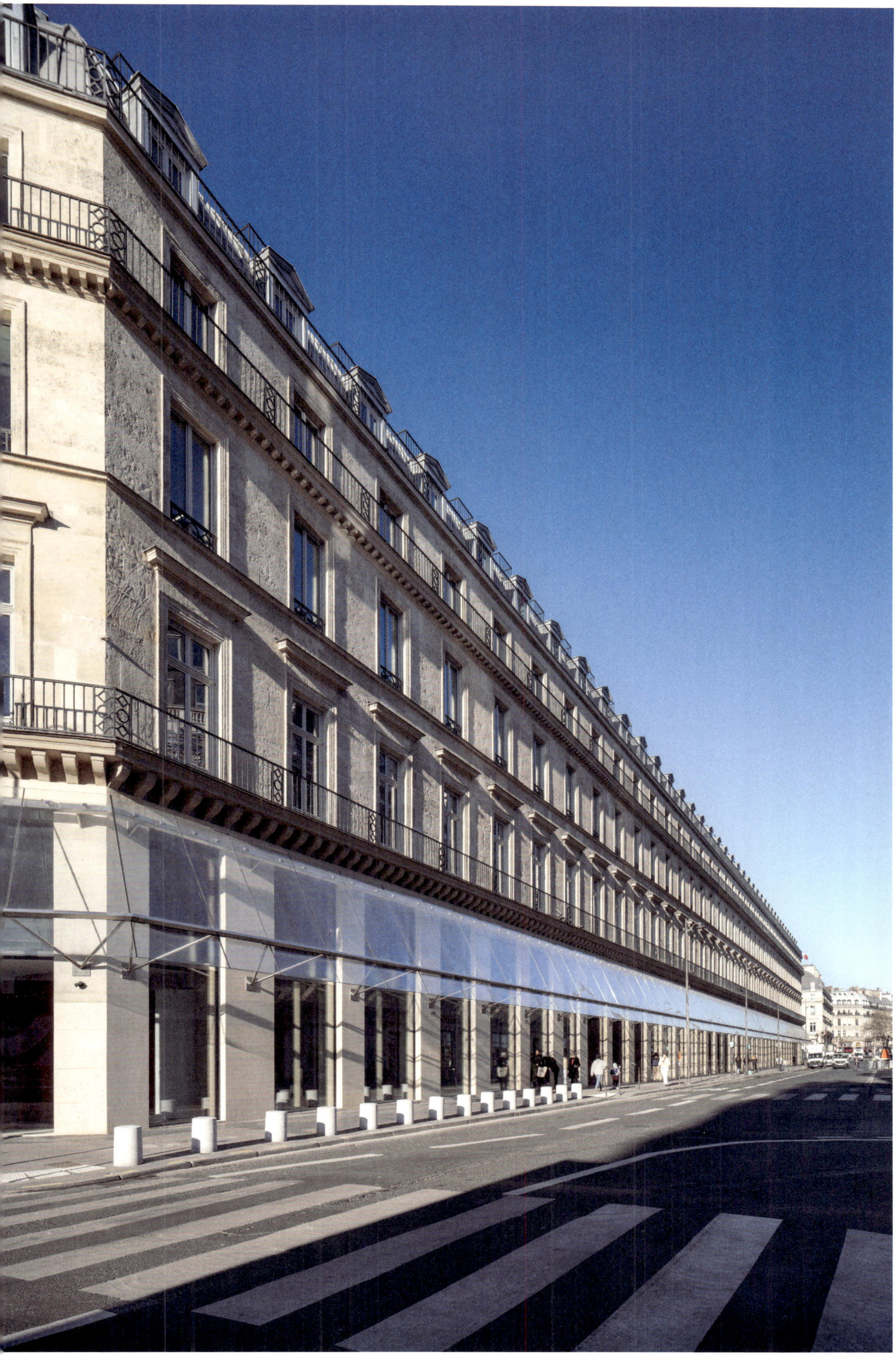

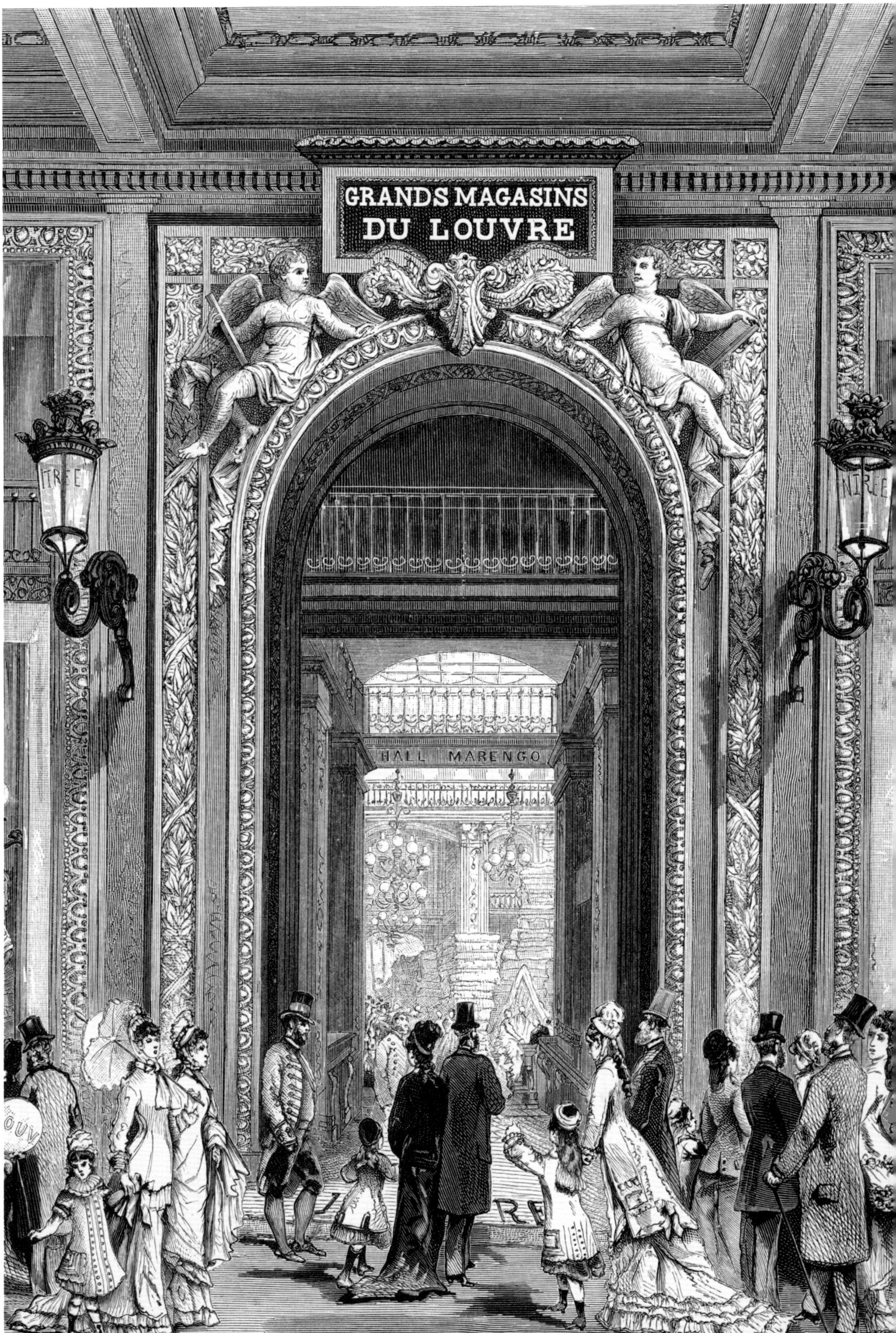

Entrance of the Grands Magasins du Louvre from Rue de Rivoli, under the arcades, 1880 (engraving by Daubron)

JEAN NOUVEL'S ARCHITECTURAL PROJECT

Mathieu Forest

Studio Director

Cyril Desroche

Project Director

Ateliers Jean Nouvel

Located on the Place du Palais-Royal in Paris, the new spaces of the Fondation Cartier pour l'art contemporain form part of the largest urban block on Rue de Rivoli. Built in 1854–1855, at the time when the street was being extended, the building is 58 meters wide and 153 meters long, following the plans specified by architects Charles Percier and Pierre Fontaine. The uniform stone facade rests on a series of arcades along the length of its Rue de Rivoli flank and continues onto the Place du Palais-Royal. Five stories high, the building housed the Grand Hôtel du Louvre for some thirty years before relinquishing its place to the Grands Magasins du Louvre, which occupied the entire building for nearly a century.

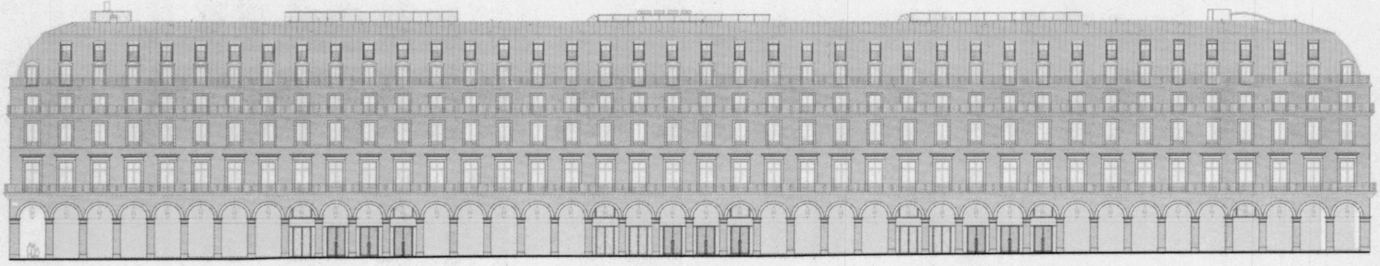

The prescribed facade of the building constructed in 1854–1855, within which Jean Nouvel designed his architectural project for the Fondation Cartier (view of Rue de Rivoli side).

In 1975, after the Grands Magasins closed, a major restructuring of the building began. The interior was almost entirely demolished. Only the exterior facades and those of the inner courtyard on the Place du Palais-Royal side remained. Basements, including a parking garage, were created, and the three other courtyards were reconstructed in concrete, their upper levels clad with mirrored curtain walls as was typical in the 1970s. The renovation was almost invisible from the outside, even though the building had become more massive: the shutters that adorned hundreds of windows were removed and the wooden facades on the ground floor were replaced by the building's new structural framework, consisting of stone-clad columns spaced every 4 meters. Inside, the building was divided into two units that functioned completely independently. The base housed the Louvre des Antiquaires, a shopping center with more than 240 antique shops on three levels—ground floor, arcade-level mezzanine, and first basement; four skylights above the four courtyards provided natural light. Office space occupied the upper floors of the building, from the second floor to the vaulted attic space under the roof. Six vertical circulation cores provided access from the ground floor, bypassing the shopping center.

In December 2013, Richard Lepeu, then CEO of the Richemont Group, asked Yvan Ansermoz, Director of Cartier Architecture and Construction, to show Jean Nouvel around the Louvre des Antiquaires so that he could envisage a project to create new exhibition spaces for the Fondation Cartier. The architect had a clear idea of what he wanted to achieve: "Everything must be removed, all that we can, except for the essential load bearers. It must be possible for the gaze to pass through an unobstructed space." He emphasized the emptiness of the site: "We need to be able to read the street across the way. Large apertures must be cut above the courtyards to maintain the view from below towards the sky. We need to gain a sense of space from above, from below, and through the transversality in the building; in short, we must expand the space." Right away, the idea of a big internal machine was asserted, large plates that could be raised and lowered under the skylights, "a kind of mechanical thing, purely mechanical."

Jean Nouvel envisioned this "machine" as five steel platforms, like mobile stages that could be used to create variable heights

DIMENSIONS OF THE BUILDING

153 M
LENGTH

58 M
WIDTH

11 M
MAXIMUM HEIGHT (ALL PLATFORMS AT BASEMENT OR CEILING)

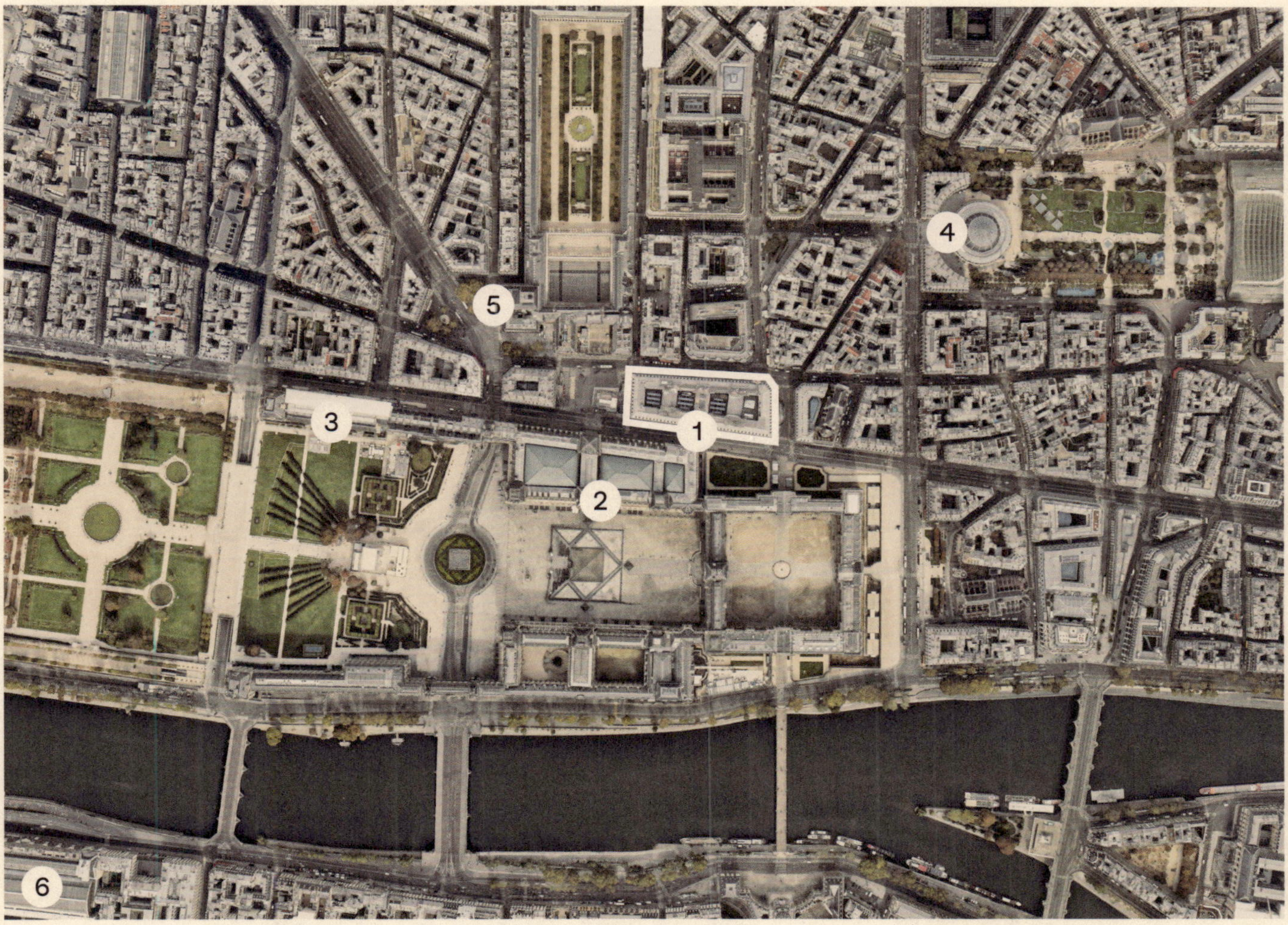

Located at 2 Place du Palais-Royal, in the 1st arrondissement of Paris, the Fondation Cartier building (1) is located in the heart of a neighborhood that brings together the most prestigious cultural institutions: Louvre (2), Musée des Arts Décoratifs (3), Bourse de Commerce – Pinault Collection (4), Comédie-Française (5) and Musée d'Orsay (6).

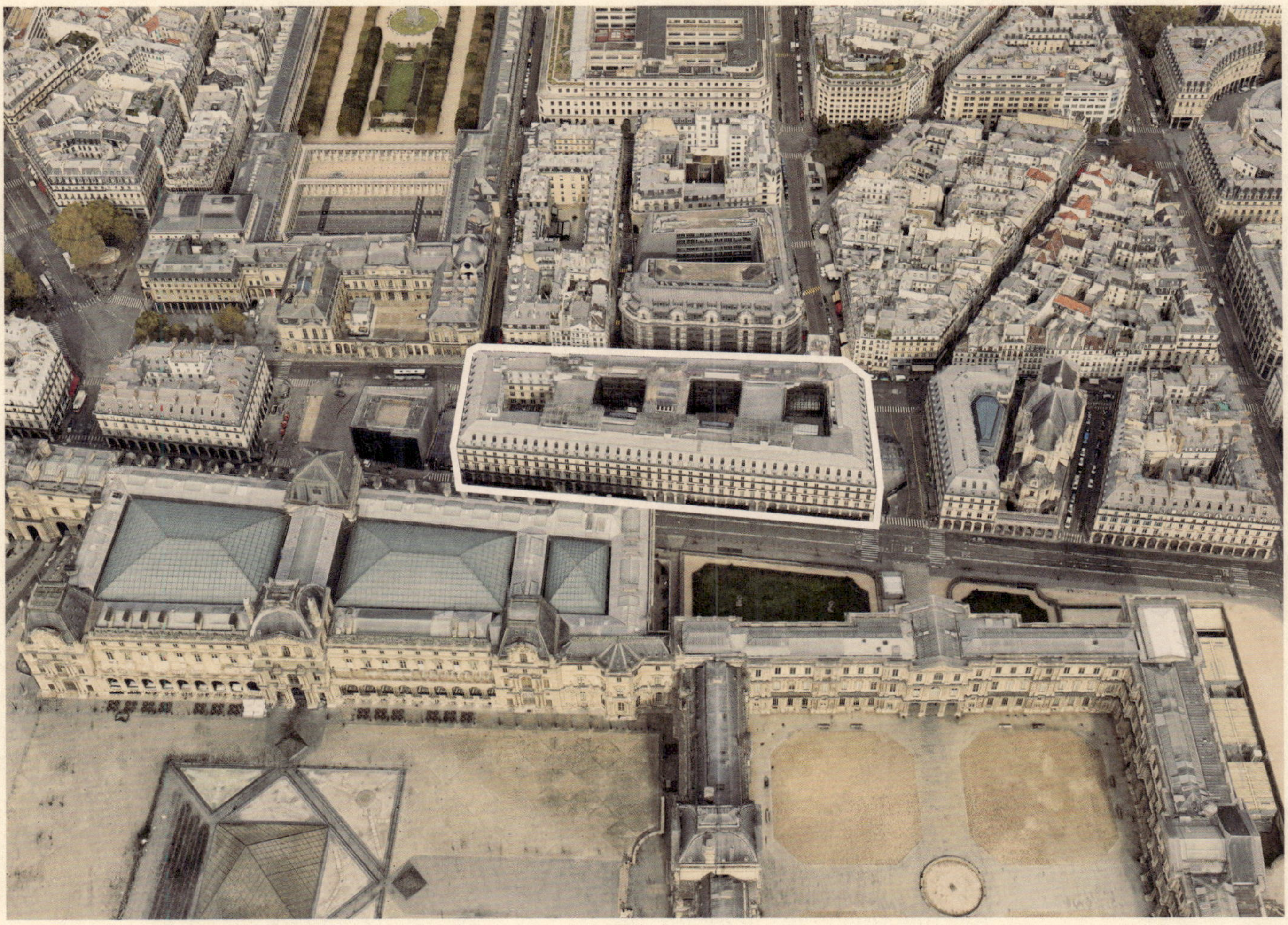

Opposite the Louvre, the Fondation Cartier building is the largest block on the Rue de Rivoli: 153 meters long and 58 meters wide.

in an infinite number of configurations, and a large continuous void. The skylights would be floors made of glass with long mobile shutters running underneath like "mechanical curtains" to selectively filter or even block out natural light. Above, hanging gardens with trees would be reminiscent of the nearby Palais-Royal gardens and the changing seasons.

SURFACE AREA OF SPACES

ENTRANCE HALL
634 M²

PETIT CAFÉ
64 M²

BOOKSTORE
132 M²

LEARNING AREA
323 M², TWO ACTIVITY ROOMS, CAPACITY: 35 PEOPLE EACH

AUDITORIUM
422 M², CAPACITY: 120 PEOPLE

RESTAURANT
295 M²

12 980 M²
TOTAL SURFACE AREA

8 500 M²
ACCESSIBLE TO THE PUBLIC

6 443 M²
OF EXHIBITION SPACE (AND A VOLUME OF 26 600 M3)

1200 M²
OF WALKWAYS

1156 M²
ON THE FIVE PLATFORMS

Installing this "machine" in this location was a huge, unprecedented challenge. Because we were not starting from scratch but faced with a heritage building that had already been renovated several times. The spaces were packed with structures, partitions, and ducts. Everything had to be opened, emptied, stripped out. Added to that, the building also housed five floors of offices, above the spaces intended for the Fondation Cartier, with six separate entrances from the street, and technical facilities, as well as underground parking. One of the first challenges was to maintain the regular operations of these offices, as relocating them was out of the question, while carrying out the work, mainly at night. From 2020 onwards, and for more than three years, 30,000 square meters of office space remained occupied, while below, nearly 10,000 square meters of flooring were being destroyed, around 100 new foundation piles installed, 11-meter-high concrete columns and walls removed or modified, and 1,000 square meters of skylights replaced. The building was gutted and transformed from the inside, stealthily, keeping it a surprise, even for those who worked there every day.

In the center of the building, a long nave measuring 85 meters long and 12.5 meters wide is open to a height of 11 meters to accommodate the "machine." Parallel to Rue de Rivoli, it passes under three of the building's four courtyards. It spans the three levels of the base and extends upward toward the sky.

Jean Nouvel and the teams at Cartier Architecture and Construction, partnered with the best engineering firms to meet this challenge and create a fully transformable architectural design, as building codes, fire safety regulations, engineering constraints, and Eurocodes do not provide for platforms of this size to be movable within a building. The right technology had to be chosen to lift floors measuring an average of 250 square meters and weighing 250 tons each in an existing, constrained space subject to regulations for buildings open to the public. The increasingly regulated construction industry prefers to stay within established boundaries, but Jean Nouvel wants to build the unprecedented. Conventions had to be circumvented and each member of the project team—technicians, engineers, architects, contractors—convincingly persuaded of the feasibility of what initially would seem impossible.

All options were examined: from racks (too large) to pistons (containing too much flammable oil), along with cables and electric motors. The expertise of gondola lift designers and engineers specializing in theater machinery was solicited. It absolutely had to work. But introducing an "aircraft carrier" into an existing building with millimeter tolerances is a real conundrum. To meet unprecedented moving load challenges, complementary engineering disciplines were brought together and coordinated: building engineering, mobile bridge engineering, and theater rigging.

The functional needs of the future Fondation Cartier determined the size of the platforms and their support structures. After extensive research and comparison studies, a cable and

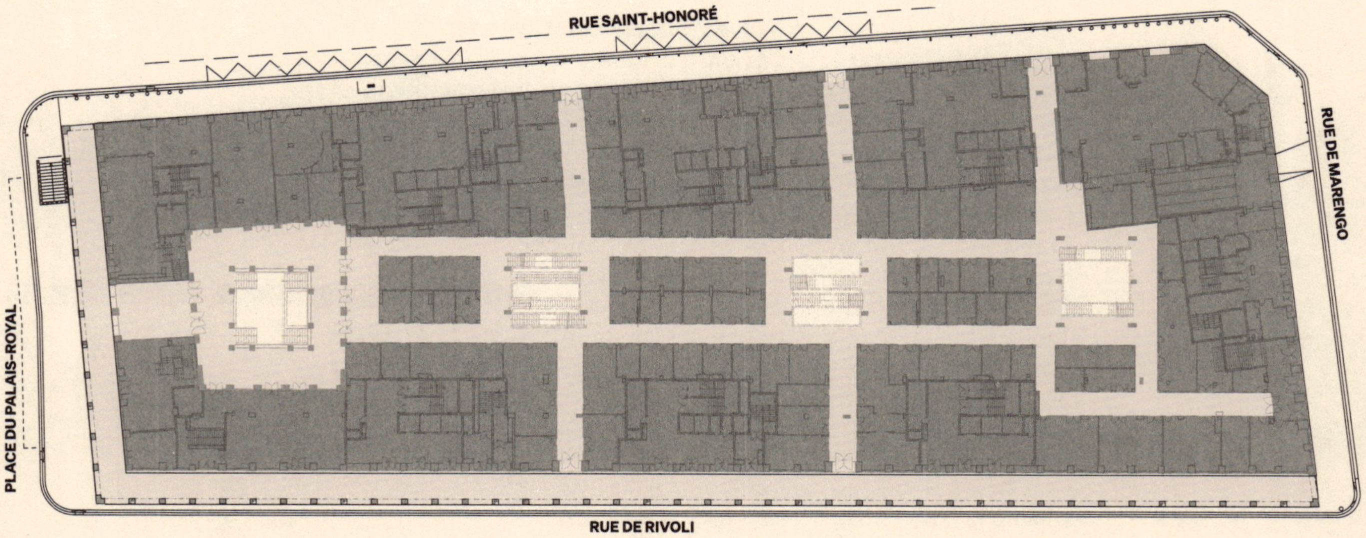

Floor plan of the ground floor of the Louvre des Antiquaires, 2014
The Louvre des Antiquaires was encumbered with walls, floors, partitions, and ducts, leaving no space suitable for an exhibition area. The facades were completely choked. Jean Nouvel's primary intention was to create as much empty space as possible by radically altering the original structure.

0 5 10 m N

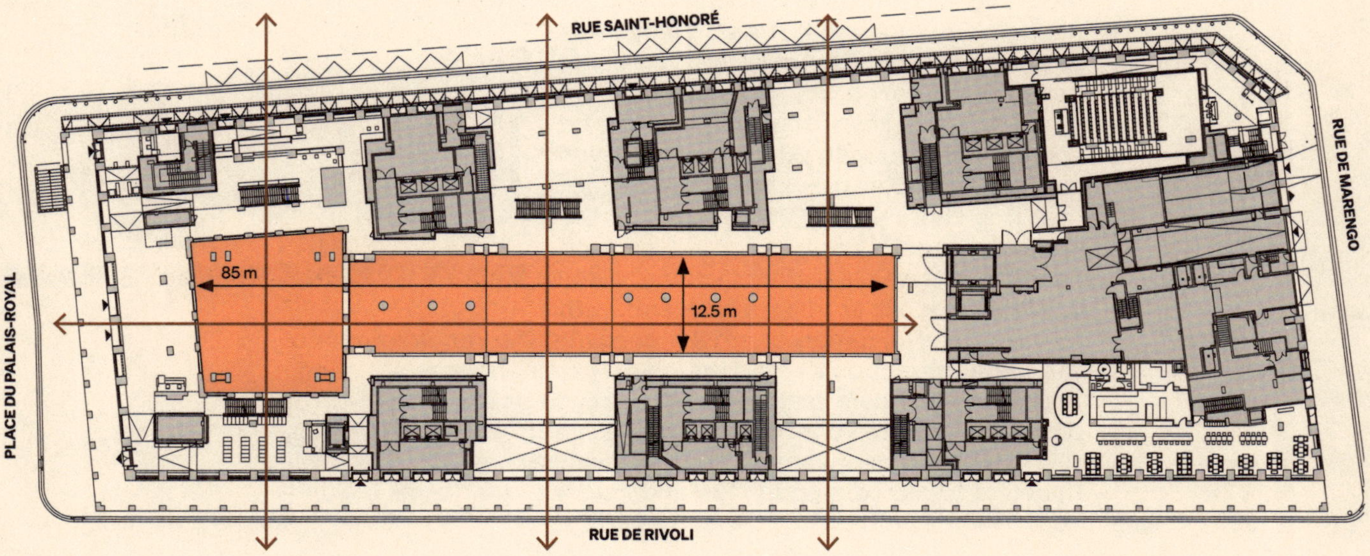

Floor plan of the ground floor of the Fondation Cartier, 2025
A central atrium measuring 85 meters long, 12.5 meters wide and 11 meters high has been created to accommodate mobile platforms. All partitions and non-essential structures have been removed. The facades have been entirely glazed, with no visible joinery, on three sides of the building. This transformation creates a set of sight lines from the Rue de Rivoli to the Rue Saint-Honoré, but also from the Place du Palais-Royal through the interior spaces of the Fondation Cartier. A glass awning has been installed along the entire length of Rue Saint-Honoré, in precisely the same place where one was in the era of the Grands Magasins du Louvre. This new awning reinforces the visual unity of the block.

0 5 10 m N

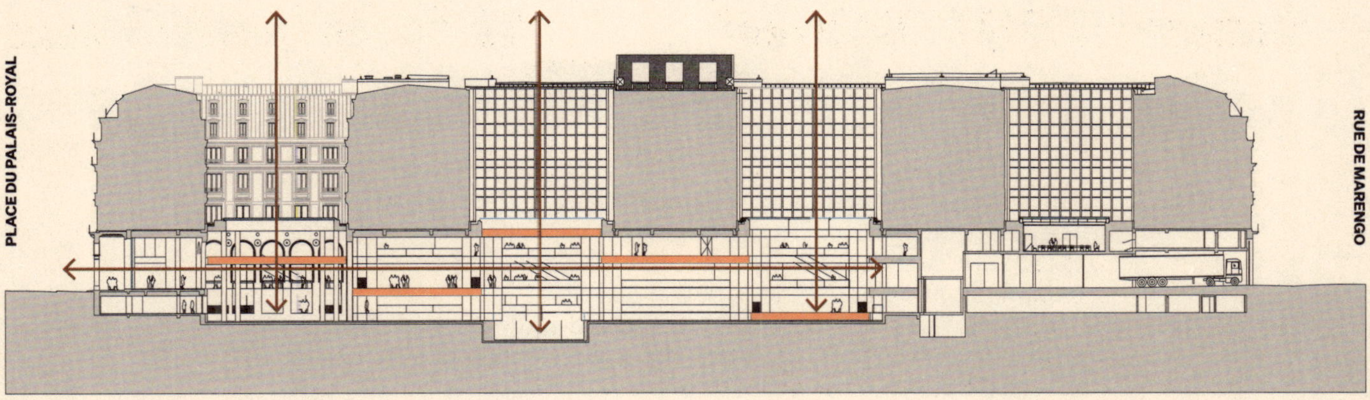

Longitudinal section of the Fondation Cartier building, 2025
10,000 square meters of permanent flooring in the center of the building have been removed, creating a central nave open to the sky through three huge skylights. The basement has been completely excavated to reveal the stone foundations and Parisian archaeology beneath. In the space created, a huge machine made up of five mobile platforms can transform the space into 117,854 different configurations.

0 5 10 m

pulley lifting system was the chosen solution. Attached to the structure of each platform on a balancing hoist, a sort of large hydraulic cylinder, eight cables run through the thickness of the platform, climb to the top of the corner uprights, act as a pulley system by making three vertical return trips, and then wind around eight drums driven by synchronized electric motors so that the platform rises perfectly horizontally. Judiciously positioned within the platform structure, all these technical components contribute to the sought-after aesthetics of the machinery. Four locking blocks ensure that a platform remains in place on its vertical structure when its position is set. Each platform can be locked in eleven different positions. Guide arms ensure that it is correctly positioned relative to its neighbor, even in the event of distention. The entire structure is braced against the existing building structure. The new posts supporting the platforms, skylights, and trees pass through the lower levels and rest on new foundations.

Safety is paramount and has been checked at every stage, meaning each mechanism is reinforced and each safety device is double-sized. The strictest safety rules, informed by aviation standards have been applied. As with any building open to the public, the space must be equipped with smoke extractors. However, given its considerable volume and the fact that it is continuously transformable, the standard regulations do not cover such conditions. It was therefore decided to design a smoke extraction system; and, with a computer simulation of smoke behavior, the requirements of the prefecture of police and the fire department were satisfied.

PLATFORMS

5
MOBILE PLATFORMS

3
PLATFORMS UNDER GLASS ROOFS AND HANGING GARDENS

11
DIFFERENT VERTICAL POSITIONS FROM BASEMENT TO CEILING

2
POLE PLATFORMS

117 854
POSSIBLE CONFIGURATIONS

The gap left by a platform that ascends or descends is protected by automatic mobile guardrails, controlled by the safety system. They disappear into the floor when the platform is positioned at the access point. The undersides of platforms become

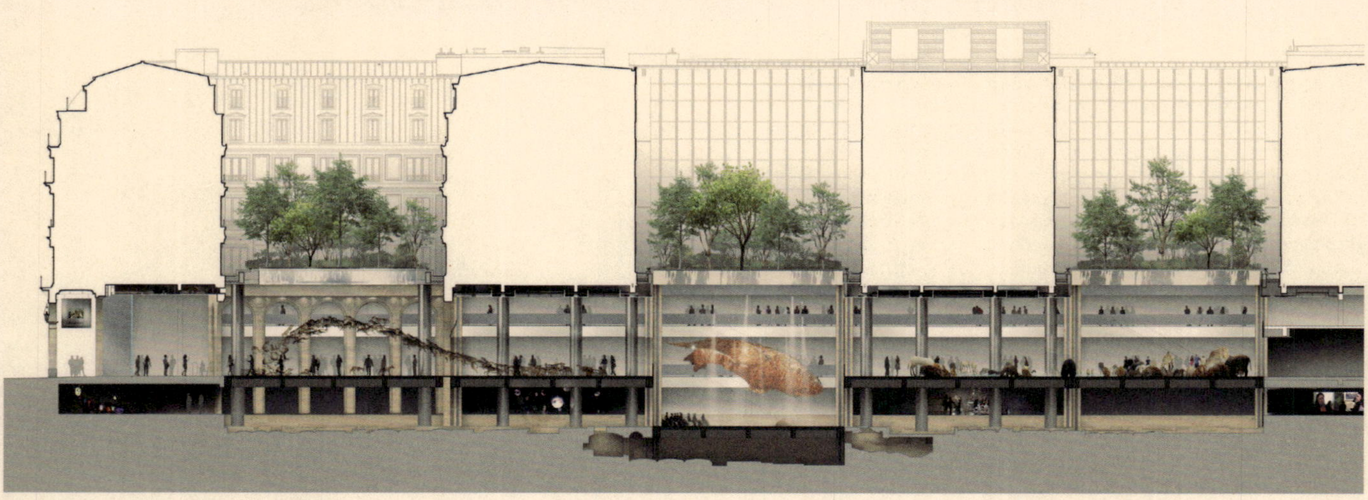

the ceilings of exhibition spaces whenever they are elevated. They are equipped with a scenographic grid allowing them to be fitted with the necessary accessories for displaying artworks and hanging lighting and various power supplies.

Around the platforms, the spaces are more conventional, in stark contrast to the "machine." The building's facades have been stripped back and huge glass panels with no visible frames have been installed between the existing columns, which have been clad in solid Saint-Maximin stone identical to that used to build the block 165 years ago. These 7-meter-high windows open onto the lower levels, upper floors, surrounding streets, glass roofs, and the sky. Along the Saint-Honoré facade, a minimalist glass canopy stretches over 150 meters, connecting the existing arcades on Rue de Rivoli and Place du Palais-Royal, thus providing pedestrians with a sheltered route around almost the entire building.

The 50-meter-wide main facade faces directly onto the Place du Palais-Royal, flanked by the headquarters of the Council of State and the Louvre Museum and facing the Hôtel du Louvre. Two majestic 7-meter-high doors in the center give onto a reception hall that is open on all sides thanks to large picture windows. The distinction between inside and outside is virtually imperceptible. The building's arcades add ambiguity to this boundary as the Place du Palais-Royal and the sidewalks outside seem to be an intrinsic part of the exhibition spaces.

Adjacent to the reception hall and nestled between four 19th-century facades, the first, and largest, platform follows the trapezoidal layout of the building's oldest courtyard. This is where the aesthetic contrast between the 21st-century machine and the historic building, which has been renovated several times, is most striking. In this architecture that brings together different eras, 8,500 square meters accessible to the public, including 6,500 square meters of exhibition space, are now spread across the lower level, ground floor, and first floor of the building.

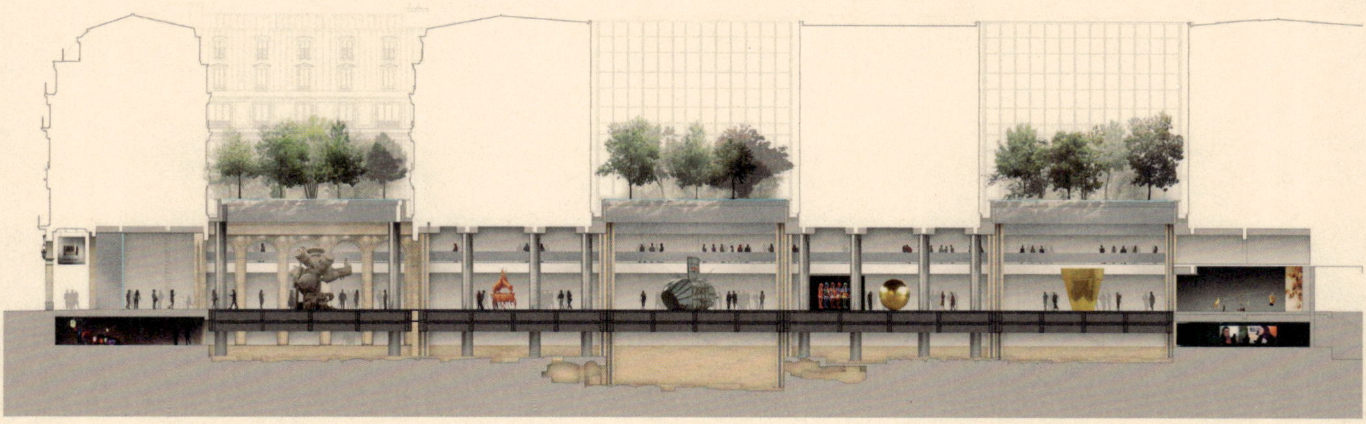

Longitudinal sections of the exhibition spaces at the Fondation Cartier
From the outset of the study, layout scenarios were conceived to convey the diversity of possible spatial configurations.

In 1994, the building designed by Jean Nouvel for the Fondation Cartier on Boulevard Raspail was designed to give the impression of having no walls. The outdoor space flowed into the interior, blurring the boundaries between the two. In 2025, Jean Nouvel took this idea even further for the Fondation Cartier at 2 Place du Palais-Royal: no walls, no floor, no ceiling. All is limitless and transformable. Everything is capable of movement.

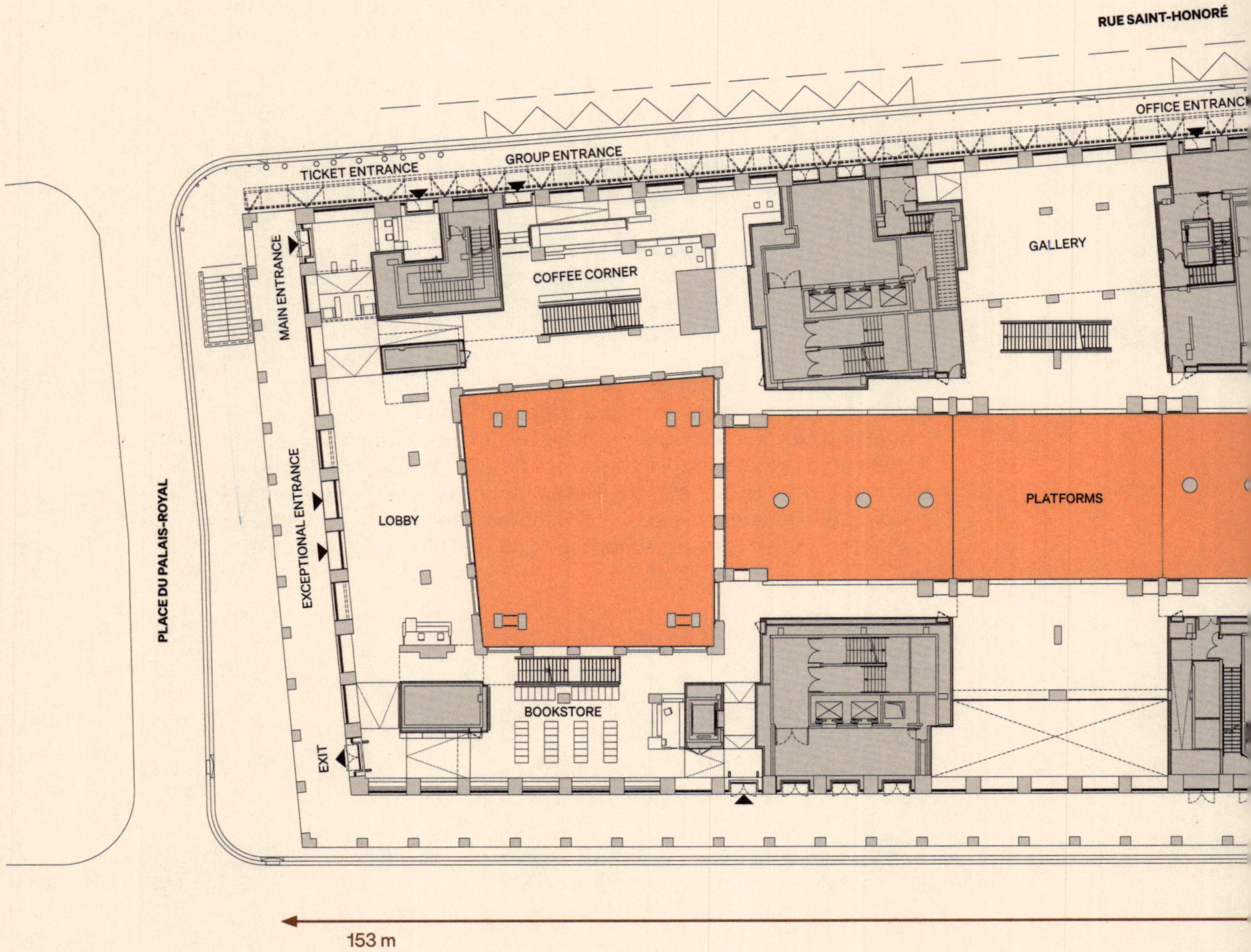

Ground floor plan of the Fondation Cartier building

☐ EXHIBITION AREA / ▩ LOGISTIC AREA

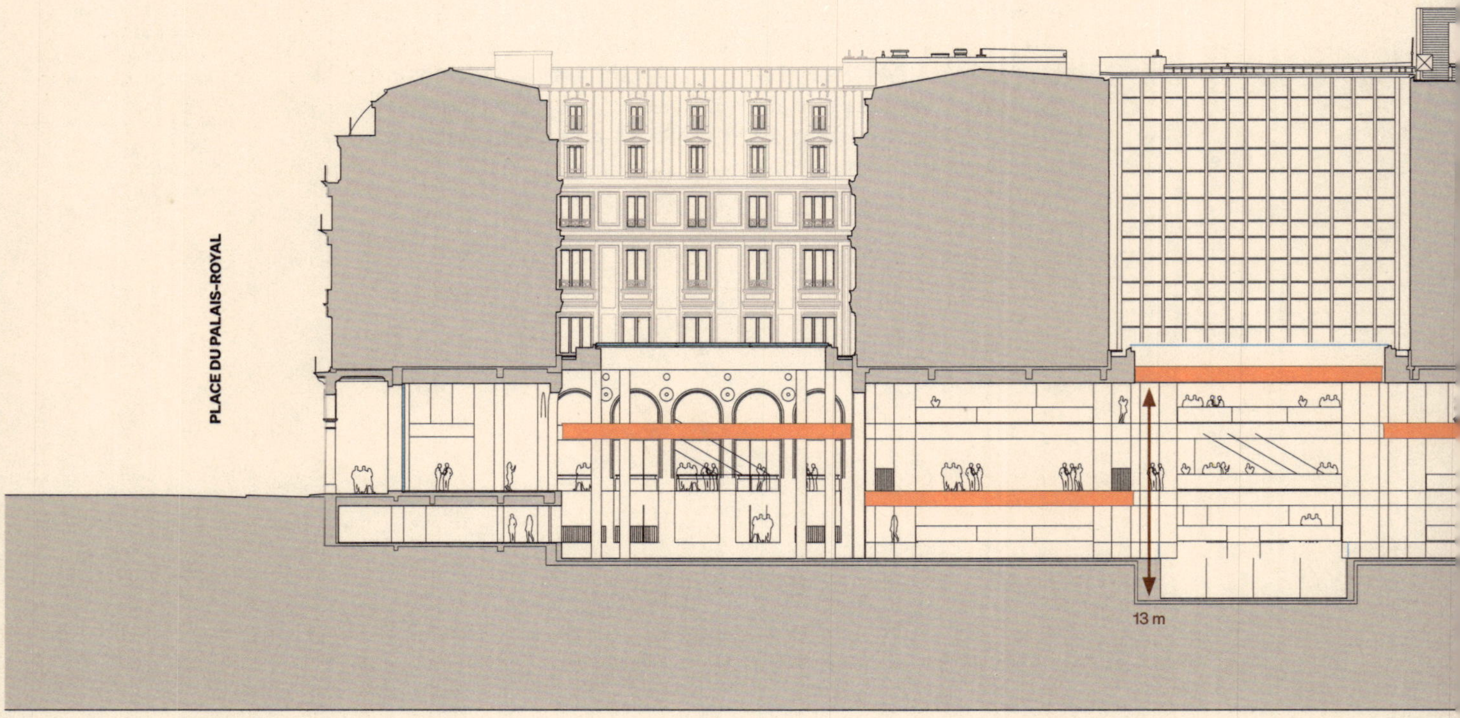

Longitudinal section of the building showing one of the possible platform configurations

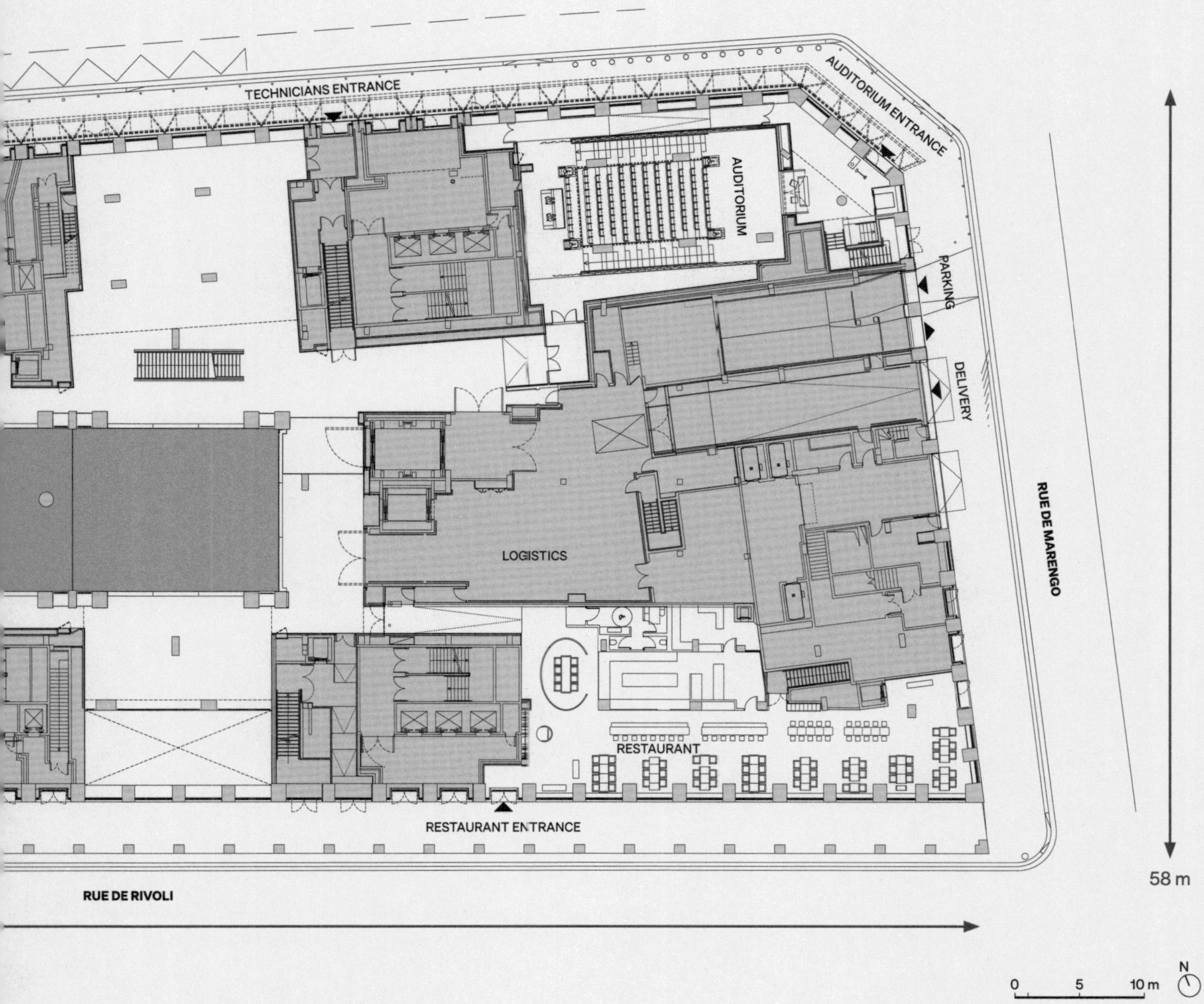
TECHNICIANS ENTRANCE
AUDITORIUM ENTRANCE
AUDITORIUM
PARKING
DELIVERY
RUE DE MARENGO
LOGISTICS
RESTAURANT
RESTAURANT ENTRANCE
RUE DE RIVOLI
58 m
0
5
10 m
N

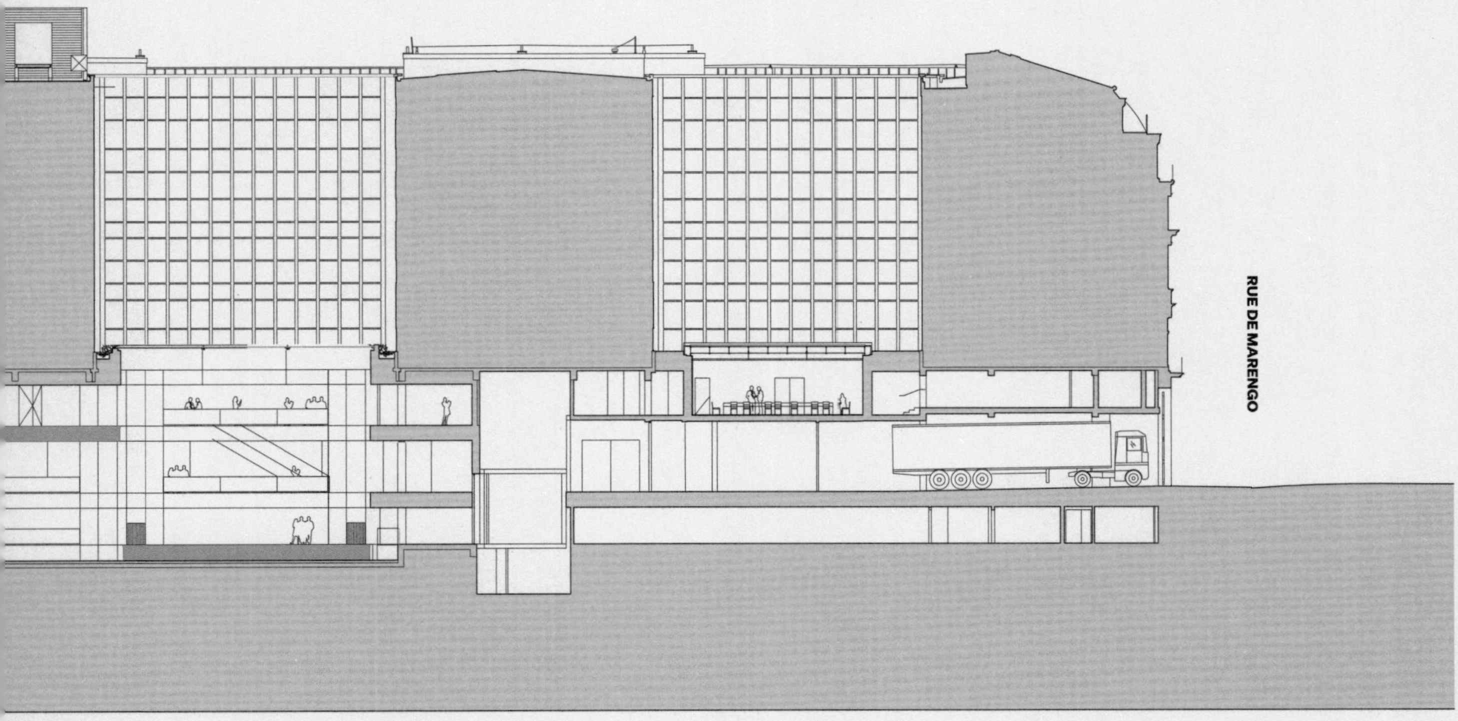
RUE DE MARENGO
0
5
10 m
N

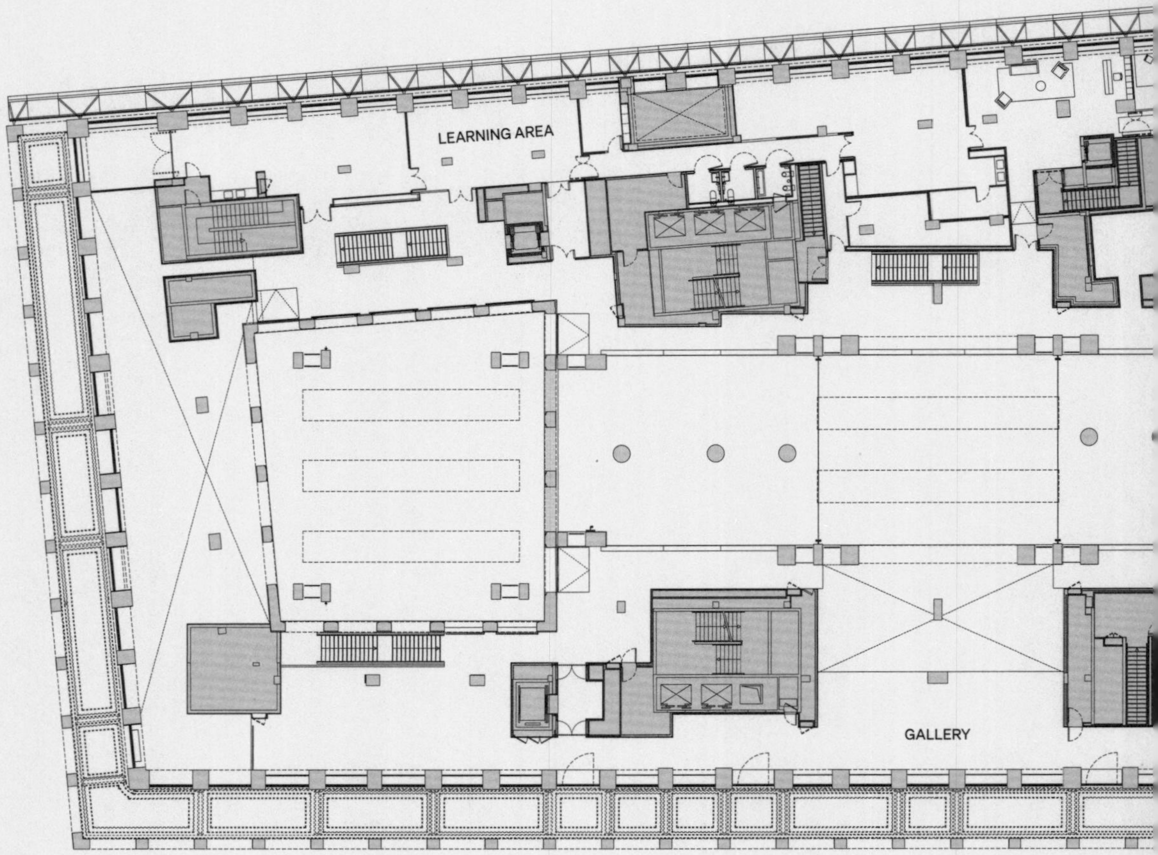

Level 1 floor plan of the Fondation Cartier building

□ EXHIBITION AREA / ■ LOGISTIC AREA

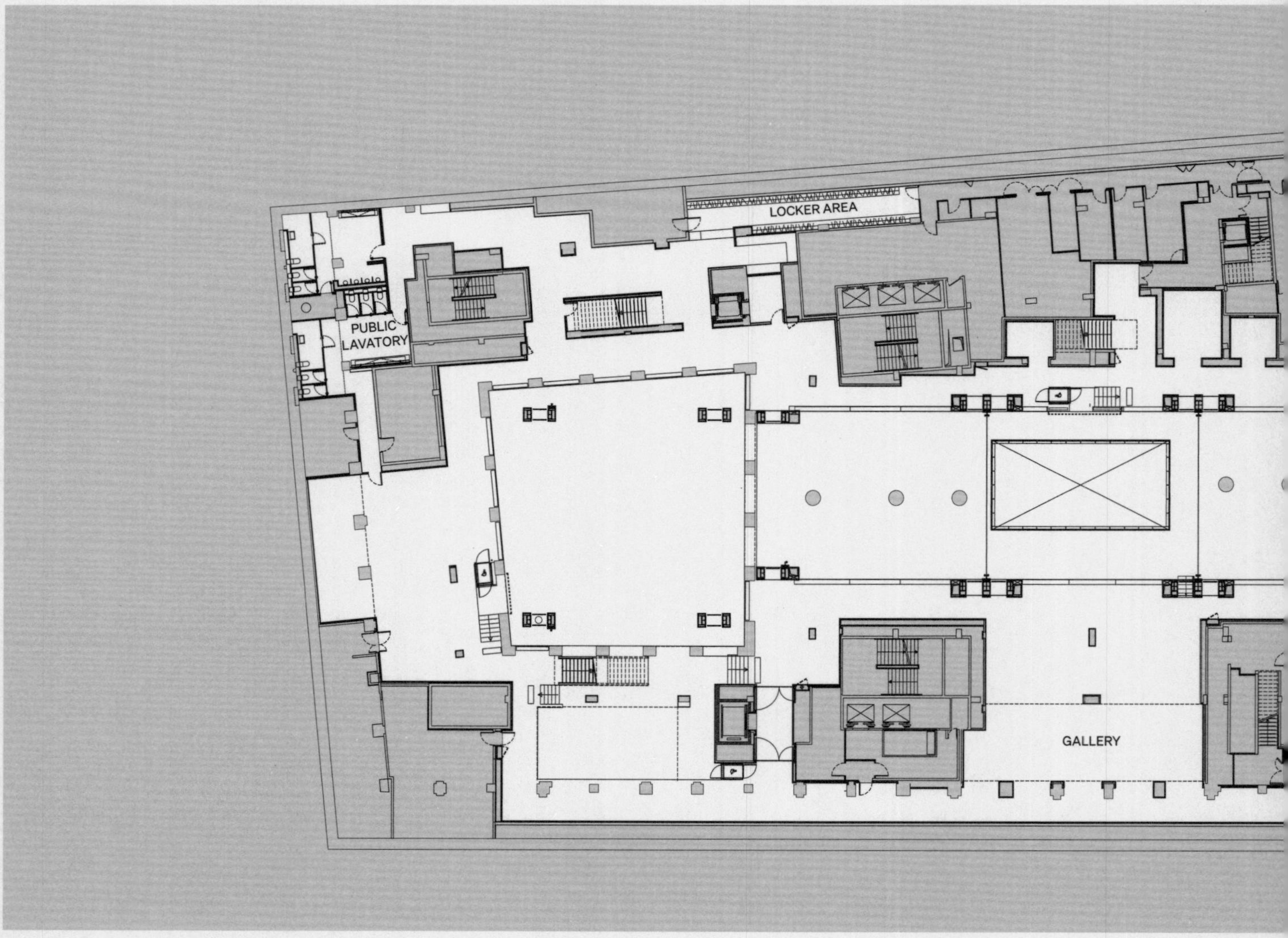

Basement floor plan of the Fondation Cartier building

□ EXHIBITION AREA / ■ LOGISTIC AREA

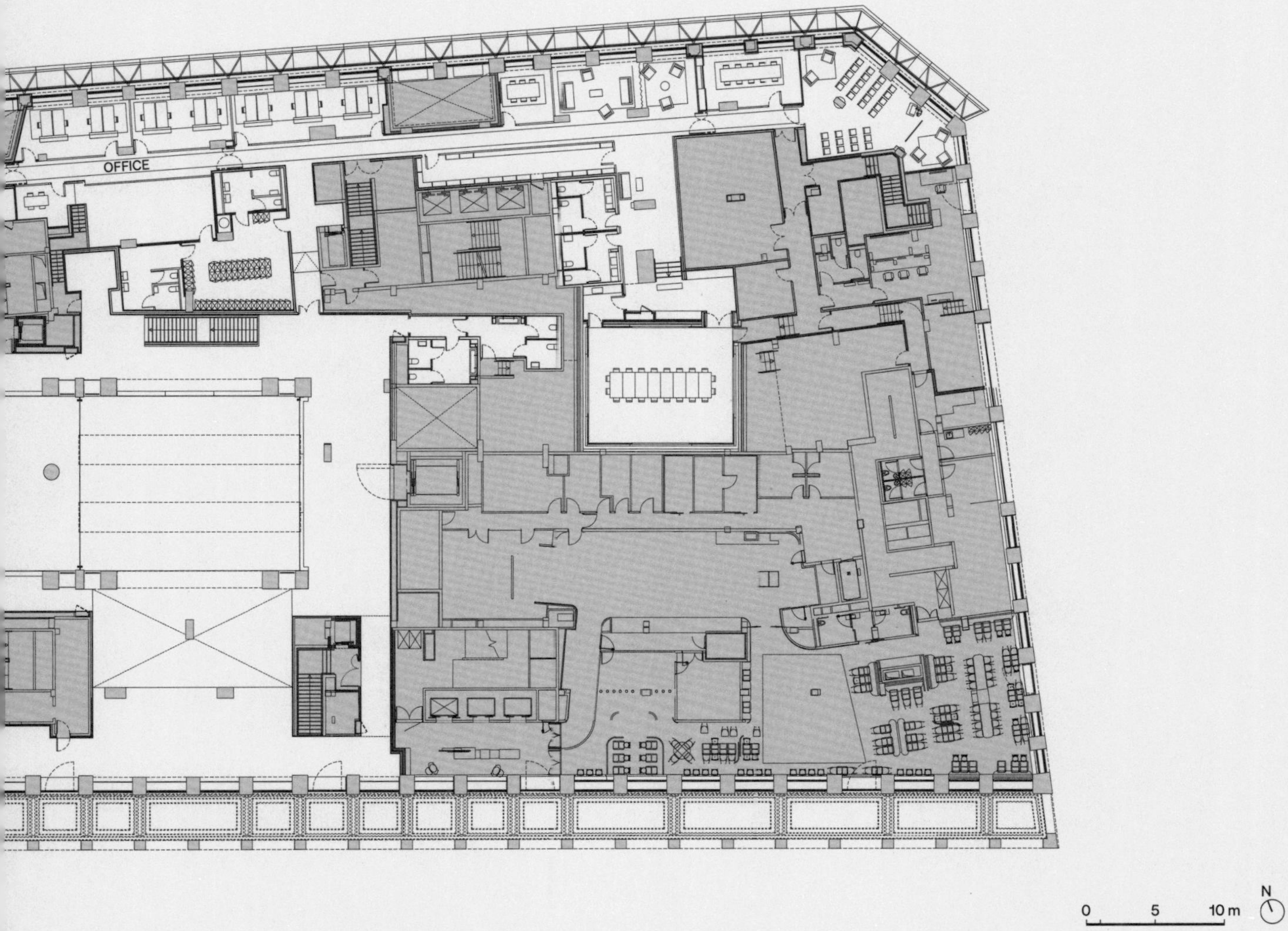
OFFICE
0
5
10 m
N

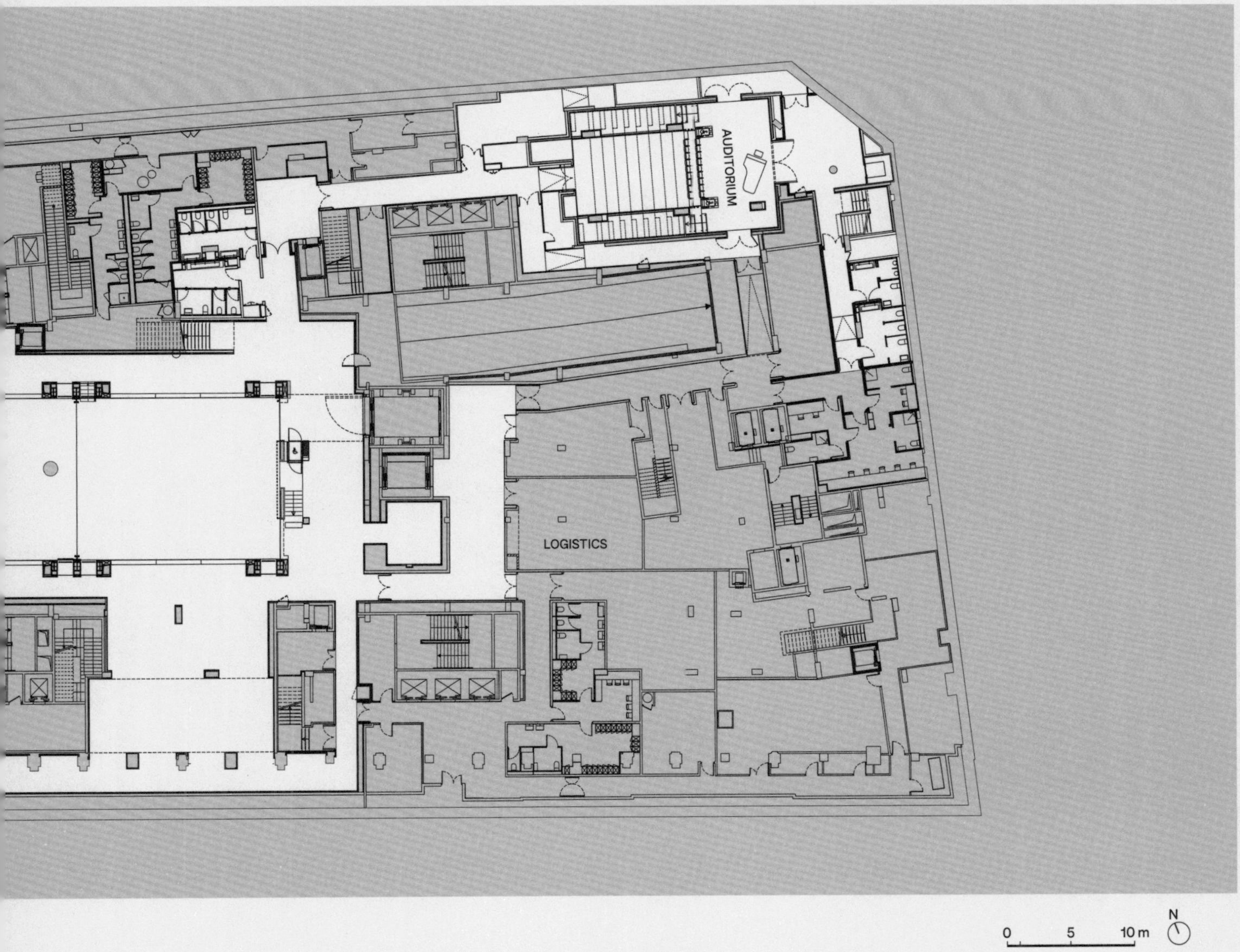
AUDITORIUM
LOGISTICS
0
5
10 m
N

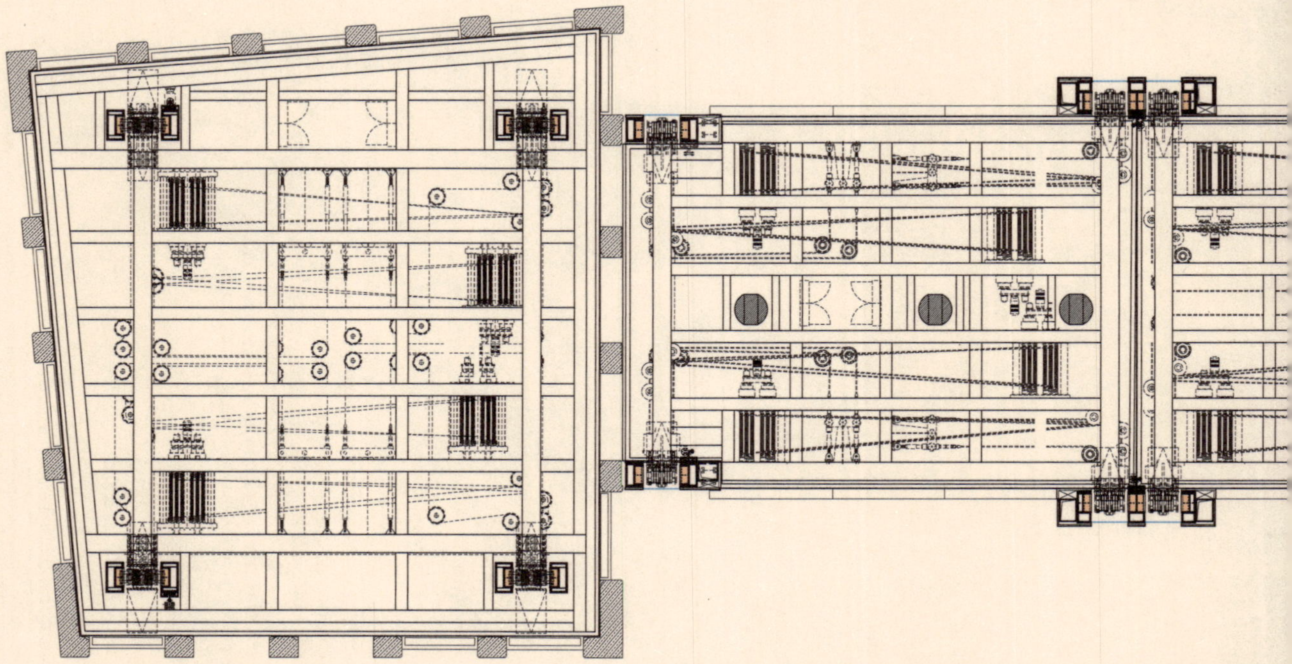

Technical plan for the undersides of the platforms
The casings placed under the platforms contain a complete technical grid for suspending heavy loads and installing lighting, speakers, projectors, and any other scenographic devices requested by the exhibition curators. All the mechanisms required to move the platforms are built into the thickness of the plates and posts: electric motors, pulleys, cables, and safety devices.

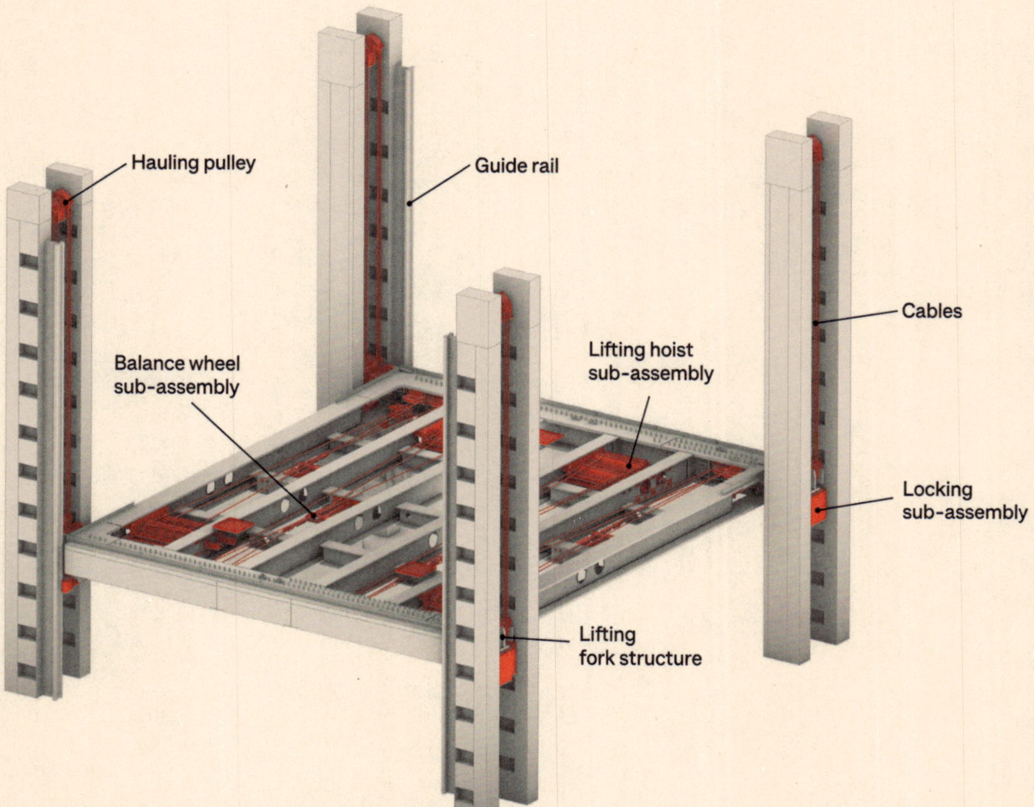

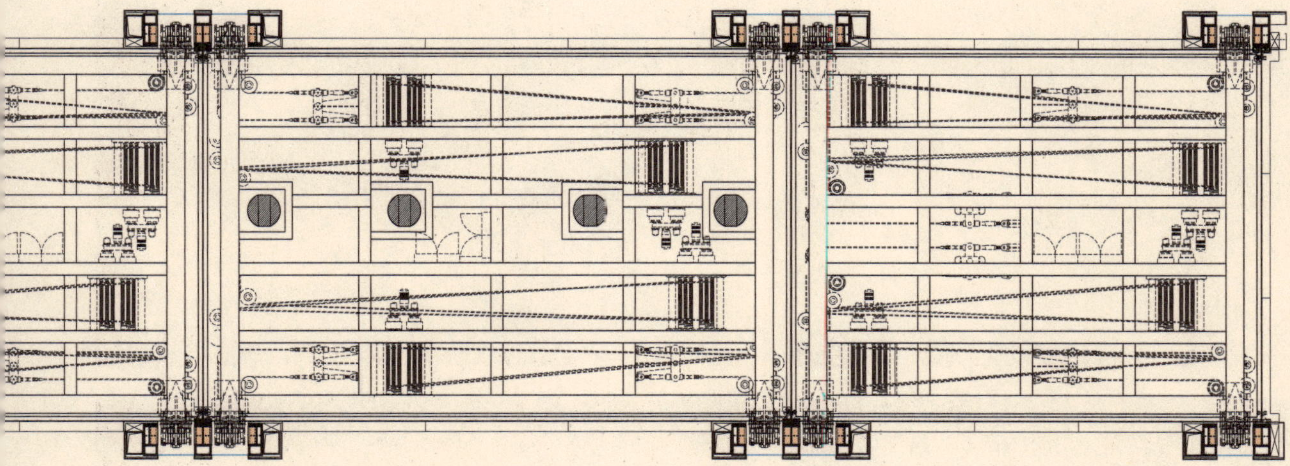

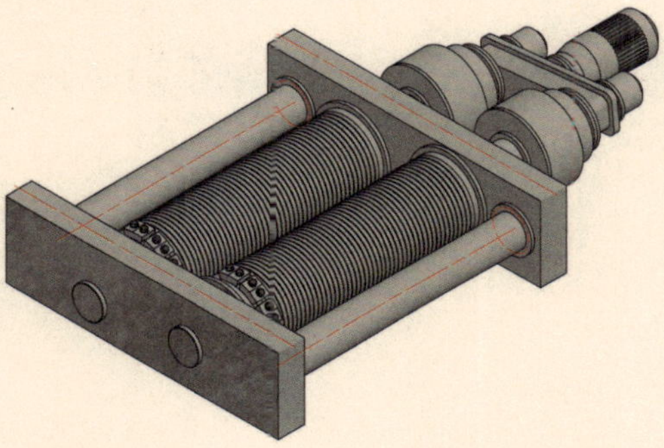

Lifting hoist sub-assembly

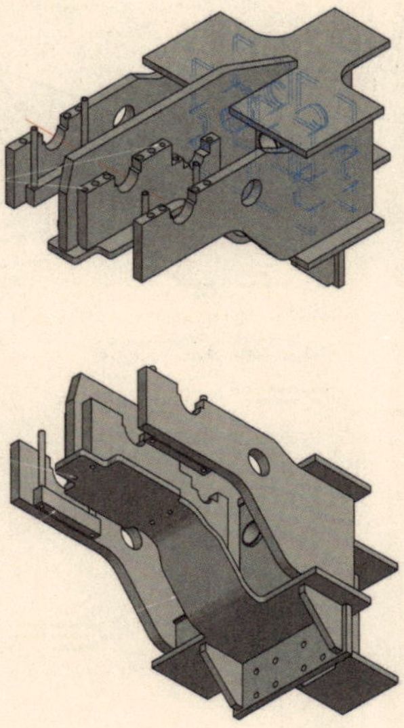

Lifting fork structure

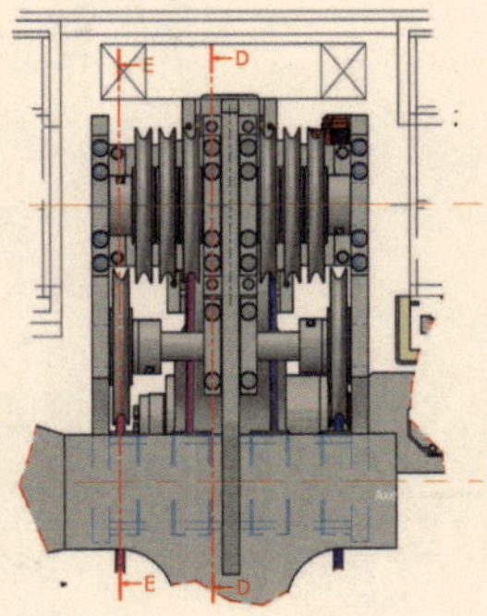

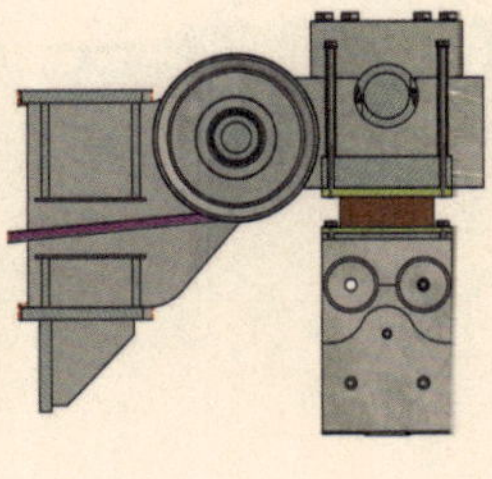

Lifting fork structure

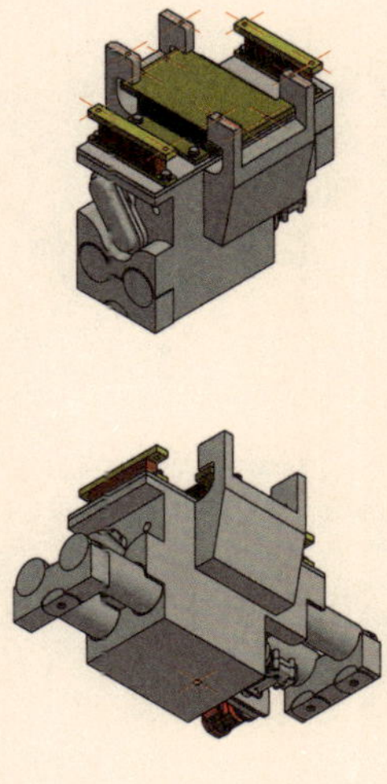

Locking sub-assembly

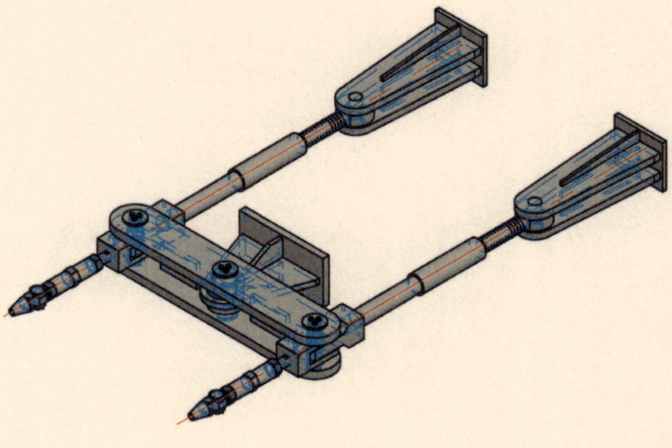

Balance wheel sub-assembly

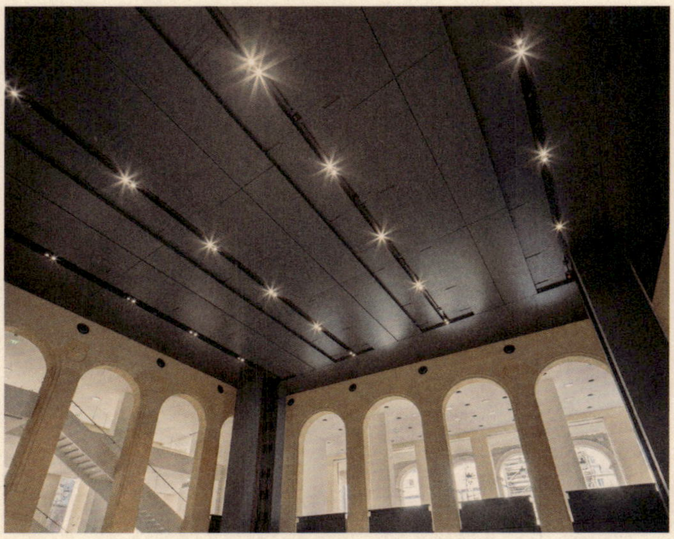
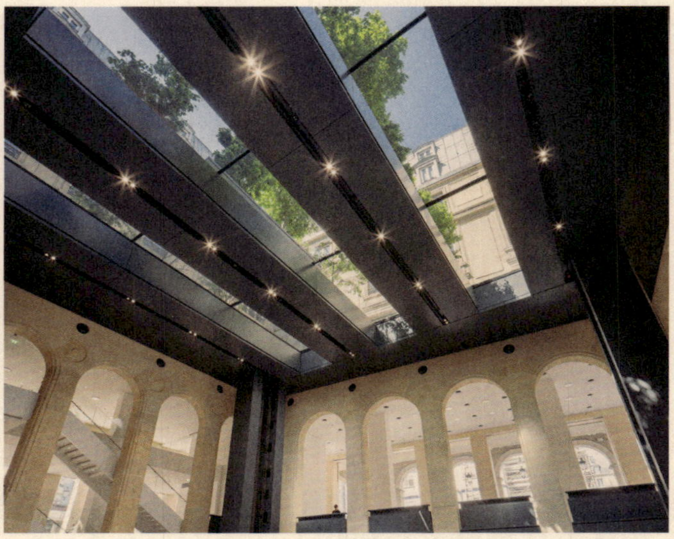
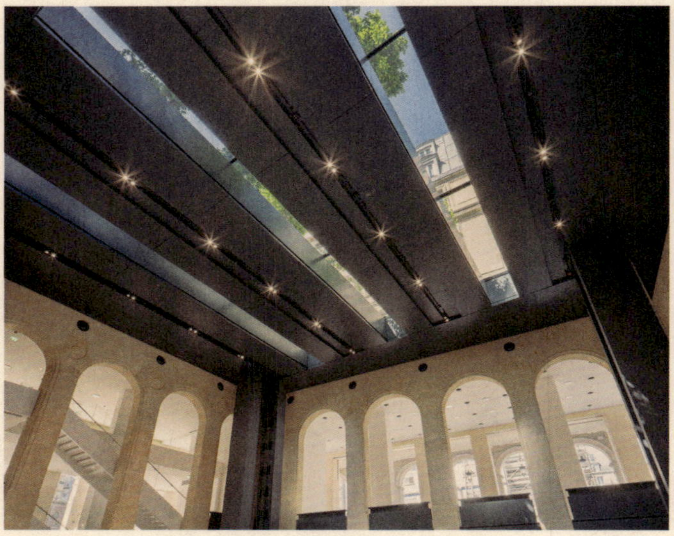
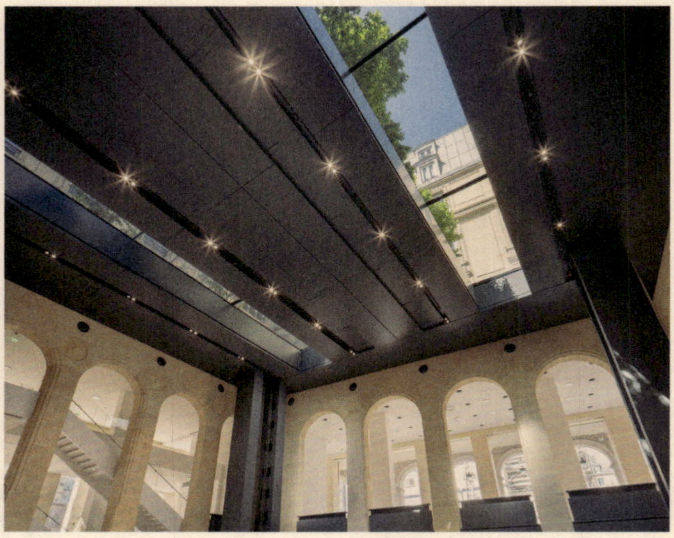

Examples of opening configurations for the movable shutters

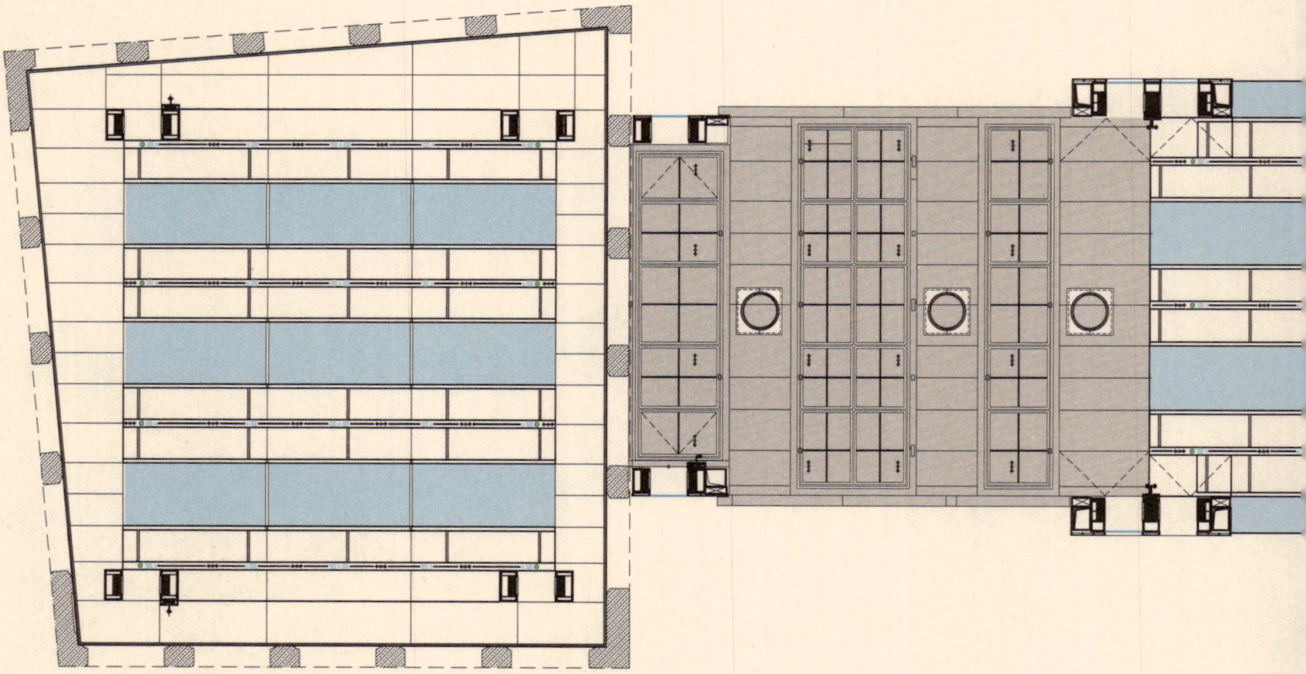

Technical plan for skylights and movable shutters
The ceilings at the level of the skylights and the upper levels of the building contain, like the platforms, a complete technical grid for suspending loads and installing scenographic devices. Under the skylights, large motorized shutters can be opened and closed to the desired position to filter the view of the trees and sky, or even screen it completely.

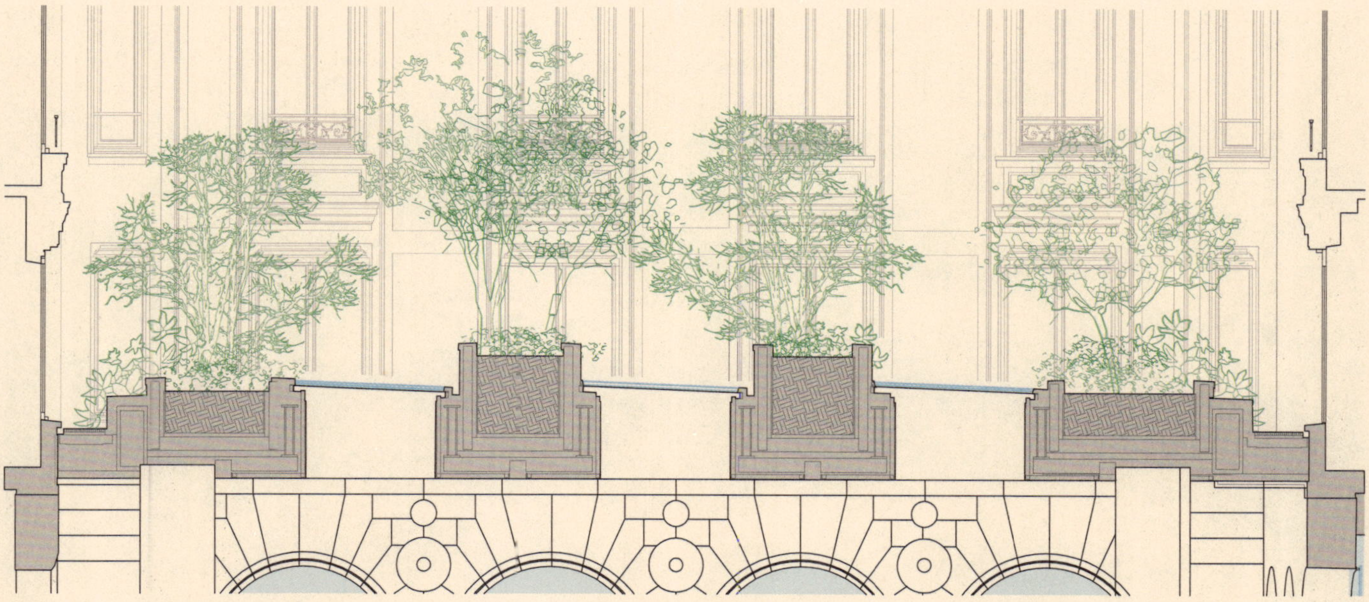

Cross-section of a skylight

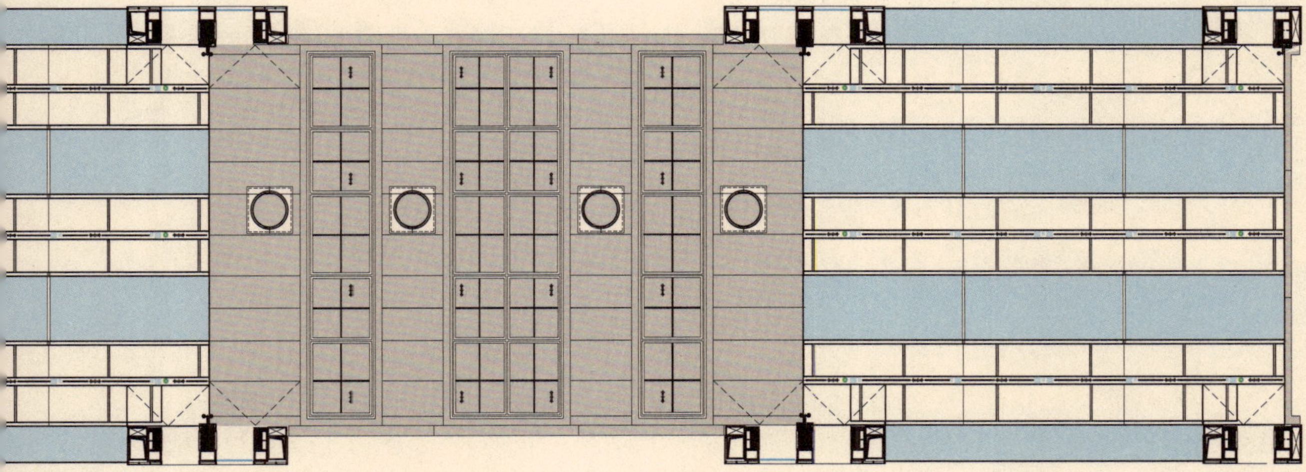

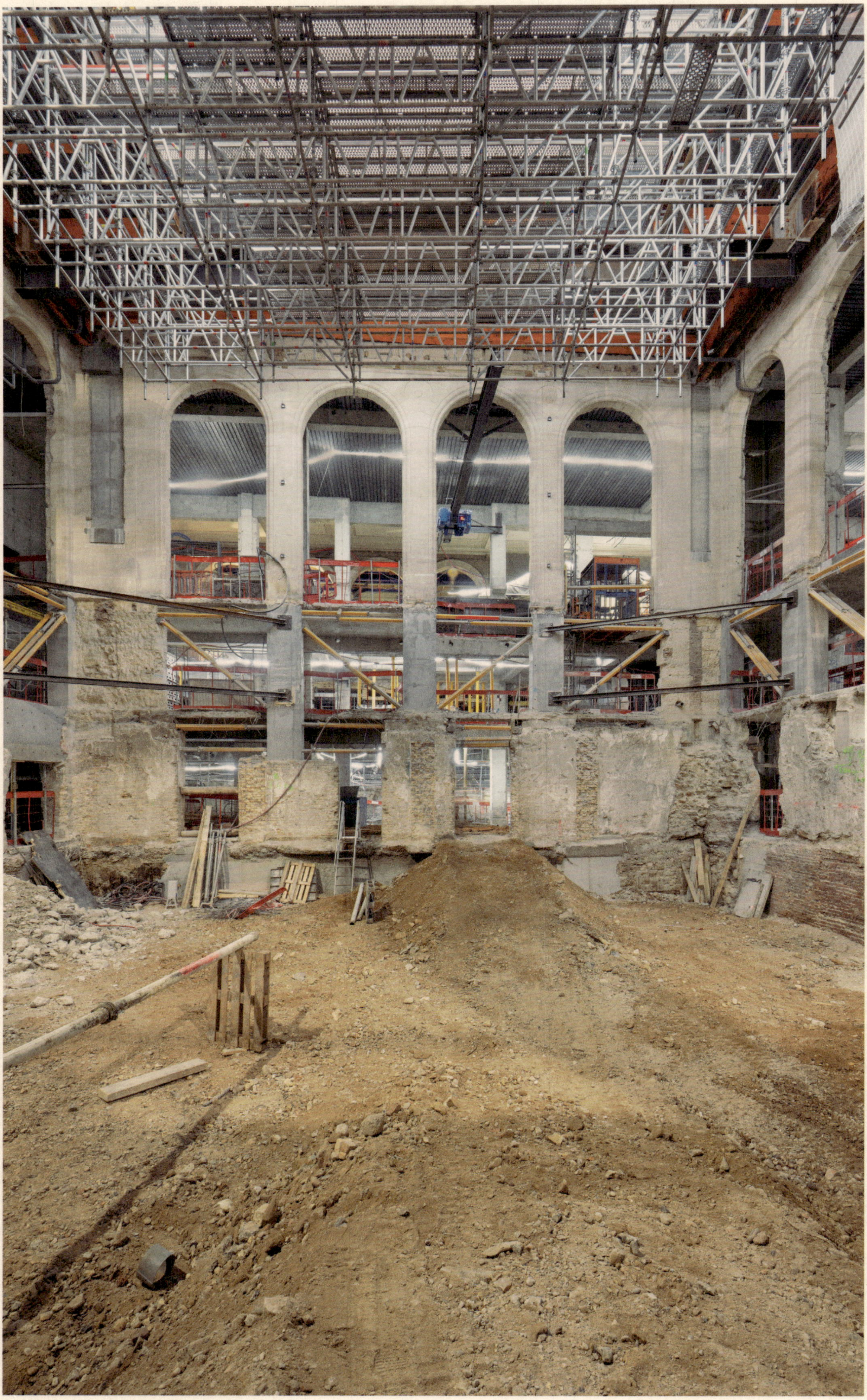

One of the inner courtyards of the Fondation Cartier building during construction, 2022

BETWEEN PRESERVATION AND MODERNIZATION: THE ARCHITECTURE OF JEAN NOUVEL

Béatrice Grenier

Strategic and International Projects Director
of the Fondation Cartier pour l'art contemporain

A city, as a collection of architectural works, can be thought of as a museum. Any new building has the potential to express the urban heritage that shaped the site on which it was erected. Jean Nouvel applies this philosophy, which he calls "contextualism," to all his architectural projects. His Louisiana Manifesto, pronounced in 2005 at the Denmark Museum of Modern Art, took the museum as its object. The architect described the theoretical principles shaping his work, both retroactively and for the future.[1] His museum projects have sought to radicalize architecture's role in relation to the city and over time have become emblematic of their respective urban environments. The new building for the Fondation Cartier pour l'art contemporain at 2 Place du Palais-Royal, in Paris, crystallizes Jean Nouvel's longstanding examination of the role of museum architecture vis-à-vis the city in establishing a dialectic between preservation and modernization.

1 — Jean Nouvel, *Louisiana Manifesto* (2005), reprinted in *Ce qui est là n'est pas ailleurs. Leçon inaugurale de l'École de Chaillot prononcée le 8 janvier 2008* (Cinisello Balsamo, Milan: Silvana Editoriale, 2009).

View of the Place du Palais-Royal and the State Council from the entrance hall of the Fondation Cartier, 2 Place du Palais-Royal, Paris, 2025

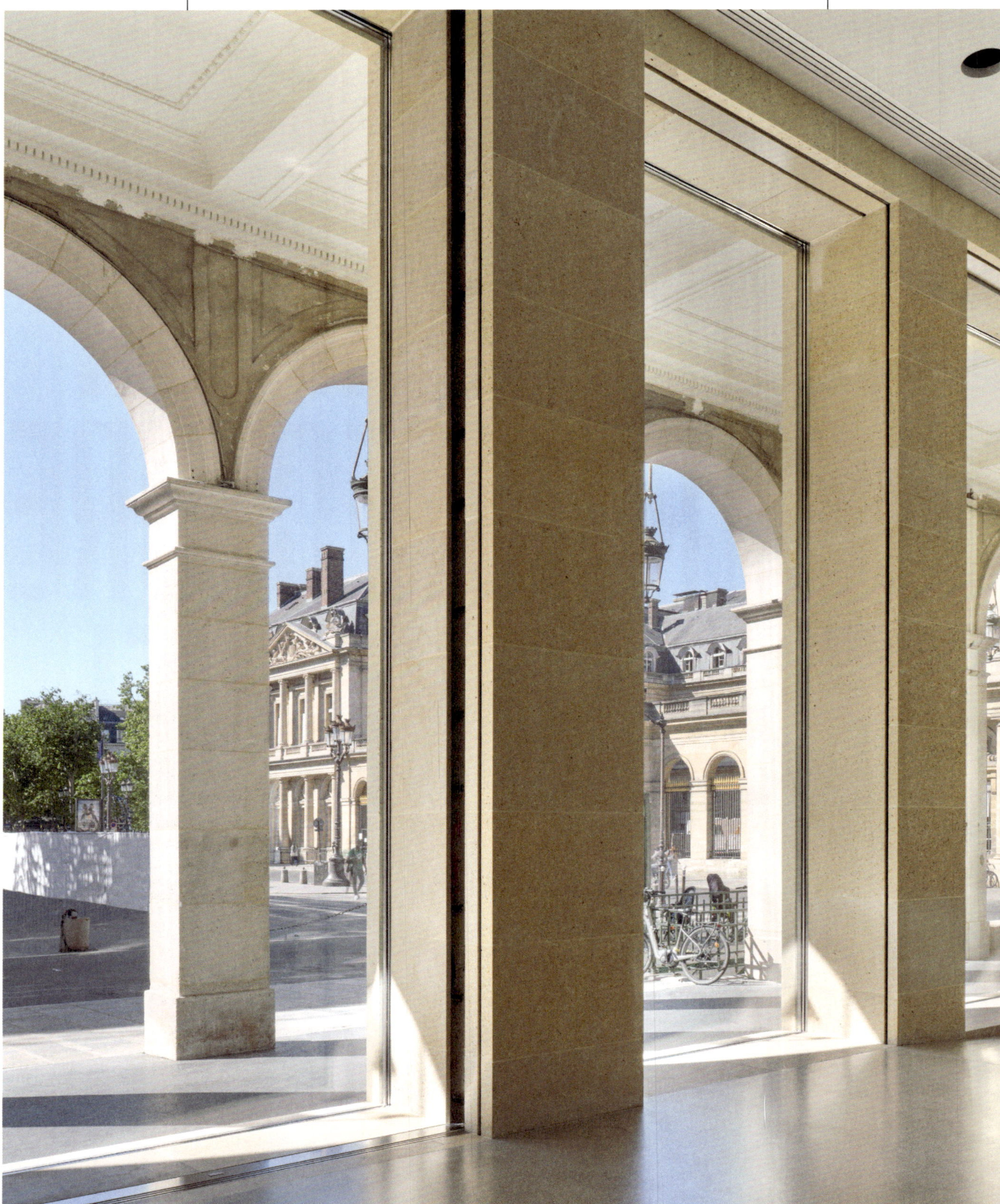

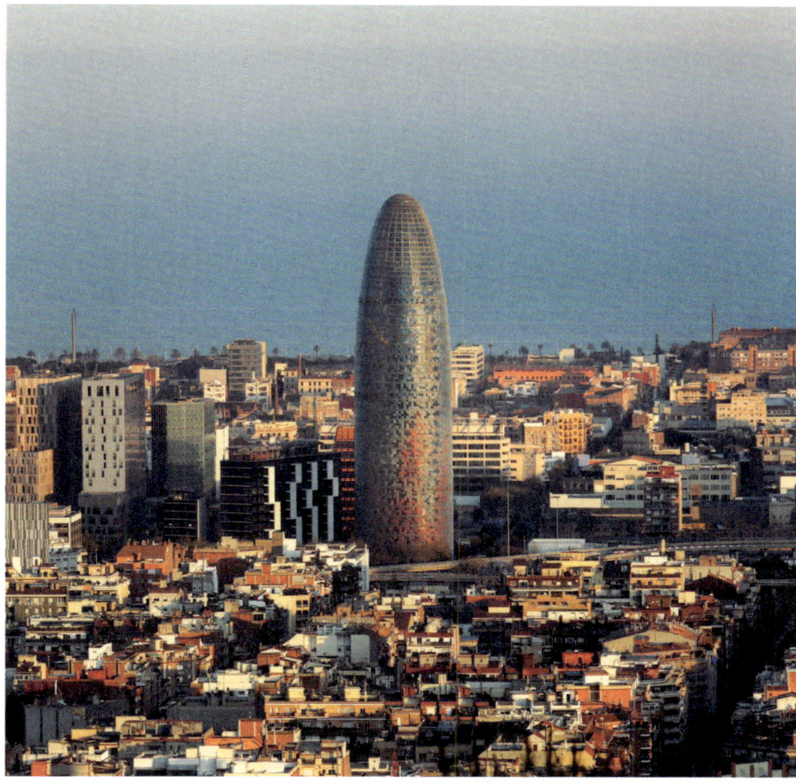

Torre Agbar, Barcelona, 2005

The City Is a Museum

On Barcelona's horizon, a singular object appears. It is held up like a mirror to the urban fabric below. It strikes the eye like a mirage, but like a mirage it seems it might vanish. Torre Agbar (2005) is a skyscraper composed of the city's fragments, a mosaic of the city's every color. Reflective of the urban landscape, it is also completely transparent. Red hues at the base prolong the horizon line of the Ciutat Vella's roofs, while shimmering silvers and blues make the tower itself disappear into the unobstructed blue sky.[2] The rounded top of the skyscraper mimics the peaks of Montserrat in the distance. When it was inaugurated in 2005, Jean Nouvel's construction was hailed as the new "totem" of Barcelona's skyline. While critics meant this cynically at the time—the economic crisis was looming and grandiose architectural gestures, emblematic of unreasonable expenditure, were viewed with disfavor[3]—it is an undeniable feat for an object so symbolic of modernity, the skyscraper, to embody as well the depth of time of a historical city like Barcelona. "Totem" is rather an appropriate word to describe not only this tower, but many architectural projects conceived by Jean Nouvel, their contradictions as well as their ambition. Indeed, this tension between preserving history and formulating the future seems to allow Jean Nouvel's soaring architecture to hold and project this totemic quality—the embodiment of a place's spirit.

A decade earlier, Jean Nouvel had expanded the Opéra de Lyon (1993) with a similar gesture. For this project, he preserved the neo-classical shell of the extant building while extending it with an abstract geometry: a spatial response proper to architecture. The volume of the existing building was doubled. The resulting architecture stood, the original with its echo hovering above, as though time had been added atop an existing structure, literally an extension of history. The skyline of Lyon, reflected in the high-tech arch, remained and remains as it ever was—yet is forever changed by this new, respectful addition.[4]

THERE IS NO OTHER MODERNITY THAN THE AGGREGATION OF PAST MODERNITIES: A CITY MUST REVEAL THE SEDIMENTATION OF TIME AND THE DIVERSITY IT CONJURES ACROSS THE AGES.

2 — After the final abandonment, in 2000, of the "Endless Tower" project for La Défense, the Torre Agbar (now known as the Glòries Tower) represented a new attempt by Jean Nouvel to capture the evanescence he had achieved in the Lucerne Culture and Congress Center (KKL, 2000) and the Fondation Cartier Boulevard Raspail (1994). See Jaume V. Aroca, "L'Art de la reconversion urbaine," in *L'Architecture d'aujourd'hui*, no. 337: Jean Nouvel, pp. 103–105, December 2001.

3 — Luis Fernández Galiano, "Tótem y catástrofe," in *El País*, October 8, 2005. Retrieved online: www.elpais.com/diario/2005/10/08/babelia/1128726382_850215.html.

4 — See "Jean Nouvel: Teatro dell'Opera a Lione," in *Domus* 752, September 1993. Retrieved online: www.domusweb.it/it/dall-archivio/2023/08/24/jean-nouvel-teatro-dellopera-a-lione.html.

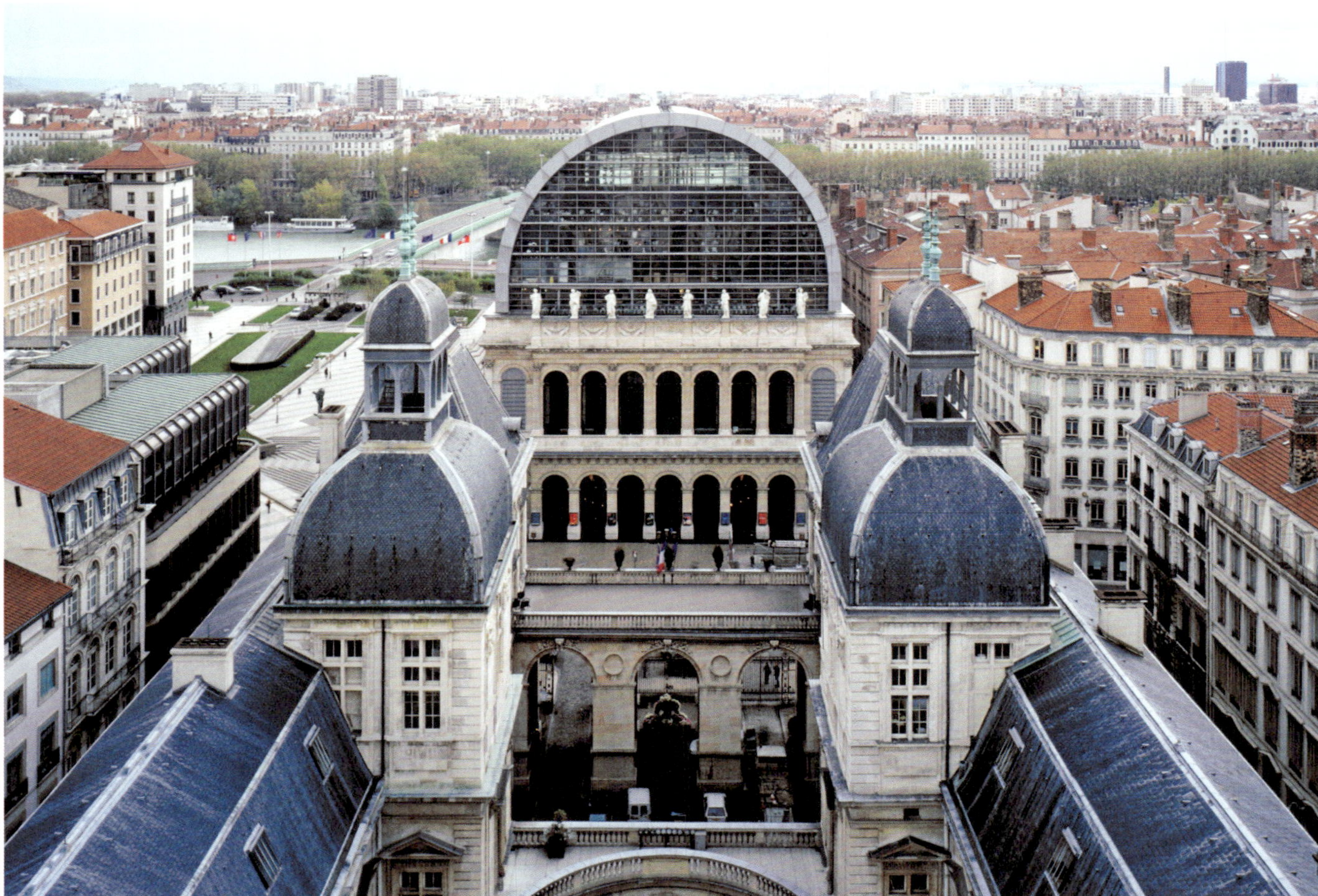

Extension of the Opéra de Lyon, 1993

The material condition of architecture presupposes division from its context, the urban space in which it inscribes itself. In the modern metropolis, architecture is the materiality that divides one finite artifact from another.[5] Yet with every building Jean Nouvel completely transcends this ontological limitation, surpassing the treatment of architecture in terms of a possible historical enclosure, separate from the city, while paradoxically the precise materiality of it suggests this very condition. By disavowing the differentiation between the city and the architectural object, for both new or extant buildings, Jean Nouvel creates the circumstances for the boundlessness of historical time to permeate the meaning of architectural content, subverting any necessity for choice between modernization and preservation. Jean Nouvel recognizes the openness and continuity of history; he addresses it with architecture. With every project, he seeks to prolong the spirit of a city as an expression of a living civilization: the urban space is also the space of the museum.[6] In Jean Nouvel's earliest ambition, this was expressed in the Théâtre Le Granit in Belfort (1984), where he simultaneously sliced through and extended an existing architecture with a glass façade as though it were as contemporary as it was past.[7] There is no other modernity than the aggregation of past modernities: a city must reveal the sedimentation of time and the diversity it conjures across the ages. Jean Nouvel's Greater Paris plan (2008–2009) aimed to express this idea on an urban scale. Its nine approaches to urban renewal placed nature, art, and elevation at the heart of a new way of living, both within the historical center and extending beyond it.[8] The project described a modernity that respected its surrounding context, in a natural and historical sense: "It is in places where history has already manifested itself that modernity has a duty to impose itself, for these places of history have in their time been places of modernity."[9] For Jean Nouvel, the historical past is projected in the future of architecture.

5 — Pier Vittorio Aureli has theorized Mies van der Rohe's use of the plinth as a direct engagement with this condition of the modern city, a political act that allows the consciousness of the collection of finite artifacts that compose the city. See *Towards an Absolute Architecture* (Cambridge: MIT Press, 2020), p. 36.

6 — For discussion on this topic, see "Jean Nouvel," in Odile Fillion, *La Ville: six interviews d'architectes* (Paris: Le Moniteur / Centre Georges Pompidou, 1994), p. 65.

7 — Working with scenographer Jacques Le Marquet, Jean Nouvel's approach was to play up the relationship between the old theater and the new intervention, enhancing each element of the old theater by pushing it to its utmost expressiveness. See Olivier Boissière (ed.), *Jean Nouvel, Emmanuel Cattani and Associates* (Zurich: Artemis, 1992), p. 48.

8 — Jean Nouvel, Jean-Marie Duthilleul and Michel Cantal-Dupart, "Neuf Mesures de transformation de la métropole parisienne : évolution des mobilités dans la métropole parisienne," Grand Pari(s) – Paris Métropole, December 2009. Study realized with oral and written contributions of Alexandre Allard, Rémi Babinet and Catherine Emprin (BETC), Olivier Boissière, Patrick Bouchain, Daniel Buren, Guy Burgel, Michel Desvigne, Yann Kersalé, Anne Lacaton and Jean-Philippe Vassal, Raphaël Ménard (Elioth), Bertrand Nouvel, Ateliers Jean Nouvel, etc.

9 — Jean Nouvel quoted in Michael Juul Holm (ed.), *Nouvel: Louisiana Manifest* (Humlebæk: Louisiana Museum of Modern Art, 2008), unpaged.

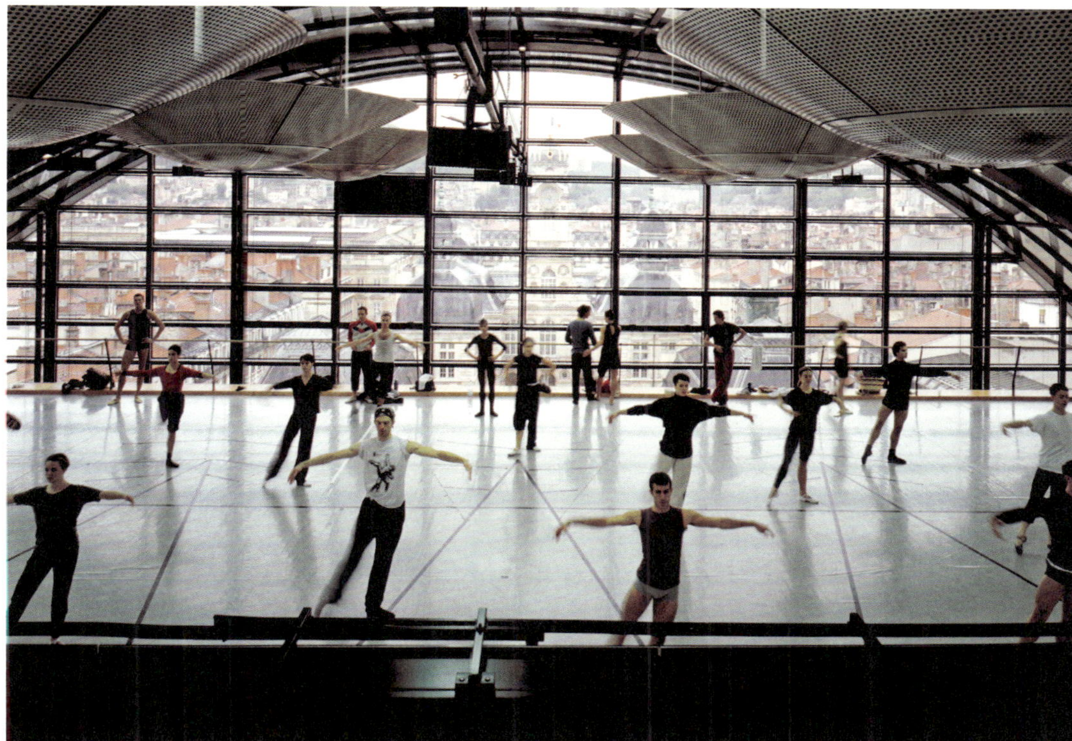

Glass wall of the main ballet studio, Opéra de Lyon, 1993

FOR JEAN NOUVEL, THE HISTORICAL PAST IS PROJECTED IN THE FUTURE OF ARCHITECTURE.

Historical facade of the Théâtre le Granit and its glass extension, Belfort, 1984

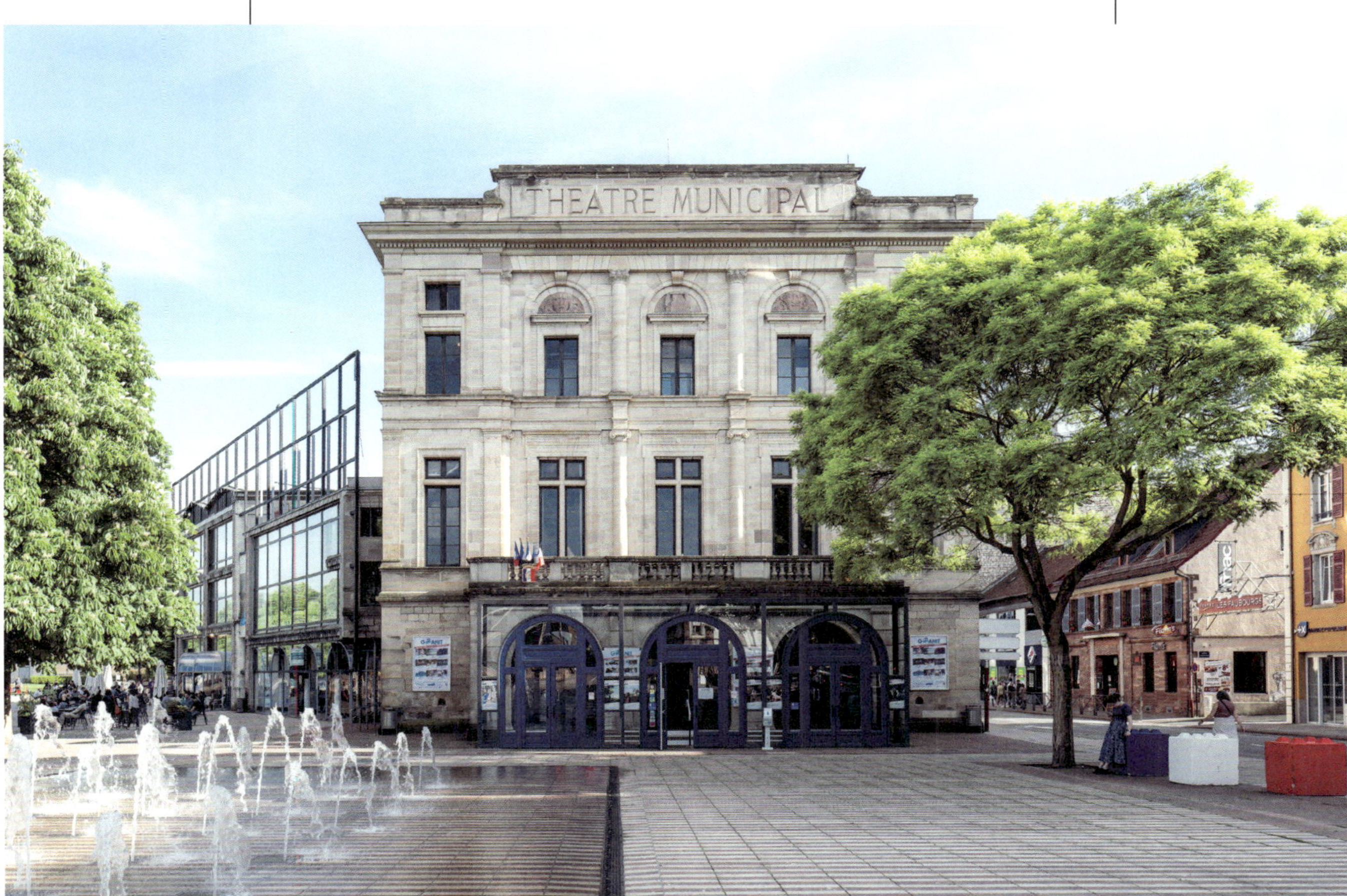

Modernization Is Also Preservation

Paris has always been the site of this ambiguous coexistence of the image of modernity and the imperative of preserving its heritage. This duality took perhaps its most ardent and irrevocable ideological stance with the construction of La Défense in the late 1950s, marking an absolute refusal to integrate modernization within Paris walls. Paris has remained a spectator to modernization, rejecting the shock of the new—save for a handful of cases, such as the Centre Georges Pompidou (1977)—after the passing of André Malraux's decisive 1962 law which officialized the historic preservation of some sectors of the city. Why was the innovation proposed by Jean Nouvel generally embraced—indeed, he may be the architect who has most marked the sanctified historical center—while that of Richard Rogers and Renzo Piano for the Centre Pompidou provoked such violent disgust?[10]

Between 1971 and 1978, Gordon Matta-Clark produced a body of work known as *Building Cuts*: sculptural transformations of abandoned buildings through the cutting and dismantling of a given architectural site. In 1975, for the Biennale of Paris, he produced *Conical Intersect*, a cut that connected two seventeenth-century buildings adjacent to the future Centre Pompidou. The two buildings had already been slated for demolition: by that time, the plateau Beaubourg and the entire Les Halles area had been subject to massive reconstruction. Looking at this photograph today is a different experience from what must at the time have been the shock of walking in front of this artwork, not yet recognizable as such. Imagine the sudden apparition in the middle of Rue du Renard of the living room of an apartment, as though the latter, with all the domesticity it represented, were the accidental result of a catastrophic demolition, about to fall into the street. The documentation of this work is perhaps still potent in illustrating the juxtaposition of the past and the future to conjure *the now* in an urban setting. Modernity's relentless pursuit of the new is literally illustrated in this work: a cyclical process of destruction and construction.

Much like the work of Matta-Clark, the architecture of Jean Nouvel crystallizes the tension between narratives of historical progress and the destruction of site as its prerequisite. The ability of Jean Nouvel's architecture to prolong historical modernity into new architectural forms may have eased its entry into the Parisian context. The Fondation Cartier building in the 14th arrondissement of Paris, inaugurated in 1994, is a prime example.

10 — Reyner Banham's was possibly the only positive review at the time of inauguration. See Reyner Banham and John Partridge, "Pompidou Cannot Be Perceived As Anything But a Monument," in *Architectural Review*, May 11, 1977. Republished online March 2012. See also Ada Louise Huxtable, "Architecture View," in *New York Times*, December 25, 1977, p. 49.

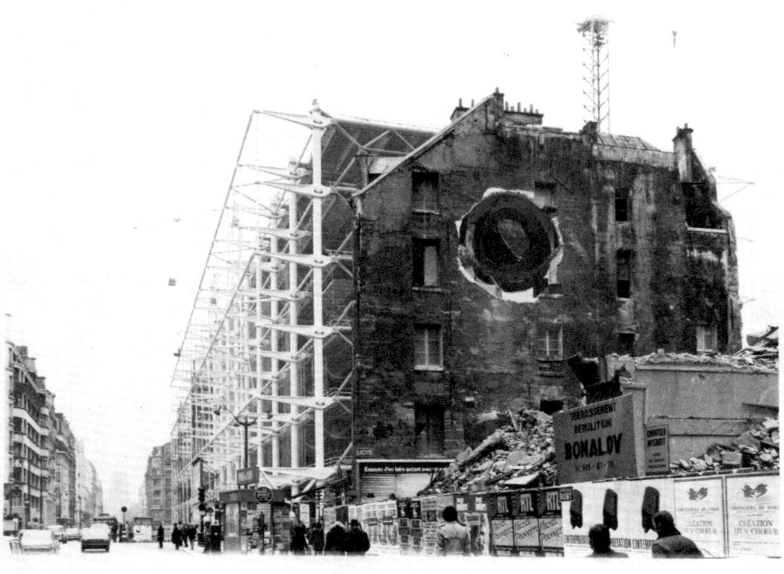

Gordon Matta-Clark, *Conical Intersect 6*, 1977 (documentation of the action *Conical Intersect*, Paris, 1975)

In 1991, the American Center, originally opened in 1934 at 261 Boulevard Raspail on the site of the old American Cathedral in Paris, moved to the Right Bank of the city. The American Center, built by architect William Bosworth,[11] had for over half a century welcomed some of America's most important artists: Merce Cunningham, John Cage, Bob Wilson, Lucinda Childs, Nam June Paik, Trisha Brown. Its foundations had been laid out, in accordance with the wishes of his descendants, to protect the roots of the cedar planted by François-René de Chateaubriand a hundred years earlier. Important masonry work was carried out to ensure the tree's survival.

Jean Nouvel's starting point for the iconic glass building of the Fondation Cartier that replaced the William Bosworth building was also the imperative of preserving the cedar. The rest was simple—a steel and glass structure, eight stories high and twice as wide, parallel to the boulevard. Framed between the two fifteen-meter-high

11 — William W. Bosworth was an American architect whose most famous designs include MIT's Cambridge campus and the AT&T building, 195 Broadway in Manhattan, New York City. Under the auspices of John D. Rockefeller Jr., his career led him to France in the 1920s, where he was put in charge of the restoration of the Palace of Versailles, Fontainebleau castle, and Notre-Dame de Reims.

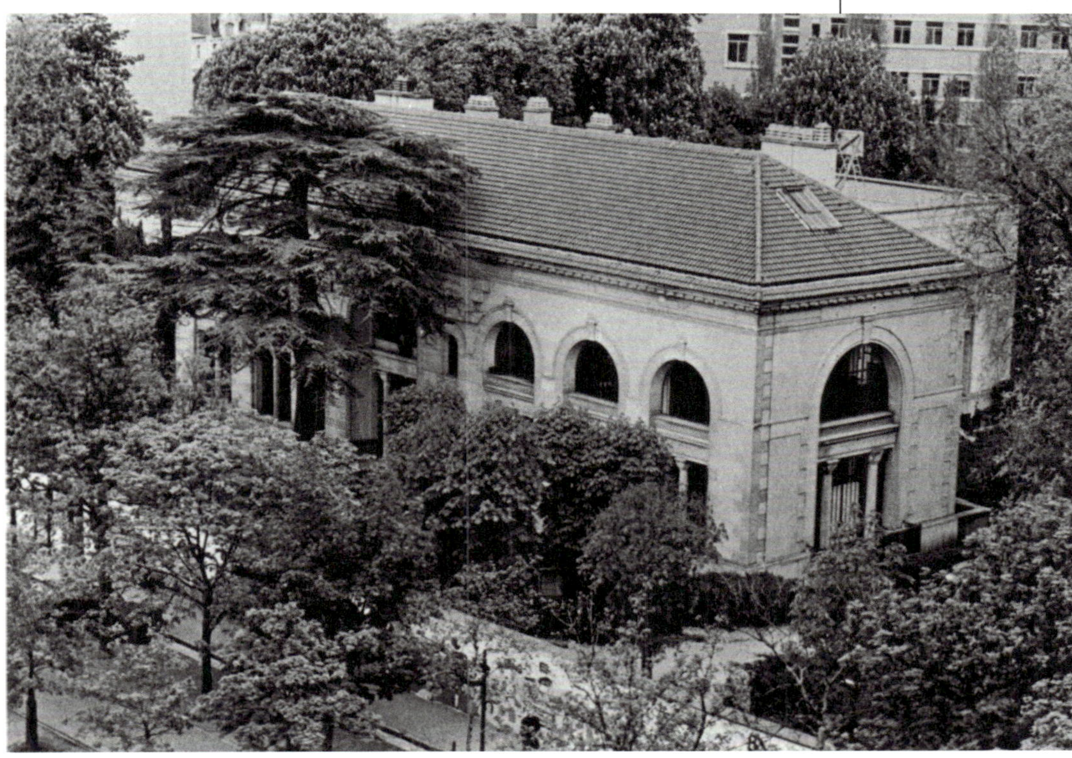

The American Center before the construction of the Fondation Cartier, 261 Boulevard Raspail, Paris, c. 1970

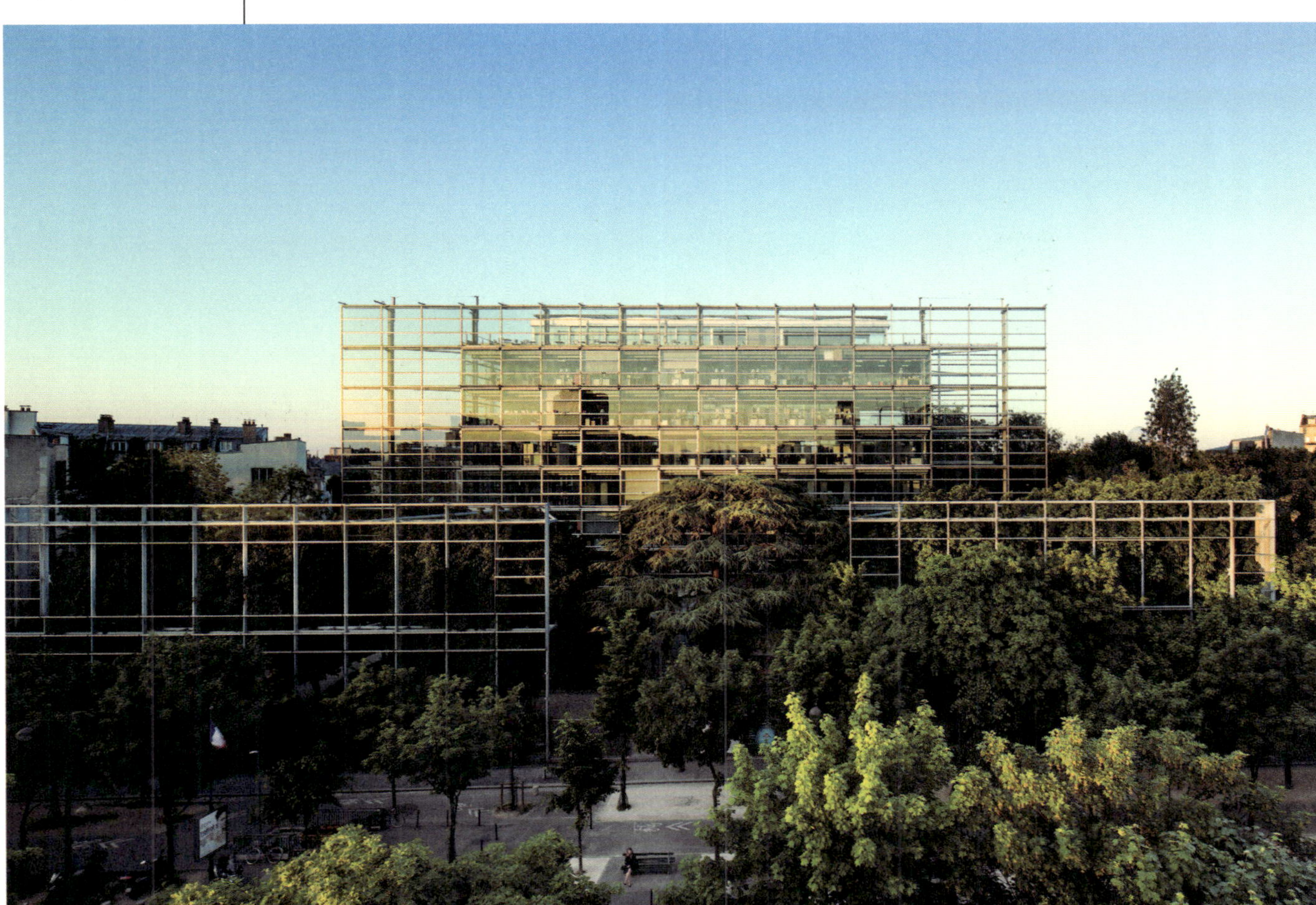

Fondation Cartier building, 261 Boulevard Raspail, Paris, 1994

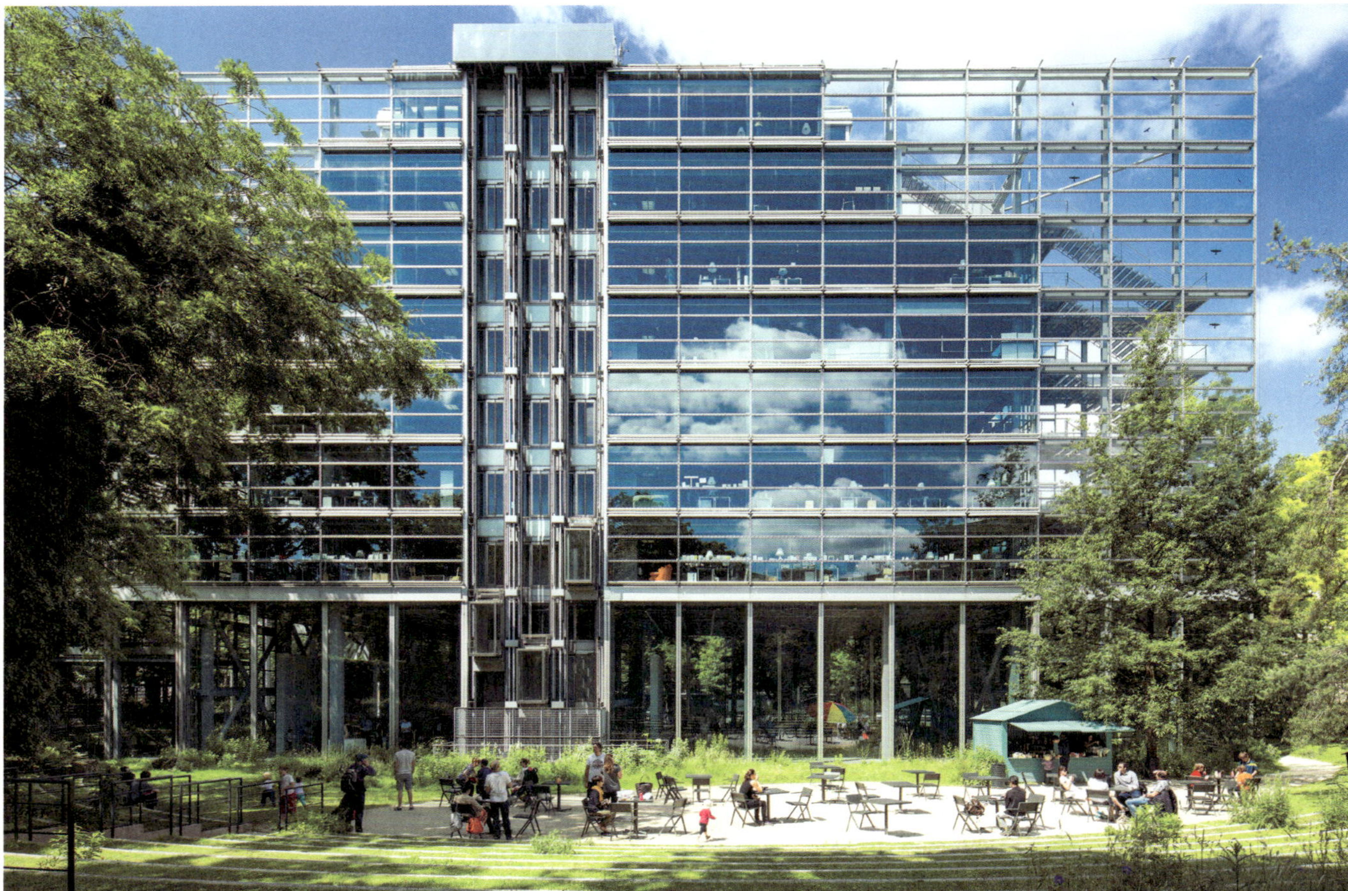

Fondation Cartier building, 261 Boulevard Raspail, Paris, 1994

TRANSPARENCY INCORPORATES THE SURROUNDING ENVIRONMENT AS AN INTEGRAL FEATURE OF THE CREATED SPACE.

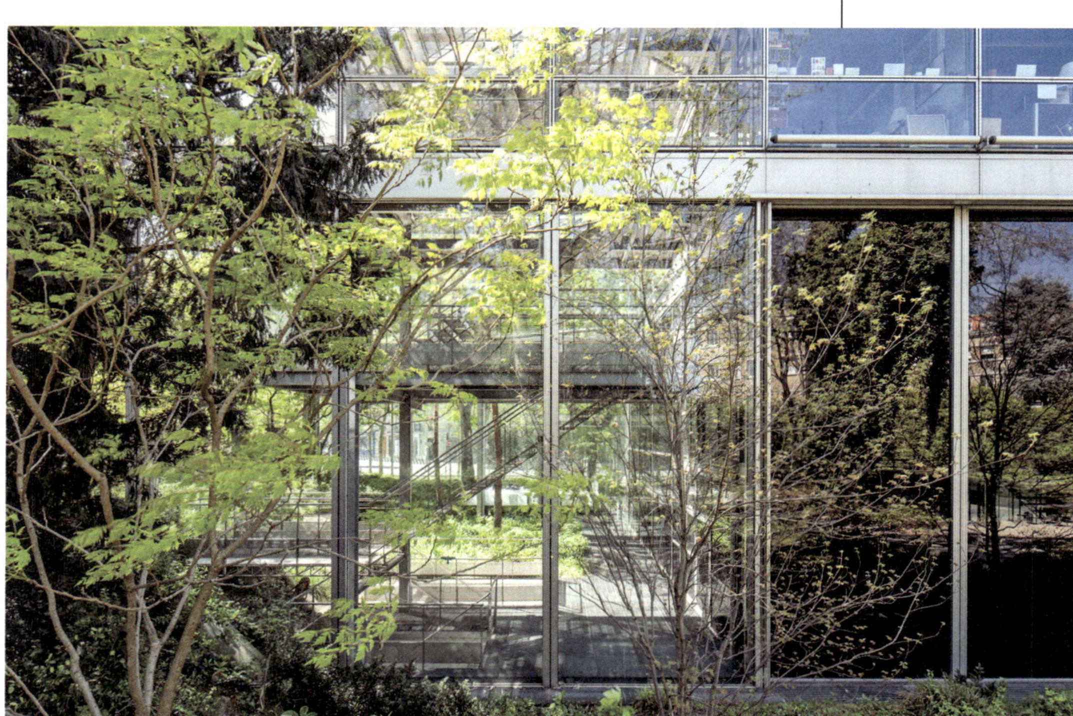

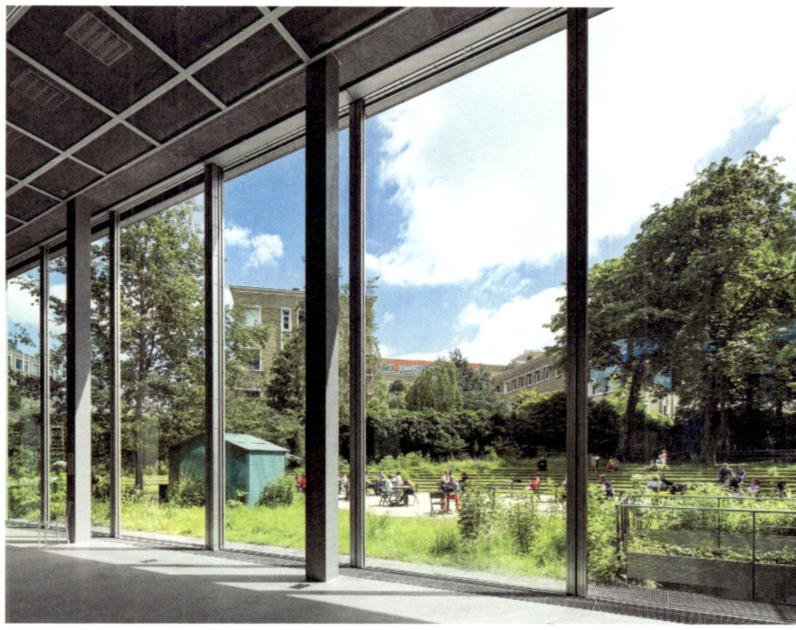

View of the Fondation Cartier garden from interior spaces

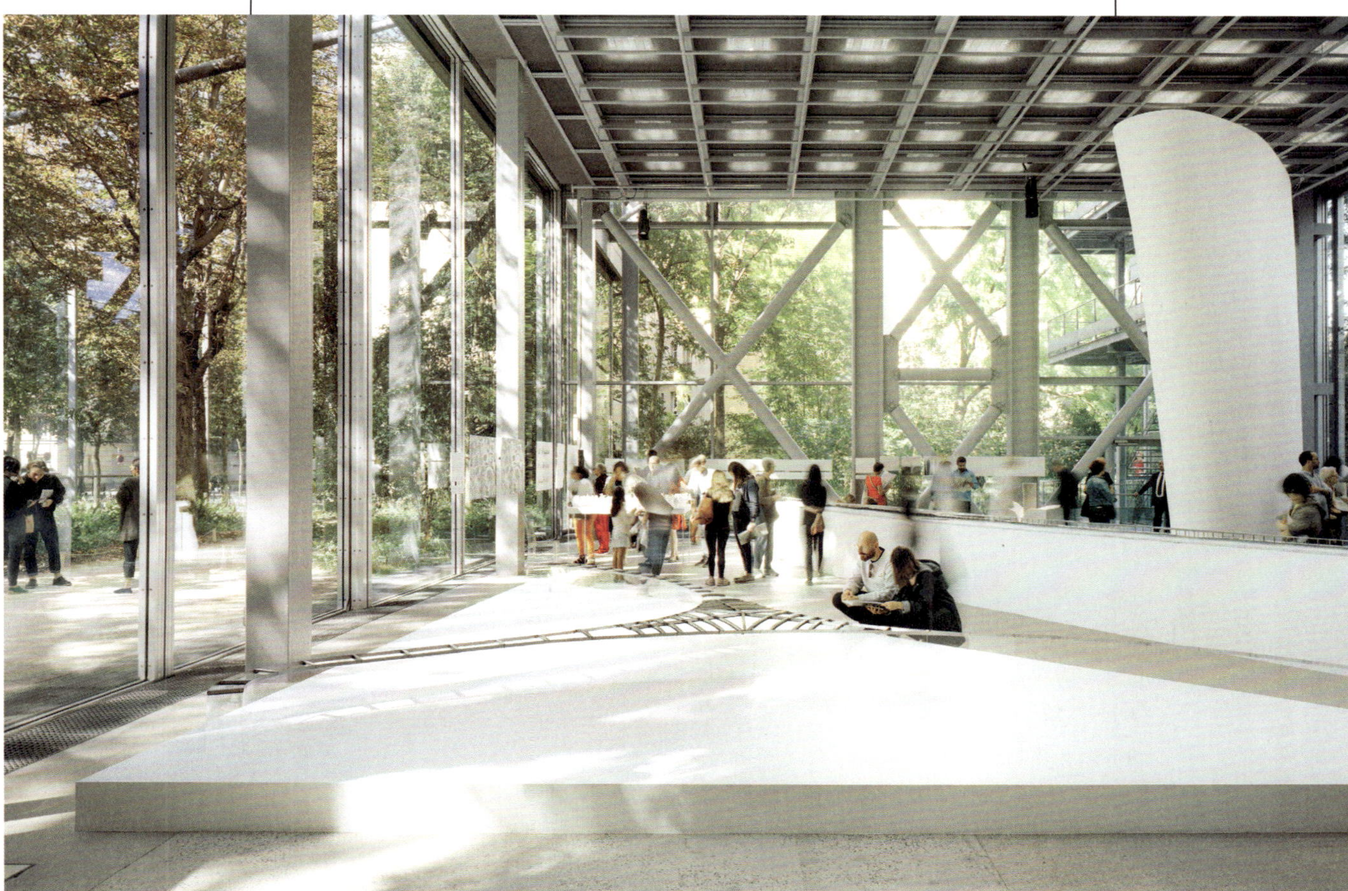

Freeing Architecture exhibition by Junya Ishigami at the Fondation Cartier in 2018

screens flanking the entrance, for over 25 years the cedar continued to welcome visitors passing from the city's streets to the garden. The point of departure for Jean Nouvel's design was respect for his predecessor, reflecting the architect's "contextualist" approach to modernization, with historical preservation at its core. The demolition of the American Center and the subsequent construction of the Fondation Cartier preserved the oldest element of the history of the original site—the tree—lodging it at the center of the new architecture.[12] Indeed, the context of the place lies as much in the narration of events that occurred within the walls of the previous American Center, whose footprint determined the new construction, as in the silent witness of the grandiose and towering Lebanese Cedar[13]: the city is everywhere, and the building merely expresses its condensed spirit.

12 — Conway Lloyd Morgan, *Jean Nouvel: The Elements of Architecture* (New York: Universe, 1998), p. 178.

13 — In 2020, the tree became terminally ill. It was extremely old and set in an environment where its soil could not be renewed. It had endured two summer heatwaves, losing so many needles in such a short amount of time that it could not regenerate and had to be removed as a danger to the building's facade.

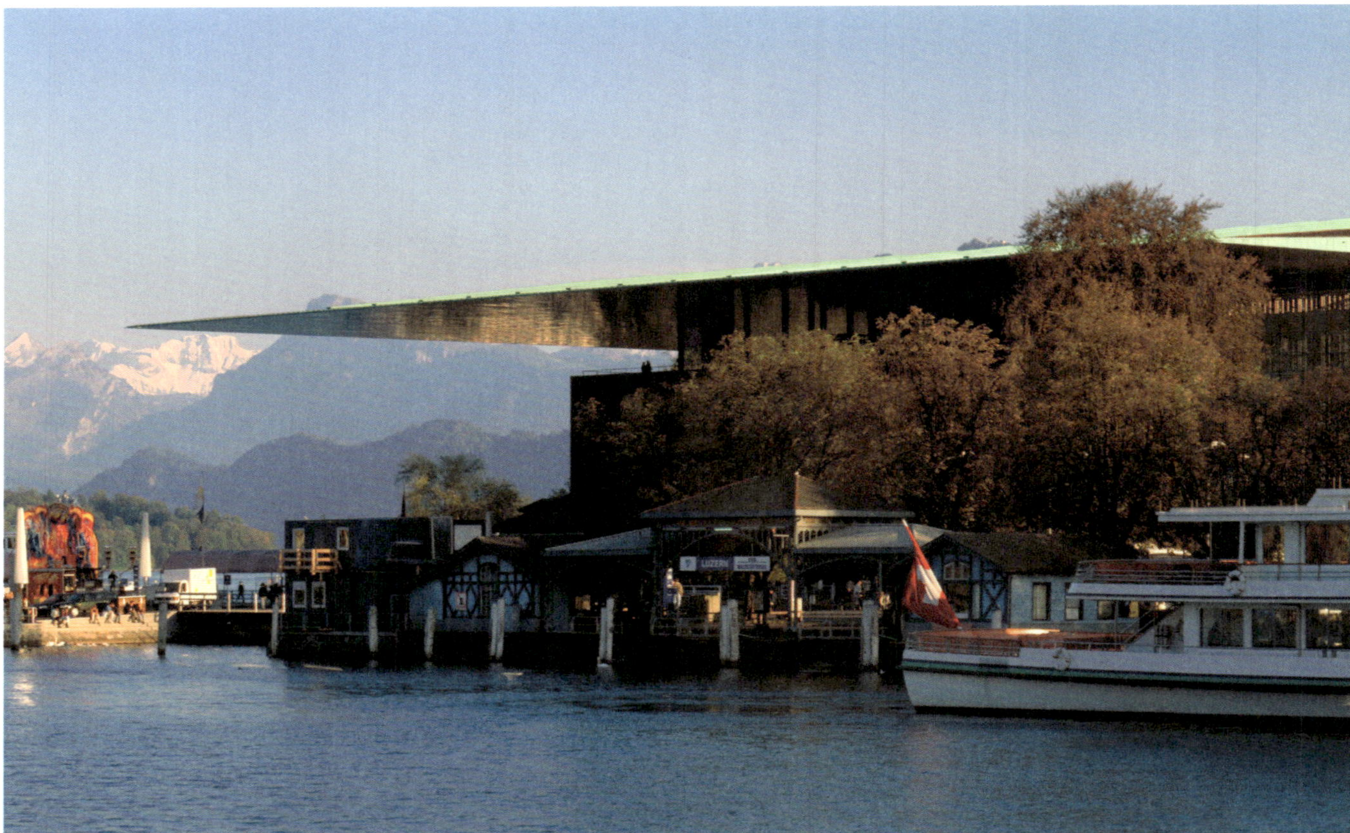

Lucerne Culture and Congress Center (KKL), 2000

For the Fondation Cartier on Boulevard Raspail and the Lucerne Culture and Congress Center (KKL, 2000), contemporaneous projects, Jean Nouvel used transparency to enter into relation with the historicity of a context.[14] A historical place is as much a natural as a built environment. In Lucerne, the competition required Jean Nouvel to retain the original architecture. His response was to construct a new building in the middle of the Quatre-Cantons lake, offering privileged views of the locally beloved historical concert hall. When the project was put on hold, Nouvel developed a second version, in which the concert hall's layout would follow and mirror the shore of the lake, the city's most defining feature.[15] The roof that unifies the building's three sections is an immense reflective surface mirroring the body of water over which it extends, suggesting the disappearance of architecture in favor of the city's natural and historical *raison d'être*—Lake Lucerne.

14 — Martino Stierli has aptly observed that one could apply Beatriz Colomina's reading of Le Corbusier's *fenêtres en longueur* to Jean Nouvel's KKL. See Martino Stierli, *Montage and the Metropolis: Architecture, Modernity, and the Representation of Space* (New Haven: Yale University Press, 2018), p. 226. See also Beatriz Colomina, *Privacy and Publicity: Modern Architecture as Mass Media* (Cambridge: The MIT Press, 1996), p. 139.

15 — Conway Lloyd Morgan, *Jean Nouvel: The Elements of Architecture*, op. cit., 1998. pp. 27–33. Patrice Goulet, "La Ville Moderne," in *Jean Nouvel*, 1987 (Paris: Institut français d'architecture / Editions du Regard, Paris 1994), p. 151.

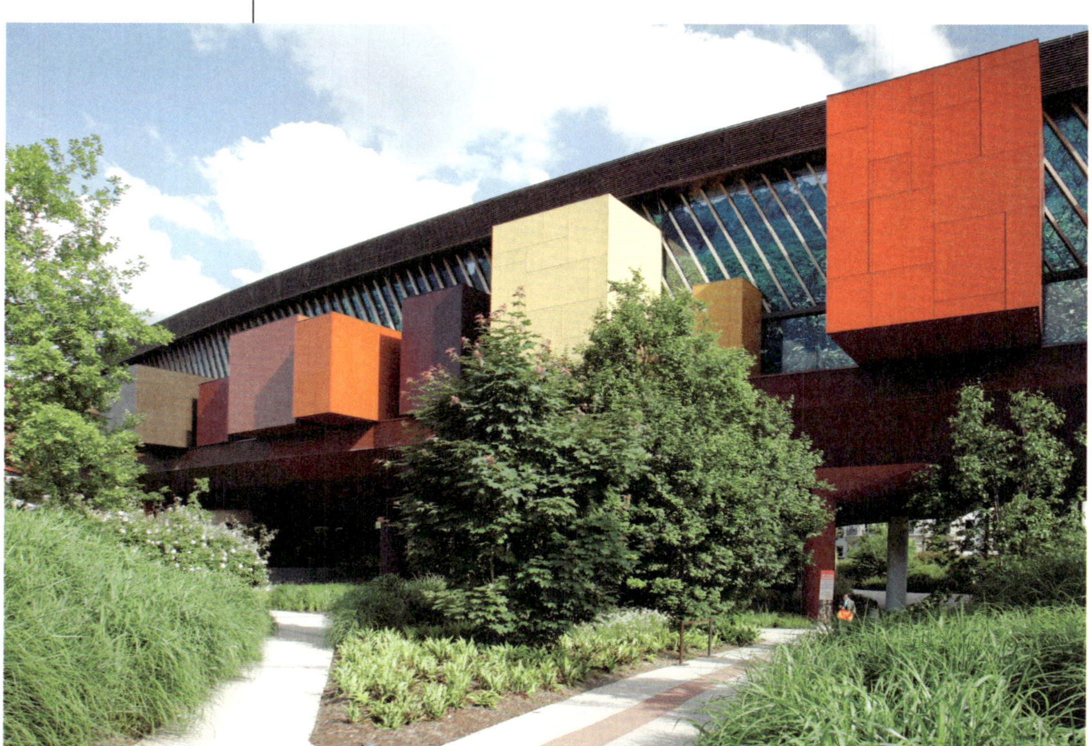

Musée du Quai Branly – Jacques Chirac, Paris, 2006

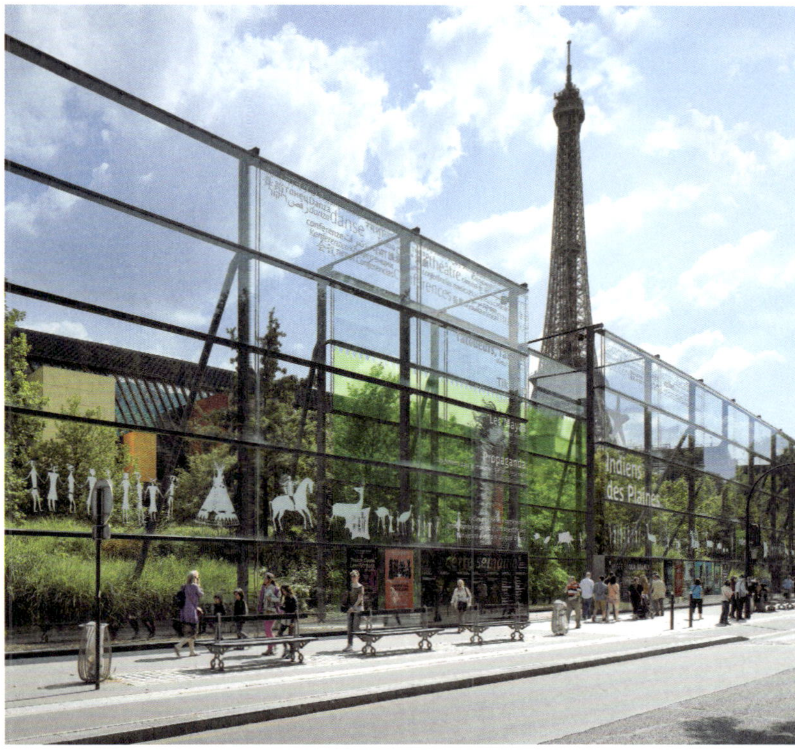

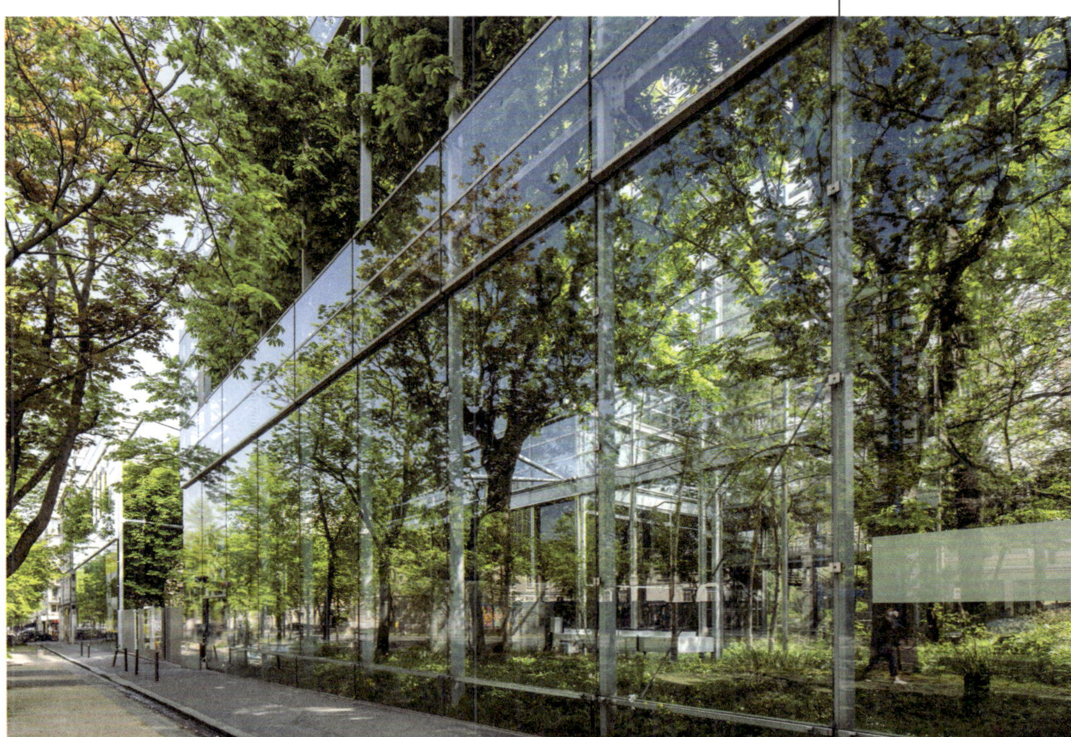

Glass walls of the Musée du Quai Branly – Jacques Chirac (opposite) and of the Fondation Cartier, 261 Boulevard Raspail (below)

This ambivalence of construction-as-preservation is achieved in both the Boulevard Raspail and Lucerne through material ambiguity. The use of reflection and transparency is what urbanist and philosopher Paul Virilio referred to as "thickness," which is to say, the presence of materiality that evokes its very disappearance.[16] Indeed, at the Fondation Cartier Boulevard Raspail, Jean Nouvel used dematerialization of architecture as a media facade sublimating the built. The glass facade contrasts sharply with the monochromatic Haussmannian monotony of Boulevard Raspail. Like an apparition, there emerges an immense volume of trees in a calculated wilderness, which Jean Nouvel would later also create for the entrance of the Musée du Quai Branly – Jacques Chirac (2006). It is only after the visitor passes the glass gates that the tangible yet blurred and evanescent boundaries at street level reveal the rest of the building. For the exhibition galleries on the ground level, Jean Nouvel designed a sliding glass structure, walls as immense screens, allowing the building to dematerialize entirely on two stories. Transparency incorporates the surrounding environment as an integral feature of the created space.

16 — Much has been written about the notion of screen and virtuality. Relevant to Nouvel see Paul Virilio, *The Aesthetics of Disappearance* (New York: Semiotext(e), 1991). Regarding the "media" quality of transparent façades and their impact on the image of the city, see also Virilio's "The Overexposed City," in *The Paul Virilio Reader*, ed. Steve Redhead (New York: Columbia University Press, 2004), pp. 83–99. For an interpretation of transparency and virtuality see also Giuliana Bruno, *Surface: Matters of Aesthetics, Materiality and Media* (Chicago: University of Chicago Press, 2014) and Olivier Boissière, "The elusive screen of reality," in *Jean Nouvel* (Paris: Terrail, 2001), pp. 127–139.

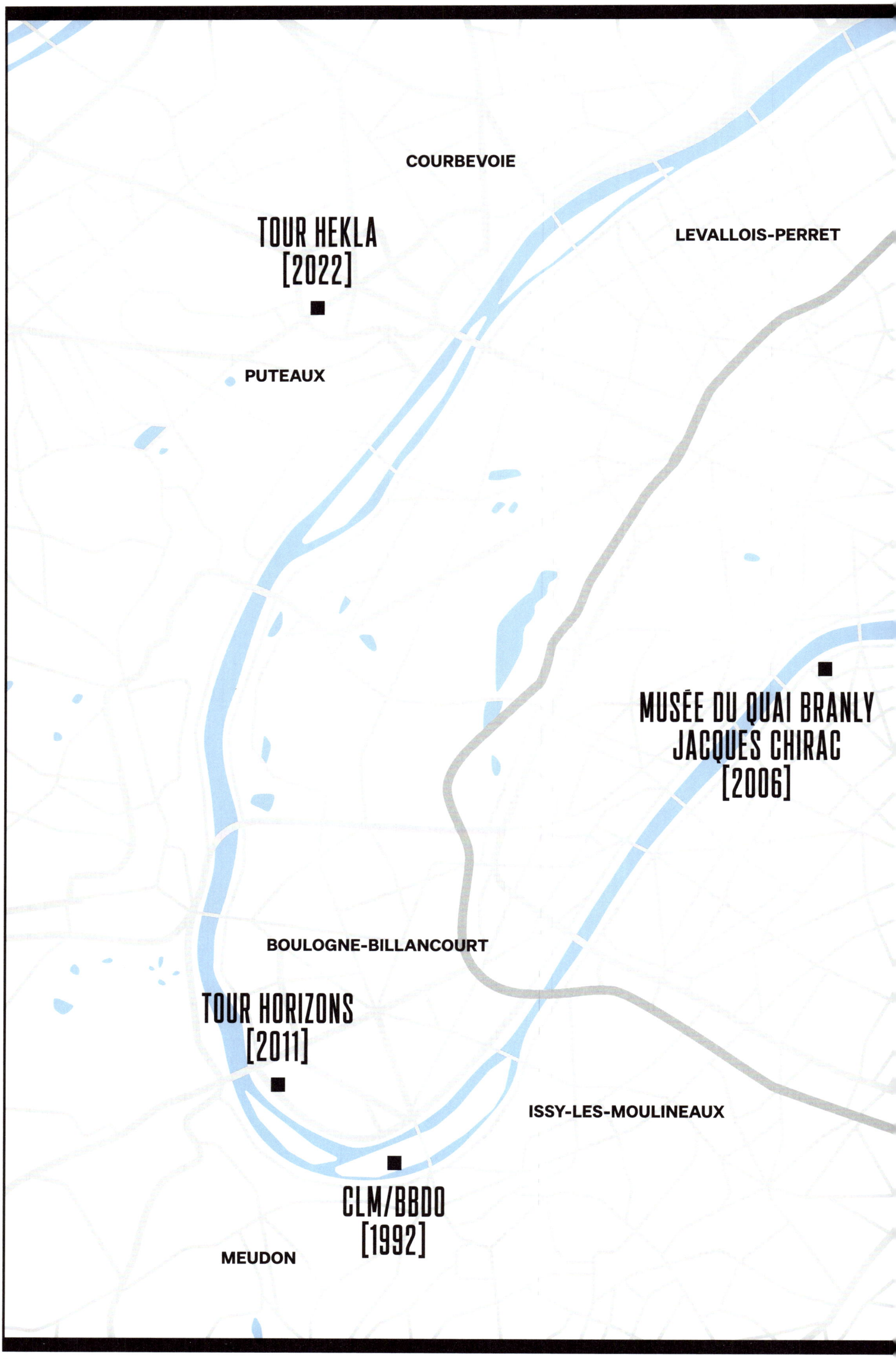

Jean Nouvel's buildings in Paris and surrounding area

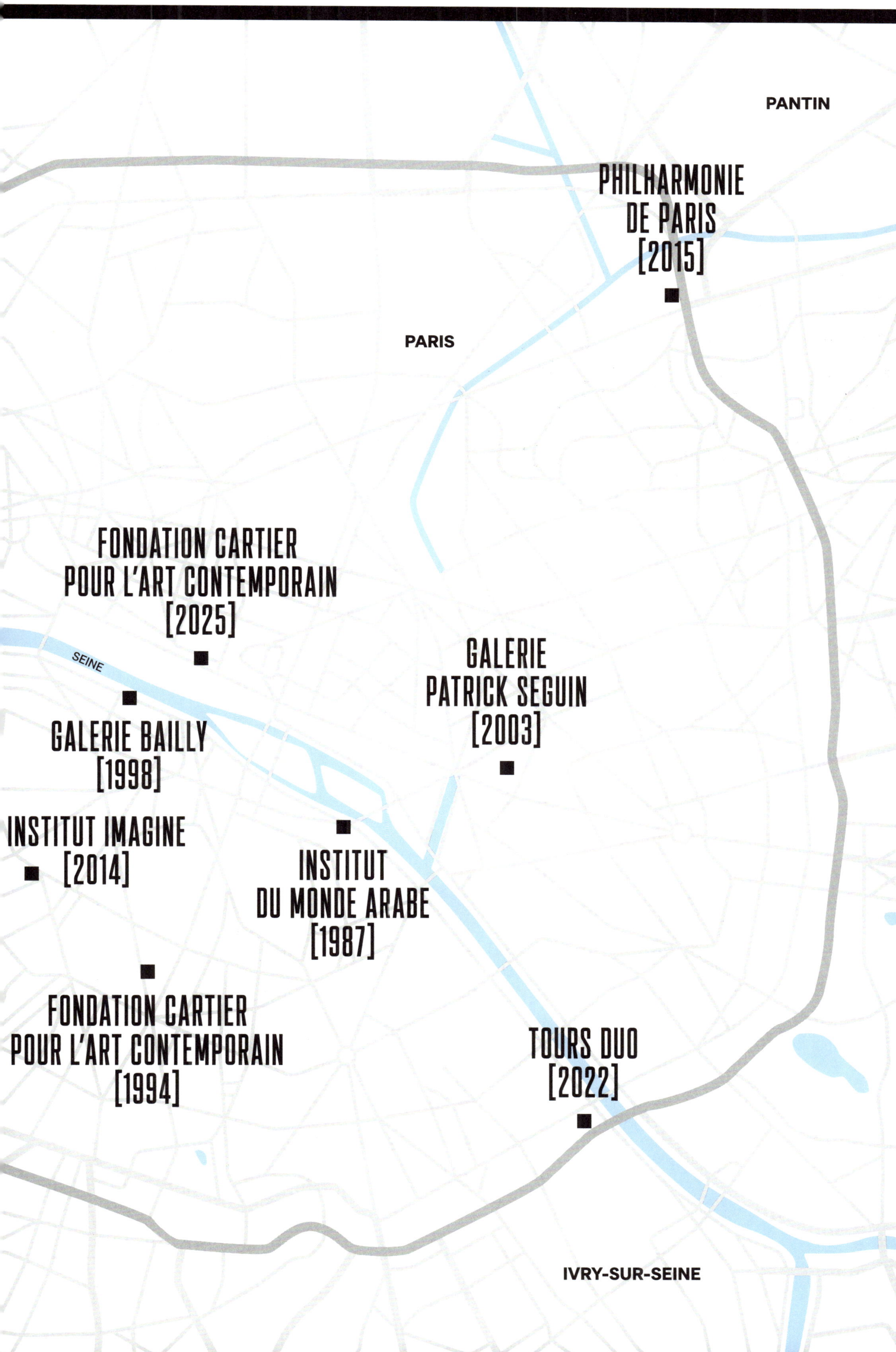
PANTIN
PHILHARMONIE DE PARIS [2015]
PARIS
FONDATION CARTIER POUR L'ART CONTEMPORAIN [2025]
SEINE
GALERIE PATRICK SEGUIN [2003]
GALERIE BAILLY [1998]
INSTITUT IMAGINE [2014]
INSTITUT DU MONDE ARABE [1987]
FONDATION CARTIER POUR L'ART CONTEMPORAIN [1994]
TOURS DUO [2022]
IVRY-SUR-SEINE

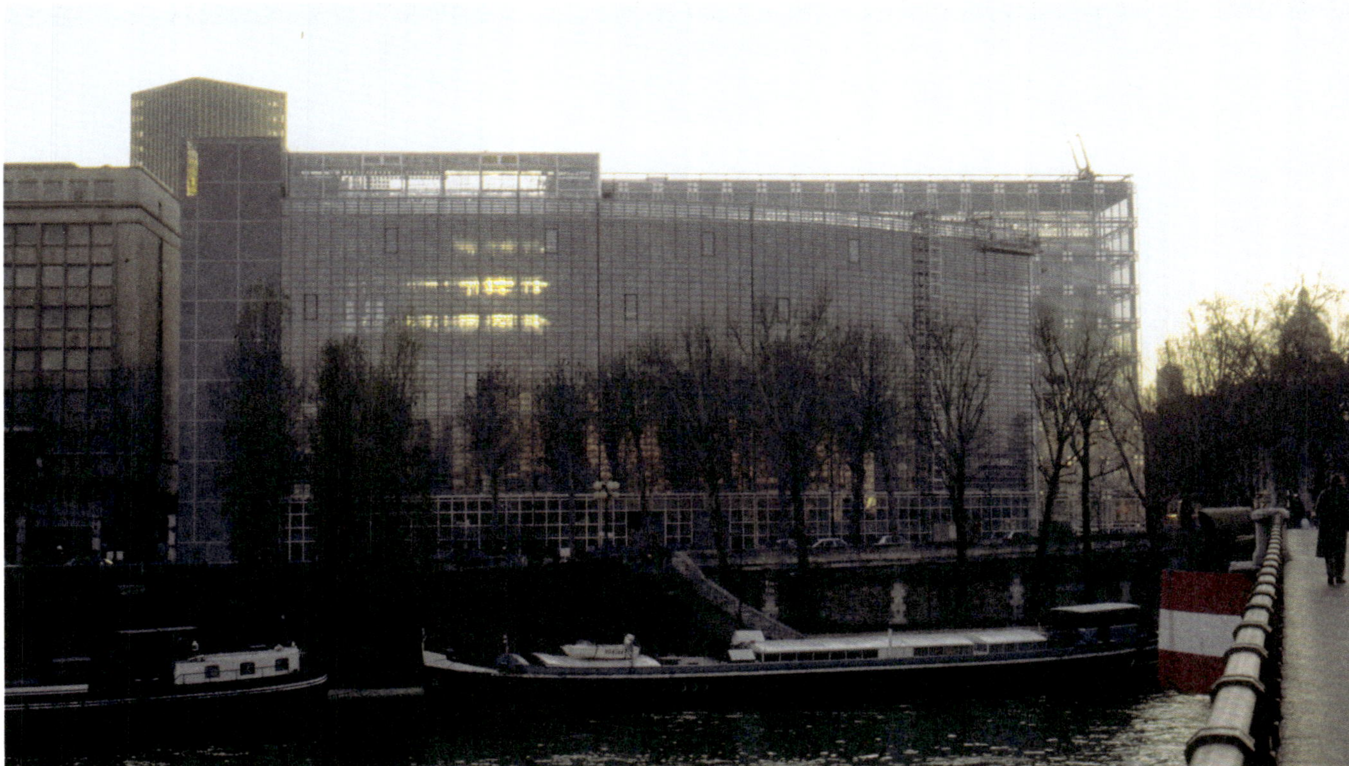

The Institut du Monde Arabe seen from the Pont de Sully, Paris, 1987

JEAN NOUVEL SEEKS TO PROLONG THE TRACES OF FORMER HISTORIES, ADD ON TO AN "UNFINISHED PARIS," ONE THAT HAS WRONGLY BEEN THOUGHT OF AS FINISHED.

Mashrabiya of the Institut du Monde Arabe, Paris, 1987

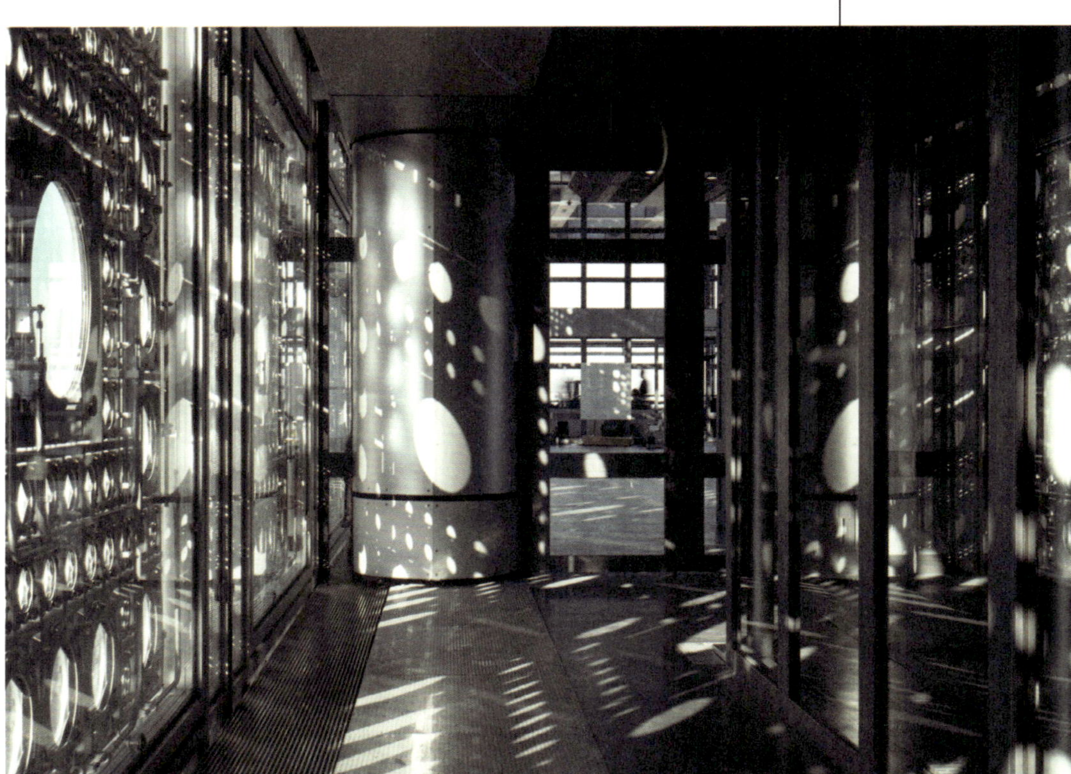

Building upon a Parisian Modernity: The Fondation Cartier pour l'art contemporain, Place du Palais-Royal

For Jean Nouvel, architecture must rely on the existing to build its future. In his Parisian projects, his relationship to the city appears most vividly, both in opposition to the avant-gardes of the previous generations and in contrast with his contemporaries.[17] This he made evident with his first project to garner international attention, the Institut du Monde Arabe in 1987, whose layout was meant as a physical continuity with the Seine itself. An extension of the oldest, most structural condition of the city, the Seine riverbanks, received a novel formal expression, an abstract reference to Arab civilization on the facade facing Haussmann's city.

With this project, Jean Nouvel declared early on in his career that he had something different in mind than Archigram (a group of avant-garde British architects of the 1960s and 1970s), whose images and aesthetics for new cities privileged a kinetic mechanism, a temporary accumulation of new forms. While architectural critic and writer Reyner Banham and Archigram saw the urban plan as archaic and static, hindering innovation,[18] Jean Nouvel considered it essential to acknowledge the past's modern ambitions. The Archigram philosophy conceived the city as a flux of merchandise, rendering urban planning impossible, even immoral: the city became an architectural object of speculation.

Another attitude towards the city, contemporary with Nouvel's and signaled by architect Rem Koolhaas, was a historical abandonment of the "West." For Koolhaas, the city had left Europe and moved on to new geographies. In *Singapore Songlines*, Koolhaas speaks of the "decline of Western influence on the making of the city" as a phenomenon contemporary with the migration of the modern urban project to other continents, especially Asia: "Europe and the United States were writing original manifestos about the modern city even as their urban populations doubled between 1900 and 1980. The rapid growth of the modern African and Asian city—three times faster than in the West—began at the very moment when 'we' stopped thinking about it."[19] Nouvel had a different conception: his dream of an architecture for the second part of the twentieth century recognized that it should

17 — See Jean Nouvel, "L'avenir de l'architecture n'est plus architectural," in *Les Cahiers de la recherche architecturale*, no. 6–7: *Architecture 1980 : doctrines & incertitudes*, Paris, October 1980, pp. 162–164.

18 — See Reyner Banham, Paul Barker, Peter Hall, and Cedric Price, "Non plan: an Experiment in Freedom," in *New Society* no. 338, March 20, 1969, pp. 435–444.

19 — Rem Koolhaas, "Singapore Songlines: Portrait of a Potemkin Metropolis... or Thirty Years of Tabula Rasa," in Rem Koolhaas and Bruce Mau, *S, M, L, XL* (New York: The Monacelli Press, 1995).

Institut du Monde Arabe, Paris, 1987

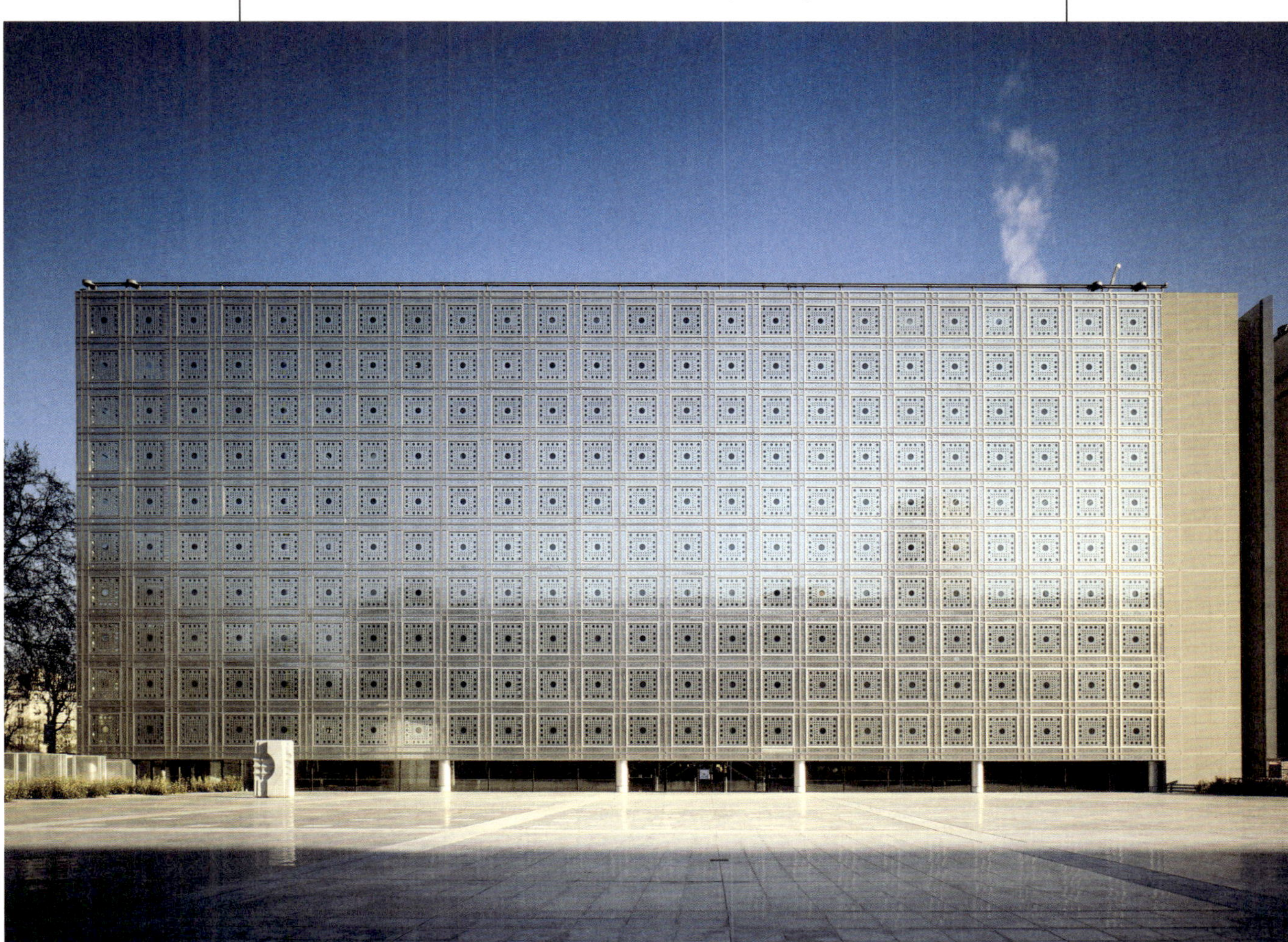

be different from the first, that it should no longer rely only on its own know-how or depend on Vitruvius's proportions to translate a living civilization.[20] Architecture should be the culture of its time, but not according to the British avant-garde's translation of contemporaneity, whose main precepts were mobility, instantaneity, and indeterminacy; Jean Nouvel seeks to prolong the traces of former histories, add on to an "unfinished Paris," one that has wrongly been thought of as finished.[21] Indeed, Jean Nouvel refuses both hypotheses which have dominated architectural discourse in the late 20th and early 21st centuries. More importantly, he refuses to abandon the city as past, as elsewhere. He insists on the role of architecture for its future:

20 — See Jean Nouvel, *Ce qui est là n'est pas ailleurs*, op. cit., p. 18.

21 — See Jean Nouvel, "L'Architecture et le monde virtuel," communication colloquium, May 20–21, 1995, Couvent de La Tourette, L'Arbresle (Rhone). Transcribed by Étienne Régent in Chantal Béret (ed.), *Jean Nouvel* (Paris: Centre Georges Pompidou, 2001), unpaged.

> Historical Paris is not finished, it is a living city...
> which must always strive asymptotically towards its apogee.
> Its heritage [...] must always be in tension with visible
> modernity, amusements, the fun of living.
> The most mythic neighborhoods and views must explore
> the gardens and roofs of Paris, the *passages*, and above
> all the botched-together neighborhoods of these last few
> decades must achieve a status equal with that of the most
> central...[22]

22 — *"Paris historique n'est pas achevé, c'est une ville en pleine forme... qui doit toujours tendre asymptomatiquement vers son apogée. Son patrimoine [...] doit toujours être en tension avec la modernité visible, les plaisirs, les bonheurs de vivre. Les quartiers et les vues les plus mythiques doivent explorer les jardins, les toits de Paris, les passages, et surtout les quartiers mal ficelés ces dernières décennies doivent conquérir un statut égal aux quartiers les plus centraux..."* Jean Nouvel quoted in Jean Nouvel, Jean-Marie Duthilleul, and Michel Cantal-Dupart, *Neuf Mesures de Transformation de la Métropole Parisienne, Évolution des Mobilités dans le Métropole Parisienne*, AJN, 2009, p. 9. [Quotation translated by Phoebe Green]

For the new exhibition spaces of the Fondation Cartier, Nouvel's stance towards the city is pushed towards the extreme in the hyper-historical center of Paris; the distinction between the city and the architectural object has radically disappeared. The building, which first housed the Grand Hôtel du Louvre (1855–1887) is historically an urban fragment which emerged on the city's map with the extension of the Rue de Rivoli during the first phase of Haussmann's works. Jean Nouvel's architectural gesture restores the building to the city—to the block of marble out of which it was carved—revealing the symbol of modernity it represents, all the while pushing it into possible futures.[23] Preservation is too pessimistic a view of time: Jean Nouvel's project for the new venue of the Fondation Cartier, inaugurated in 2025, shows that time's passage, in the heart of Paris, does not incur the dissolution of the city, but conversely, with the architectural mutation he proposes, captures its most contemporary expression. Indeed, in the Fondation Cartier Place du Palais-Royal there is no divide between construction and preservation, city and architecture, past and future. The building is at once an extension of the urban landscape and an image of its history. Along the Rue de Rivoli, a series of picture windows seven meters high allow passersby to look not only inside the building but also through the entire city block and see the city. From within, one looks up and beholds the facade of the Louvre. Beneath every other courtyard punctuating the building, hanging gardens offer a view of the sky amidst greenery that, referencing the Palais Royal gardens, is undeniably Parisian. The entrance, at street level, joins the address to the Place du Palais-Royal—one of Paris' oldest squares, linking the gardens to the Louvre—thus creating an absolute continuity with history, allowing it to permeate modernity's future within.[24]

23 — The Grand Hôtel du Louvre was built during the first phase of Haussmann's works which were conducted in preparation for the 1855 Paris Exposition. The succeeding arcades that repeat the rhythm of the opened-up boulevards are emblematic of the new aesthetic and architectural order of the Boulevard de l'Opéra and Rue de Rivoli.

24 — Prior to the opening of the new venue of the Fondation Cartier, the Place du Palais-Royal became emblematic of the architecture of Jean Nouvel with a mirror-clad scaffolding to mask the makeshift architecture of the construction site offices and highlight the architectural ensemble of the plaza, which is to say the State Council, the facade of the Louvre and the Hotel du Louvre (a facade symmetrical with that of the building of the Fondation Cartier).

In Abu Dhabi, the heritage of the Louvre looms, and there, Jean Nouvel built a city to house it. The edge of this city is a dome that unites different galleries, emblems of different civilizations, into one singular village. In an image of universality, it unites its different buildings, boxes or houses with a play of light that enhances a unique aesthetic experience and makes it recognizable as an urban context. Opaque materiality, as opposed to transparency—elsewhere used to inhabit history—here composes the fabric of museography to suggest different temporalities: marble, leather and granite vividly identify the experience of this "city" where time is the frontier of its different districts: Ancient Worlds, Middle Ages, Early Modern and Contemporary. In Paris, next to the Louvre, the omnipresent heritage of the city spills into the preserved shell, the heretofore anonymous Haussmannian architecture of the Grands Magasins du Louvre (1887–1974) and then the Louvre des Antiquaires (1978–2019) and fills the succession of architectural voids that await the visitor. As one enters the Fondation Cartier conceived by Jean Nouvel, the surrounding hyper-density

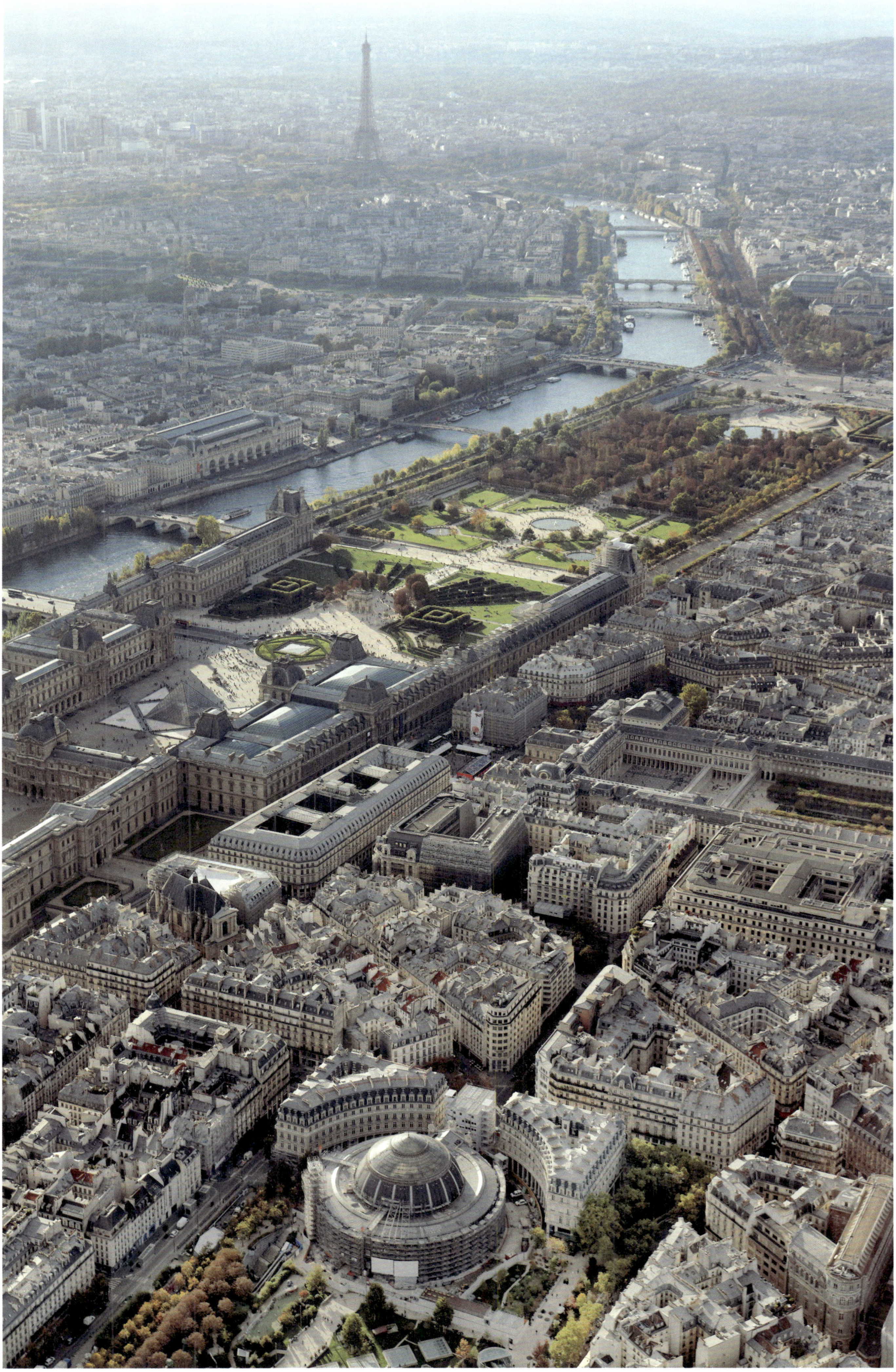

Aerial view of Paris, the Louvre district, and its surroundings, 2017

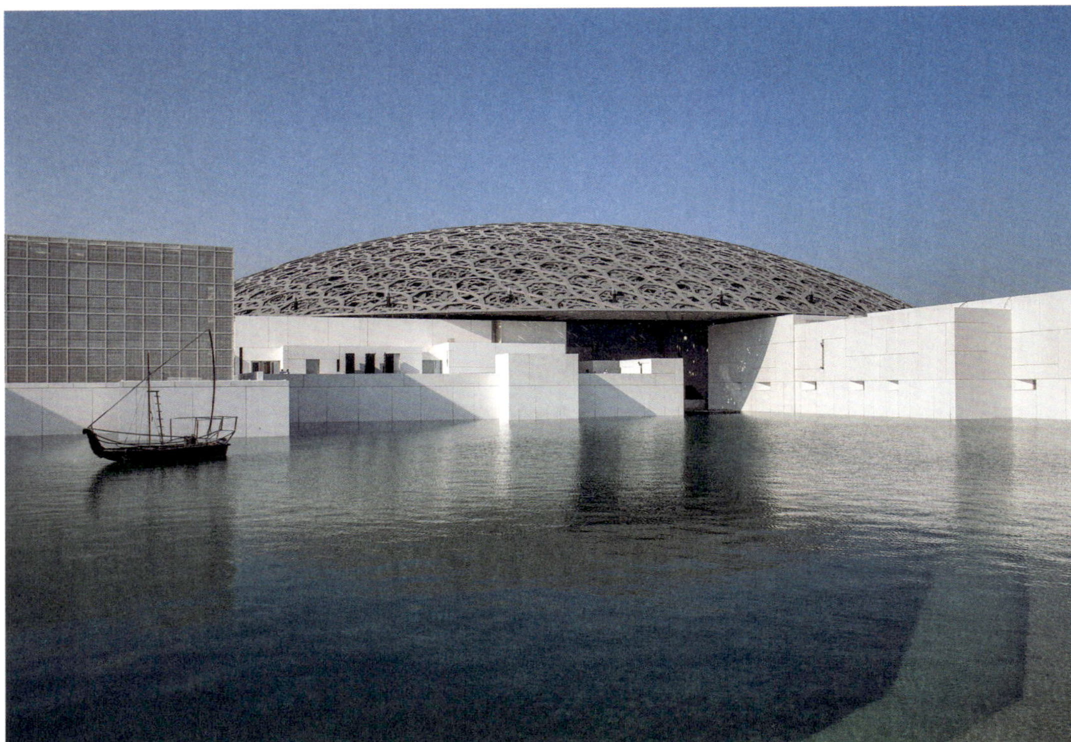

of material history is thrilling, almost a museum in itself. All at one glance: the superimposition of the historical seat of power of Napoleon's empire, later to become the embodiment of the ideals of Republican France, its first museum, temple of the fine arts, the most important public space of the city, theater of bygone revolutions. Below the visitor's feet, in subterranean Paris, lie the remains of Philippe II's medieval castle, dormant, adjacent to the metro line that pierced through the first boulevards to demarcate the advent of modern urban life.

Louvre Abu Dhabi museum, 2017

Five platforms of two hundred square meters, which can be adjusted to different heights, suggest the abstraction of any possible city to be built above the historical foundations of Lutèce. Kinetic floors and ceilings punctuated by cables and pulleys evoke the

Interior spaces of the Louvre Abu Dhabi museum, 2017

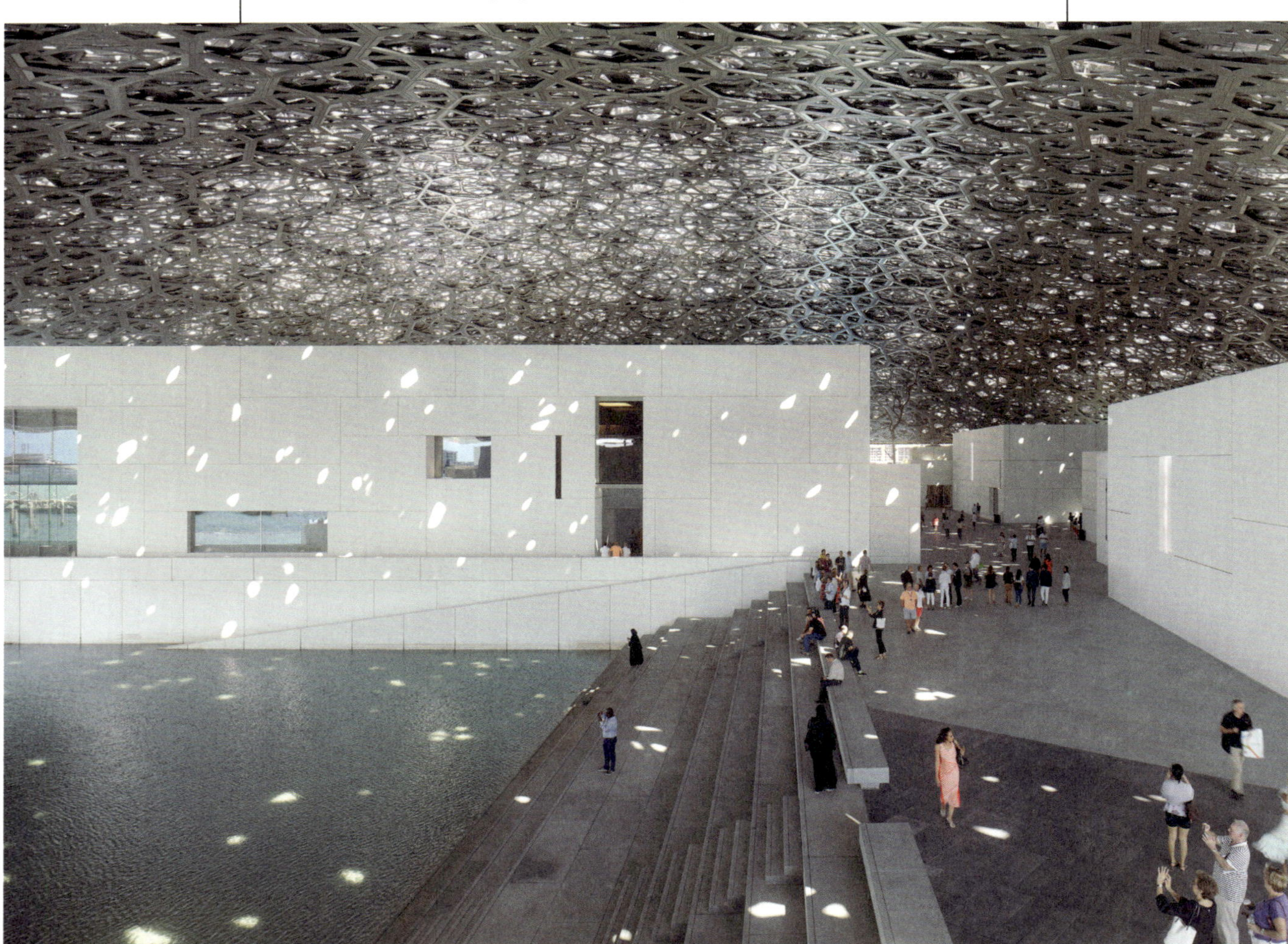

25 — For a complete history, refer to "The History of the Building," p. 182.

specter of the industrial age that saw the birth of the original architecture of the Grand Hôtel du Louvre.[25] The possibility of perpetual mutation evoked by the dormant mobility of the exhibition armature with which Jean Nouvel has equipped the Fondation Cartier building captures the ambition of a nascent modern Paris at the time of the first Universal Exposition the city hosted in 1855. The interior architectural landscape is an impressive sight: retractable ceilings temper the amount of light that punctuates the day, marking the passage of time, while movable floors are potentially interchangeable with ceilings; mechanical guardrails that operate according to the platforms' designated heights add or subtract possible interior lookouts. History has transformed the face of the Paris in which we are immersed; Jean Nouvel invites us to speculate on its possible futures. With the infinite possibility of exhibition making, the architecture inserted into an emblematic past modernity is projected into all possible formulations of the future.

At the Fondation Cartier, 2 Place du Palais-Royal, Jean Nouvel has made the city and the museum one and the same, sublimating any possible distinction between modernization and preservation. One enters to discover that the city is a collection of possibilities, and that its future hypothetical iterations might manifest on these speculative platforms.

Interior spaces of the Fondation Cartier building, 2 Place du Palais-Royal, Paris, 2025

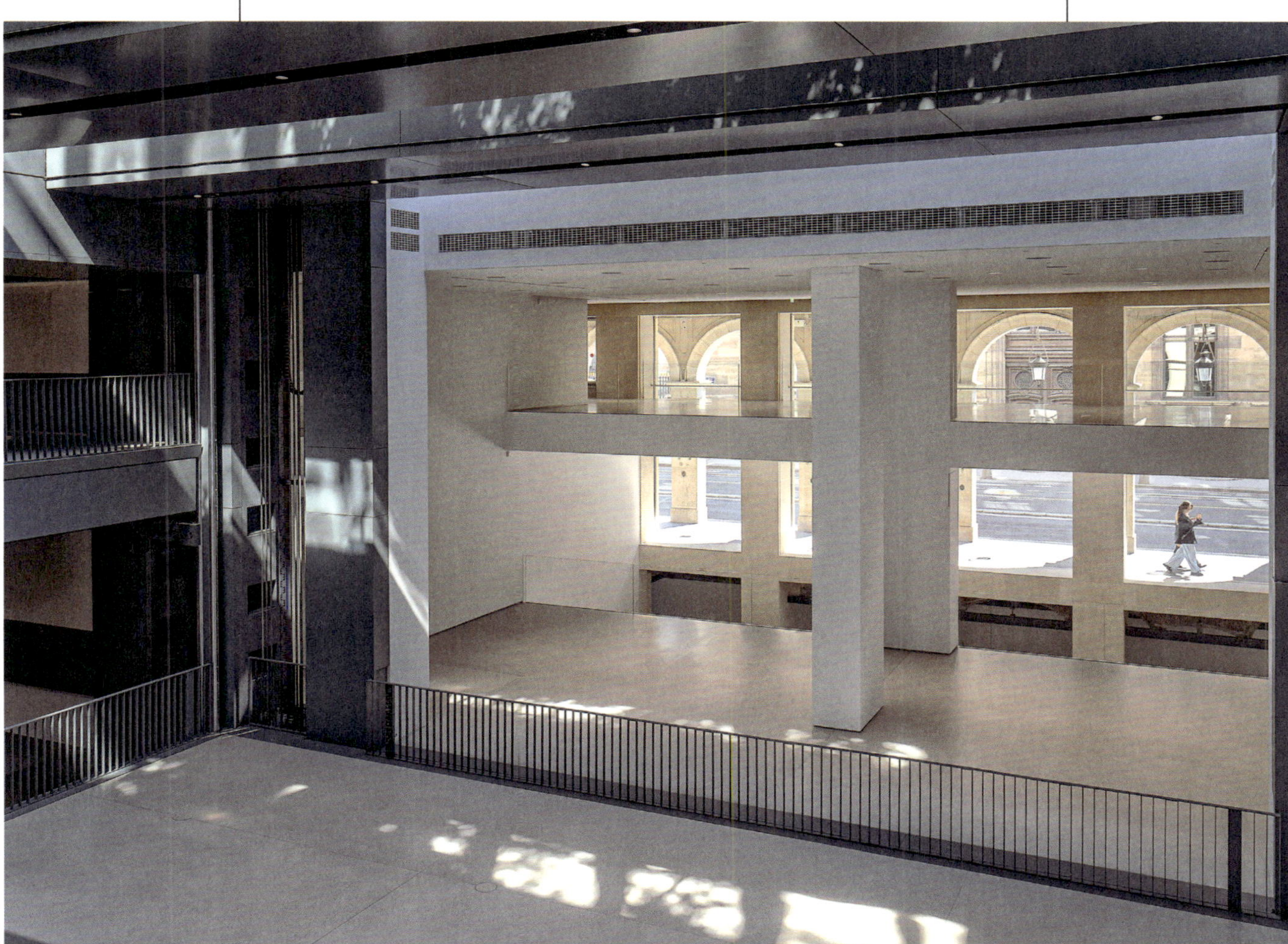

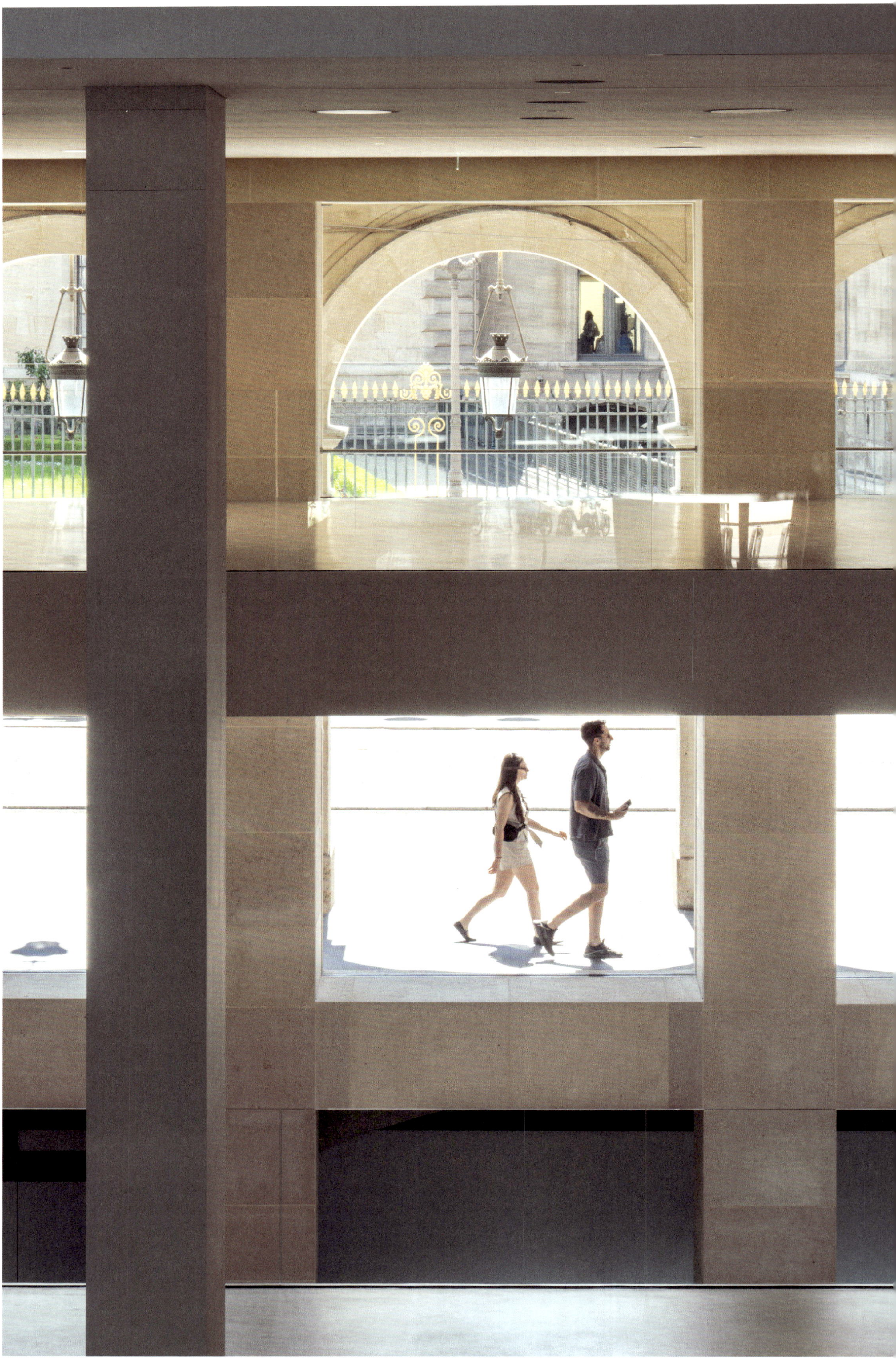

View of Rue de Rivoli from interior spaces of the Fondation Cartier

Photographs by

MARTIN ARGYROGLO

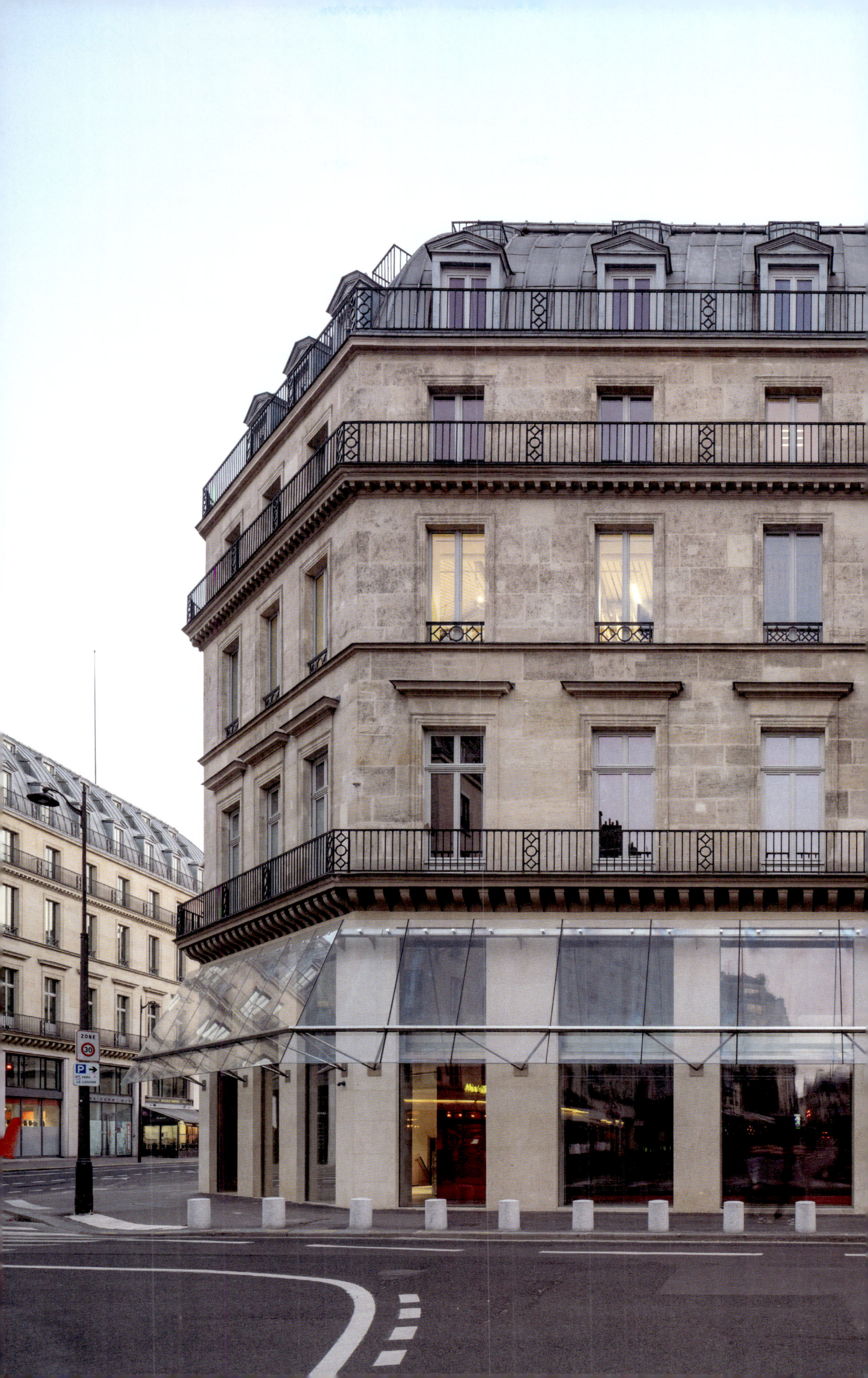
ZONE
30

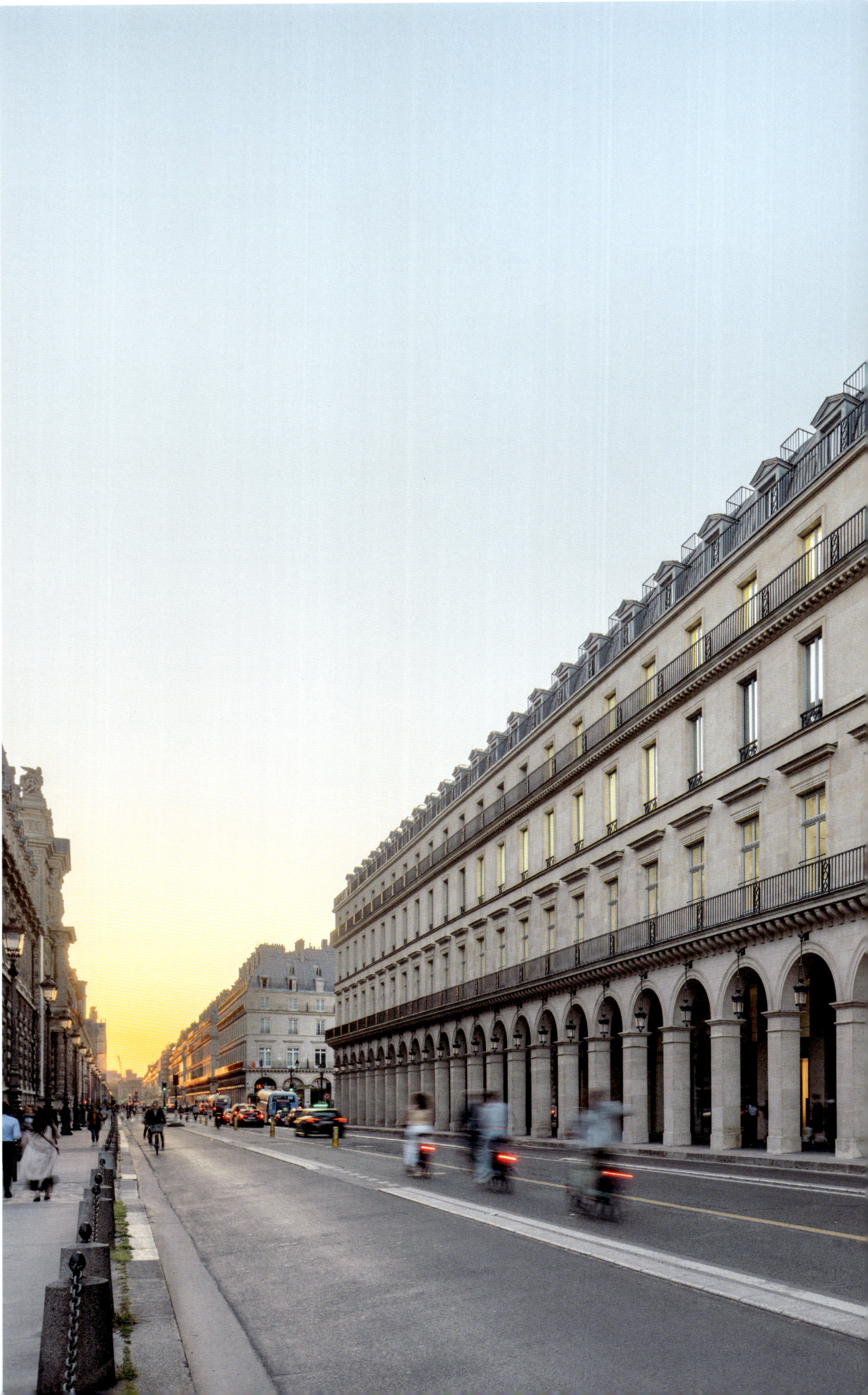

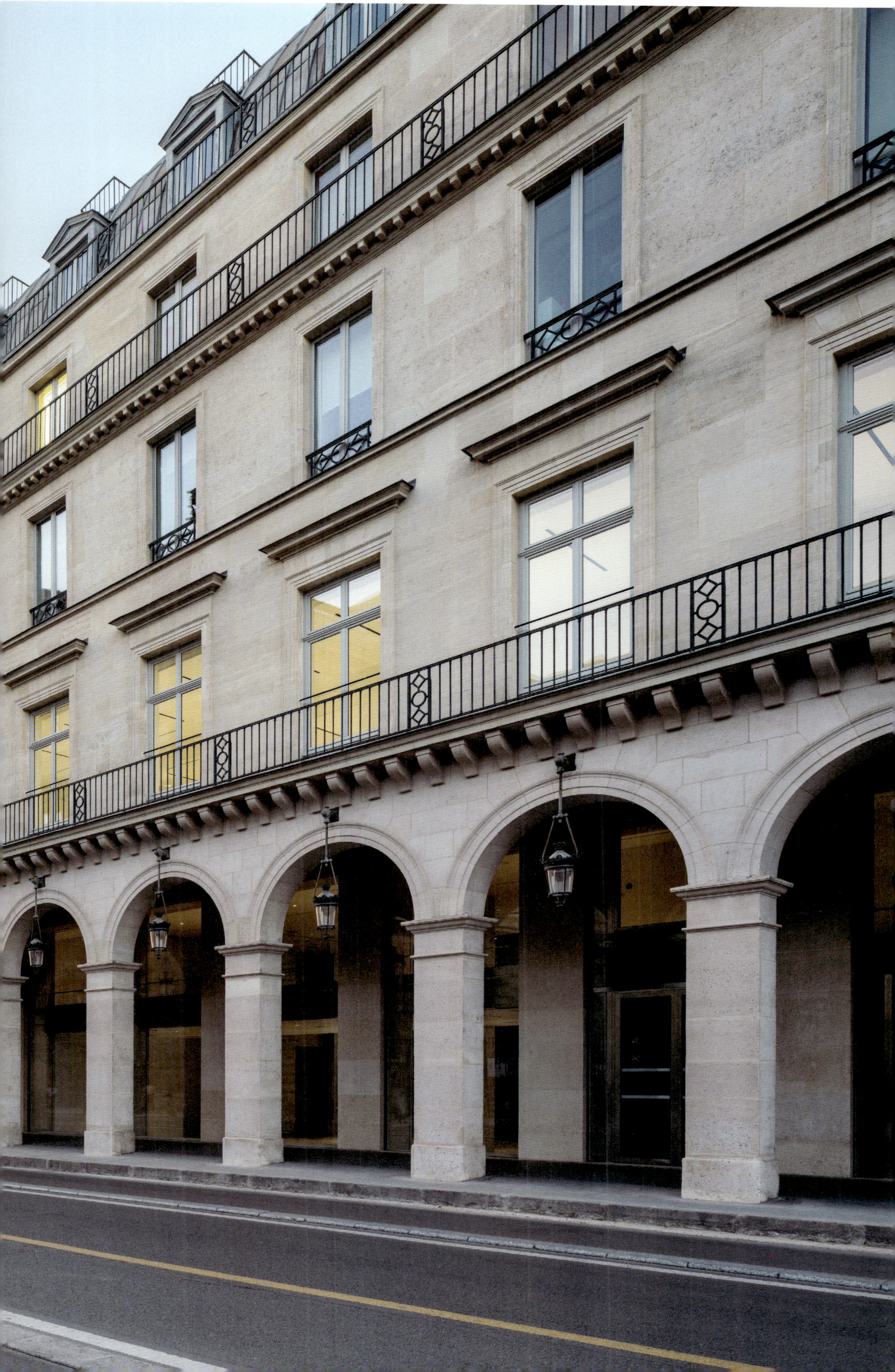

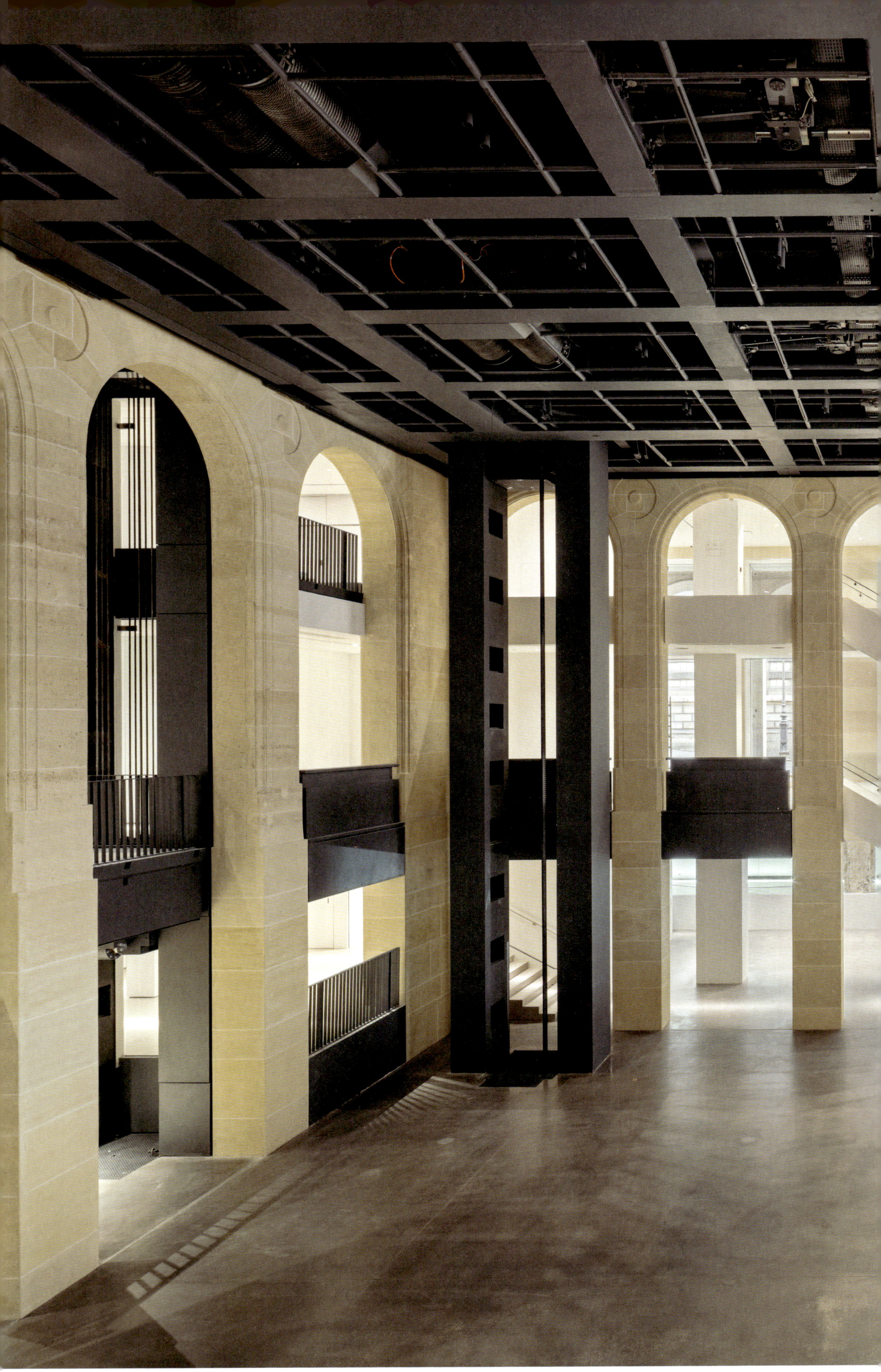

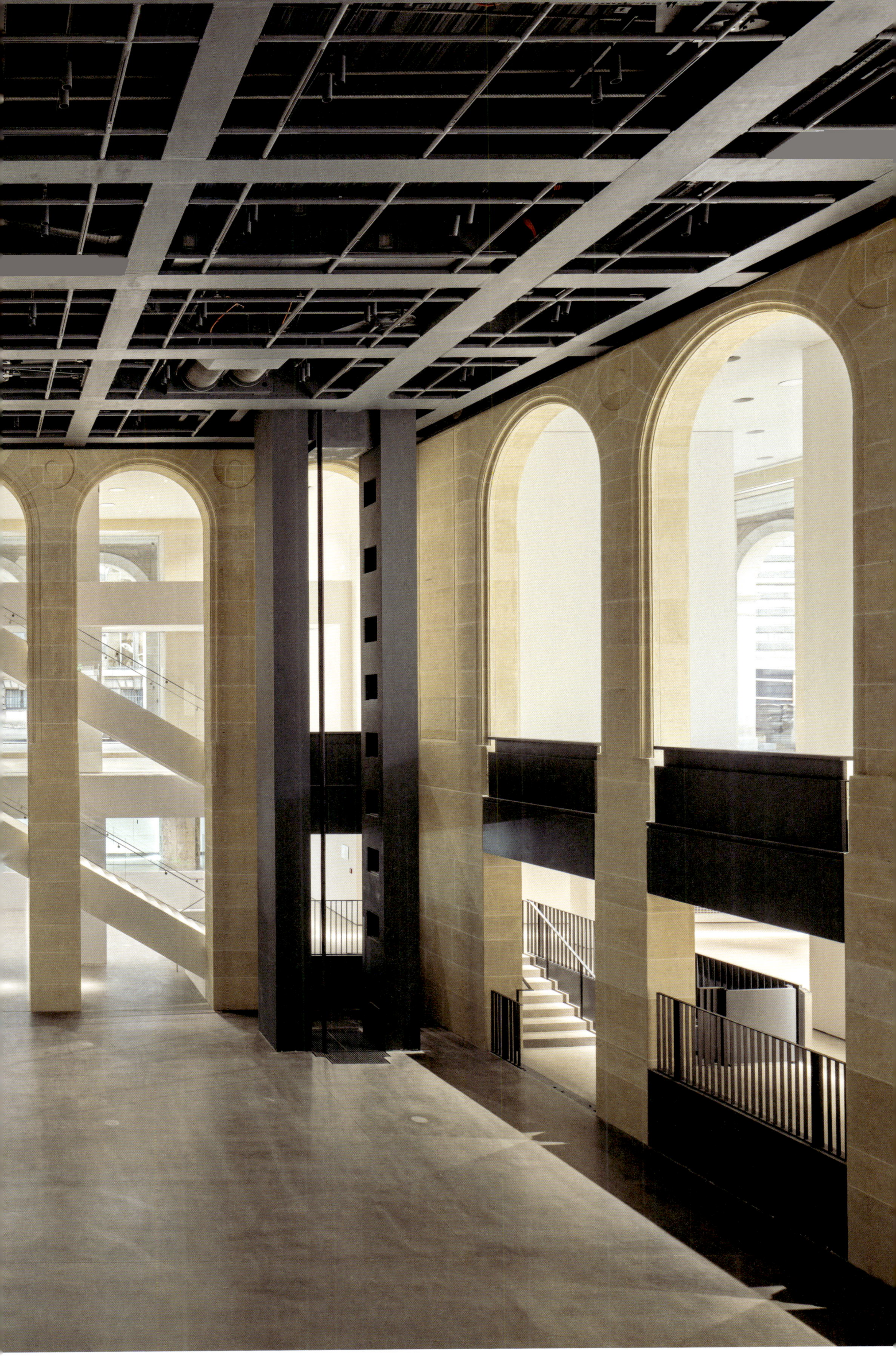

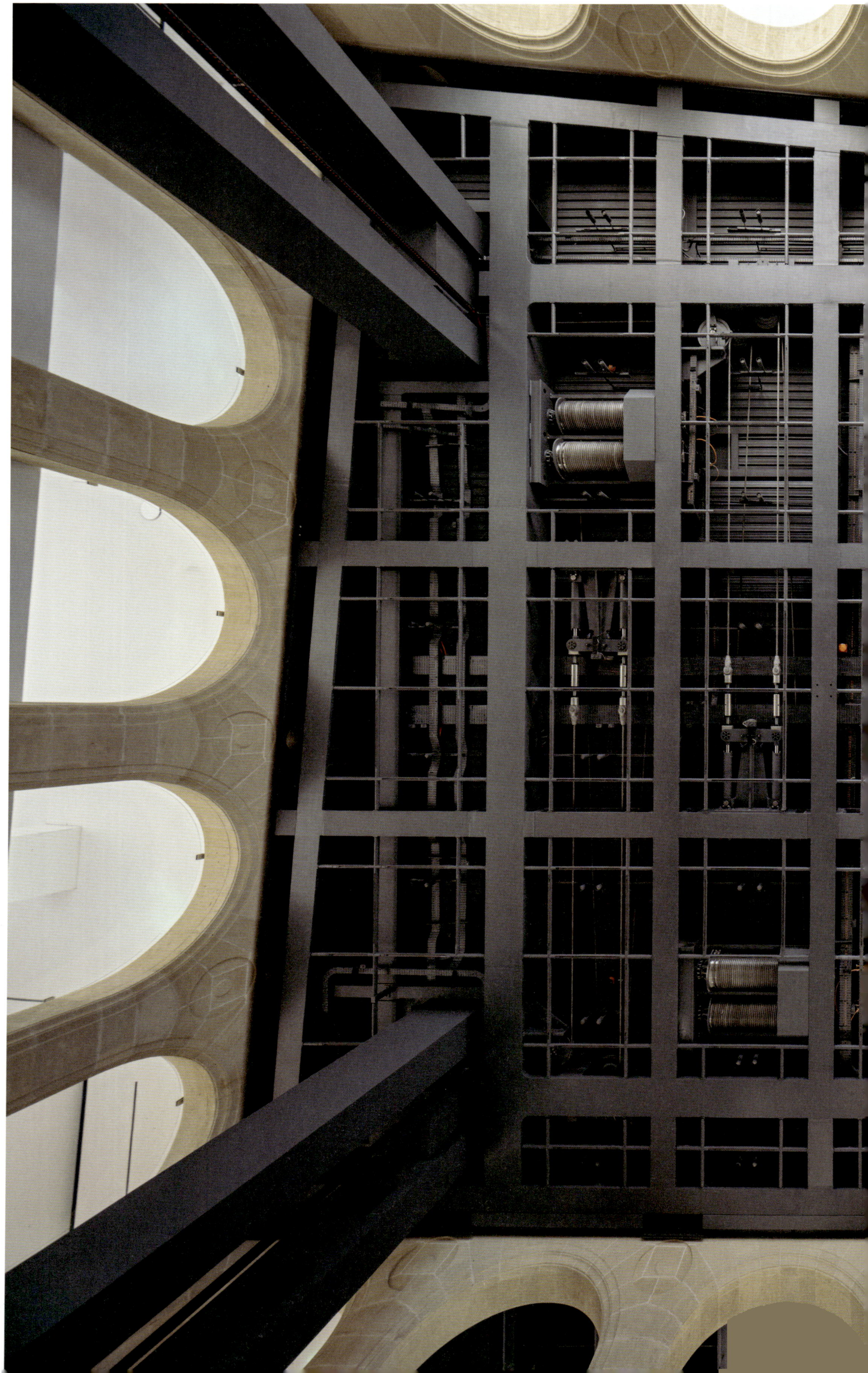

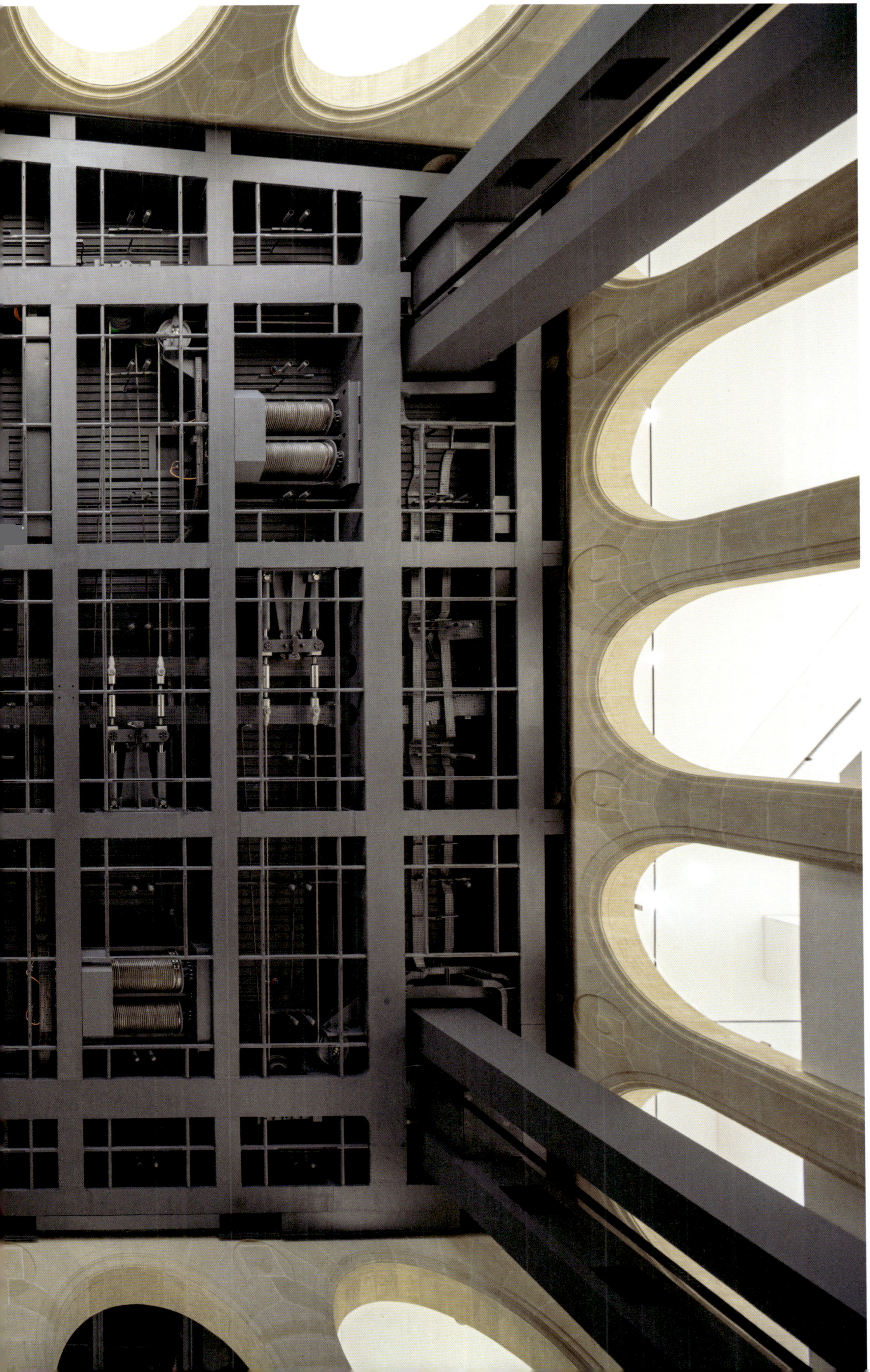

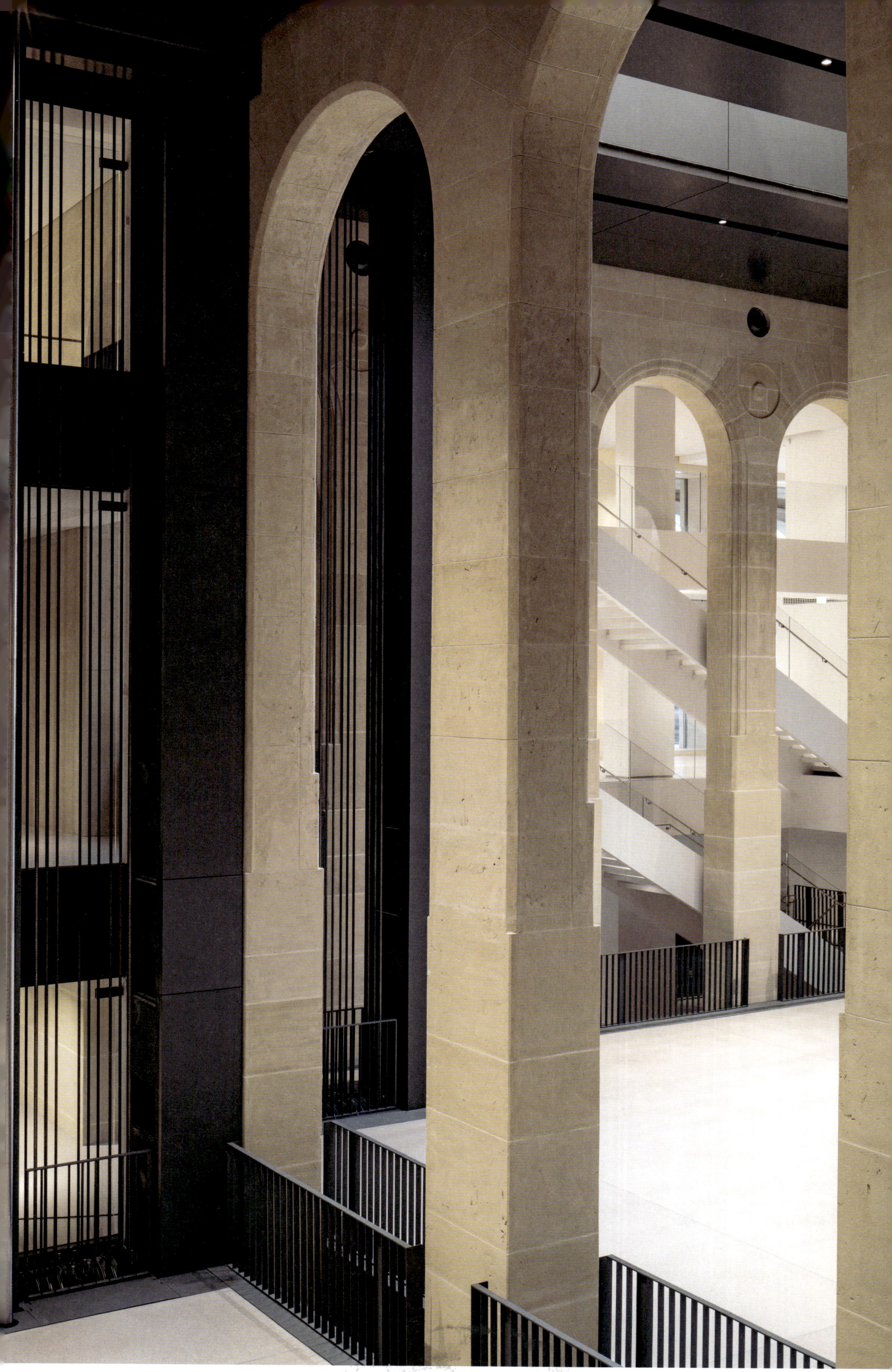

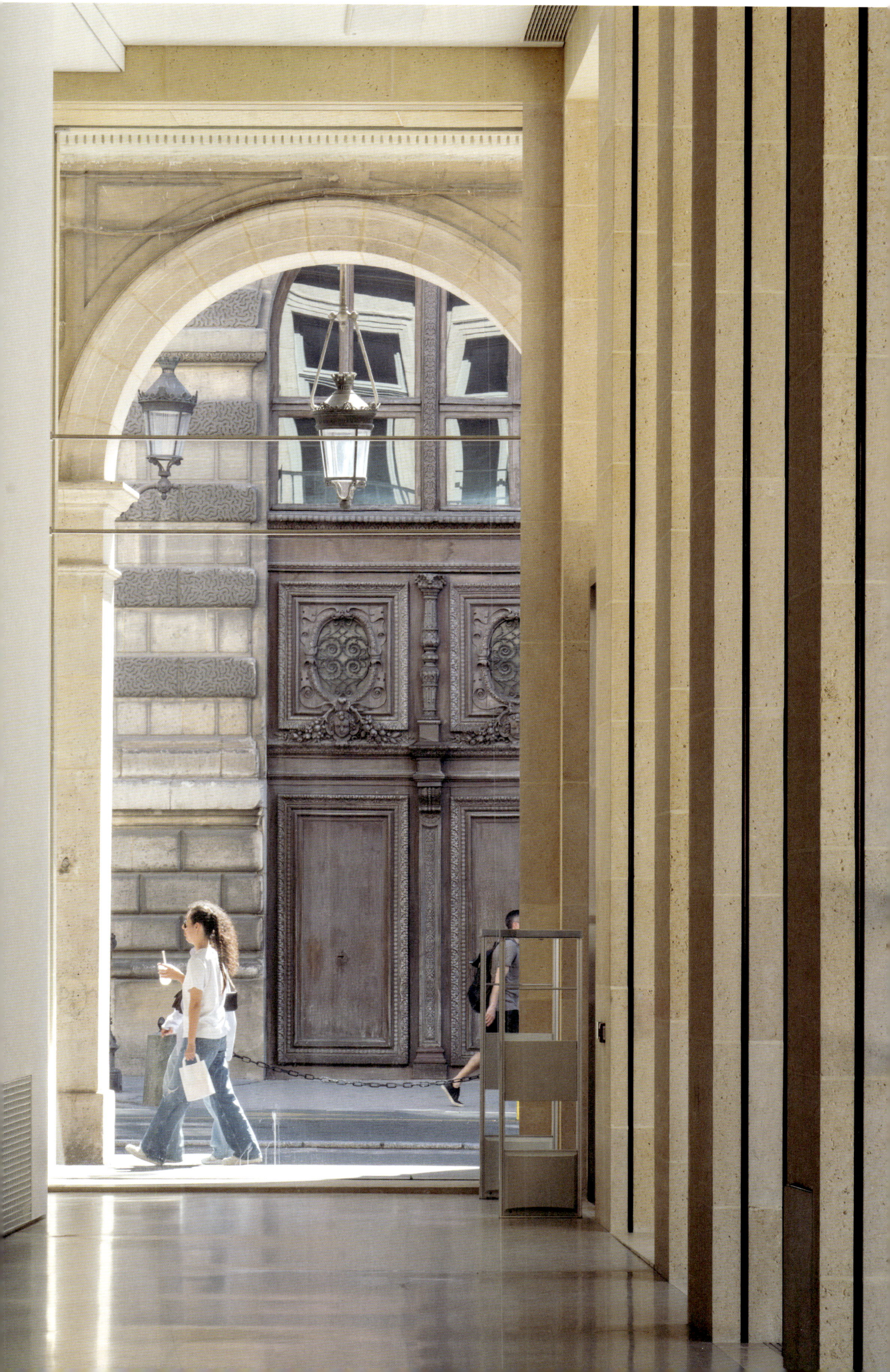

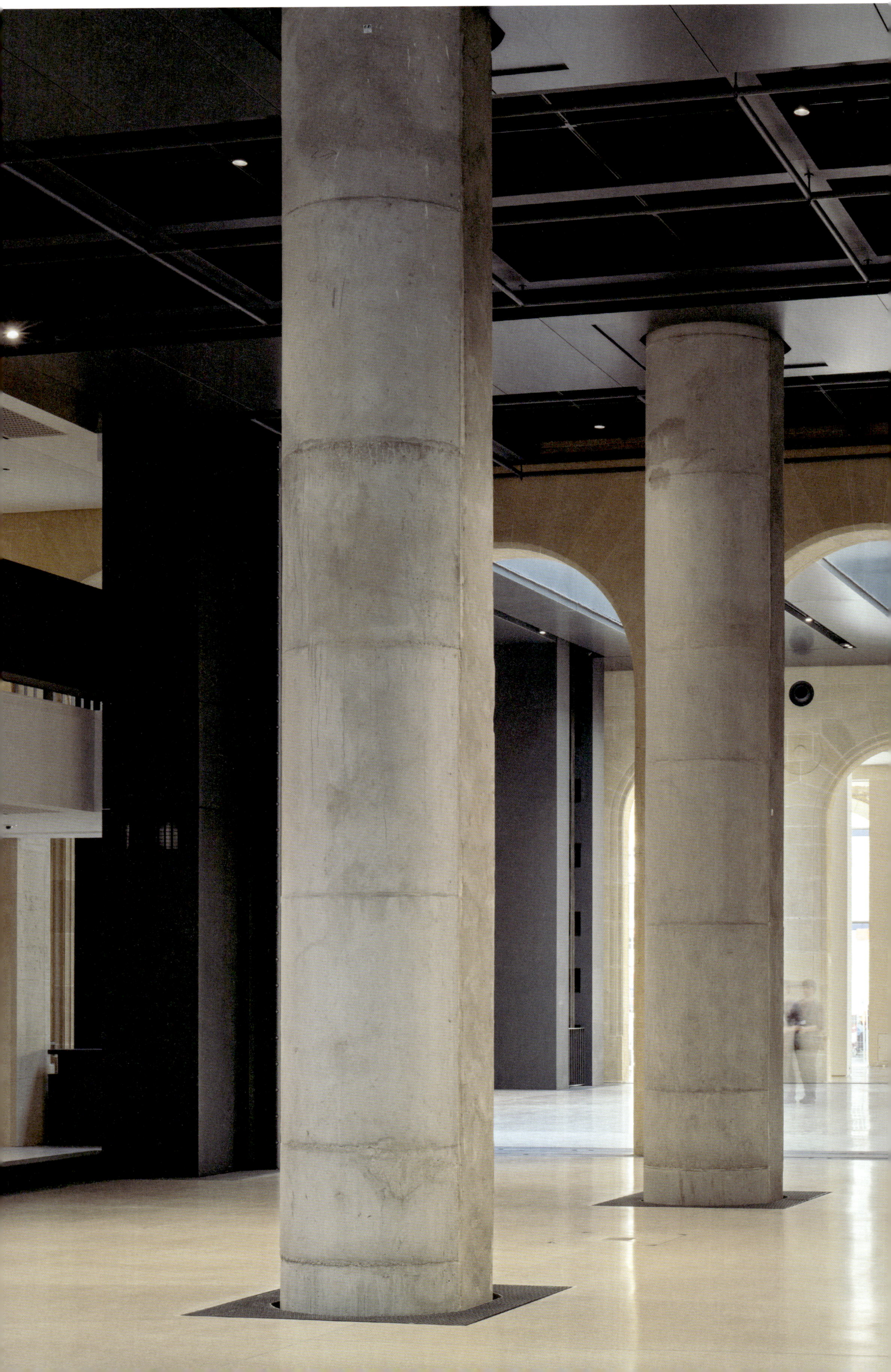

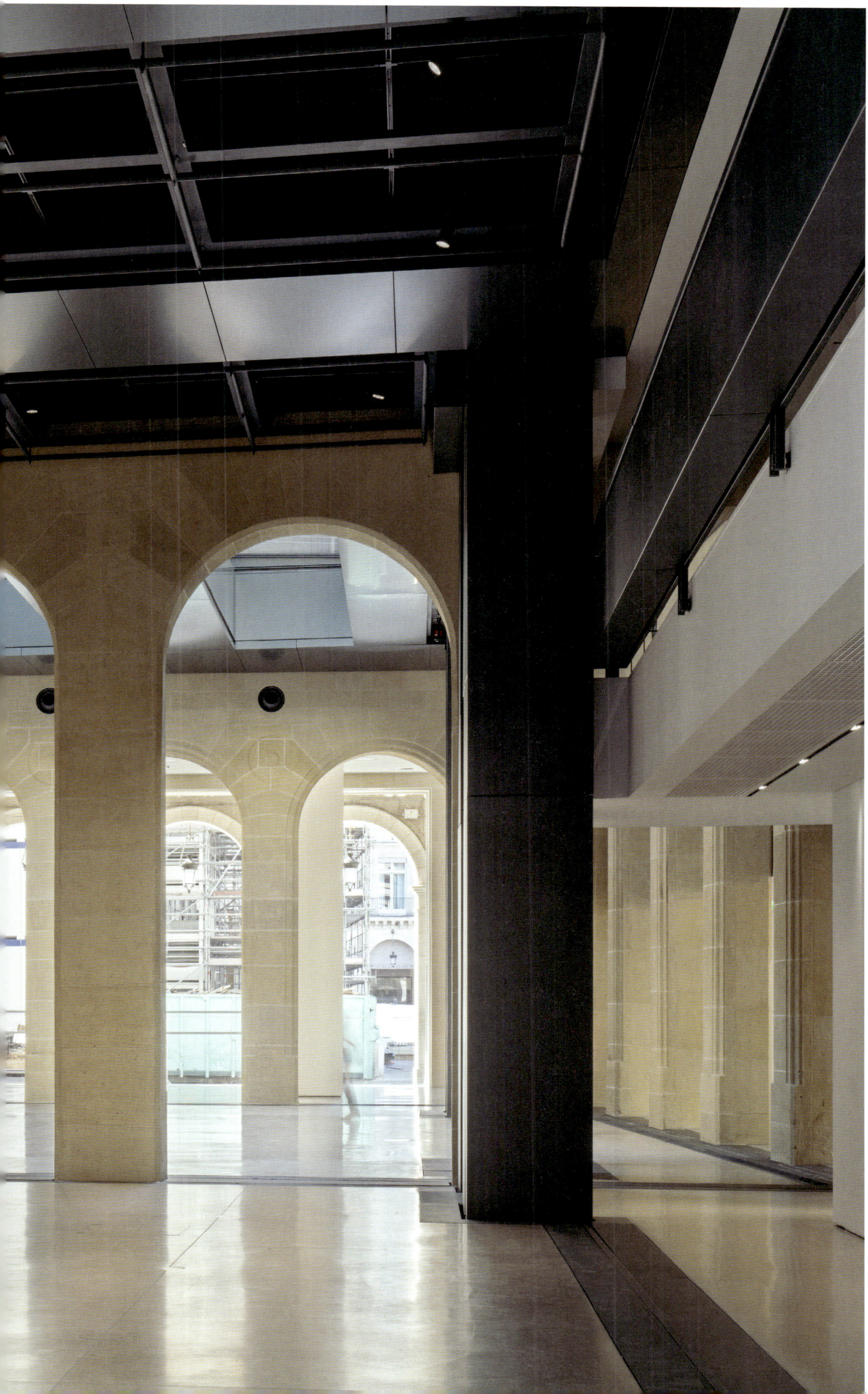

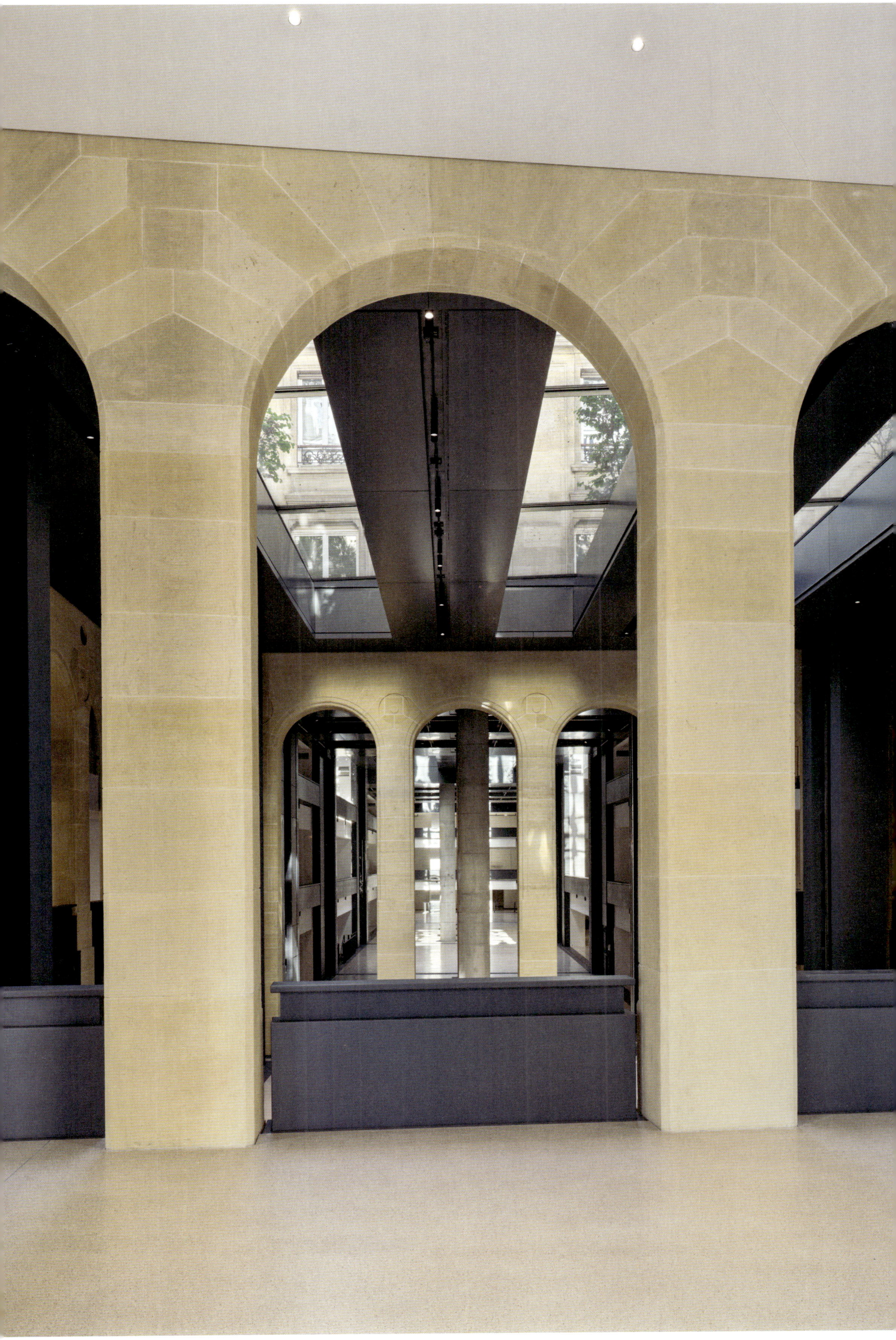

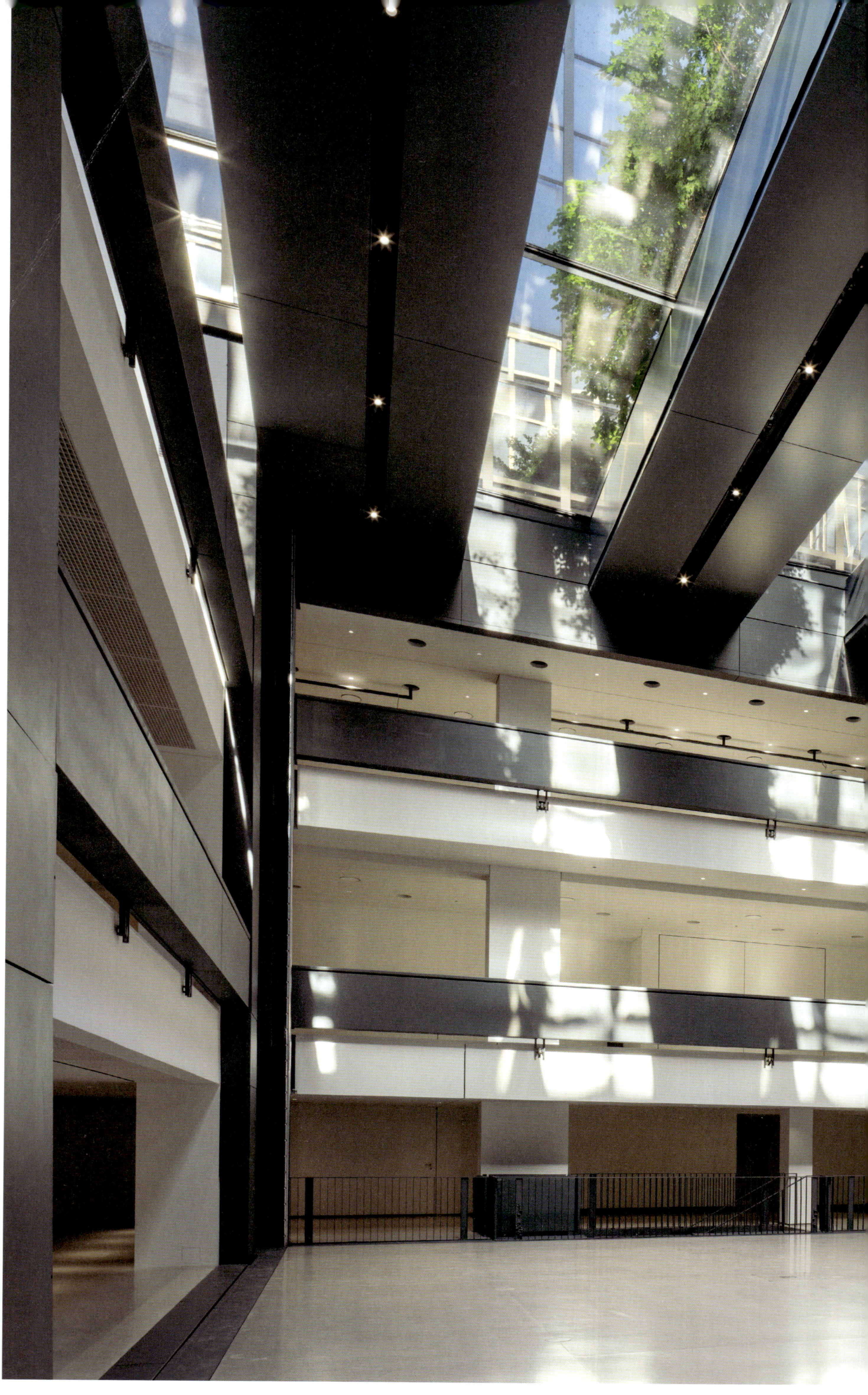

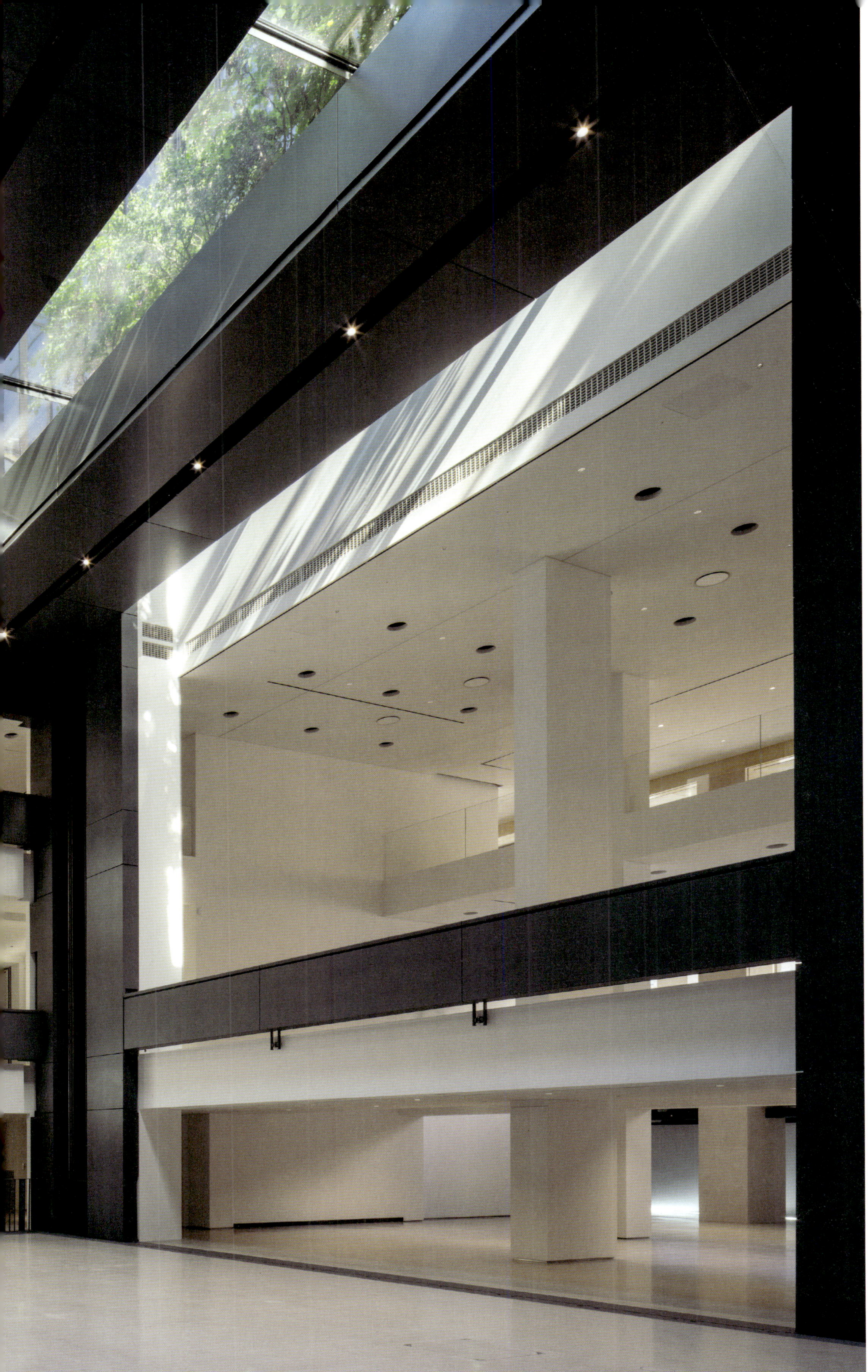

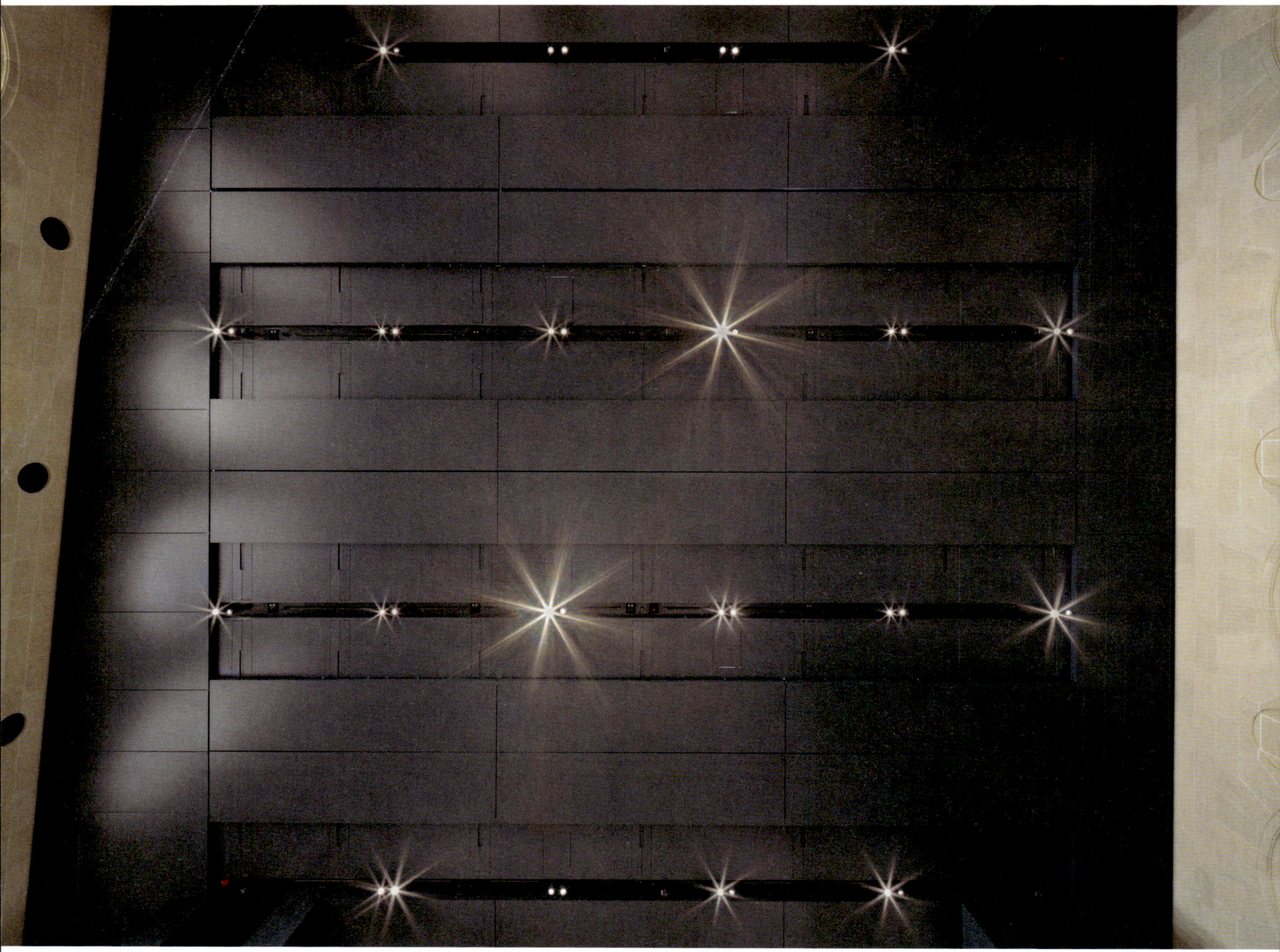

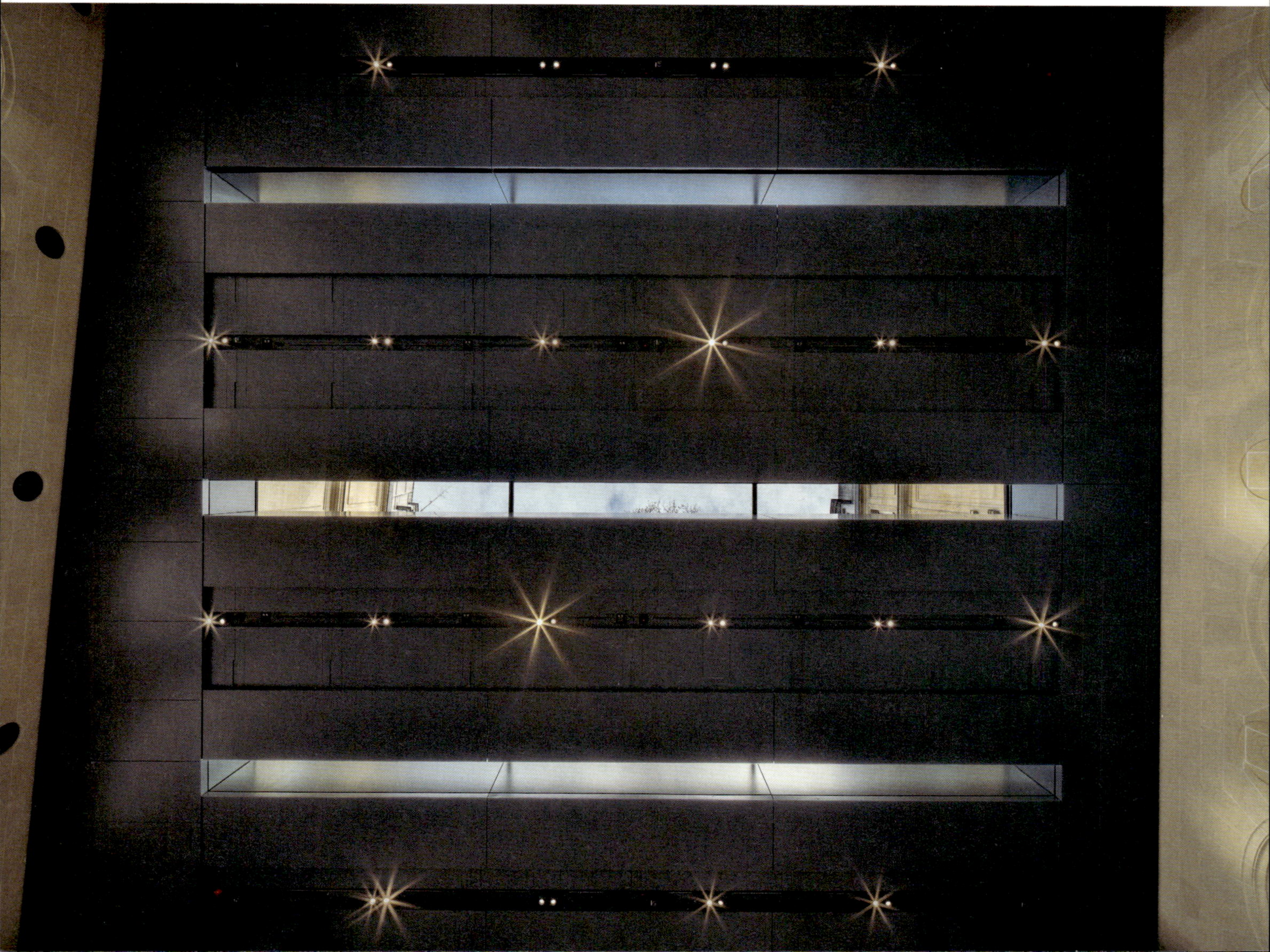

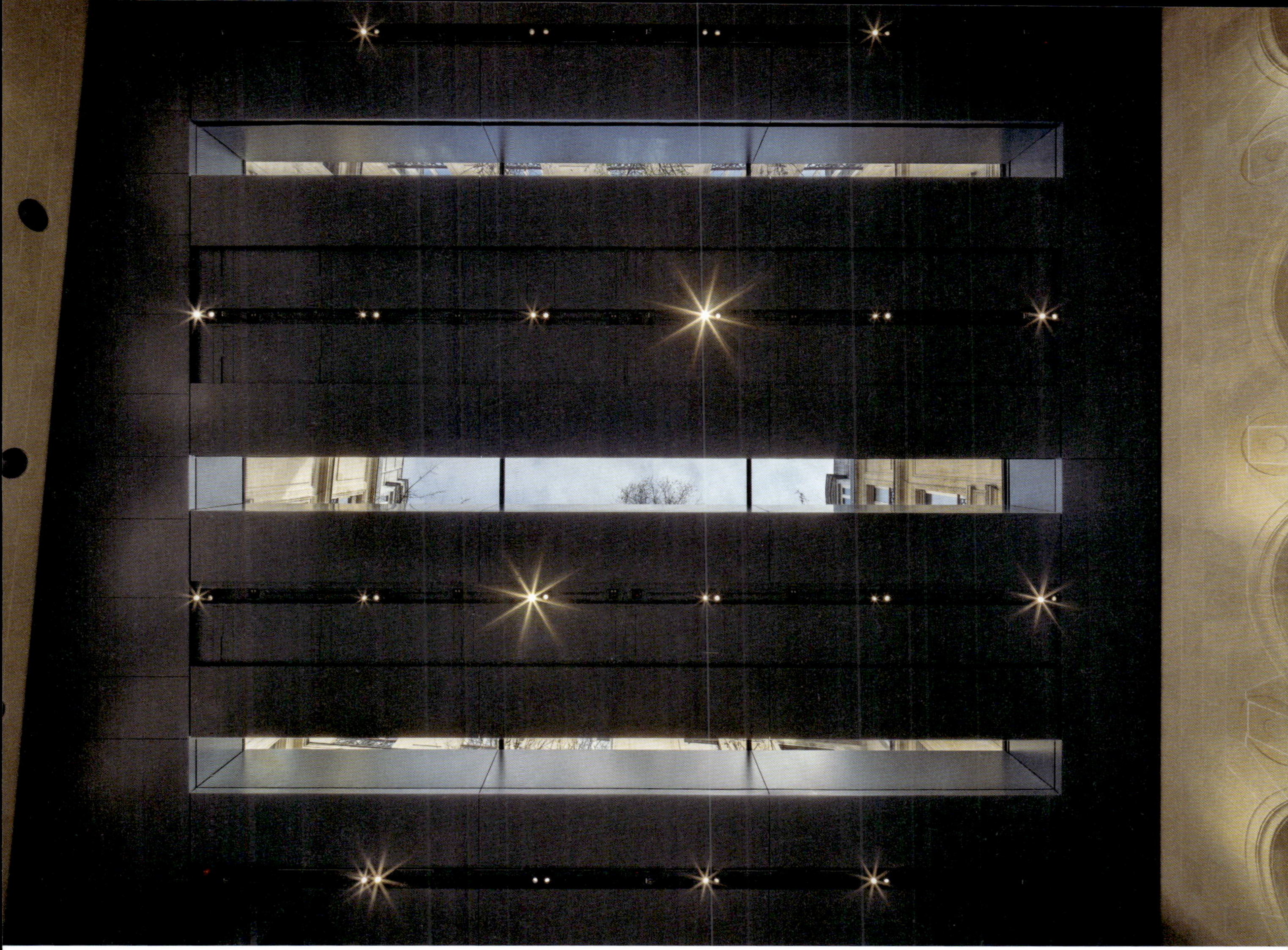

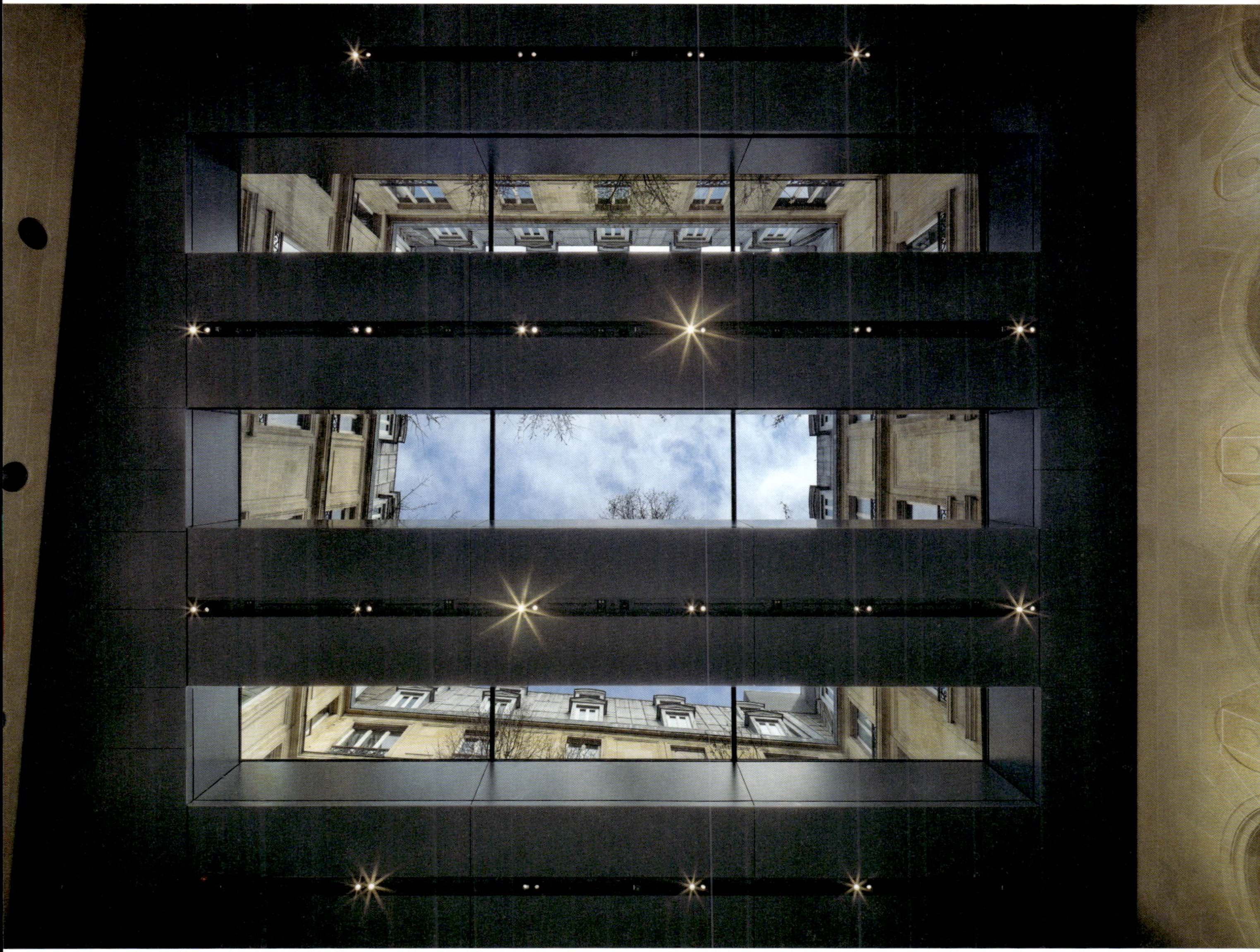

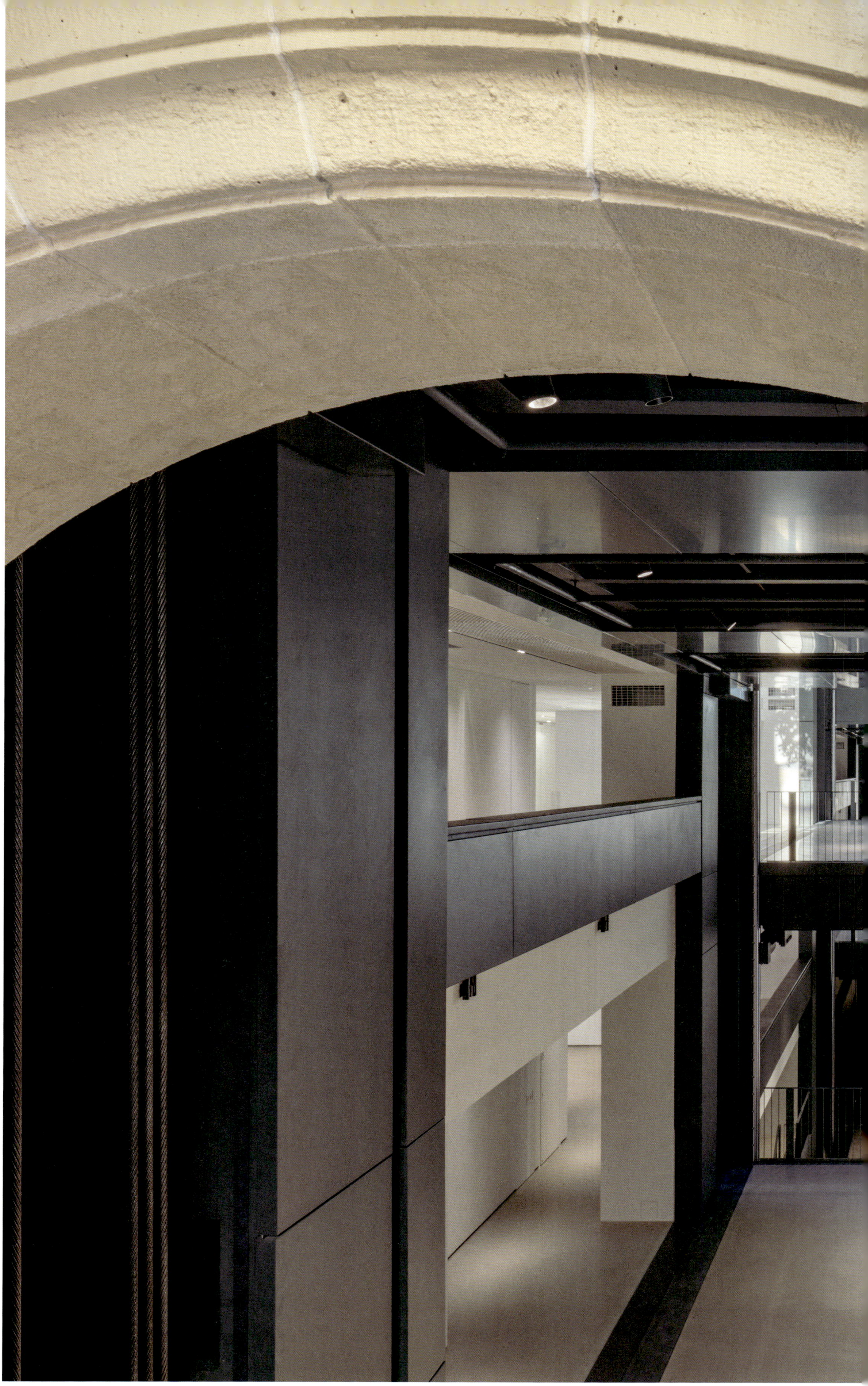

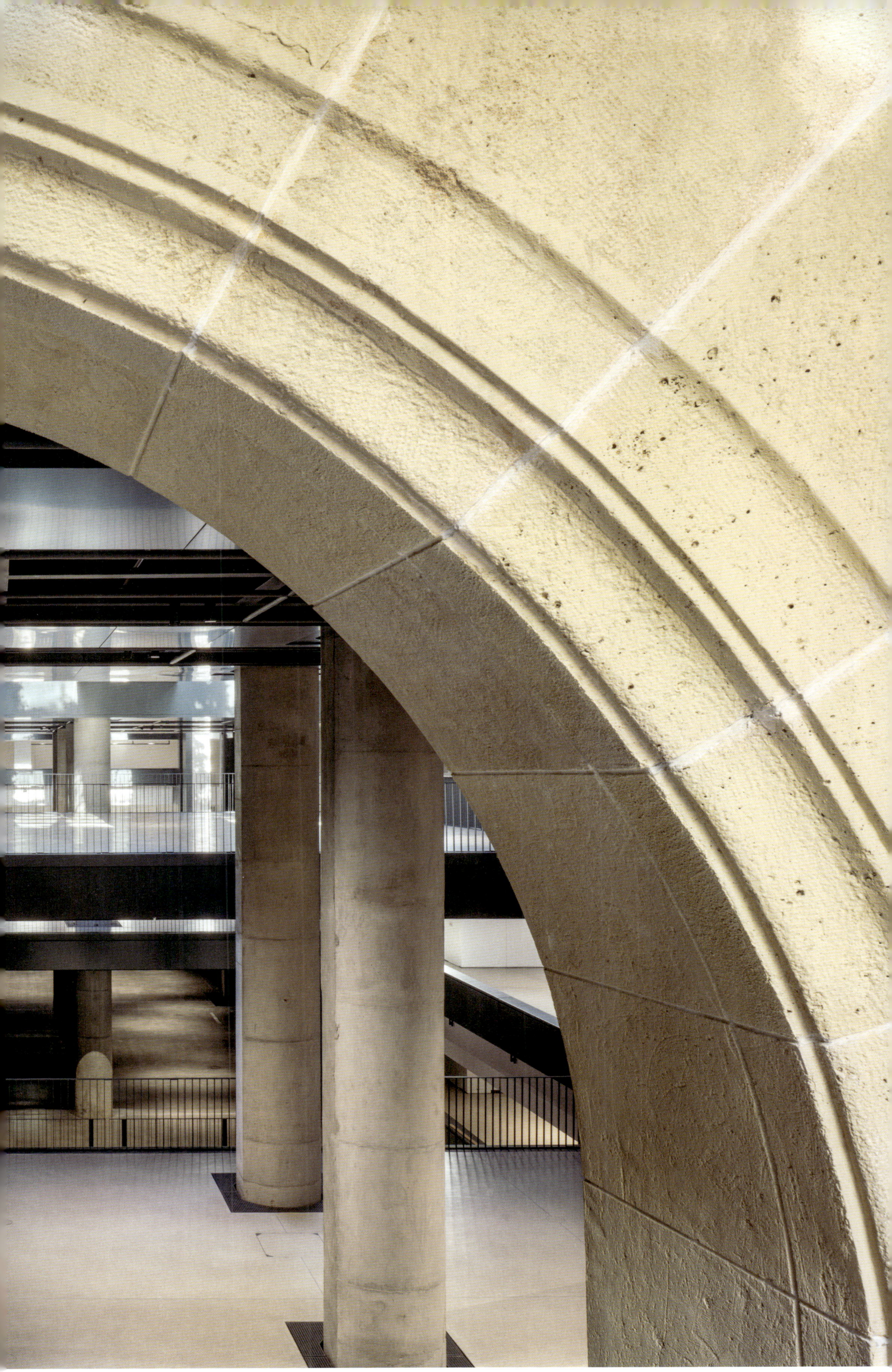

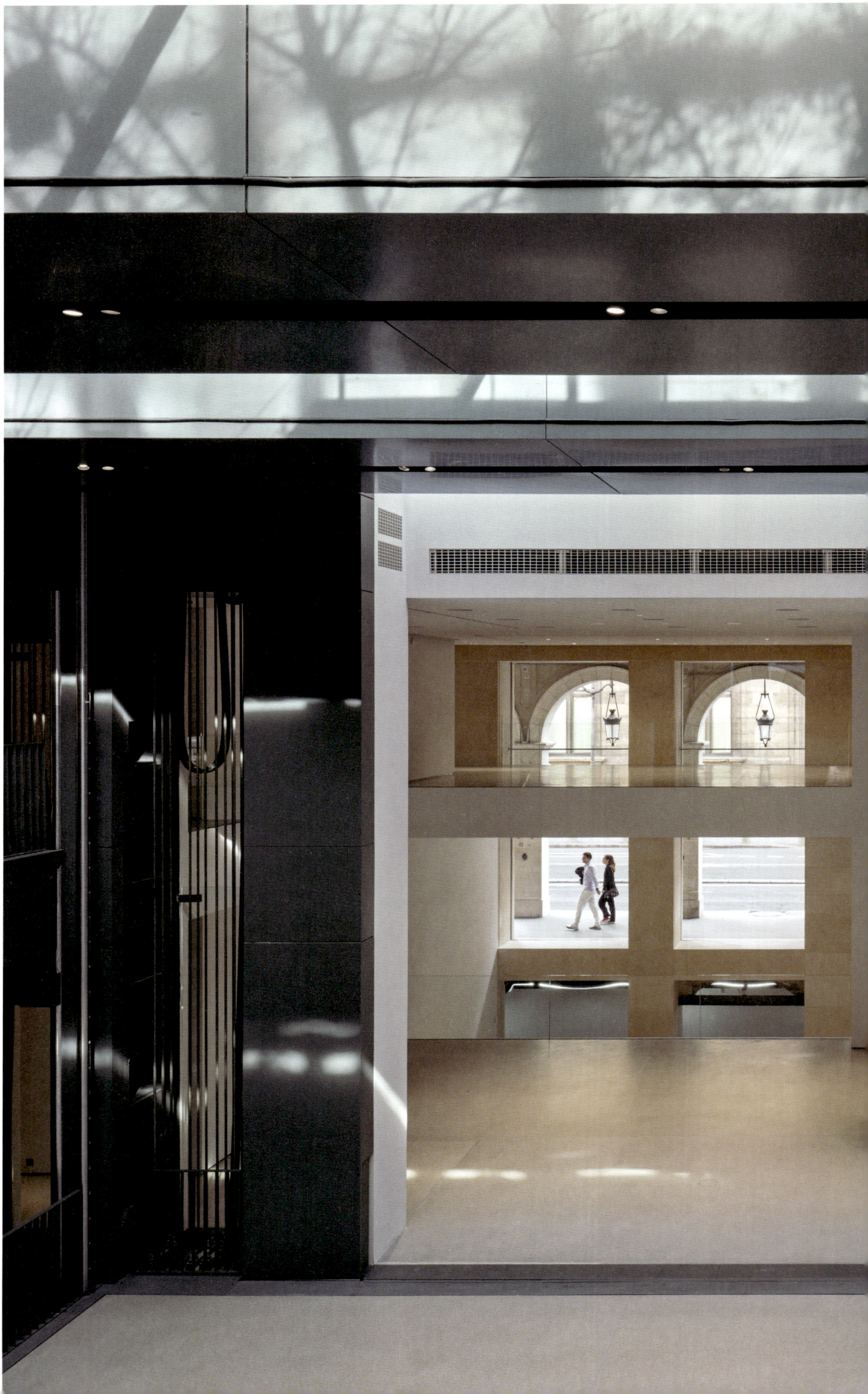

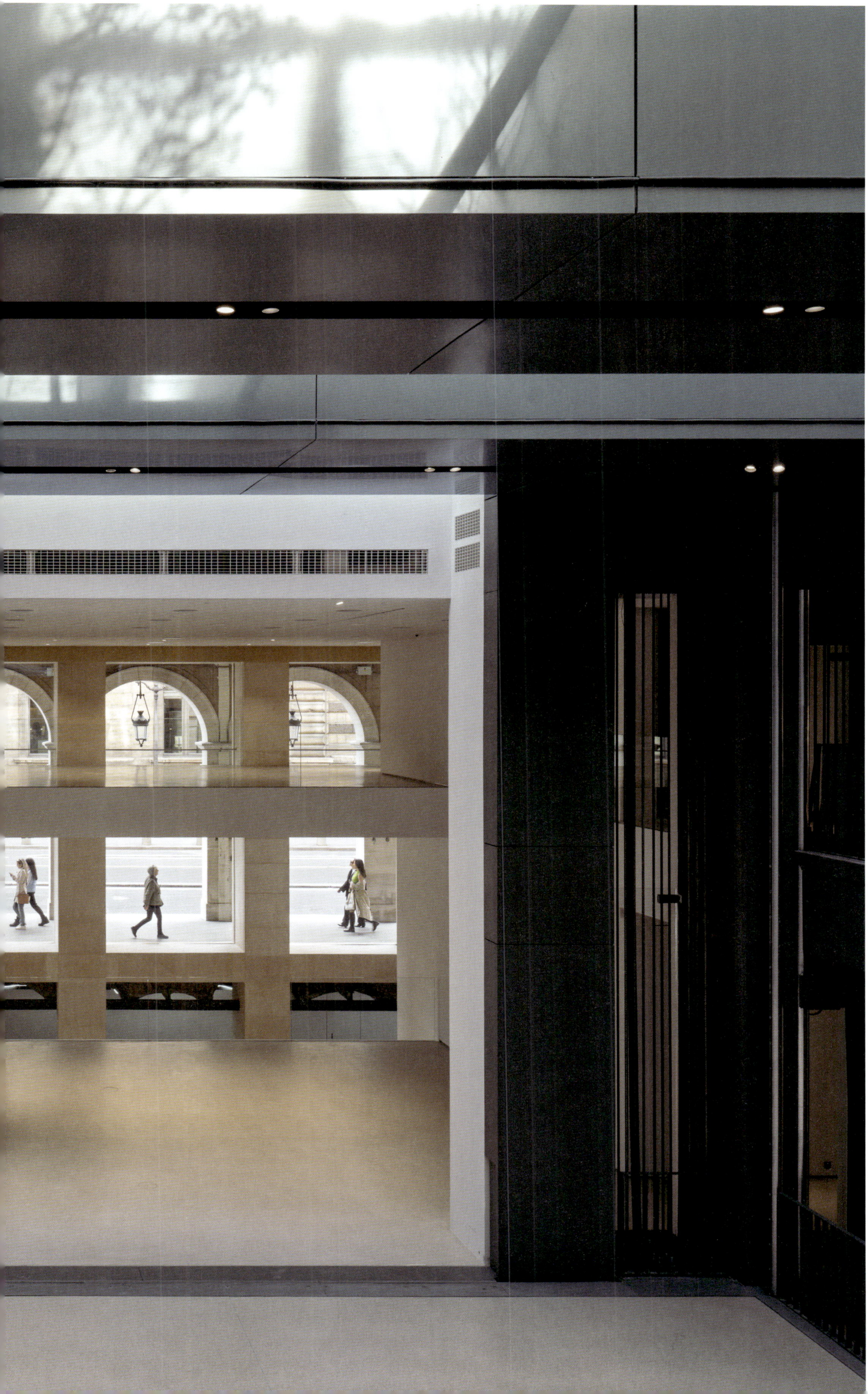

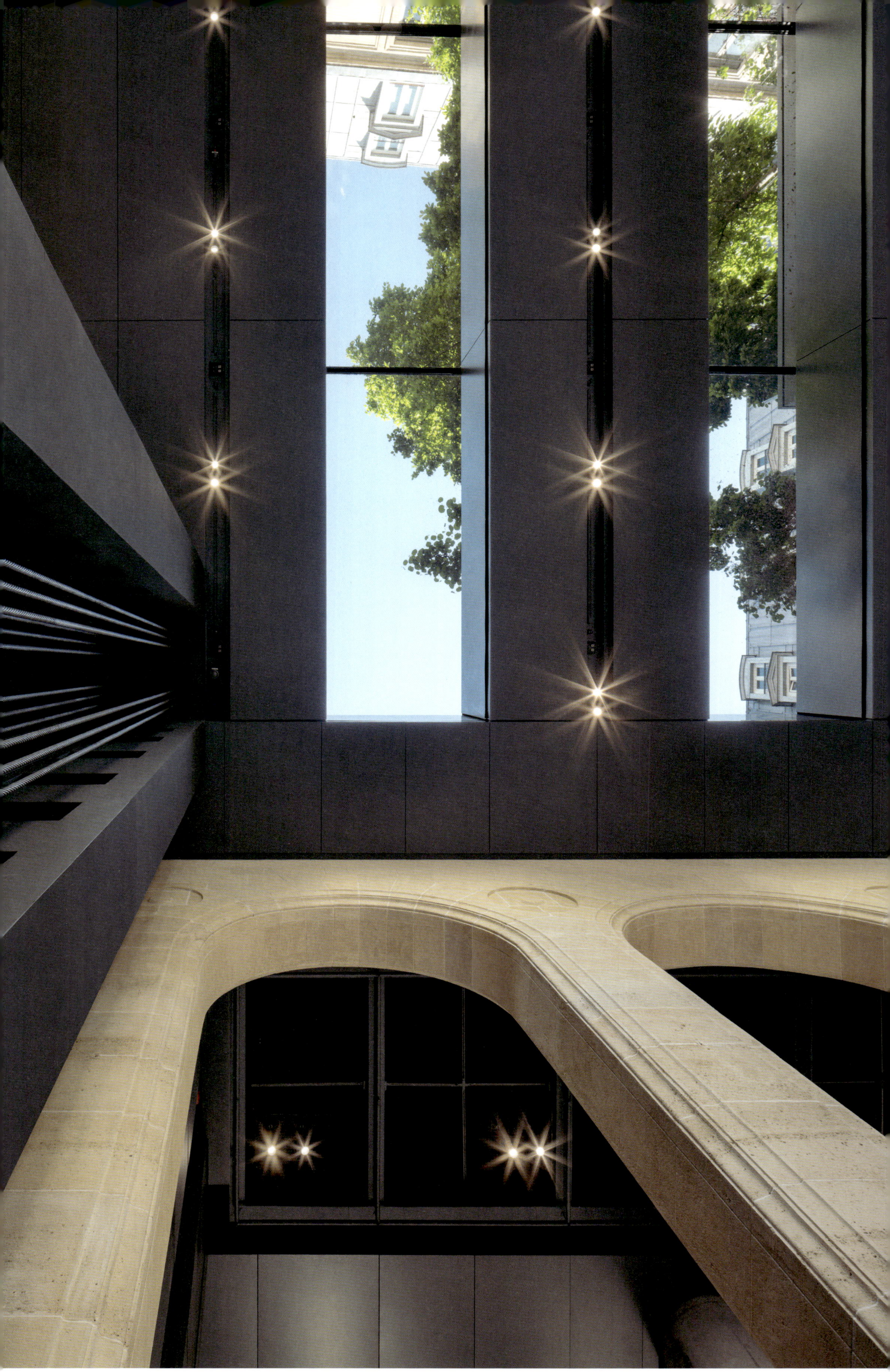

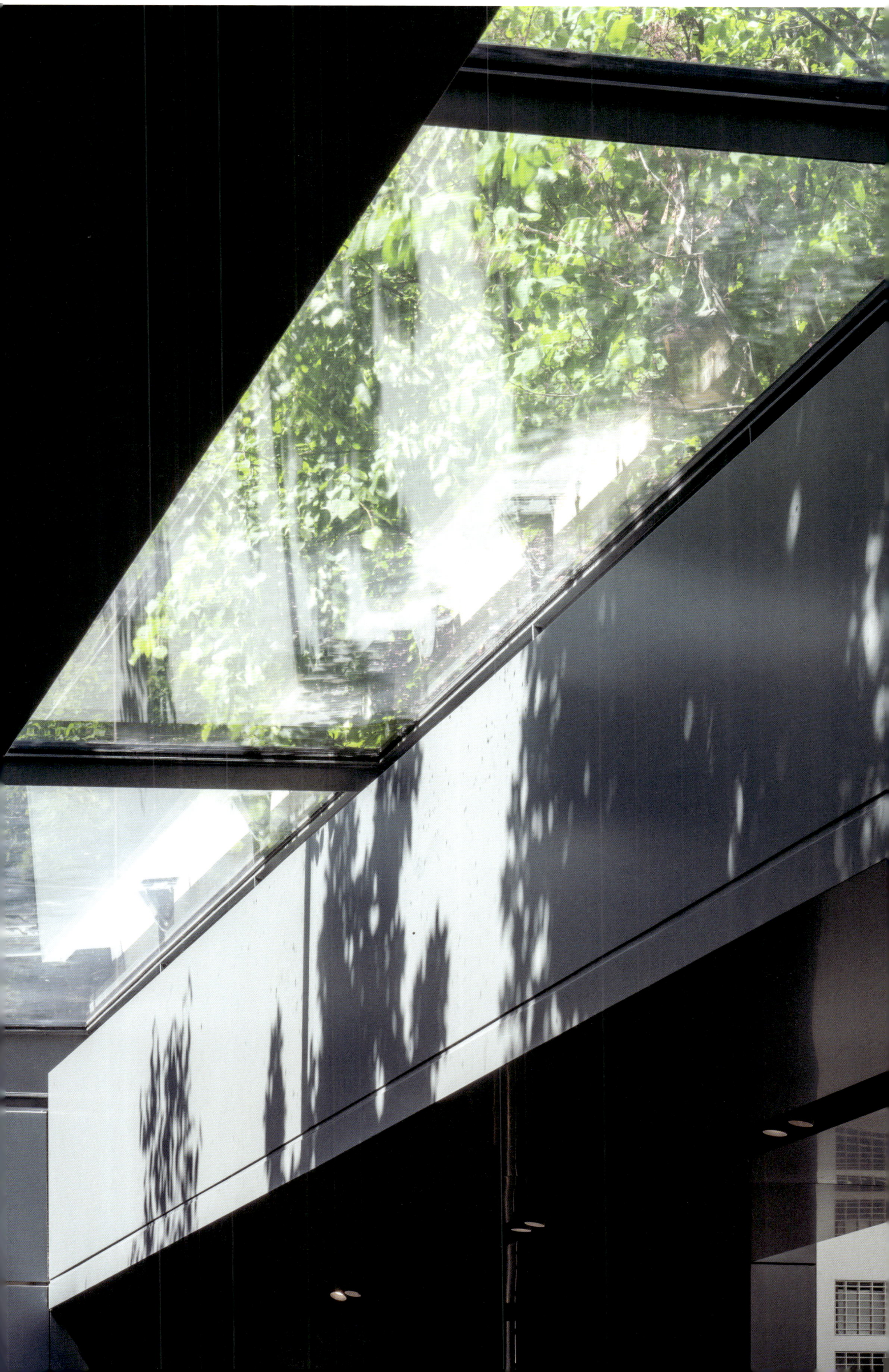

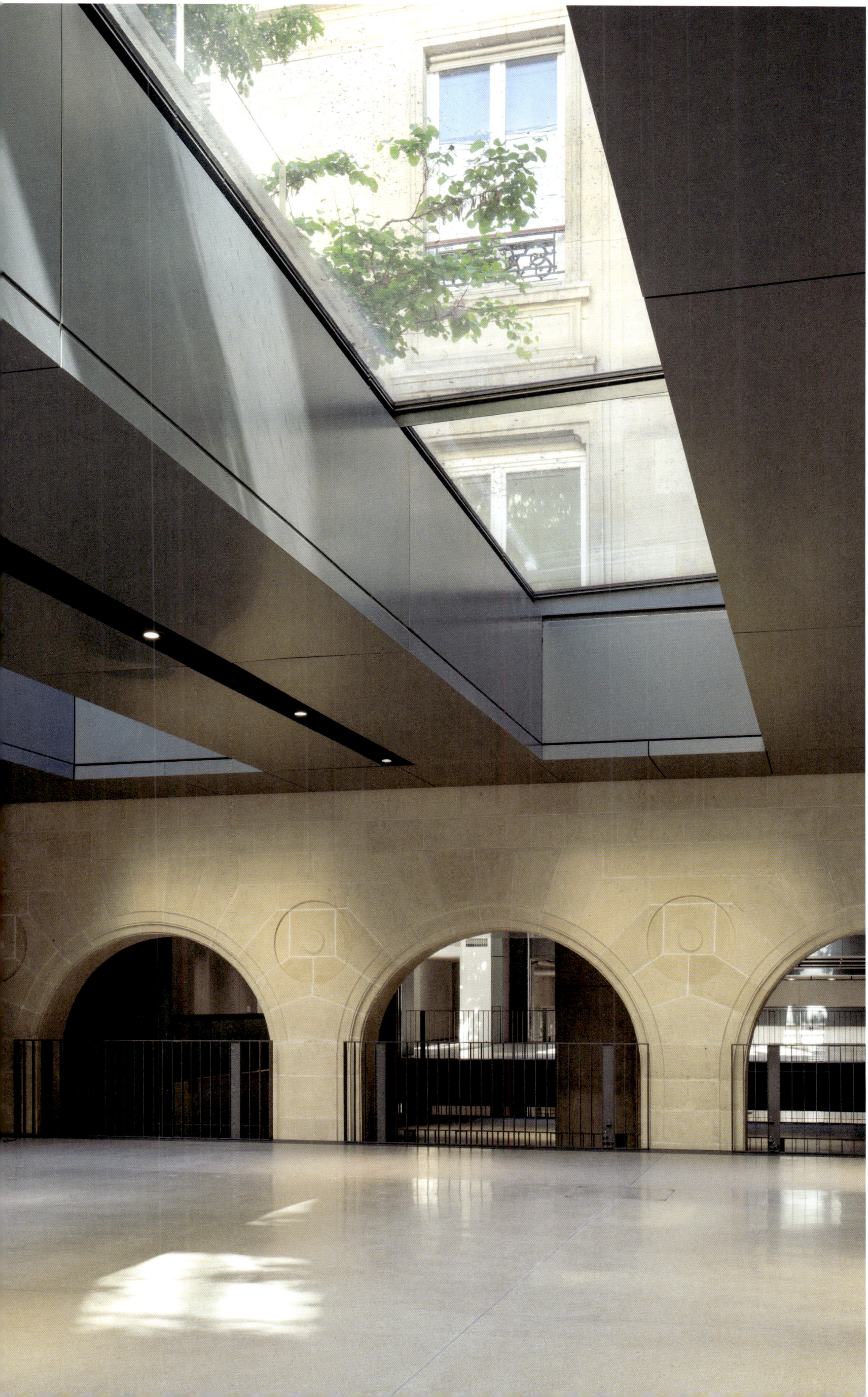

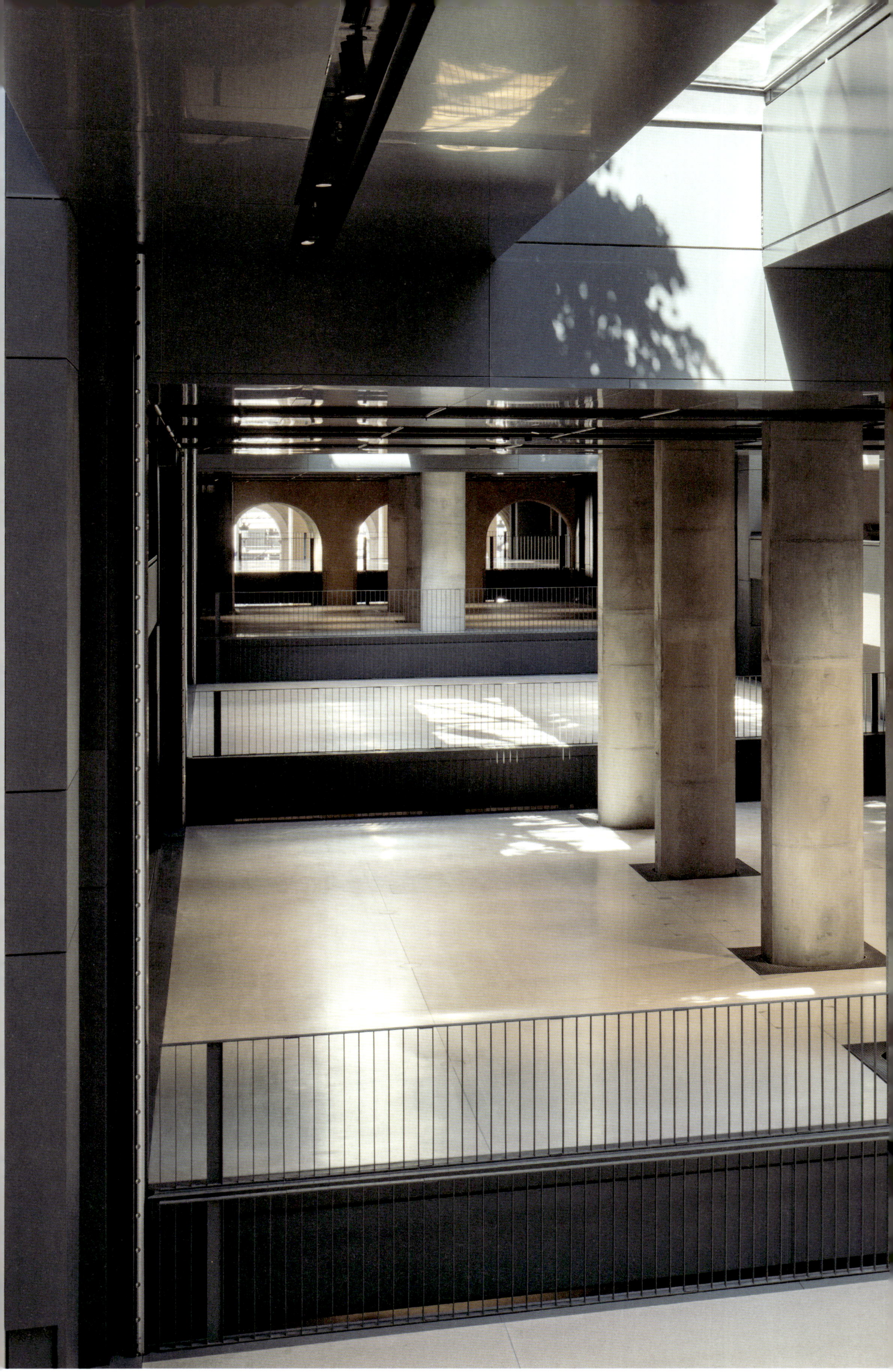

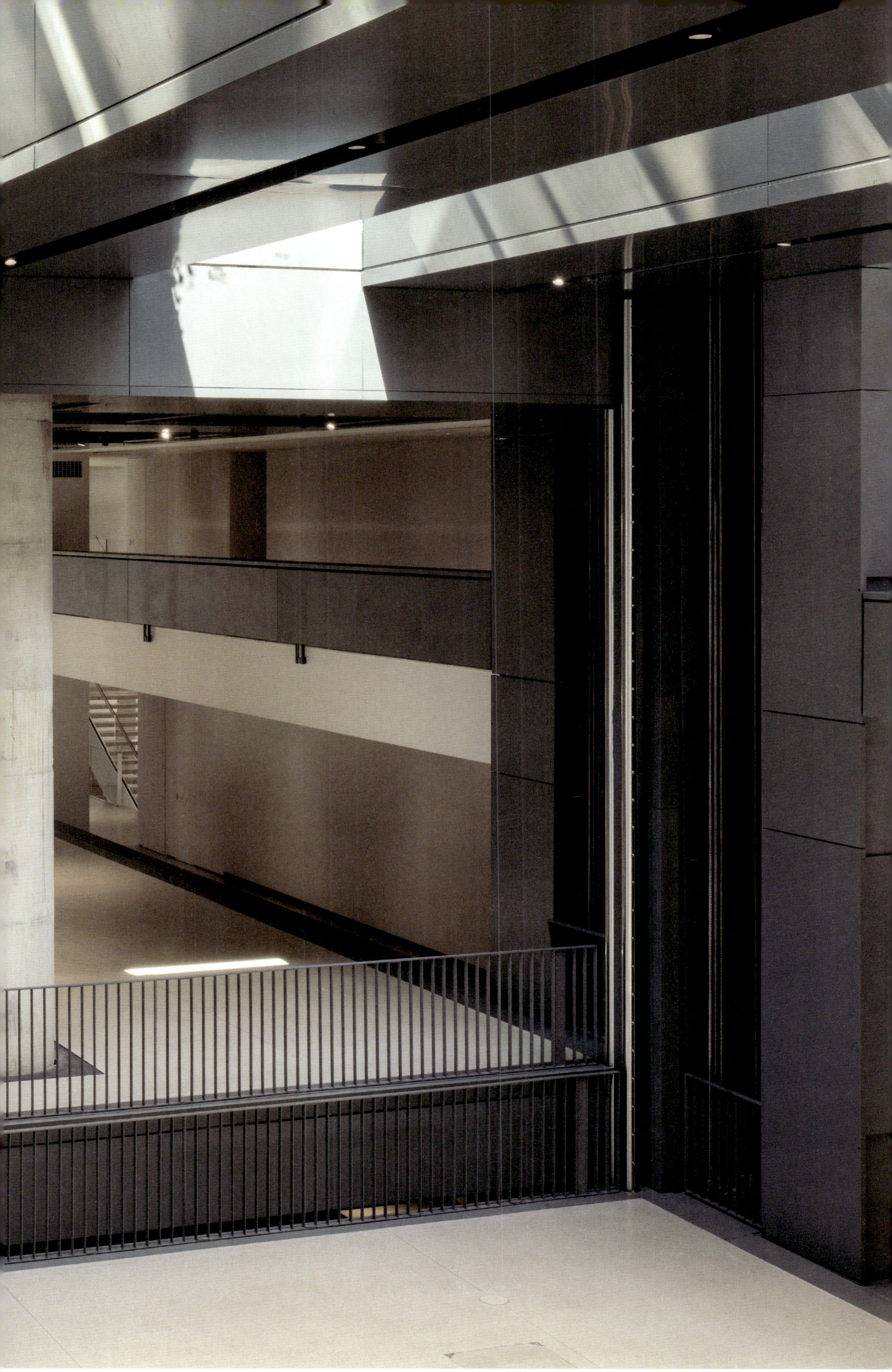

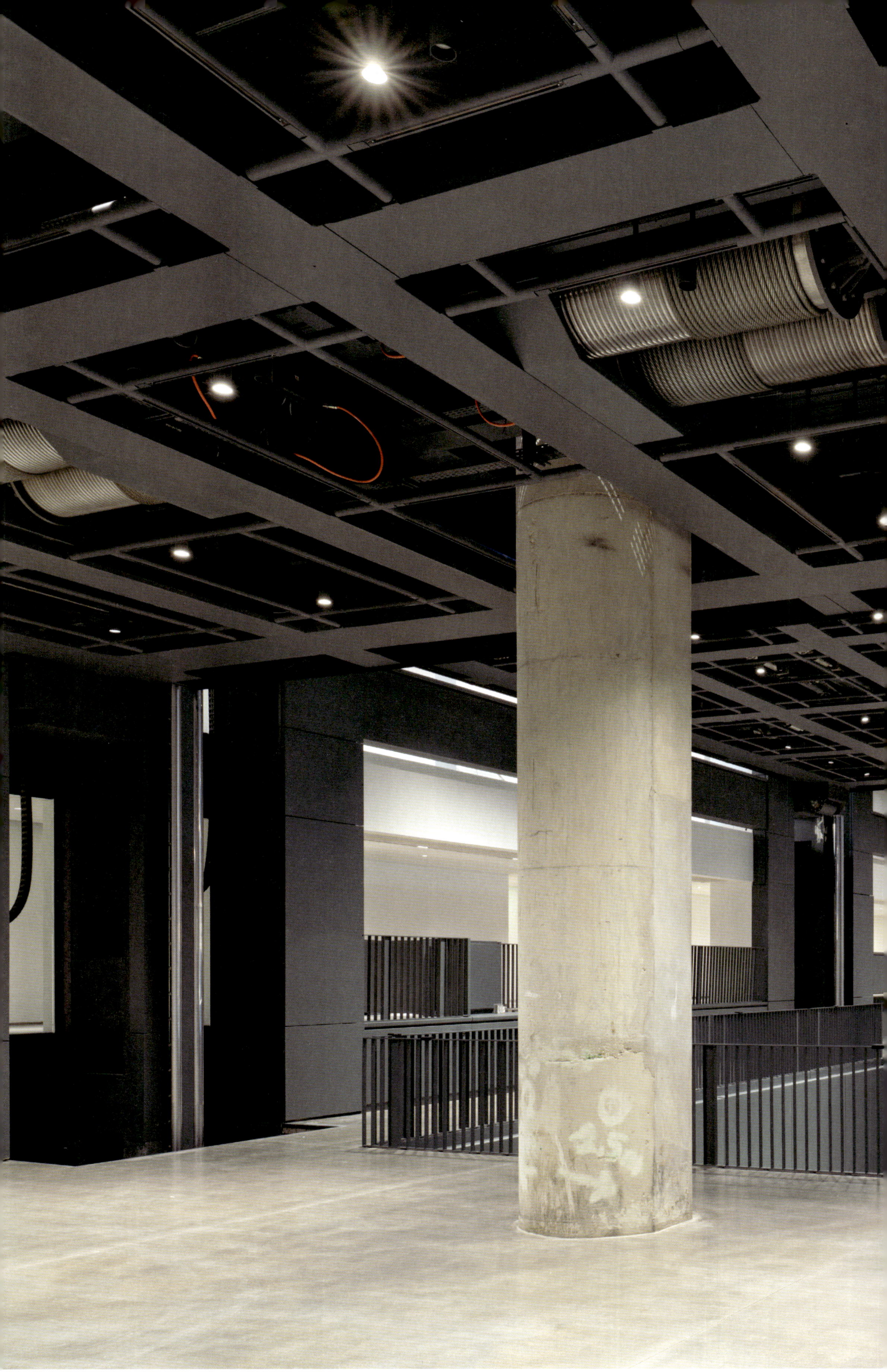

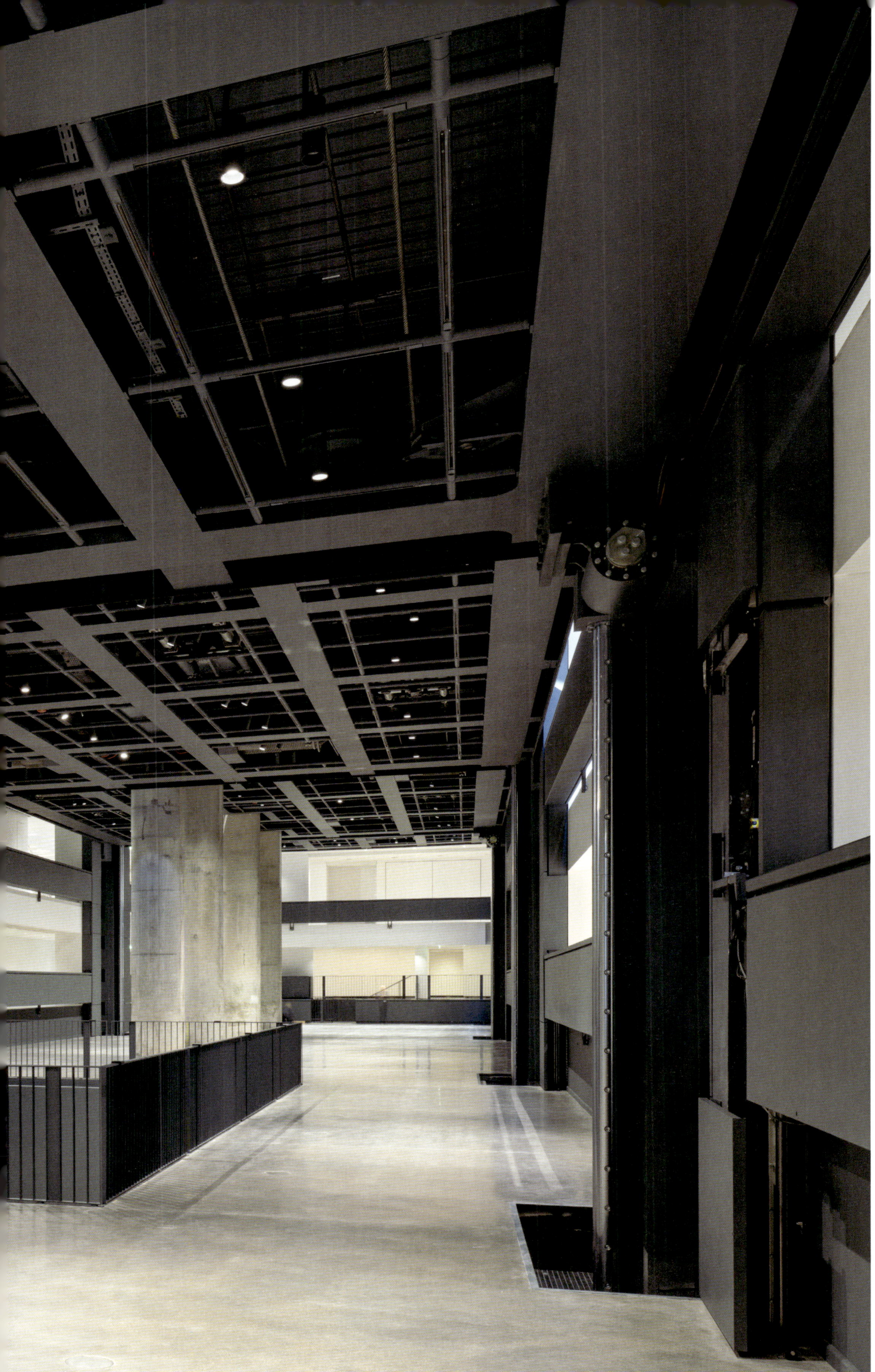

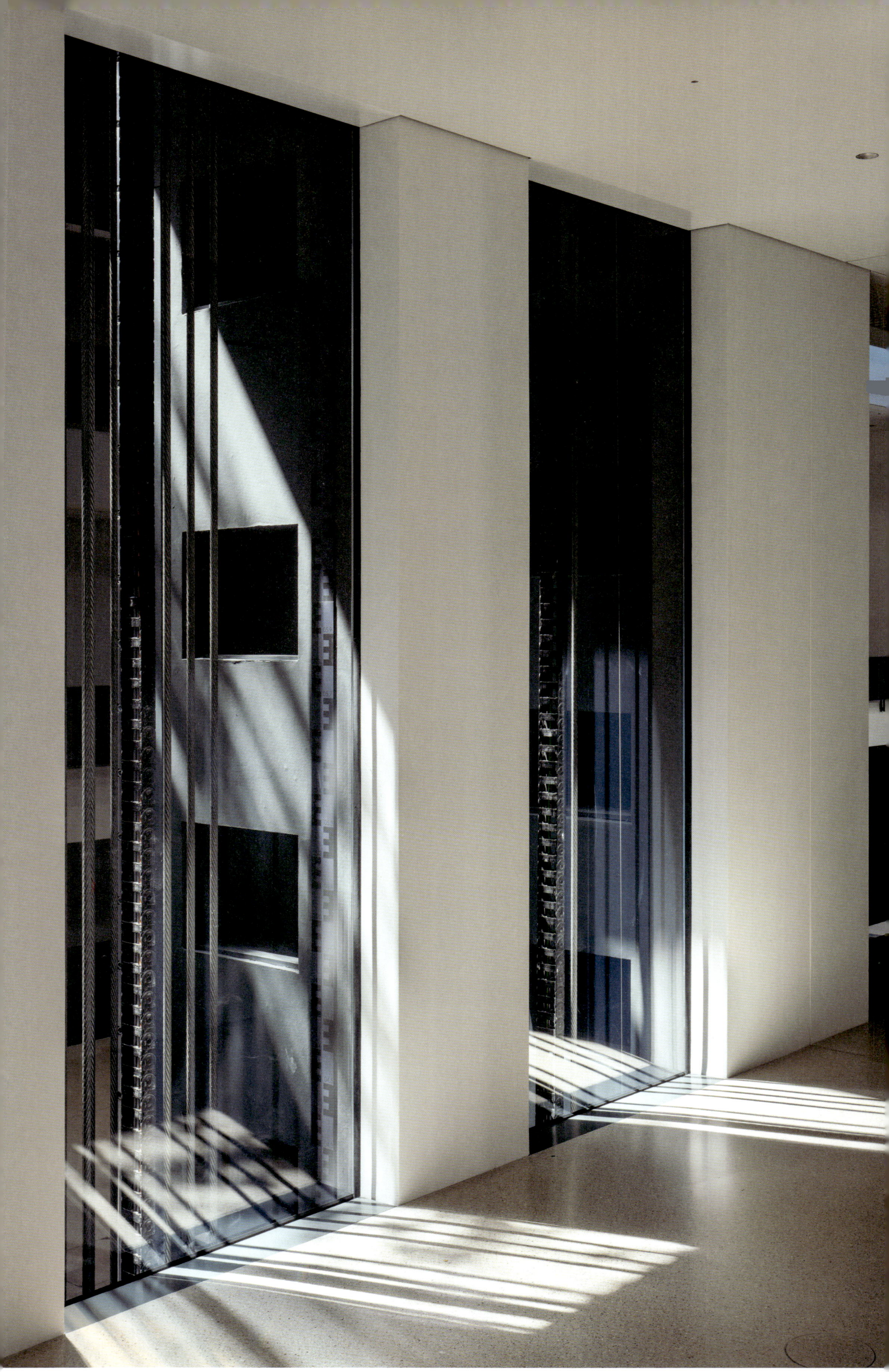

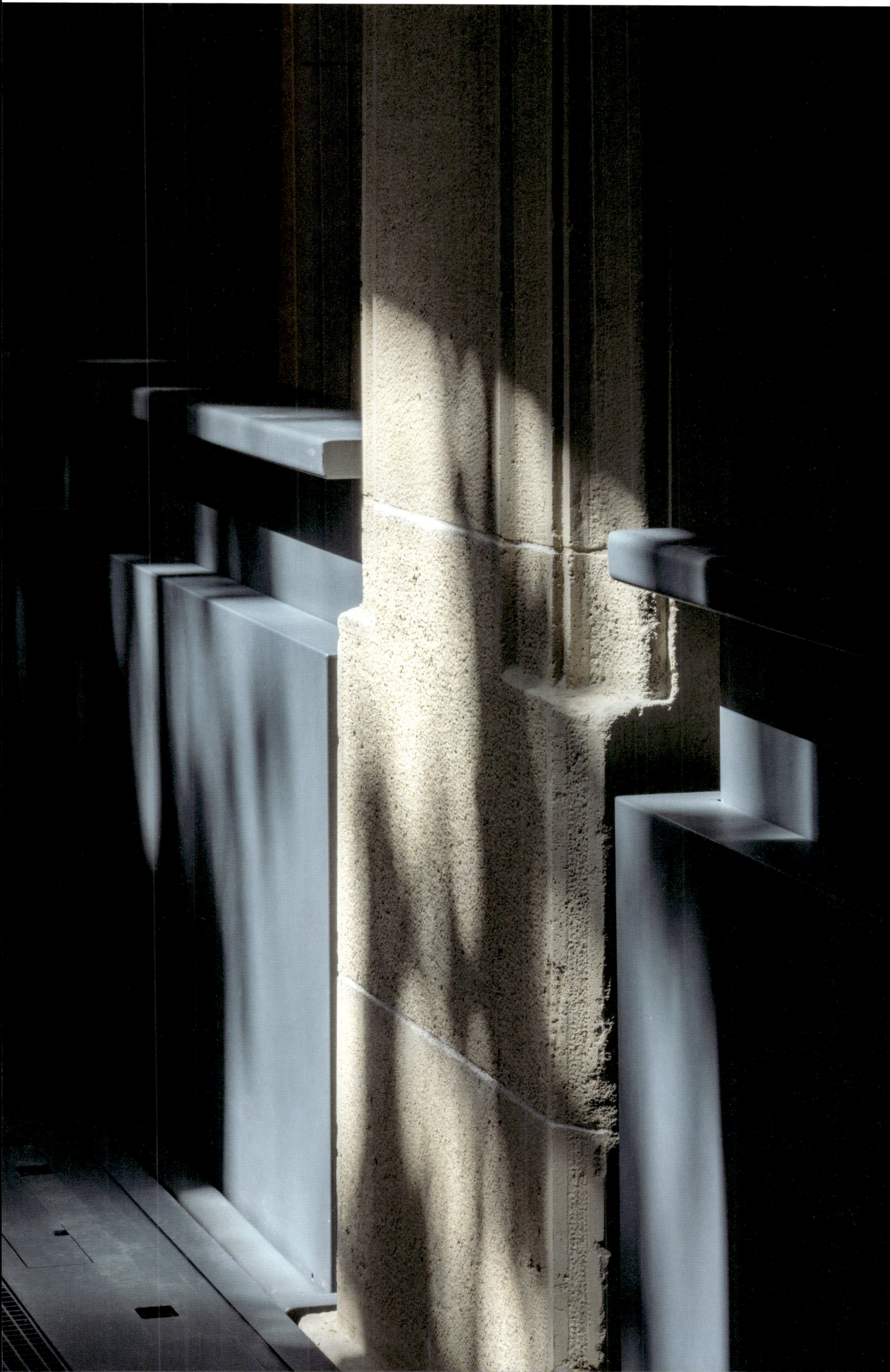

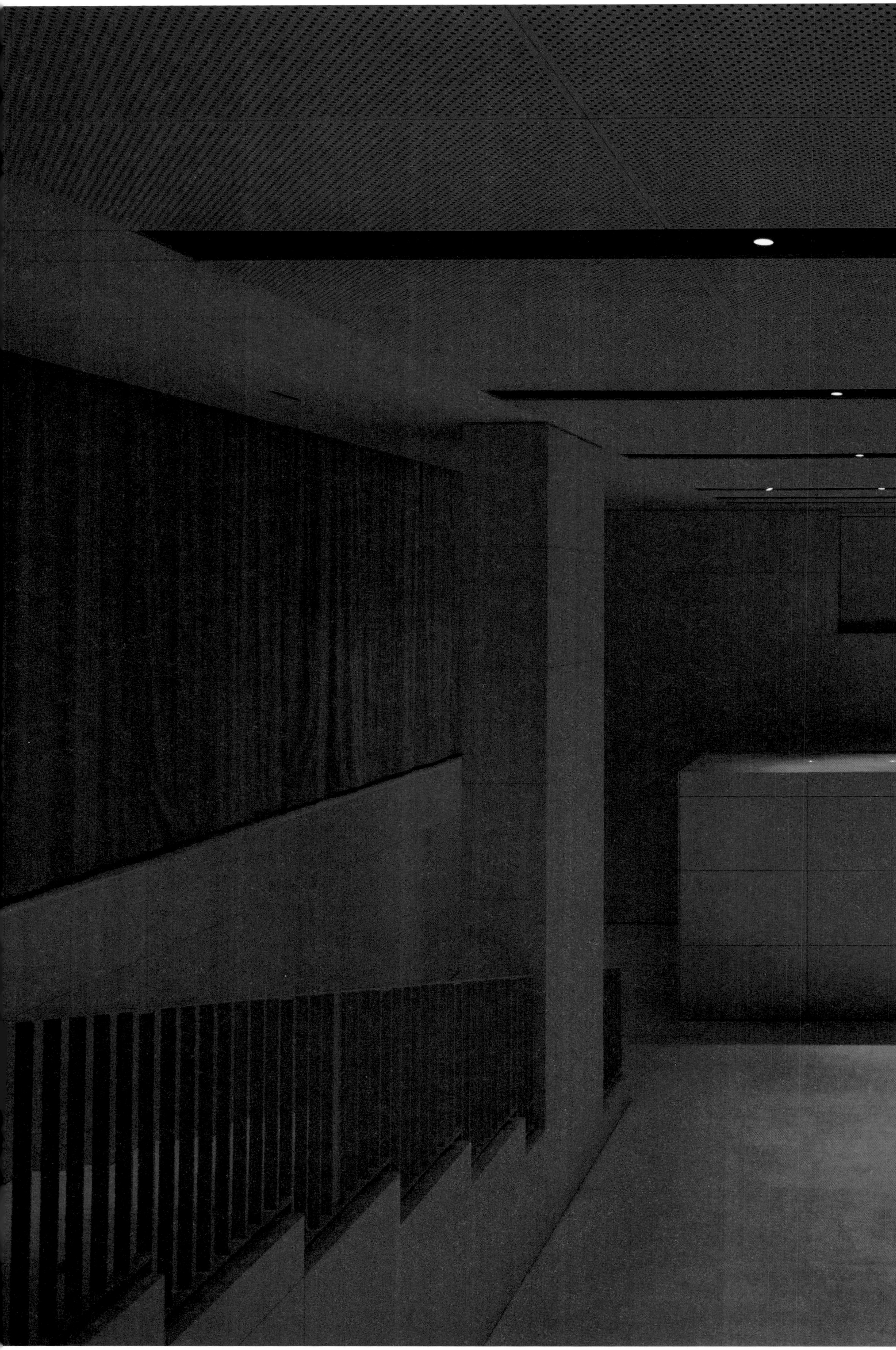

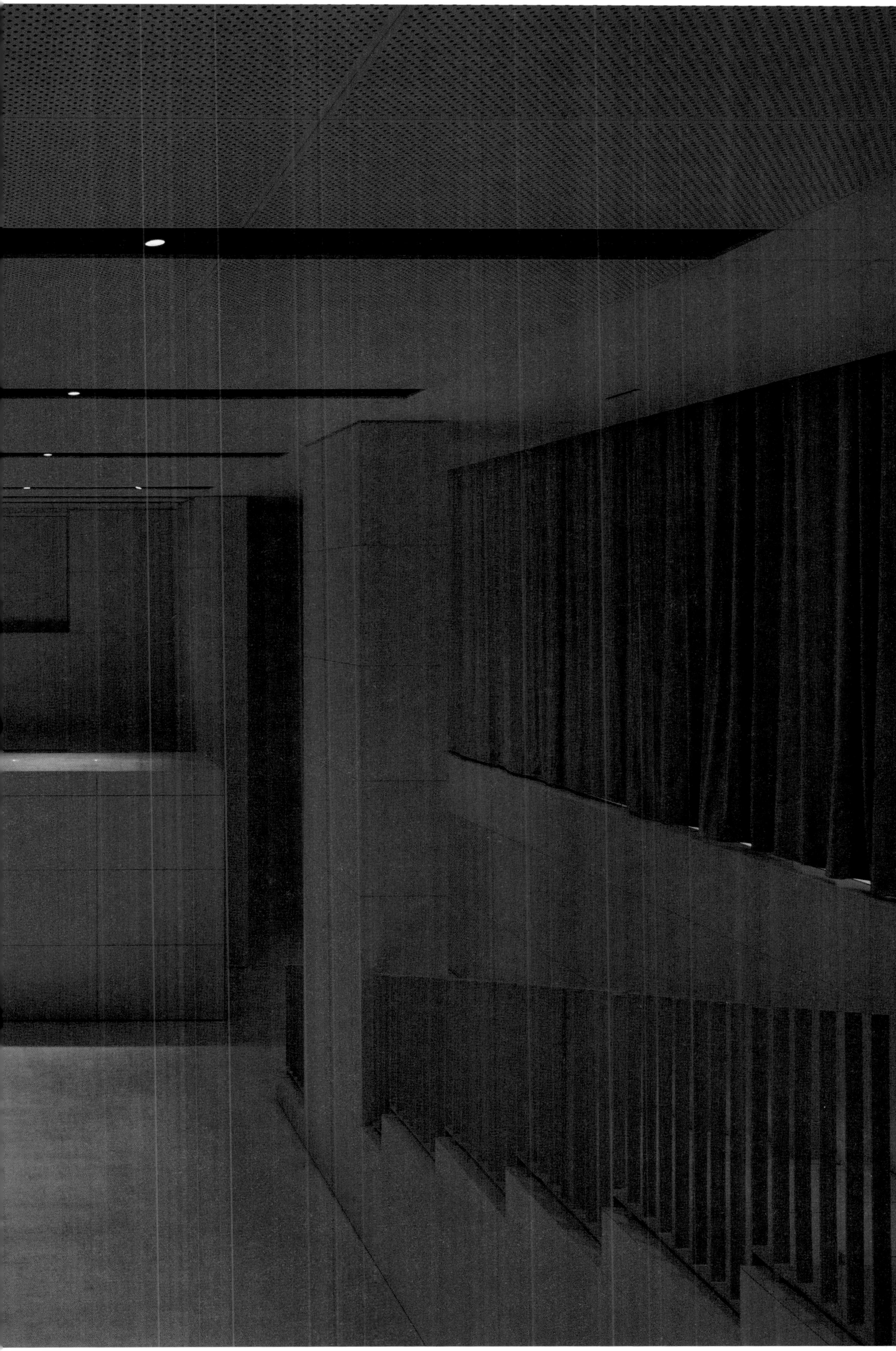

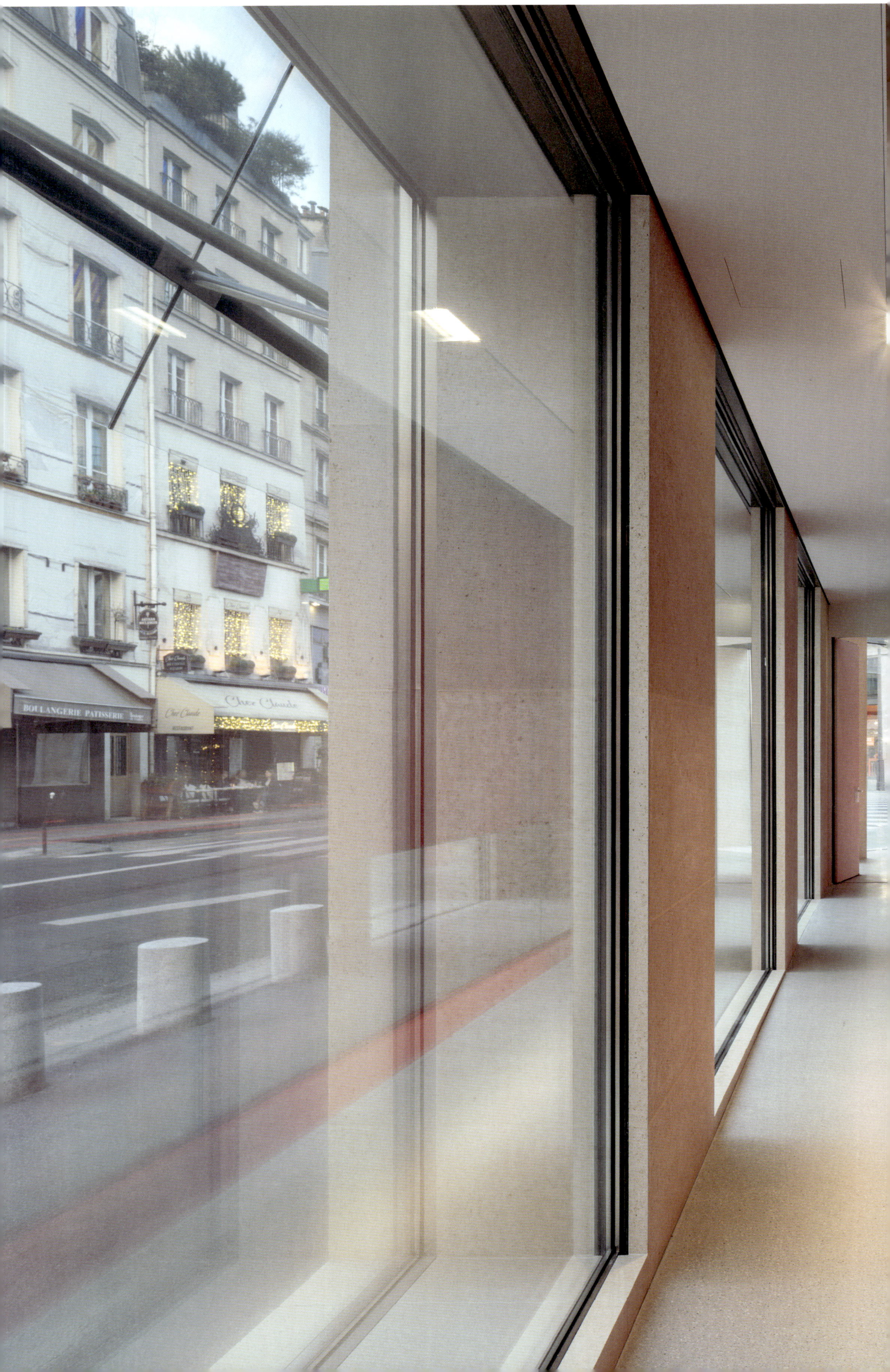
BOULANGERIE PATISSERIE
Chez Claude

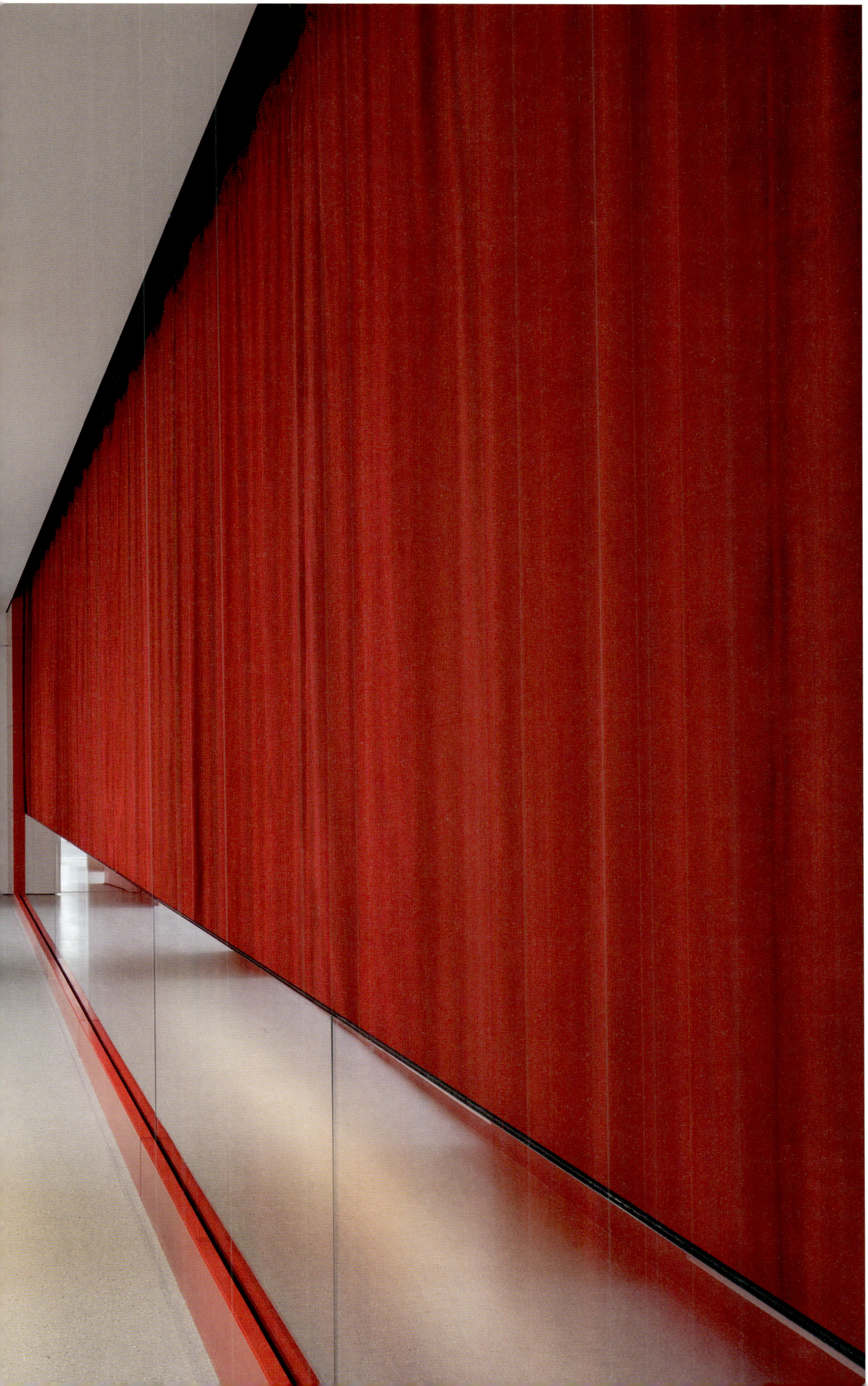

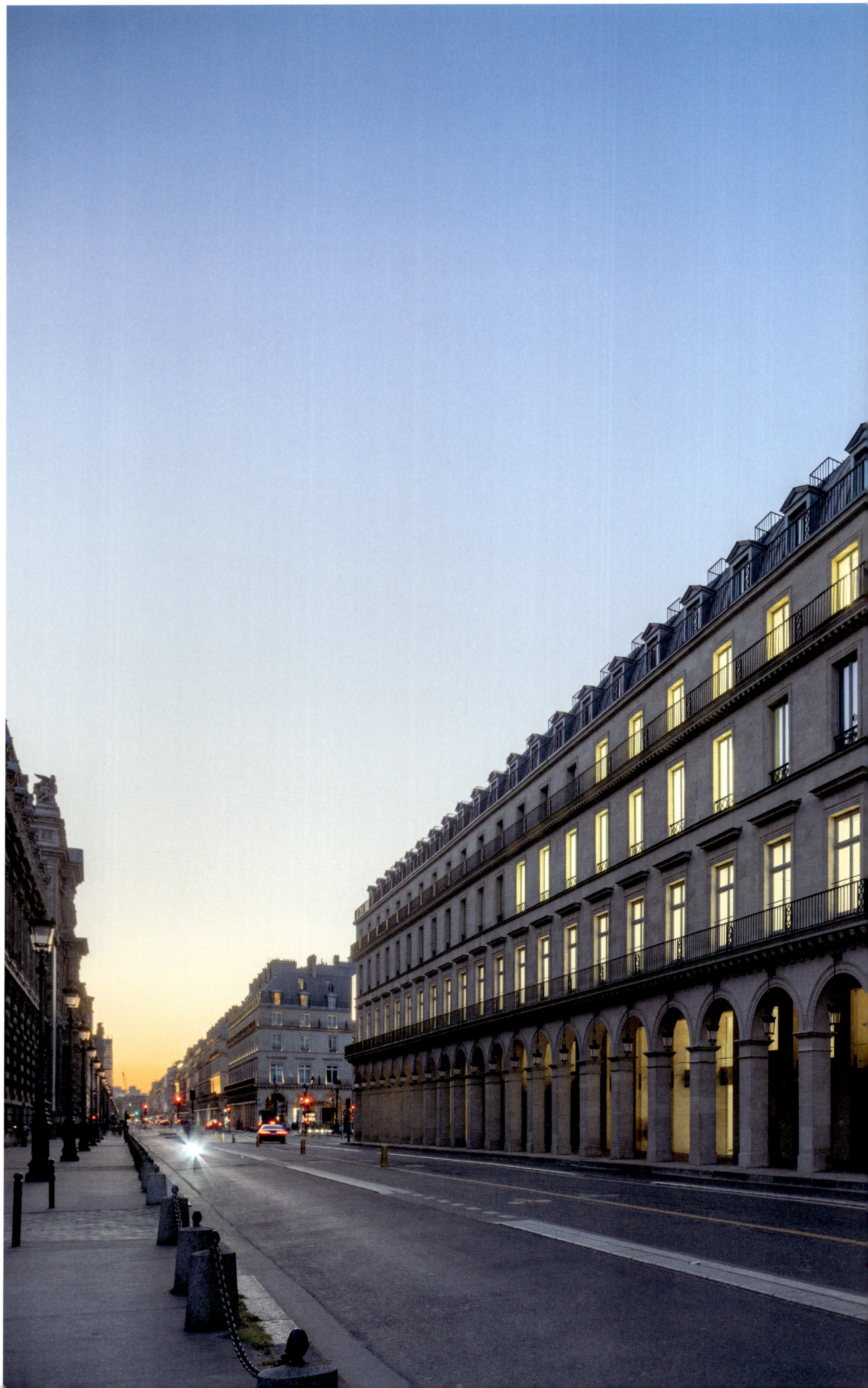

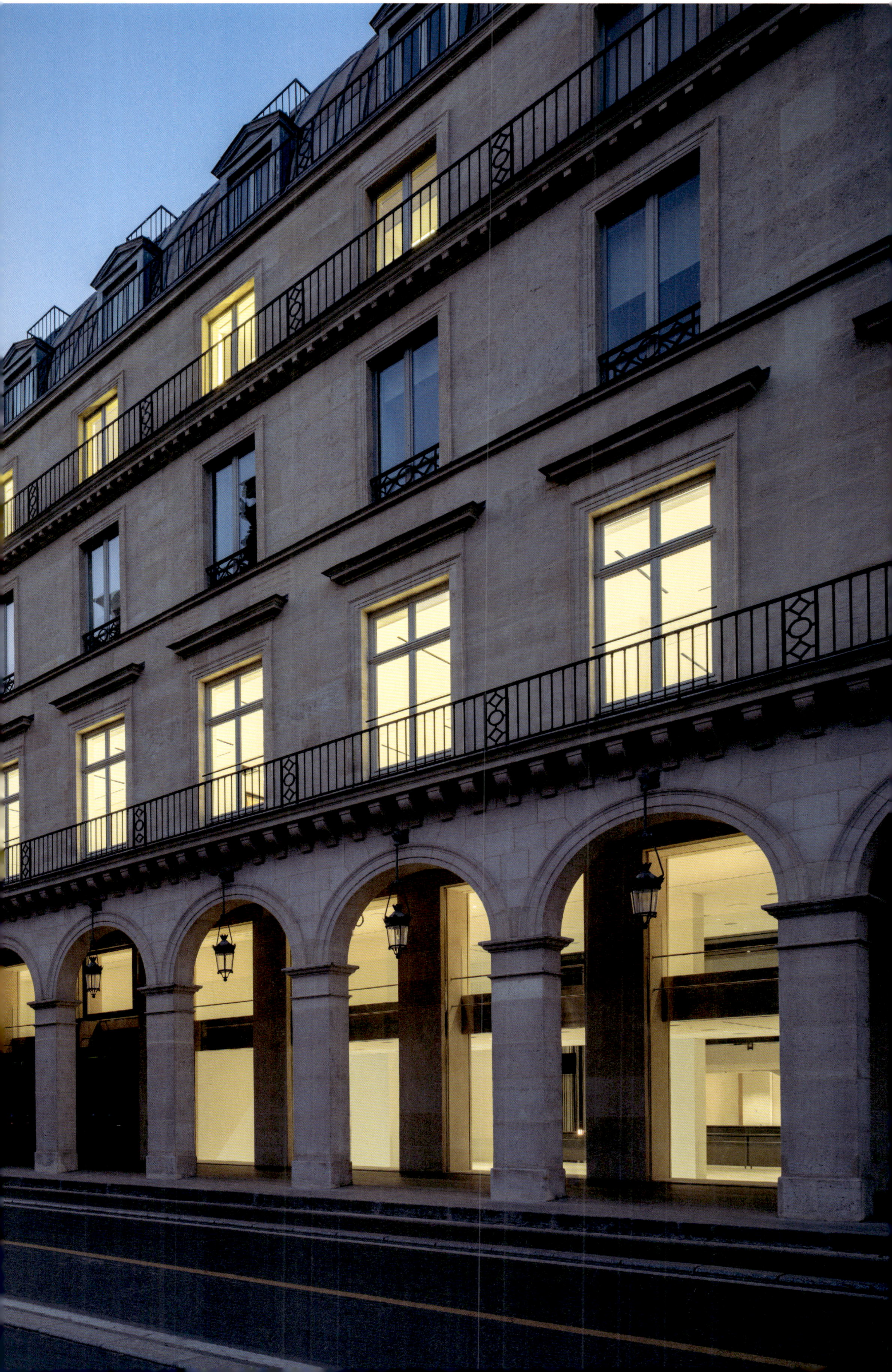

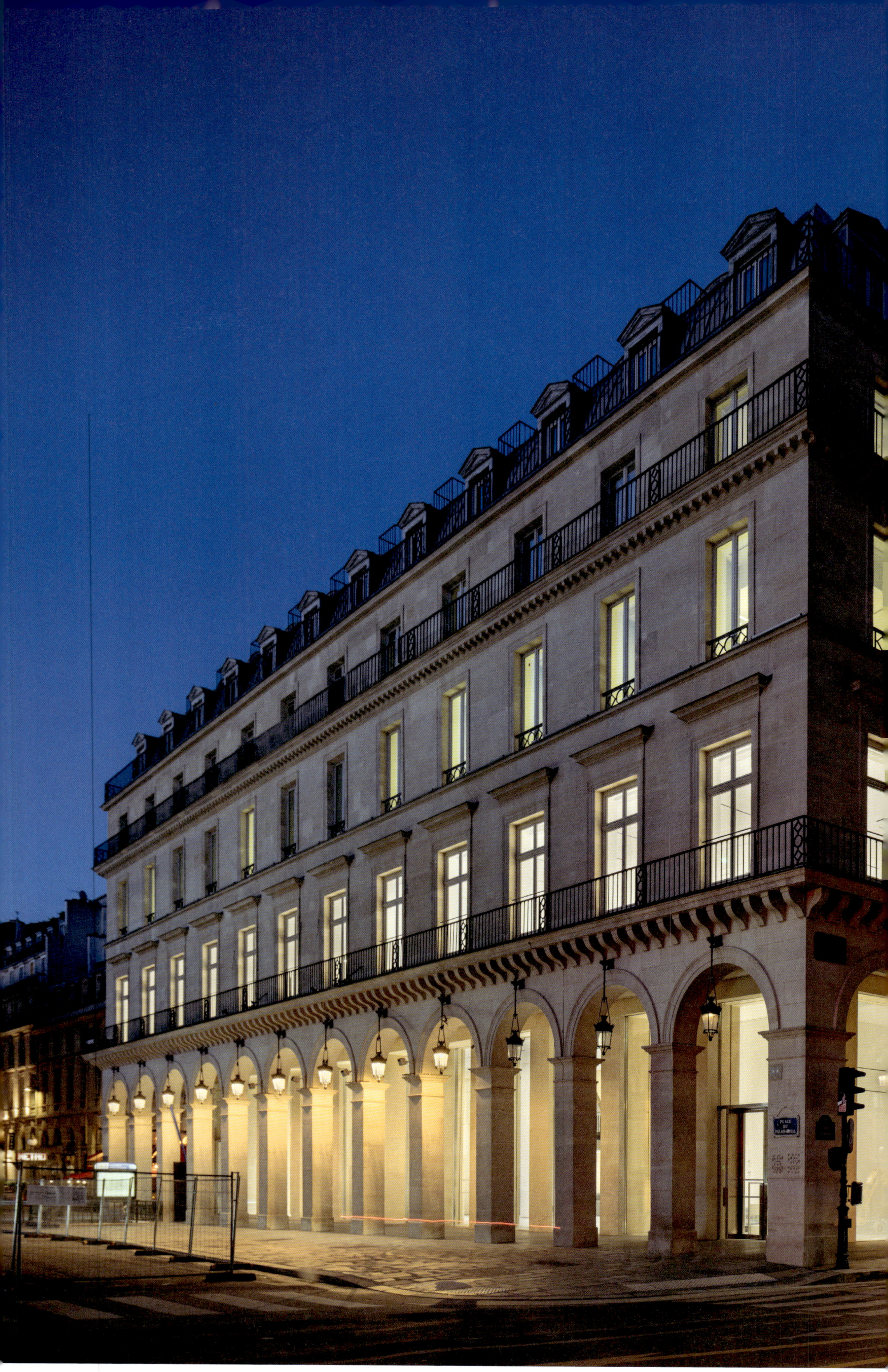

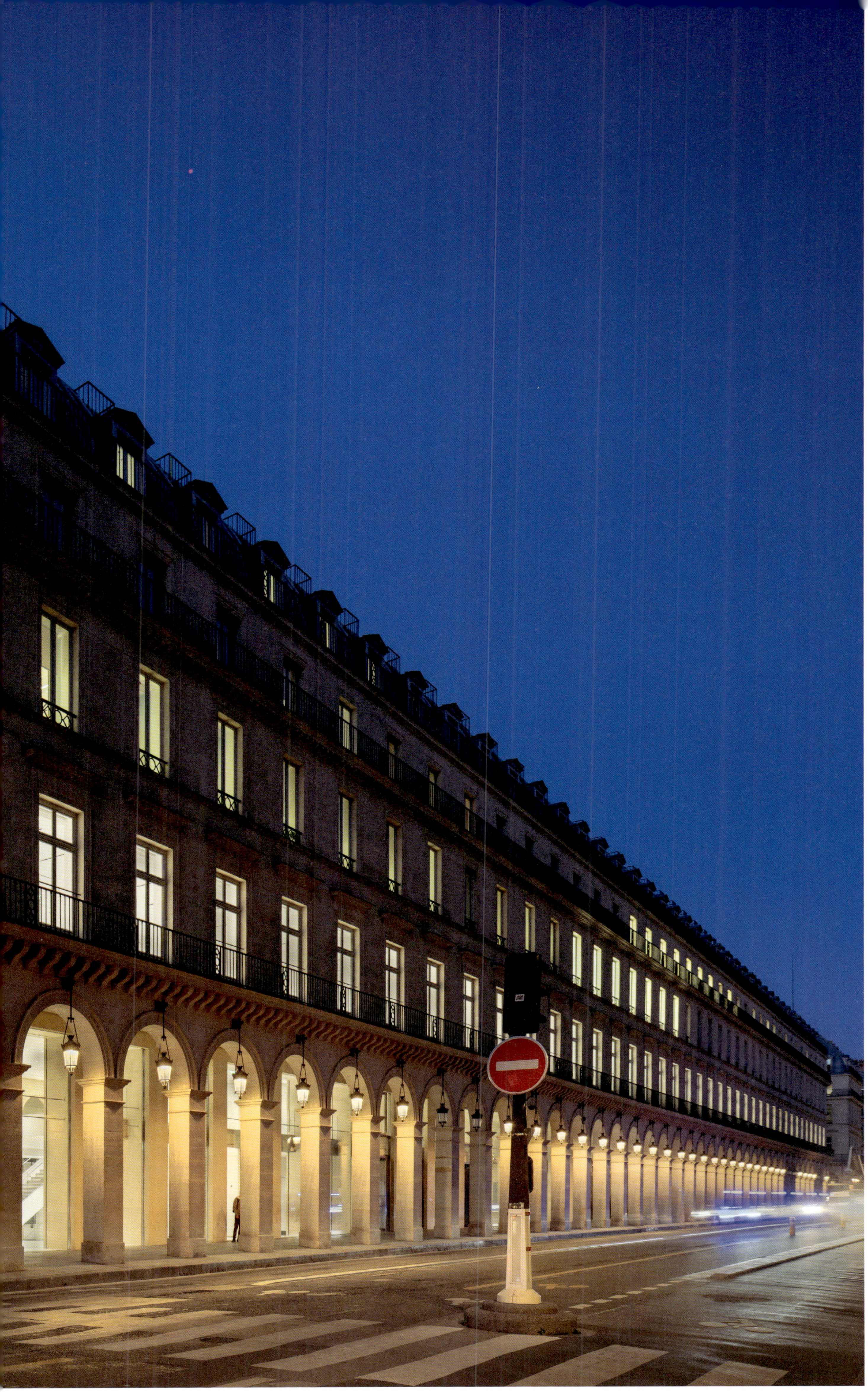

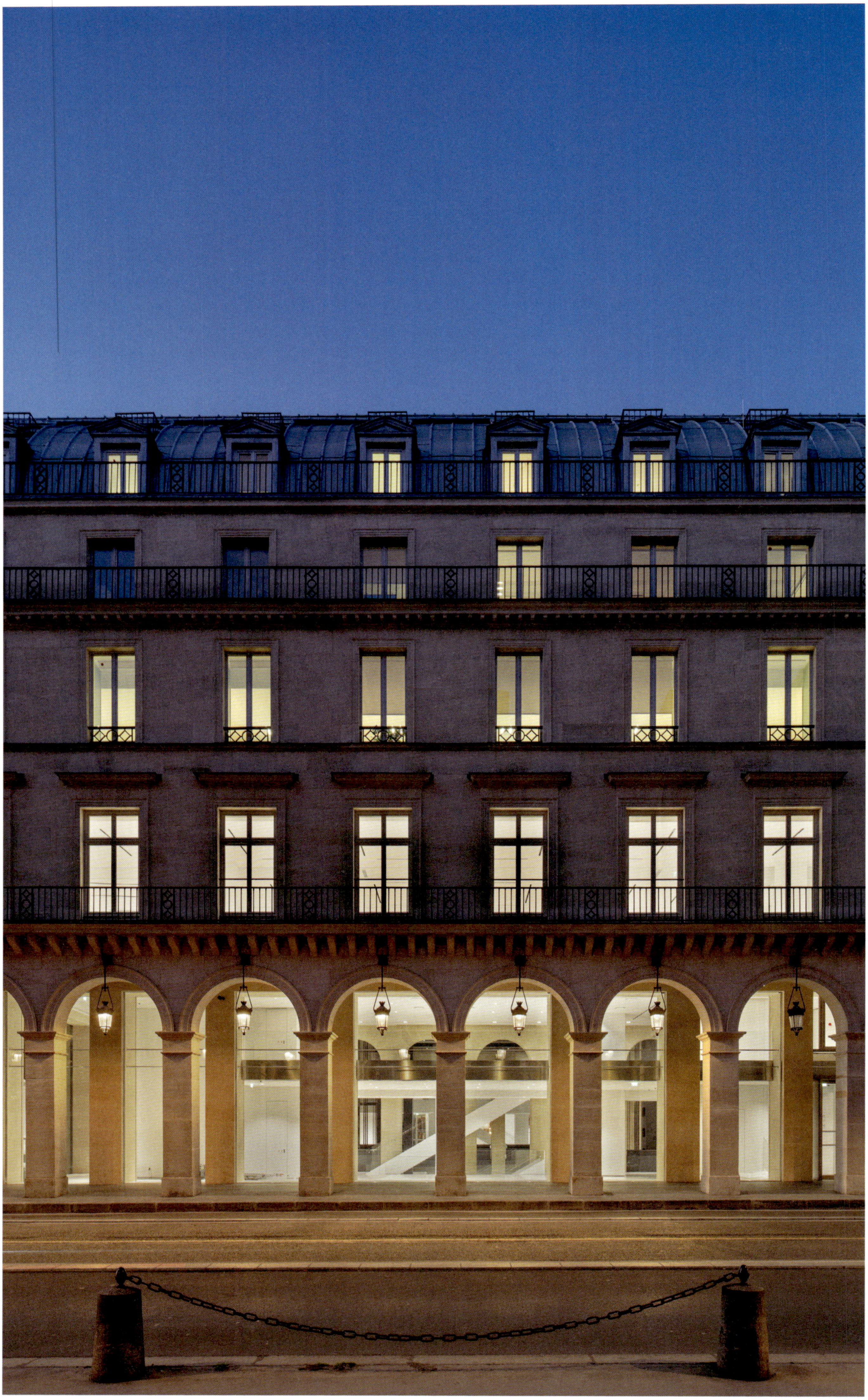

The Fondation Cartier building seen from Rue de Rivoli

AFTERWORD

Louis Ferla

President and CEO, Cartier International

Cyrille Vigneron

Chairman, Cartier Culture & Philanthropy

The architectural project of the Fondation Cartier pour l'art contemporain in Place du Palais-Royal is unique and symbolic. It demonstrates that the architecture of transformation can apply as much to a building as to general urbanism, and to cultural urbanism in particular. The project has transformed one space, that of the Louvre des Antiquaires, into another, that of the Fondation Cartier, while also respecting its immediate environment. It is a sublime expression of introverted architecture, defined not by its external appearance but by its usage and internal life. Rather than a rigid space fixed in a structure, its mobile platforms make it a living space, open to creation and permanent metamorphosis.

Set close to the Louvre, it shares with the latter the physical foundations of the Louvre Castle: the machine of the 21st century has been combined with the foundations of the 12th century and the building of the 19th.

This opus is thus an atemporal architectural creation connected not to any specific aesthetic period, but to all those by which it has been preceded and will be followed. The space-time represented by the Fondation Cartier is a center and a ubiquity, a present and an eternity.

This architectural machine is not simply the new setting for experimentation and expression by the Fondation Cartier pour l'art contemporain—as enriched by its forty-year history as by the promise of the forty years to come—but also as the point of departure for a new form of dynamic architecture. A foundational act par excellence.

THE HISTORY OF THE BUILDING

1. The Grand Hôtel du Louvre seen from Place du Palais-Royal, 1860

2. The reading room of the Grand Hôtel du Louvre, 1877

3. The Grands Magasins du Louvre seen from Rue de Rivoli, c. 1910

4. The Louvre des Antiquaires before the start of the Fondation Cartier construction, 2019

5. The construction site facilities conceived by Jean Nouvel for the Fondation Cartier, 2024

THE TRANSFORMATION OF THE LOUVRE DISTRICT, 1802–1855

The modernization of Paris was set in motion by Napoleon Bonaparte at the start of the 19th century. In 1802, construction began in the heart of the city for the Rue de Rivoli, with its famous arches designed by architects Charles Percier and Pierre Fontaine. In 1835, a first section running from the Place de la Concorde to the Rue des Pyramides was completed. In the 1850s, under the aegis of Napoleon III and Baron Haussmann, the Rue de Rivoli was extended, and the "Grand Louvre" project expanded to the rest of the district, with new blocks taking shape between the freshly completed thoroughfare and the Rue Saint-Honoré. In 1854, the construction of the Grand Hôtel du Louvre, designed by the architect Alfred Armand, could begin.

THE GRAND HÔTEL DU LOUVRE, 1855–1887

Preparation for the Exposition Universelle of 1855 included construction of several large hotels to accommodate the expected five million visitors. Erected in just over a year, the Grand Hôtel du Louvre opened its doors on October 15, 1855. Boasting five floors, each divided into three "districts" (Palais-Royal, Rivoli and Saint-Honoré) built around three courtyards, and fitted with gas lighting, a ventilation system, and a telegraph room, the hotel was a showcase for France's industrial and technological prowess during the Second Empire. It offered its guests numerous leisure facilities: cafés, game rooms, function rooms, and reading rooms.

THE GRANDS MAGASINS DU LOUVRE, 1887–1974

From the time of its inauguration, the Grand Hôtel du Louvre housed the shops of the Galeries du Louvre on the ground floor and mezzanine. These commercial spaces were first renamed "Au Louvre," altered in 1863 to "Grands Magasins du Louvre." In 1887, the building was entirely turned over to commerce and the Grand Hôtel moved to the other side of the Place du Palais-Royal. The Grands Magasins du Louvre offered a vast range of goods and organized "exhibitions" of new articles, toys, and fabrics. "Shopping" became an activity in its own right. Over almost the next hundred years, the building underwent restructuring and modernization: elevators and a small tramway were installed, entrances and internal spaces were reorganized—a fourth courtyard was notably added—and in 1899–1900 an underground passage leading to the metro was built.

THE LOUVRE DES ANTIQUAIRES, 1978–2019

In 1973, owing to financial difficulties suffered by its owner, the Société du Louvre, the building was sold, and a year later the Grands Magasins were permanently closed. Extensive renovation work was undertaken in 1975 to transform the building into the "Louvre des Antiquaires": the internal structure was almost entirely demolished, the external facades were glazed, and pyramid-shaped skylights installed. Only one of the four courtyards survived this redevelopment. The Louvre des Antiquaires opened in 1978 with more than 240 antique shops distributed across three floors, while the upper levels were rented out as business offices. Various art galleries also staged temporary exhibitions in the building. However, faced with declining foot traffic, in 2019 the Louvre des Antiquaires closed its doors.

THE FONDATION CARTIER POUR L'ART CONTEMPORAIN, 2025

In 2020, the Maison Cartier and the Société Foncière Lyonnaise, owner of the building since 1995, initiated new development work under the direction of Jean Nouvel for the purpose of accommodating the Fondation Cartier pour l'art contemporain. Covering a total area of 6,500 m^2 (basement, ground floor, and first floor), the fully modular structure gives the institution almost five times more space than it had at 261 Boulevard Raspail. The upper floors house offices, including those of the Fondation Cartier.

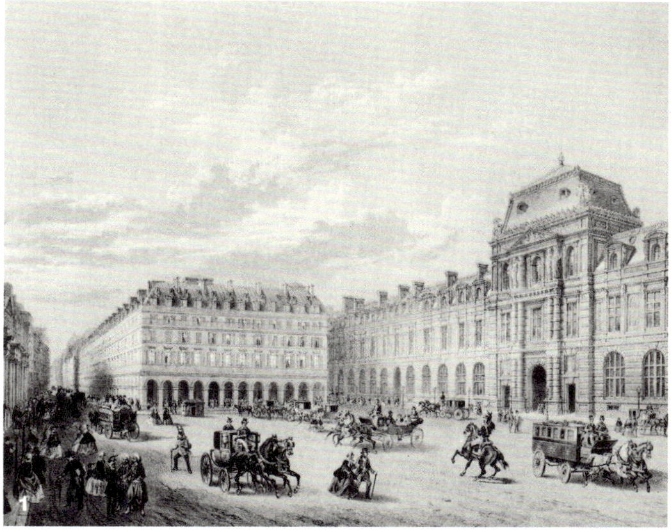
1

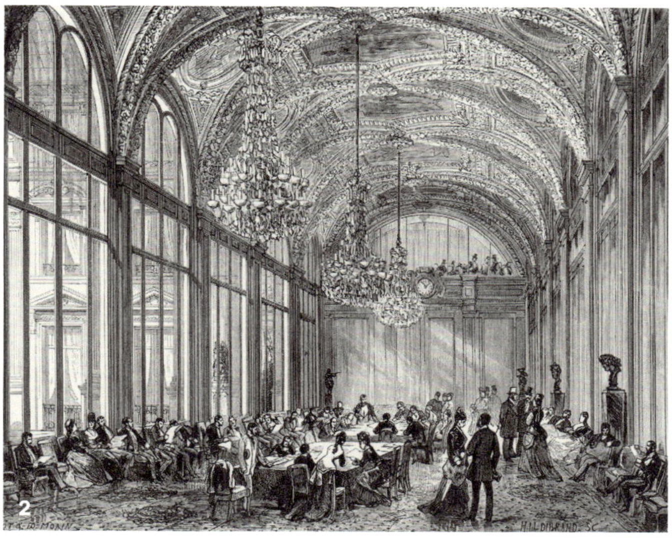
2

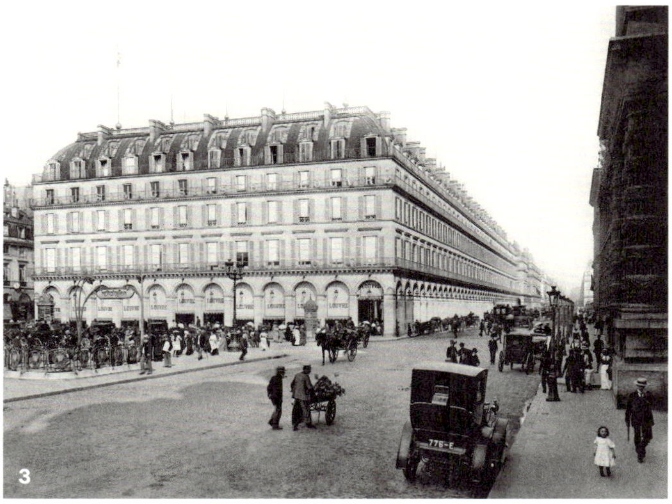
3

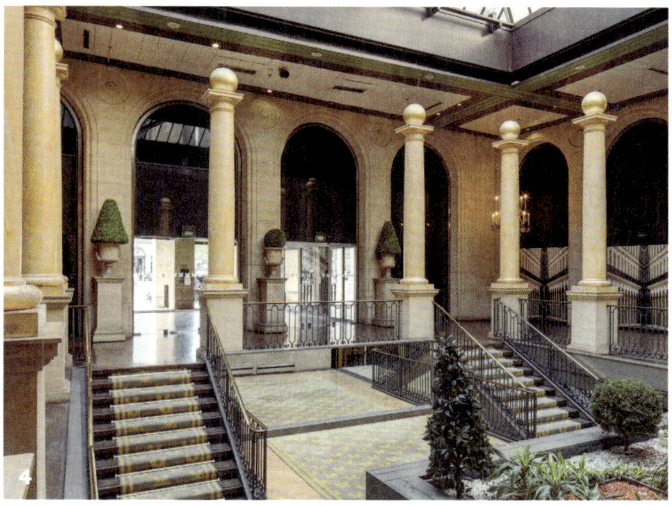
4

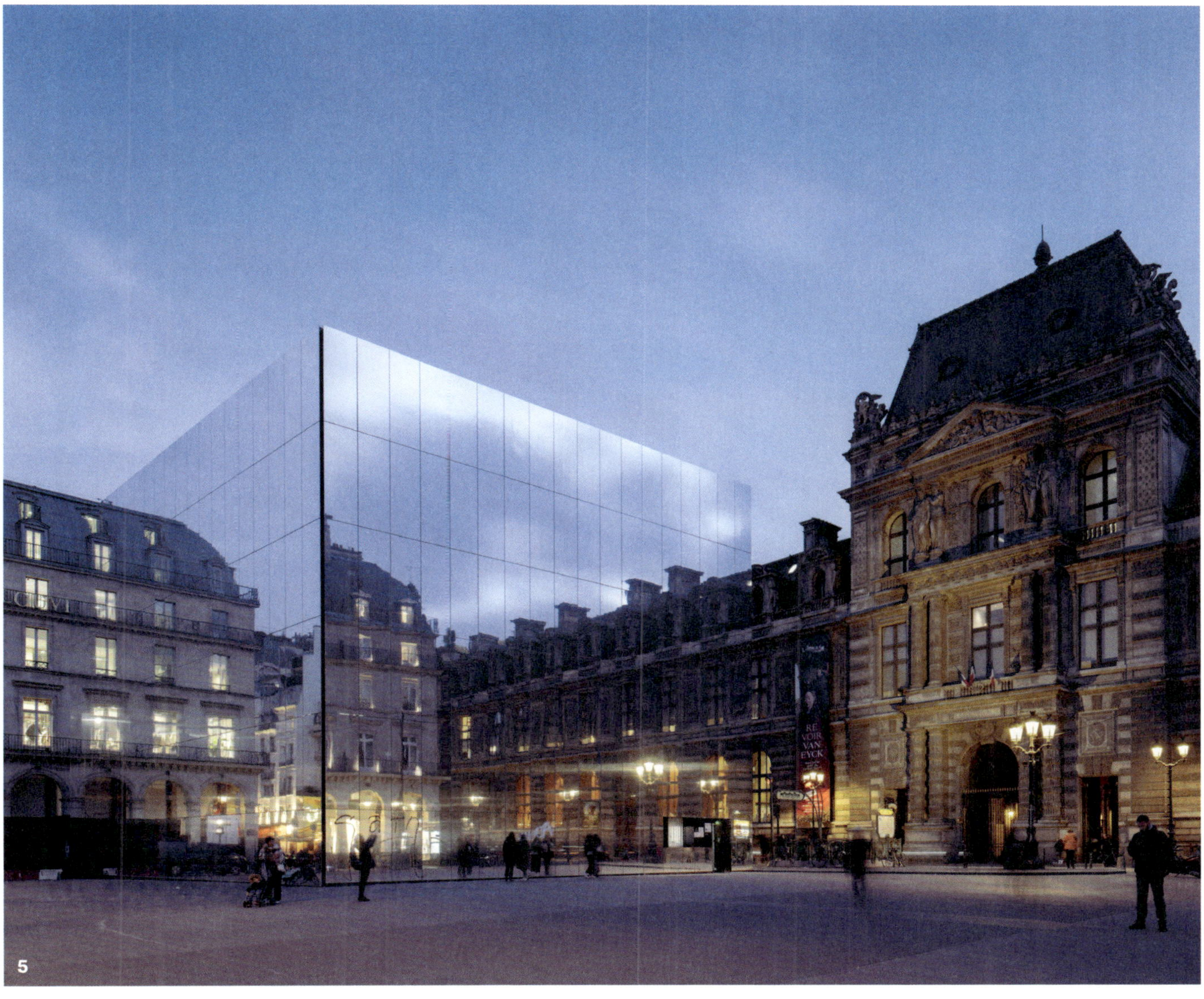
5

JEAN NOUVEL AND THE FONDATION CARTIER POUR L'ART CONTEMPORAIN

1. Unrealized project for the Fondation Cartier in Jouy-en-Josas, 1987

2. Production unit of the Maison Cartier in Saint-Imier, 1992

3. Fondation Cartier building, 261 Boulevard Raspail, 1994

4. Unrealized project for the Fondation Cartier on the Île Seguin, 2009

5. Unrealized extension of the Fondation Cartier on the site of the Hôpital Saint-Vincent-de-Paul, 2018

THE FONDATION CARTIER, JOUY-EN-JOSAS, 1986–1988

In 1984, the Fondation Cartier pour l'art contemporain was created by Alain Dominique Perrin, then the President of Cartier, and, following a suggestion from the artist César, set up its offices on the Montcel estate in Jouy-en-Josas. In 1986, Marie-Claude Beaud, the Fondation's first director, introduced Jean Nouvel to Alain Dominique Perrin. With the intention of enlarging the Fondation, Perrin commissioned the architect to design a building that would fit in with the landscape. Jean Nouvel envisioned a glass and steel L-shaped building to be sited on a hill on the grounds of the estate. Although the project did not receive planning permission from the authorities, it marked the start of the relationship between Jean Nouvel and the Fondation Cartier.

JEAN NOUVEL AND MAISON CARTIER, 1989–2006

While Alain Dominique Perrin searched for a site in Paris to accommodate the Fondation Cartier, he commissioned Jean Nouvel to design a production unit for the Maison Cartier, and between 1989 and 1992 the architect built a watch factory, production workshops, storage rooms, and offices in Saint-Imier, Switzerland, for the company. These were followed in 2006 by the headquarters of the Richemont Group in Bellevue, near Geneva.

THE FONDATION CARTIER, 261 BOULEVARD RASPAIL, PARIS, 1992–1994

Alain Dominique Perrin turned once again to Jean Nouvel when he identified the site of the former American Center, in the 14th arrondissement in Paris, as the new setting for the Fondation Cartier. Taking the site's history as his point of departure, the architect conceived a building all in glass, without internal walls, in which the sky and surrounding trees would be reflected and the boundary between interior and exterior would disappear. This "Parisian monument," as Alain Dominique Perrin described it, was inaugurated in 1994. Encircling Jean Nouvel's building, the *Theatrum Botanicum* designed by artist Lothar Baumgarten was a true garden-cum-theater in the heart of the city. Over the years, a dialogue emerged between Jean Nouvel, his building, and the artists and scenographers who designed exhibitions for the Fondation Cartier. In 1999, Jean Nouvel himself designed the solo exhibition of artist Gottfried Honegger. In 2008, the architect also curated and designed the retrospective exhibition held in honor of his friend César.

THE URBAN DEVELOPMENT PLAN FOR THE ÎLE SEGUIN, BOULOGNE-BILLANCOURT, 2009

In 2009, the Fondation Cartier and Jean Nouvel teamed up once again with a proposal for the urban development of the Île Seguin, to the west of Paris. To be sited on this huge industrial wasteland, the architect planned a complex of cultural, musical, and artistic facilities, as well as shops, offices, and hotels. Included in his project were plans for a 5,000 m² concrete and glass structure to accommodate the Fondation Cartier at one end of the island. The project was not put into execution.

THE PROJECT FOR EXTENSION OF THE FONDATION CARTIER TOWARDS HÔPITAL SAINT-VINCENT-DE-PAUL, PARIS, 2018

In 2018, Jean Nouvel worked to expand the Fondation Cartier onto the site of the neighboring Hôpital Saint-Vincent-de-Paul, which had been closed for several years. He proposed to raise the height of an existing building and create additional exhibition spaces for the Fondation Cartier Collection, and to construct a screening room, a restaurant, offices, and a terrace overlooking Paris. This project did not advance beyond the planning stage.

THE FONDATION CARTIER, 2 PLACE DU PALAIS-ROYAL, PARIS, 2020–2025

In 2020, to provide future accommodation for the Fondation, Maison Cartier commenced major renovation work on an enormous Haussmannian building on the Place du Palais-Royal, between the Rue de Rivoli and the Rue Saint-Honoré. Jean Nouvel reconceived the whole of the building's interior, making natural light not only a central component of his architectural project, but also an integral element of the setting. The 6,500 m² of exhibition space, in combination with five large mobile platforms that can be positioned at different heights, offer this historic building multiple possible configurations. This exceptional project is the fruit of nearly forty years of dialogue between the Fondation Cartier and Jean Nouvel.

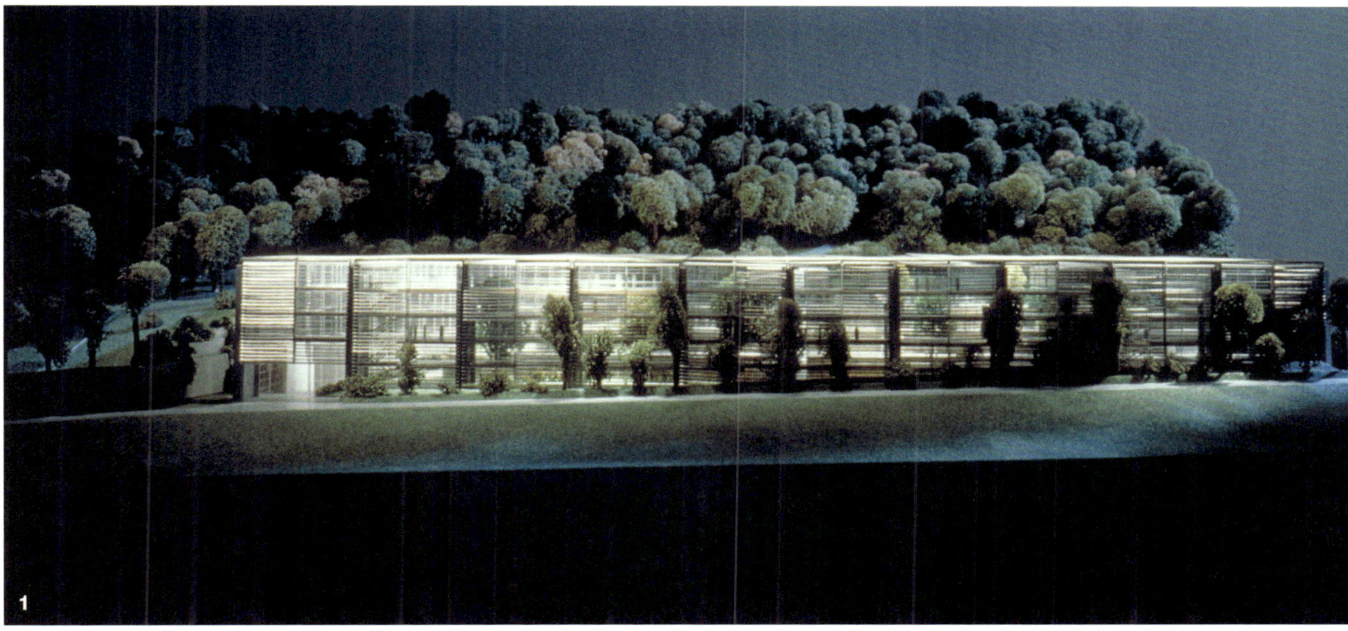
1

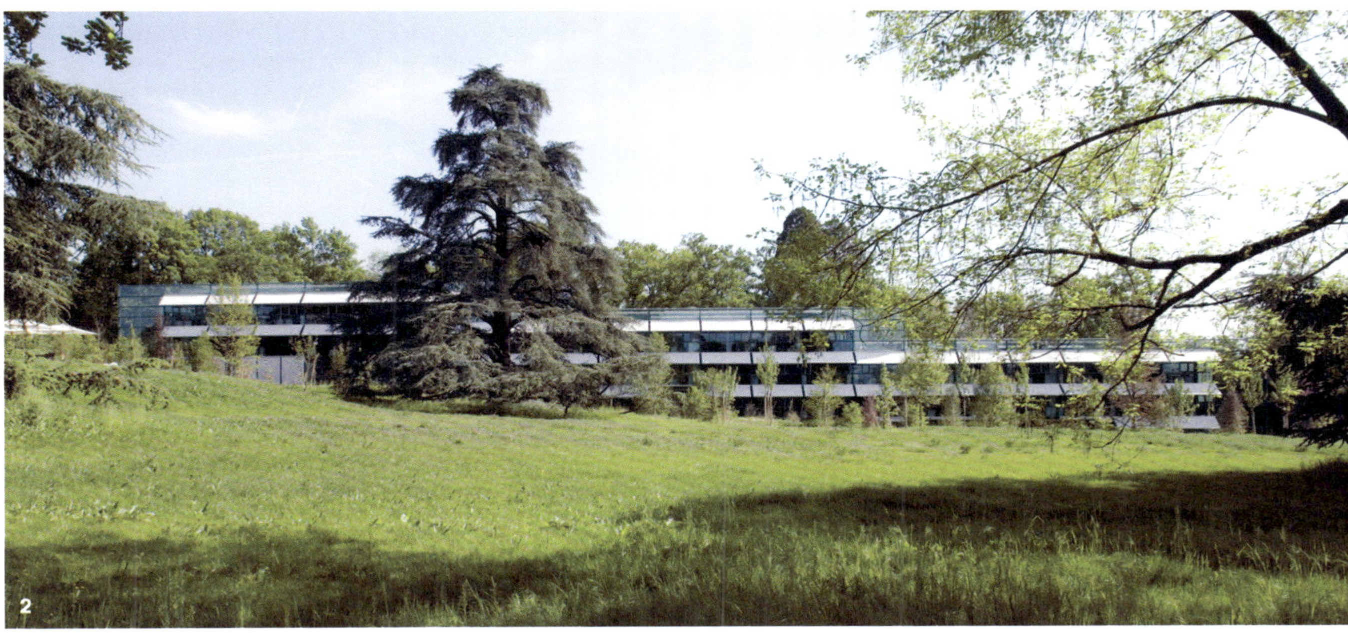
2

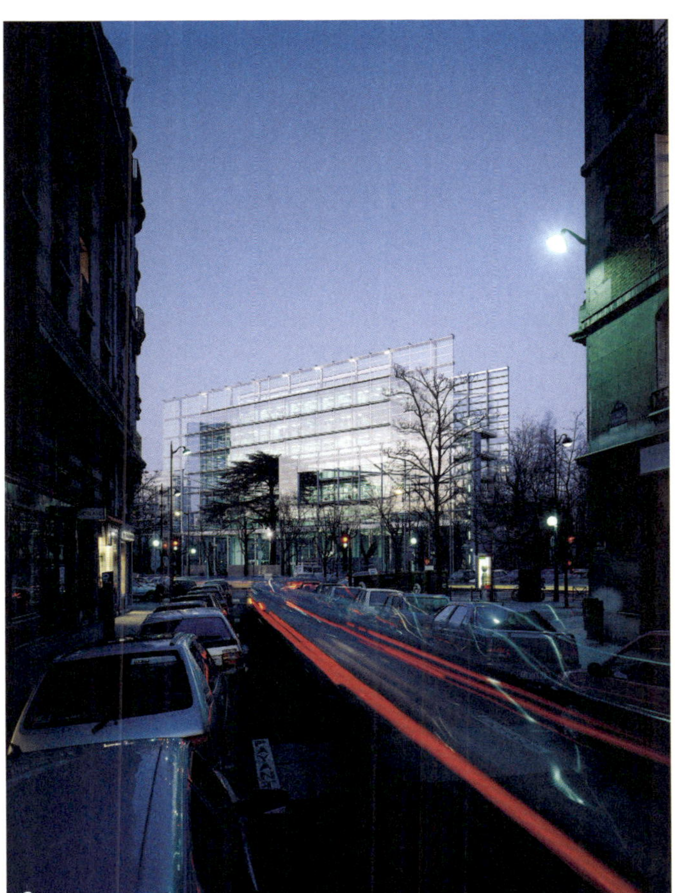
3

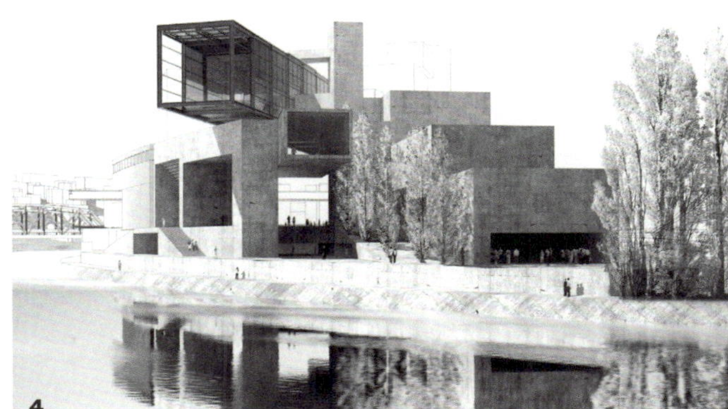
4

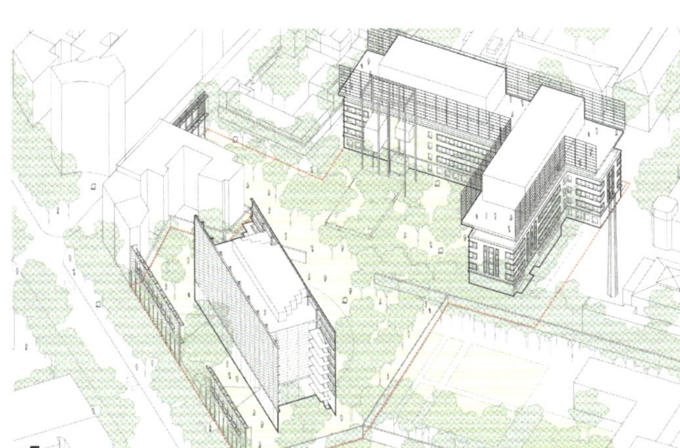
5

JEAN NOUVEL

Jean Nouvel was born in Fumel (France) in 1945. Following studies at the École supérieure des beaux-arts de Bordeaux, in 1966, he entered the École nationale supérieure des beaux-arts de Paris, graduating in 1971. His first job was as assistant to the architect Claude Parent. He then worked with the urbanist and essayist Paul Virilio before opening his own practice in 1970. A co-founder of the Mars 1976 movement, formed to fight corporatism among architects, he also participated in the creation of the labor union Syndicat de l'architecture. Scenographer for the Biennale de Paris since 1971, he founded its Architecture section, opening with the exhibition *À la recherche de l'urbanité : savoir faire la ville, savoir vivre la ville*, held at the Centre Georges Pompidou in 1980.

Jean Nouvel's approach to architecture—guided by context, history, and culture of the site—has brought him international renown. His first major project was the Institut du Monde Arabe on the left bank of the Seine in Paris, between 1981 and 1987. Since then, he has designed many architectural projects and cultural venues in Europe and around the world. In Paris he has designed the Fondation Cartier pour l'art contemporain Boulevard Raspail (1994), the Musée du quai Branly – Jacques Chirac (2006), the Philharmonie de Paris (2015), and more recently the Hekla Tower and Duo Towers (2022). The extension of the Museo Nacional Centro de Arte Reina Sofía in Madrid, the Torre Agbar in Barcelona (2005), the two vertical garden towers at One Central Park in Sydney (2014), the Louvre Abu Dhabi museum (2017), the National Museum of Qatar in Doha (2019), 53W53 Tour Verre next to the MoMA in New York (2019), and the Museum of Art Pudong in Shanghai (2021) are some of Jean Nouvel's international projects that have helped to stretch the boundaries of contemporary architecture. In late 2025, another project was inaugurated in Paris, the new spaces of the Fondation Cartier pour l'art contemporain at 2 Place du Palais-Royal.

Alongside his many architectural projects, Jean Nouvel has also taken part in the consultation process regarding Grand Paris (2008–09), in which, with the aid of French artists, designers, and intellectuals, he envisioned the transformation of the Paris metropolis and proposed how its transportation networks, among other elements, might evolve.

Jean Nouvel's work has received numerous accolades in France and internationally. In 1989 the Institut du Monde Arabe brought him the Aga Khan Award for Architectural Excellence, especially for "its role as a successful bridge between the French and Arab cultures." In 2000 he won the Golden Lion at the 7th Biennale di Architettura in Venice. The following year, he received three of the highest international distinctions: the Royal Gold Medal from the Royal Institute of British Architects (RIBA), the Praemium Imperiale from the Japanese Association of Fine Arts, and the Francesco Borromini Prize for the Lucerne Culture and Congress Center (KKL). He was awarded an *honoris causa* doctorate from the Royal College of Art in London in 2002. In 2006, in Frankfurt, he received the International High-Rise Award for the Torre Agbar in Barcelona, in recognition of "his exceptional contribution to the debate on buildings of great height," and two years later the prestigious Pritzker Prize.

Major Projects
Institut du Monde Arabe (Paris, 1987), Opéra de Lyon (1993), Fondation Cartier pour l'art contemporain (261 Boulevard Raspail, Paris, 1994), Galeries Lafayette (Berlin, 1996), Lucerne Culture and Congress Center – KKL (2000), Palais de justice de Nantes (2000), Dentsu Tower (Tokyo, 2002), Torre Agbar (Barcelona, 2005), extension of the Museo Nacional Centro de Arte Reina Sofía (Madrid, 2005), Musée du Quai Branly – Jacques Chirac (Paris, 2006), Guthrie Theater (Minneapolis, 2006), Richemont headquarters (Geneva, 2006), 40 Mercer building (New York, 2008), Danish Radio Concert Hall (Copenhagen, 2009), Ferrari factory (Maranello, 2009), One New Change (London, 2010), 100 11th Avenue building (New York, 2010), Sofitel Hotel (Vienna, 2010), Montpellier City hall (2011), Doha Tower (Doha, 2011), Renaissance Barcelona Fira Hotel (Barcelona, 2012), Fondation Imagine (Paris, 2014), One Central Park Towers (Sydney, 2014), Anderson 18 & Nouvel Ardmore Towers (Singapore, 2015), The White Walls Tower (Nicosia, 2015), Philharmonie de Paris (2015), Le Nouvel KLCC Towers (Kuala Lumpur, 2016), Louvre Abu Dhabi (2017), Fondazione Alda Fendi – Esperimenti (Rome, 2018), La Marseillaise Tower (Marseille, 2018), Stelios Ioannou Learning Resource Center – Cyprus University (Nicosia, 2018), Ycone Tower (Lyon, 2019), National Museum of Qatar (Doha, 2019), 53W53 including the MoMA galleries extension (New York, 2019), CEVA stations (Geneva, 2019), flagship store Dolce & Gabbana of Seoul (2021), Marc Ladreit de Lacharrière gallery of the Musée du Quai Branly (Paris, 2021), Henderson Cifi Tiandi – The Roof (Shanghai, 2021), Museum of Art Pudong – MAP (Shanghai, 2021), The Artists' Garden (Qingdao, 2021), Rosewood Tower and Hotel (Sao Paulo, 2022), Duo and Hekla Towers (Paris, 2022), Start Museum (Shanghai, 2022), facade and lobby of the Paris 2024 Samsung pop-up store, Paris 2024 Samsung pavilion, UBS headquarters (Monaco, 2024), Fondation Cartier pour l'art contemporain (2 Place du Palais-Royal, Paris, 2025)...

In Progress: Major Projects and Studies
Sharaan Desert Resort (Al-'Ula), Shenzhen Opera House, Tencent Tower (Guangzhou), La Querola d'Ordino accommodations (Andorra), humanization and extension projects of the Palais du Peuple (Paris) and William Booth residence (Marseille), Galeries Lafayette transformation (Berlin), environmentally friendly campus Ecotone Antibes (Sophia Antipolis), Aviation Academy (Singapore), residential project in Japan, The national Art Museum of China – NAMOC (Beijing)...

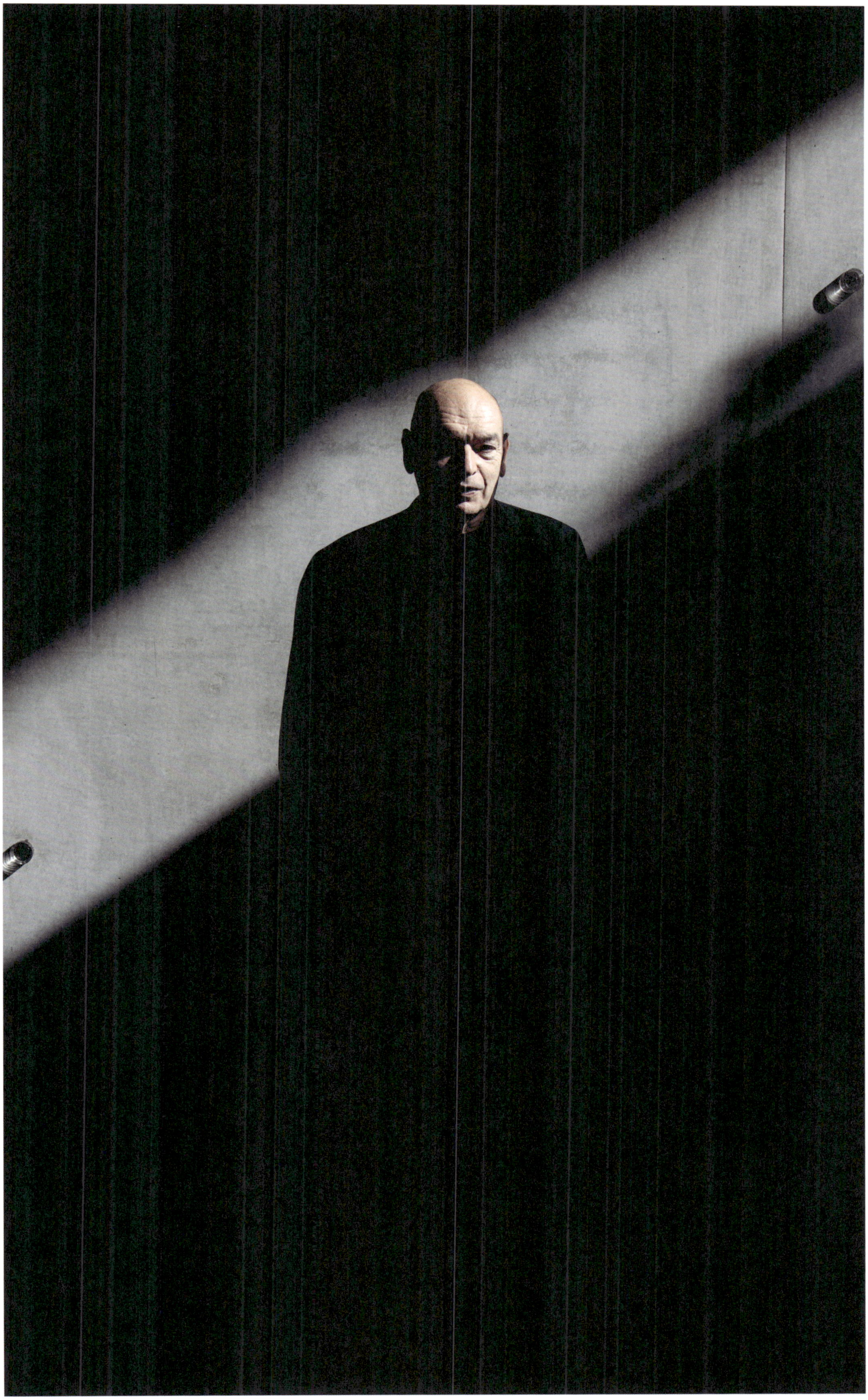

BIOGRAPHIES OF CONTRIBUTORS

MARTIN ARGYROGLO

Martin Argyroglo is an independent photographer specializing in the fields of architecture, art, and culture. After completing a program of literary studies, he attended the École des Gobelins in 2001, followed by the Beaux-Arts in Paris in 2003. It was during this period that he embarked on a career as a professional photographer, acting for seven years as assistant to Marc Riboud (1923–2016). Since 2008 he has worked on his own projects, participating in collective exhibitions in France and abroad as well as solo shows. In 2012, the École Nationale Supérieure d'Architecture de Paris-La Villette hosted his exhibition *La plaine est belle*. Between 2021 and 2025, Martin Argyroglo documented the different stages of the renovation project at 2 Place du Palais-Royal in Paris for the Fondation Cartier.

BEATRIZ COLOMINA

Beatriz Colomina is the Howard Crosby Butler Professor of the History of Architecture, the Director of Graduate Studies in the School of Architecture, and the founding director of the Interdisciplinary Media and Modernity program at Princeton University. She writes and curates on questions of design, art, sexuality, and media and her work has been translated in more than 25 languages.

Her books include *Sexuality and Space* (New York: Princeton Architectural Press, 1992), *Privacy and Publicity: Modern Architecture as Mass Media* and *Domesticity at War* (Cambridge: MIT Press, 1994 and 2007), *Clip/Stamp/Fold* (Barcelona: Actar Publishers, 2010), *Are We Human? Notes on an Archaeology of Design* and *X-Ray Architecture* (Zürich: Lars Müller Publishers, 2016 and 2019), as well *as Radical Pedagogies* (Cambridge: MIT Press, 2022).

Her exhibitions include *Clip/Stamp/Fold* at the Storefront for Art and Architecture gallery in New York in 2006, *Playboy Architecture* at NAiM / Bureau Europa in Maastricht in 2012, *Radical Pedagogies* at the 14th Venice Biennale of Architecture in 2014, and *Sick Architecture* at CIVA in Brussels in 2022.

In 2016 she was co-curator with Mark Wigley of the 3rd Istanbul Design Biennial. In 2018 the KTH Royal Institute of Technology in Stockholm made her Doctor Honoris Causa and in 2020 she was awarded the Ada Louise Huxtable Prize for her contributions to the field of architecture. She is currently curating with Mark Wigley the exhibition *We the Bacteria: Notes Toward Biotic Architecture* for the 2025 Milan Triennale.

CYRIL DESROCHE

A graduate architect from ENSA Paris-Malaquais, Cyril Desroche joined the Ateliers Jean Nouvel in March 2000. He participated in numerous projects during their phases of conception, study, and construction: the Nantes Law Courts, the Musée du Quai Branly – Jacques Chirac Museum in Paris, the Danish Radio Concert Hall in Copenhagen, the Le Havre Aquatic Complex, and Bucklersbury House in London, a 150,000 m² project directed by the Atelier Foster Nouvel, an agency that teamed Jean Nouvel and Norman Foster, created specifically for this project.

In 2005, Cyril Desroche left the Ateliers Jean Nouvel for California, where he joined Frank Gehry's studio. For six years, he worked principally on the development of the Louis Vuitton Foundation, and then on projects for the Luma Foundation in Arles and the Guggenheim Museum in Abu Dhabi. In 2011, he returned to the Ateliers Jean Nouvel and joined the team for the Paris Philharmonic Hall project. In 2015, he was appointed project director in the team for the creation of new exhibition spaces for the Fondation Cartier pour l'art contemporain in Paris.

Cyril Desroche is co-author, with Caroline Desroche, of the book *Los Angeles Standards*, a photographic portrait of the city through 15 typologies which identify the unique Los Angeles environment, postfaced by Frank Gehry (Arles: Poursuite, 2020).

MATHIEU FOREST

A graduate of the École d'Architecture de la Ville et des Territoires Paris-Est, Mathieu Forest joined the Ateliers Jean Nouvel in 1997. He has participated in numerous projects, such as the Zlaty Andel building in Prague, the Danish Radio Concert Hall in Copenhagen, the Archipel Theatre in Perpignan, the Nouvel KLCC in Kuala Lumpur, as well as various competitions, among them the redevelopment of the Halles district in Paris and the new Gazprom headquarters in St. Petersburg. From 2007 to 2015, he was project director for the construction of the Paris Philharmonic Hall, then for the preliminary studies and competition for the National Art Museum of China in Beijing and the Museum of Art Pudong in Shanghai. Since 2015, he has been the studio director in charge of the transformation of the Palais-Royal building for the Fondation Cartier pour l'art contemporain.

BÉATRICE GRENIER

Béatrice Grenier is Strategic and International Projects Director at the Fondation Cartier. In 2025, she curated an exhibition in Venice, presenting Jean Nouvel's architectural project for the Fondation Cartier on the Place du Palais-Royal in Paris, as part of the collateral program of the 19th Venice Architecture Biennale. She also curated, with Grazia Quaroni, *Exposition Générale,* the inaugural exhibition dedicated to the Collection of the Fondation Cartier in its new spaces. In 2024, she was a contributor to the Mondrian Initiative annual residence, where she and Emanuele Coccia co-curated "Metropolitan Nature: The New Modern," a series of conversations with international architects published in *e-flux architecture* (2025). Béatrice Grenier is currently collaborating with Professor Aziza Chaouni at the University of Toronto to research expanding heritage in the UNESCO world heritage city of Stone Town and Ng'ambo, Zanzibar, Tanzania.

Béatrice Grenier is the author of books and essays at the intersection of global contemporary architecture and art such as *Architecture for Culture: Rethinking Museums* and *Tashkent: A Modernist Capital* (New York: Rizzoli, 2025 and 2024); she directed *Infinite Memory* (ed.), the first monograph dedicated to the work of Caroline Poggi and Jonathan Vinel (Milan: Lenz Press / Paris: Fondation Cartier pour l'art contemporain, 2024). She is the Paris desk editor of *ArtAsiaPacific* and a regular contributor to contemporary art and architecture publications such as *Domus*, *Pin-Up*, and the *Journal of Curatorial Studies*. Béatrice Grenier was previously based in New York, where she worked with internationally acclaimed artist Cai Guo-Qiang to realize large-scale public art projects.

DANICA O. KUS

Danica O. Kus is an independent architecture and fine art photographer. Born in Slovenia, she received her education in photography at the RHoK Academy of Visual Arts in Brussels between 1999 and 2005. Her work focuses on photographing buildings, from modern museums to urban structures, in collaboration with architects, designers, and cultural institutions. Her photographs have been exhibited in solo and group exhibitions around the world and appear regularly in architecture and design publications. Her work has entered the collections of the Bibliothèque Nationale de France, the Museum of Fine Arts Houston, and the Musée Rodin, as well as private collections.

Danica O. Kus has received numerous awards, including a 2024 IPA International Photography Award (First Prize, Architecture/Industrial category); 2023 Architecture Photography MasterPrize Awards (Best of Best, Exterior Detail and Interior Detail categories), and first prize in the 2008 Vitra Belgium competition.

ANTOINE PICON

A graduate of the École Polytechnique and the École Nationale des Ponts et Chaussées, Antoine Picon is also an architect and a PhD in history. A historian of architecture, cities, and technologies, he is a professor at the Harvard Graduate School of Design. He was president of the Fondation Le Corbusier from 2013 to 2024.

Antoine Picon has published numerous articles and books on the history of engineering, utopian thought, architecture, and cities, among which are *Ornament: The Politics of Architecture and Subjectivity* (Hoboken: Wiley, 2013), *Smart Cities: A Spatialised Intelligence* (Chichester: John Wiley & Sons Ltd., 2015), *The Materiality of Architecture* (Minneapolis: University of Minnesota Press, 2021), and more recently, with Carlo Ratti, *Atlas of the Senseable City* (New Haven: Yale University Press, 2023). A focus of his studies is the relationship between architectural practice and scientific and technological developments. More recently, he has directed his attention to the impact of the digital revolution on architecture and the city, and the interactions between cities, nature, and technology.

Antoine Picon has been a member of the Académie des Technologies since 2010 and of the Académie d'Architecture since 2015. In 2014, he was named Chevalier des Arts et des Lettres, and since 2024 he has also been an honorary doctor of the Estonian Academy of Arts.

SELECTED BIBLIOGRAPHY

PUBLICATIONS ON JEAN NOUVEL

Jean Nouvel, *Mes convictions* (Paris: Flammarion, 2025)

"Jean Nouvel," in *Voir venir, venir voir* (Paris: Fondation Cartier pour l'art contemporain, 2024), pp. 97–104

Philip Jodidio, *Jean Nouvel by Jean Nouvel, 1981–2022* (Cologne: Taschen, 2022)

Jean Nouvel, in my head, in my eye... belonging..., exhibition catalog (Shanghai: Power Station of Art, 2019)

Olivier Boissière (ed.), with Jean Nouvel, *Louvre Abu Dhabi: The Story of Jean Nouvel's Architectural Project* (Abu Dhabi / Paris: Louvre Abu Dhabi / Skira, 2019)

GA Document, no. 145: *Jean Nouvel. Louvre Abu Dhabi*, February 2018

El croquis, no. 183: *Jean Nouvel, 2007–2016*, 2016

Odile Fillion (ed.), *Jean Nouvel : mes meubles d'architecte, sens et essence*, exhibition catalog (Paris: musée des Arts décoratifs / Flammarion, 2016)

Coloriages avec Jean Nouvel (Paris: Fondation Cartier pour l'art contemporain, 2014)

"Jean Nouvel and Hans Ulrich Obrist in Conversation," in *Thirty Years for Contemporary Art*, vol. 1 (Paris: Fondation Cartier pour l'art contemporain, 2014), pp. 101–122

Jean Nouvel: Recent Project (Tokyo: Ada Edita Global Architecture, 2014)

Philip Jodidio, *Nouvel, 1945: donneur de formes* (Cologne: Taschen, 2012)

Abitare, no. 518: Olivier Boissière, Maria Giulia Zunino and Mario Piazza (eds.), *Being Jean Nouvel*, December 2011 – January 2012

Ruth Peltason and Grace Ong-Yan (eds.), *Architect: The Pritzker Prize Laureates in Their Own Words* (London: Thames & Hudson, 2011)

Kathryn Rattee and Melissa Larner (eds.), *Red Summer in Kensington Gardens by Jean Nouvel*, exhibition catalog (London: Serpentine Gallery / Koenig Books, 2010)

Jean Nouvel, *Ce qui est là n'est pas ailleurs. Leçon inaugurale de l'École de Chaillot prononcée le 8 janvier 2008* (Cinisello Balsamo, Milan: Silvana Editoriale, 2009)

Jean Nouvel, Jean-Marie Duthilleul, and Michel Cantal-Dupart, *Naissances et renaissances de mille et un bonheurs parisiens* (Paris: Éditions du Mont-Boron, 2009)

Philip Jodidio, *Jean Nouvel by Jean Nouvel: Complete Works, 1970–2008* (Cologne: Taschen, 2008)

a+u: Architecture and Urbanism, special issue: *Jean Nouvel, 1987–2006*, April 2006

Jean Baudrillard and Jean Nouvel, *The Singular Objects of Architecture* (Minneapolis: University of Minnesota Press, 2005)

El croquis, no. 112–113: *Jean Nouvel, 1994–2002*, 2003

Jaume V. Aroca, "L'Art de la reconversion urbaine" in *L'Architecture d'aujourd'hui*, no. 337: Jean Nouvel, December 2001

Chantal Béret (ed.), *Jean Nouvel*, exhibition catalog (Paris: Centre Georges Pompidou, 2001)

Vincent Lasserre and Françoise Pannetier (eds.), *L'Inattendu muséal selon Jean Nouvel*, exhibition catalog (Bordeaux: Le Festin, 2001)

El croquis, no 65-66 (third edition): *Jean Nouvel, 1987–1998*, 1999

GA Document Extra, no 7: *Jean Nouvel* (1999)

Conway Lloyd Morgan, *Jean Nouvel: The Elements of Architecture* (New York: Universe, 1998)

Kenchiku Bunka, vol. 51, no. 597, 599 and 602: *The Unbuilt Jean Nouvel: 100 Projects*, 1996

Olivier Boissière, *Jean Nouvel* (Paris: Terrail, 1996)

Odile Fillion, *La Ville: six interviews d'architectes* (Paris: Centre Georges Pompidou / Le Moniteur, 1994)

Patrice Goulet, *Jean Nouvel* (Paris: Institut français d'architecture / Éditions du Regard, Paris 1994)

Hubert Tonka and Jeanne-Marie Sens, "*Le Bateau ivre" de Jean Nouvel: immeuble Cartier, 261, boulevard Raspail à Paris* (Paris: Sens & Tonka, 1994)

"Jean Nouvel: Teatro dell'Opera a Lione" in *Domus* 752, September 1993

Olivier Boissière (ed.), *Jean Nouvel: Jean Nouvel, Emmanuel Cattani and Associates* (Zurich: Artemis, 1992)

Georges Fessy, Jean Nouvel, and Hubert Tonka, *Institut du monde arabe : une architecture de Jean Nouvel, Gilbert Lézénès, Pierre Soria, Architecture Studio* (Seyssel: Champs Vallon, 1988)

Patrice Goulet, *Jean Nouvel*, exhibition catalog (Paris: Institut français d'architecture / Electa Moniteur, 1987)

Jean Nouvel, "L'avenir de l'architecture n'est plus architectural," in *Les Cahiers de la recherche architecturale*, no. 6–7: *Architecture 1980 : doctrines & incertitudes*, Paris, October 1980

PUBLICATIONS ON MUSEUM ARCHITECTURE AND DYNAMIC ARCHITECTURE

Béatrice Grenier, *Architecture for Culture: Rethinking Museums* (New York: Rizzoli, 2025)

Pippo Ciorra and Maddalena Scimemi (eds.), *Restless Architecture: Diller Scofidio + Renfro* (Florence: Forma, 2024)

Julian Rose, *Building Culture: Sixteen Architects on How Museums Are Shaping the Future of Art, Architecture, and Public Space* (New York: Princeton Architectural Press, 2024)

András Szántó, *Imagining the Future Museum: 21 Dialogues with Architects* (Berlin: Hatje Cantz, 2022)

Krzysztof Pomian, *Le Musée, une histoire mondiale*, three volumes (Paris: Gallimard, 2020–2022)

Dario and Libero Gamboni, *The Museum as Experience. An Email Odyssey through Artists' and Collectors' Museums* (Turnhout: Brepolis, 2020)

Lukas Feireiss (ed.), *Space is... The Place: Current Reflections on Art and Architecture* (Leipzig: Spector Books, 2020)

Antoine Picon, *The Materiality of Architecture* (Minneapolis: The University of Minnesota Press, 2020)

Penelope Curtis and Dirk van den Heuvel, *Art on Display: 1949–69* (Lisbon: Calouste Gulbenkian Museum, 2019)

Jean-Philippe Hugron, *Lafayette Anticipations. Fondation d'entreprise Galeries Lafayette / OMA* (Paris: Archibooks, 2019)

Catherine de Smet, *Le Corbusier penseur du musée* (Paris: Flammarion, 2019)

Guillaume Houzé, Rem Koolhaas, and François Quintin, *Neuf Plâtre. Un bâtiment d'OMA / Rem Koolhaas* (Paris: Lafayette Anticipations, 2018)

Martino Stierli, *Montage and the Metropolis: Architecture, Modernity, and the Representation of Space* (New Haven: Yale University Press, 2018)

Penny Harvey, Casper Bruun Jensen, and Atsuro Morita (eds.), *Infrastructure and Social Complexity: A Companion* (Abingdon, New York: Routledge, 2017)

Konstantinos Chatzis, Gilles Jeannot, Valérie November and Pascal Ughetto (eds.), *Les Métamorphoses des infrastructures, entre béton et numérique* (Brussels: Peter Lang, 2017).

Rem Koolhaas, *Études sur (ce qui s'appelait autrefois) la ville*, (Paris: Payot & Rivages, 2017)

Eva-Maria Troelenberg and Melania Savino (eds.), *Images of the Art Museum: Connecting Gaze and Discourse in the History of Museology* (Berlin / Boston: Walter de Gruyter GmbH, 2017)

Philip Ursprung, *Der Wert der Oberfläche: Essays zu Architektur, Kunst und Ökonomie* (Zurich: gta, 2017)

Chris Dercon and Nicholas Serota (eds.), *Tate Modern: Building a Museum for the 21st Century* (London: Tate Publishing, 2016)

Donatien Grau (ed.), *Jean Nouvel / Claude Parent : musées à venir* (Paris: Association Azzedine Alaïa; Arles: Actes Sud, 2016)

Giuliana Bruno, *Surface: Matters of Aesthetics, Materiality and Media* (Chicago: University of Chicago Press, 2014)

Hans Ulrich Obrist (ed.), *Lucius Burckhardt, Cedric Price. A stroll through a Fun Palace*, exhibition catalog (Zurich: Swiss Arts Council Pro Helvetia, 2014)

Regina Bittner and Wilfried Hackenbroich, *Architektur aus der Schuhbox. Baťas internationale Fabrikstädte* (Leipzig: Stiftung Bauhaus Dessau / Spector Books, 2012)

Pier Vittorio Aureli, *The Possibility of an Absolute Architecture* (Cambridge, MA: MIT Press, 2011)

Hal Foster, *The Art–Architecture Complex* (London / New York: Verso, 2011)

Béatrice Simonot, *La Maison du Peuple. Beaudouin, Lods, Prouvé, Bodianski. Un bijou mécanique* (Blou: Monografik, 2010)

Jacques Lucan, *Composition, non-composition. Architecture et théories, XIXe-XXe siècles* (Lausanne: Presses polytechniques et universitaires romandes, 2009)

Sigfried Giedion, *Space, Time and Architecture. The Growth of a New Tradition* (Cambridge, MA: Harvard University Press, 2009; first published 1941)

Wouter Davidts, *Bouwen voor de Kunst? Museumarchitectuur van Centre Pompidou tot Tate Modern* (Ghent: A&S Books, 2006)

Brian Hatton, *Cedric Price: Austrian Frederick Kiesler Prize for Architecture and the Arts 2002* (Vienna: Österreichische Friedrich und Lilian Kiesler – Privatstiftung, 2002)

John Elderfield (ed.), *Imagining the Future of the Museum of Modern Art* (New York: Museum of Modern Art, 1998)

Beatriz Colomina, *Privacy and Publicity: Modern Architecture as Mass Media* (Cambridge, MA: The MIT Press, 1996)

Sigfried Giedion, *Building in France, Building in Iron, Building in Ferroconcrete,* trans. J. Duncan Berry (Santa Monica: The Getty Center For The History Of Art, 1995; originally published in French, 1928)

Paul Virilio, *The Aesthetics of Disappearance* (New York: Semiotext(e), 1991)

S. Frederick Starr, *Melnikov: Solo Architect in a Mass Society* (Princeton: Princeton University Press, 1978)

Ada Louise Huxtable, "Architecture View," *New York Times*, December 25, 1977

Reyner Banham and John Partridge, "Pompidou cannot be perceived as anything but a monument," in *Architectural Review*, May 11, 1977

Reyner Banham, Paul Barker, Peter Hall and Cedric Price, “Non plan: an Experiment in Freedom,” in *New Society* no. 338, 20 March 1969

F. Kiesler, “Merchandise That Puts You on the Spot. Some Notes on Show Windows,” undated typescript, circa 1930, Österreichische Friedrich und Lilian Kiesler – Privatstiftung

Friedrich J. Kiesler, *Contemporary Art Applied to the Store and its Display* (New York: Brentano's, 1930)

PUBLICATIONS ON THE HISTORY OF THE BUILDING AND THE LOUVRE DISTRICT

Elvira Férault and Isabelle Marquette (eds.), *La Saga des Grands Magasins*, exhibition catalog (Paris: Cité de l'architecture et du patrimoine / Grand Palais – RMN Editions 2024)

Amélie Gastaut (ed.), *La Naissance des Grands Magasins, 1852-1925 : mode, design, jouets, publicité*, exhibition catalog (Paris: Musée des Arts Décoratifs, 2024)

Bernard Marrey, *Les Grands Magasins, des origines à 1939* (Saint-André-de-Roquepertuis: Le Linteau, 2018; originally published 1979)

Jan Whitaker, *The World of Department Stores* (London / New York: Vendome Press, 2011)

Cabinet Recherches & Études Appliquées, *Centre d'affaires Le Louvre / Louvre des Antiquaires: étude historique et architecturale (rapport)* (Société Foncière Lyonnaise: February 2008)

Walter Benjamin, *The Arcades Project* (Cambridge, MA / London: Belknap Press of Harvard University Press, 2002)

Michel Carrouges, *Les Machines célibataires* (Paris: Arcanes, 1954)

Georges d'Avenel, *Le Mécanisme de la vie moderne*, part 1, in “Les Grands Magasins,” in *Revue des deux mondes*, July 15, 1894

Alfred d'Aunay, *Le Louvre. Grand Hôtel et Grands Magasins* (Paris: Firmin-Didot and Cie, 1880)

G. Clerc, “Les Nouvelles Galeries des Grands Magasins du Louvre,” *Le Monde Illustré* supplement, October 4, 1879

Paul de Saint-Victor, “L'Hôtel du Louvre,” *La Presse*, October 15, 1855

THE STAKEHOLDERS OF THE ARCHITECTURAL PROJECT

FONDATION CARTIER POUR L'ART CONTEMPORAIN

Alain Dominique Perrin
President

Chris Dercon
Managing Director

Julie Auriol
Marketing and Digital Director

Veerle Dobbeleir
Collection Director

Isabelle Gaudefroy
Artistic Director

Béatrice Grenier
Strategic and International Projects Director

Bénédicte Jarosz
Strategy and Development Director

Adeline Pelletier
Heritage Director

Tanguy Pelletier
Public Progamming Director

Grazia Quaroni
Collection Director

Céline Riou
Human Resources Director

Lisa Seantier
Production Director

Naïa Sore
Image and External Relations Director

Caroline Valentin
Administrative and Financial Director

Project Team

Béatrice Grenier
Strategic and International Projects Director

Philippe Lê
Building Director

Cédric Alaphilippe
Safety and Security Director

Oscar Lecuyer
Chief of Staff

Lucie de Saint-Blanquat
Curator

Vanja Merhar
Bookstore Director

RICHEMONT

Johann Rupert
Chairman

Nicolas Bos
Group CEO

Richard Lepeu
Fondation Cartier Administrator

Didier Battiston
Richemont Senior Advisor

CARTIER

Louis Ferla
President and CEO

Cyrille Vigneron
Chairman Cartier Culture & Philanthropy

Arnaud Carrez
Senior Vice-President and Chief Marketing Officer

DELEGATED PROJECT OWNERSHIP

Cartier SA – Architecture and Construction

Yvan Ansermoz
Architecture and Construction Director

Thomas Brunet
Architecture and Construction Deputy Director

Arthur Lablanchy
Architecture and Construction Senior Manager

Benoit Pierrecy
Architecture and Construction Senior Manager

PROJECT MANAGEMENT

Jean Nouvel
Design Architect

Ateliers Jean Nouvel

Mathieu Forest
Studio Director

Cyril Desroche
Project Director

Architects
Luisa Alderighi, Nathalie Aouad, Lydie Bot, Anne-Sophie Bourdais, Aurélien Bru, Ilaria Cazzato, Fabrice Diakok, Karim Fattal, Gweltaz Keromnes, Louis Mounis, Julien Pasteau, Giulia Piana, Matthias Raasch, Jean-Marc Rio, Urszula Tyszkiewic, Clara Veci, Amaury Villien De Gabiole, Francesco Virgillito

Computer-Generated Images
Mitzu Kishi, Tanguy Nguyen, Ala Rassaa, Antoine Wendling

JIGEN Interactive Studio

Furnishings and Fittings
Jean Nouvel Design

Nina Bargoin, Martine Bedin, Félix Heger, Bastien Lafont, François Lafortune

STRUCTURAL AND FLUID ENGINEERING

SETEC Bâtiment

Daniel Abittan
Engineering Operations Manager

Vincent Baumann
Structural Engineer

David Gata
Plumbing Engineer

Michael Guin
Fluid Project Manager

Michel Plociennick
HVAC Engineer

Abdel Togou
ELV/HV/Security Engineer

Thomas Gallina
ELV/HV/Security Engineer

Mechanical Engineering
SETEC – ISM

Philippe Lecomte
Expert Engineer,
Project Manager

Evin Johannes
Expert Engineer

Scenic Engineering
Ducks Scéno

Clément Dréano
Project Leader

Kevin Larcade
Project Manager

Cyril Benhaim
Project Manager

Lighting Engineering
L'Observatoire International

Hervé Descottes
Principal

Acoustic Engineering
AVEL Acoustique

Cost Planning and Construction Management Support
BMF

Renaud Chanceaulme
Construction Management Support Managing Director

Jérôme Guillerm
Cost Planner

Cécile Muninger
Cost Planning Project Manager

Juliette Barach
Cost Planning Project Manager

Renaud Farrenq
Construction Management Support

Alexandre Masson
Construction Management Support

FQR

David Faugere
Construction Management Support

FIRE PROTECTION

Fire Safety Officer and Fire Safety Systems Coordinator
BATISS

Quentin Coutureau
Fire Safety Systems Coordinator

Romain Kolodjiej
Safety Commission Coordinator

Nathalie de Villers
Safety Officer

Fire Engineering
CERIB

Fabienne Robert
Director

Christian Labetoulle
Department Manager

Lafdal Bouaza
Research and Development Engineer

Smoke Extraction Engineering
LISI

Elizabeth Blanchard
Director

Ugo Mattei
Project Manager Engineer

BET FAÇADES

TESS

Tom Gray
Associate Director

Riccardo Vanigli
Facade Engineer

TECHNICAL INSPECTION SERVICES

BTP Consultants

Rony Chebib
Managing Director

Farah Badreddine
Agency Director

Alexis Arra
Technical Inspection Group Manager

Bureau Veritas

Gérard Klyss
Consultant

Laetitia Atlan
Operations Manager

TECHNICAL CONSULTANTS

BET Cuisine

Rémi Philippe
Technical and Design Manager

OPC - Setec Opency

Olivier Delle Castelle
Deputy Managing Director

Commissioning Engineer

Cédric Faux
Technical Installations Commissioning Engineer

ARCHITECTURAL PROGRAMMING

Chiara Alessio
Architectural Programmer

GRAPHIC DESIGN AND SIGNAGE

deValence

Alexandre Dimos
Associate Graphic Designer

Ghislain Triboulet
Associate Graphic Designer

Clément Frassi
Graphic Designer

Locomotion

Laurence Guichard
Founder

ENVIRONMENTAL CONSULTANTS

Le Sommer Environnement

Michel Le Sommer
Agency Director

Stefania Barberio
Project Manager

Yousfi Driss
Project Manager

HISTORICAL CONSULTANT

Grahal (Groupe de recherche Art Histoire Architecture Littérature)

Michel Borjon
President and Founder

LEGAL AND INSURANCE SERVICES

Cabinet Racine

Nicolas Boytchev
Partner

Philippe Johnston
Lawyer

Gras Savoye

Claude Noel
Construction Director

Sihem Bissad
Project Manager

Cartier SA / Richemont

Canelle Axus
Intellectual Property Counsel

Simon Coutaz
Risk and Compliance Manager

Jacqueline Ronconi
Chief Legal Counsel

Alexandre Calcat
Group Physical Security Associate Director

Magdalena Matusiak
Head of Group Insurance and Risk

Sophie Geliot
Insurance Manager

LESSOR

SFL
(Société Foncière Lyonnaise)

Aude Grant
Chief Executive Officer

Dimitri Boulte
Chief Executive Officer
(through October 2024)

Éric Oudard
Technical and Development Director

Pierre-Yves Bonnaud
Asset Manager and Client Manager

Emilie Germane
Legal Director

DELEGATED PROJECT OWNERSHIP

VINCI Immobilier

Marie-Laure Recard
Project Director

Flora Gladin
Deputy Project Director

Gary Atlan
Program Manager

LESSOR'S PROJECT MANAGEMENT

B. Architecture, AJN, AIA, ARTELIA, TERRELL, BATISS, SOCOTEC, AE75, TESS, Green Affair, LASA

PROJECT MANAGEMENT ASSISTANCE

Ma

Justine Culioli
Founder

Nicolas Hector
Project Director

GENERAL CONTRACTOR AND GROUP MEMBERS

PETIT
branch of **VINCI Construction**
Group Representative

Cyrille Giboux
Deputy Director

Julien Ischer
Operations Director

Zakaria Zerrouki
Project Director

SMB-TAMBE
Group Member

Metal Structures, Mechanisms, and Mobile Platforms

SUBCONTRACTORS

Tunzini, Uxello, LPP, IDFP, Transversal-Granito, Micholet, Metalesca, Somen, Framatec, Master Industrie, Pasquinelli SAS, Cyb Stores, Uni-marbres, Gesop, Shaw, Bellapart, AEEN, Ineo, Saga Tertiaire, Otis, Parquetsol, Bonnardel, Les Marbreries de la Seine, Sofrastyl, SETCR

Our thanks to the elected officials of the City of Paris and to the departments responsible for reviewing the project, as well as the Direction régionale des affaires culturelles, the Paris Police Prefecture, and the regional prefecture of Île-de-France and Paris.

PUBLICATION

Graphic Design

Undo-Redo, Paris

Editorial Team

Adeline Pelletier
Heritage Director

Cécile Provost
Publishing Department Manager

Bérengère Gouttefarde
Editor

Roxane Paillou
Editorial Assistant

Translation
Monique Gross
(text by Mathieu Forest
and Cyril Desroche)

Emma Lingwood
(Foreword)

Timothy Stroud
(texts by Jean Nouvel
and Antoine Picon)

Copyediting and Proofreading
Phoebe Green

Production
Camille Desproges
Actes Sud, Arles

Photoengraving
Clément Regard
Les Artisans du Regard, Paris

The editorial team would like
to thank:

Charlotte Kruk
Personal Assistant to Jean Nouvel

Béatrice Grenier
Strategic and International
Projects Director, Fondation Cartier
pour l'art contemporain

Lucie de Saint-Blanquat
Curator, Fondation Cartier
pour l'art contemporain

Pierre-Édouard Couton
Studio PE

Yvan Ansermoz
Director, Cartier Architecture
and Construction

Thomas Brunet
Deputy Director, Cartier
Architecture and Construction

CREDITS

Unless otherwise stated, plans, sections, blueprints, and models of the interior spaces designed by Jean Nouvel for the building 2 Place du Palais-Royal were produced by © Ateliers Jean Nouvel

For all the spaces of the Fondation Cartier pour l'art contemporain: © Jean Nouvel

Cover, opening and closing pages (except first image), pp. **16**, **36**, **85**, **91**, **94**, **97**, **99**, **101**, **116** (top), **118**, **120**, **138**, and from **139** to **180**: © Martin Argyroglo
From pp. **37** to **78**, **92**, **95**, and **137**: © Danica O. Kus
Closing pages: © Cédric Corroy – Lumento (first image, retouched)
Back cover: © Luc Boegly

Interior pages:
pp. **10–11**: © Ateliers Jean Nouvel, © Dominique Ehrhard
pp. **14–15**: © Luc Boegly
p. **18** (top): SFL Collection, Société Foncière Lyonnaise, owner of the building complex, photo © SUMMUM 3D / Benoit Touchard
p. **18** (bottom): Courtesy of Brown University Library
pp. **19** (top), **23**, **25**, **28**, **102**, and **183** (top, right): Alfred d'Aunay, *Le Louvre, Grand Hôtel et Grands Magasins* (Paris: Firmin-Didot et Cie, 1880)
p. **19** (bottom): Library of Congress, Prints & Photographs Division, LC-DIG-pga-14316 (digital file from original print)
pp. **20–21**: CC0 Paris Musées / Musée Carnavalet – Histoire de Paris
p. **22**: Bibliothèque nationale de France
p. **24** (top): Bibliothèque historique de la Ville de Paris / Ville de Paris
p. **24** (bottom): © F. Harand / Musée Carnavalet / Roger-Viollet
p. **26**: Bibliothèque nationale de France
p. **27**: Universal Images Group / via Getty Images
p. **29** (top): © Renzo Piano, Adagp, Paris, 2025; Piano & Rogers Architects Fonds; Archives and Museum Activities Unit, Politecnico di Milano, ACL
p. **29** (bottom): Fonds Cedric Price, Collection Centre Canadien d'Architecture, © CCA
p. **30**: © Jean Prouvé, Adagp, Paris, 2025; © All rights reserved; © Vladimir Bodiansky; Eugène Beaudouin, Adagp, Paris, 2025; © Centre Pompidou, MNAM-CCI Bibliothèque Kandinsky, Dist. GrandPalaisRmn / Fonds Prouvé
p. **31**: © Mary Evans / Grenville Collins / Postcard Collection / Bridgeman Images
p. **33** (top): © Jean Nouvel, Emmanuel Cattani & Associés, photo © Centre Pompidou, MNAM-CCI, Dist. GrandPalaisRmn / Philippe Migeat | Christian Bahier
p. **35**: © 2025 Austrian Frederick and Lillian Kiesler Private Foundation, Vienna
p. **80**: CC0 Paris Musées / Musée Carnavalet – Histoire de Paris
p. **81** (top): Bibliothèque nationale de France
p. **81** (center): CC0 Paris Musées / Musée Carnavalet – Histoire de Paris
p. **81** (center): SFL documentation, Archiveco 500/126
pp. **82–83**: Bibliothèque nationale de France
p. **84**: Museo Nazionale della Scienza e della Tecnologia "Leonardo Da Vinci," Milan, Italy © Icas94 / © NPL – DeA Picture Library / Bridgeman Images
p. **87** (top): SFL documentation, Basement archives
p. **88**: © Bibliothèque Mazarine
p. **89** (top): The Metropolitan Museum of Art, New York, The Elisha Whittelsey Collection, The Elisha Whittelsey Fund, 1951
p. **89** (bottom): © Bibliothèque Mazarine
p. **93**: © Thomas Salva – Lumento
pp. **96** and **98**: *Les Grands Magasins du Louvre - Les plus beaux et les plus vastes du monde*
p. **100**: CC0 Paris Musées / Musée Carnavalet – Histoire de Paris
pp. **104** and **107** (top): All rights reserved
p. **105**: © Google Earth
p. **121**: © Ateliers Jean Nouvel. Local architect: b720 - Fermin Vazquez, photo © Manuel Cohen
pp. **122** and **123** (top): © Jean Nouvel & Associés (Jean Nouvel and Emmanuel Blamont), photo © Georges Fessy
p. **123** (bottom): © Jean Nouvel, Gilbert Lézénès, Dominique Lyon, photo © GRRRANIT SN
p. **124**: © Gordon Matta-Clark, Adagp, Paris, 2025; Whitney Museum of American Art, New York; gift of Harold Berg; Digital image Whitney Museum of American Art / Licensed by Scala
p. **125** (top): photograph from the John Rounds Collection, part of the American Center archives deposited at IMEC by Nelcya Delanoë upon completion of her book *Le raspail vert, l'American Center à Paris, 1934-1994* (Paris: Seghers, 1994). This photograph is featured on page 41. American Center Archives / IMEC
pp. **125** (bottom), **126** (top), and **127** (top): © Jean Nouvel, Emmanuel Cattani & Associés, photo © Luc Boegly
pp. **126** (bottom) and **129** (bottom): © Jean Nouvel, Emmanuel Cattani & Associés, photo © Martin Argyroglo
p. **127** (bottom): © Jean Nouvel, Emmanuel Cattani & Associés, © JUNYA.ISHIGAMI+ASSOCIATES, photo © Axel Dahl
p. **128** (top): © Ateliers Jean Nouvel, photo © Philippe Ruault
p. **128** (bottom): © Ateliers Jean Nouvel, photo © imageBROKER.com / Alamy Stock Photo
p. **129** (top): © Ateliers Jean Nouvel, photo © Roland Halbe
p. **132** (top): © Jean Nouvel (representative), Gilbert Lézénès, Pierre Soria, Architecture Studio, photo All rights reserved
pp. **132** (bottom) and **133**: © Jean Nouvel (representative), Gilbert Lézénès, Pierre Soria, Architecture Studio, photo © Georges Fessy
p. **135**: Ph.Guignard / Air-Images
p. **136** (top): © Ateliers Jean Nouvel, photo © Danica O. Kus
p. **136** (bottom): © Ateliers Jean Nouvel, photo © Roland Halbe
p. **183** (top, left): © Roger-Viollet
p. **183** (center, left): © Neurdein / Roger-Viollet
p. **183** (center, right): © Yves André
p. **183** (bottom): © Ateliers Jean Nouvel, photo © Martin Argyroglo
p. **185** (top): © Jean Nouvel, Emmanuel Cattani & Associés, photo All rights reserved
p. **185** (center): © Ateliers Jean Nouvel. Associated architect: Eric Maria, photo © Yves André
p. **185** (bottom, left): © Jean Nouvel, Emmanuel Cattani & Associés, photo © Philippe Ruault
p. **185** (bottom, right): © Ateliers Jean Nouvel
p. **187**: © Gérard Julien / AFP

This book was published by
Fondation Cartier pour l'art contemporain
2, Place du Palais-Royal
75001 Paris
fondationcartier.com

ISBN 978-2-86925-194-6

Distributed in the USA and Canada by
ARTBOOK | D.A.P.
75 Broad Street, Suite 630,
New York, NY 10004, USA
www.artbook.com

Distributed in all other countries by
Thames & Hudson Ltd
6–24 Britannia Street
London WC1X 9JD
United Kingdom
www.thamesandhudson.com

Printed and bound in July 2025 by EBS,
Verona, Italy.

Legal deposit: October 2025
First edition

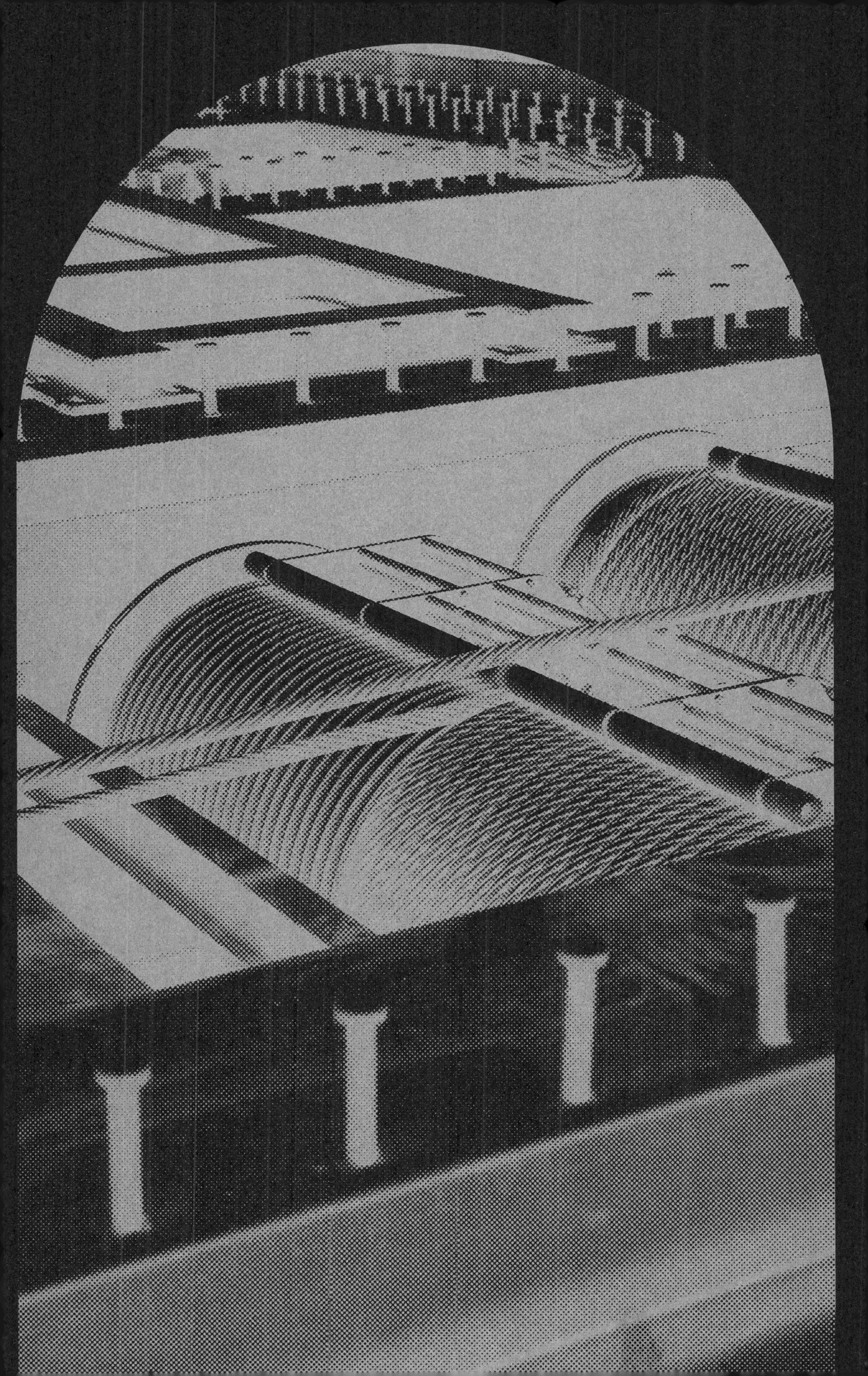

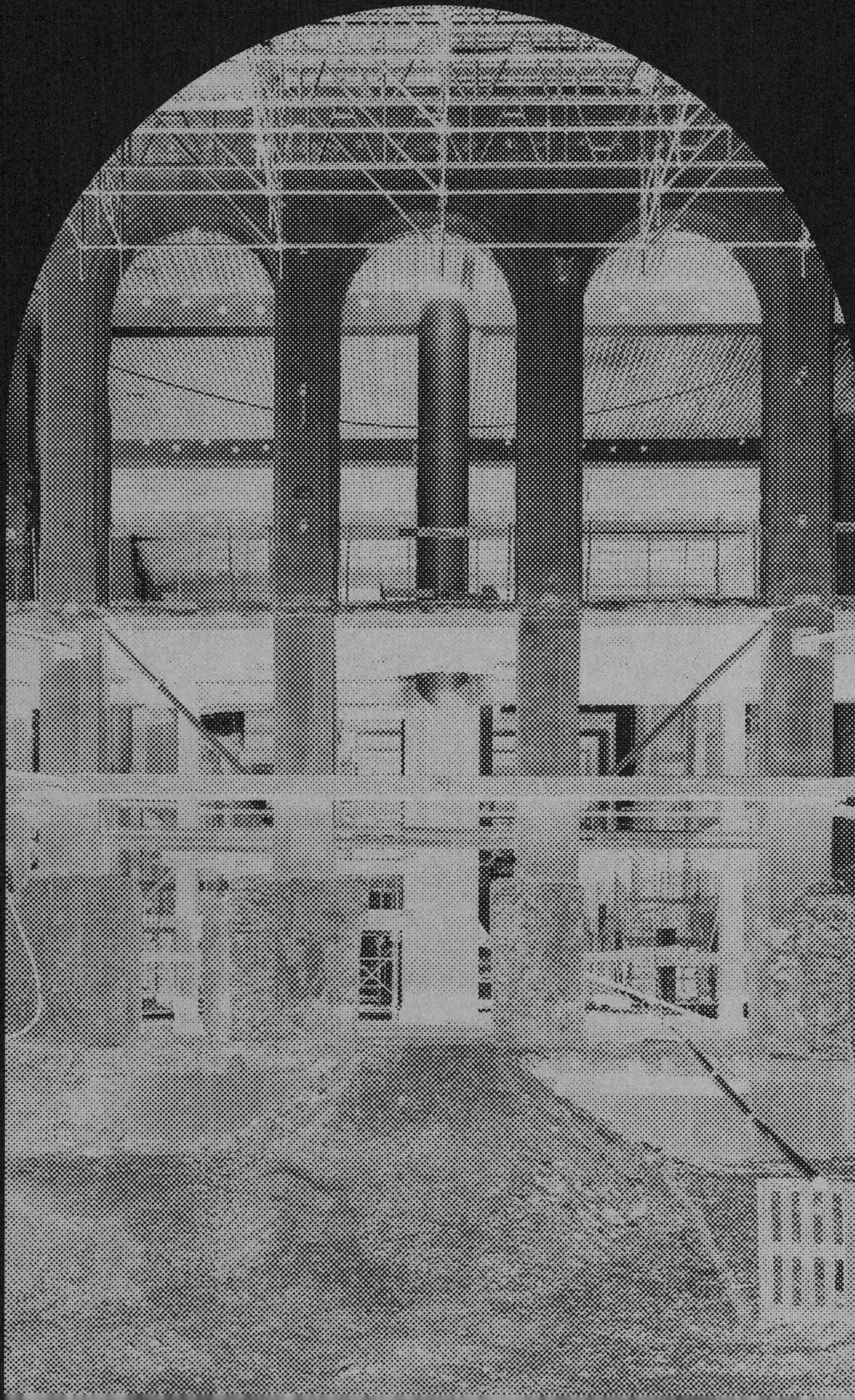

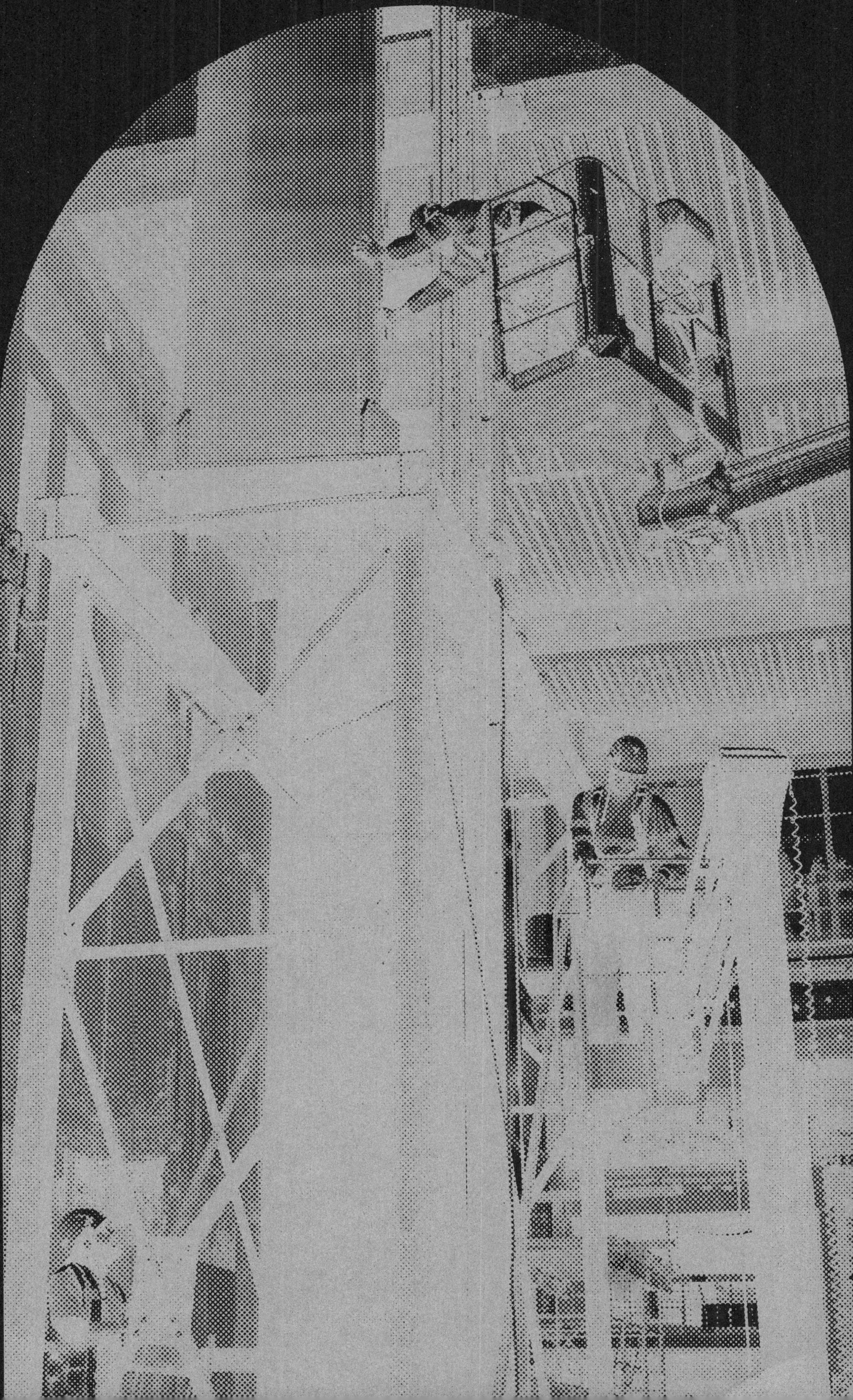

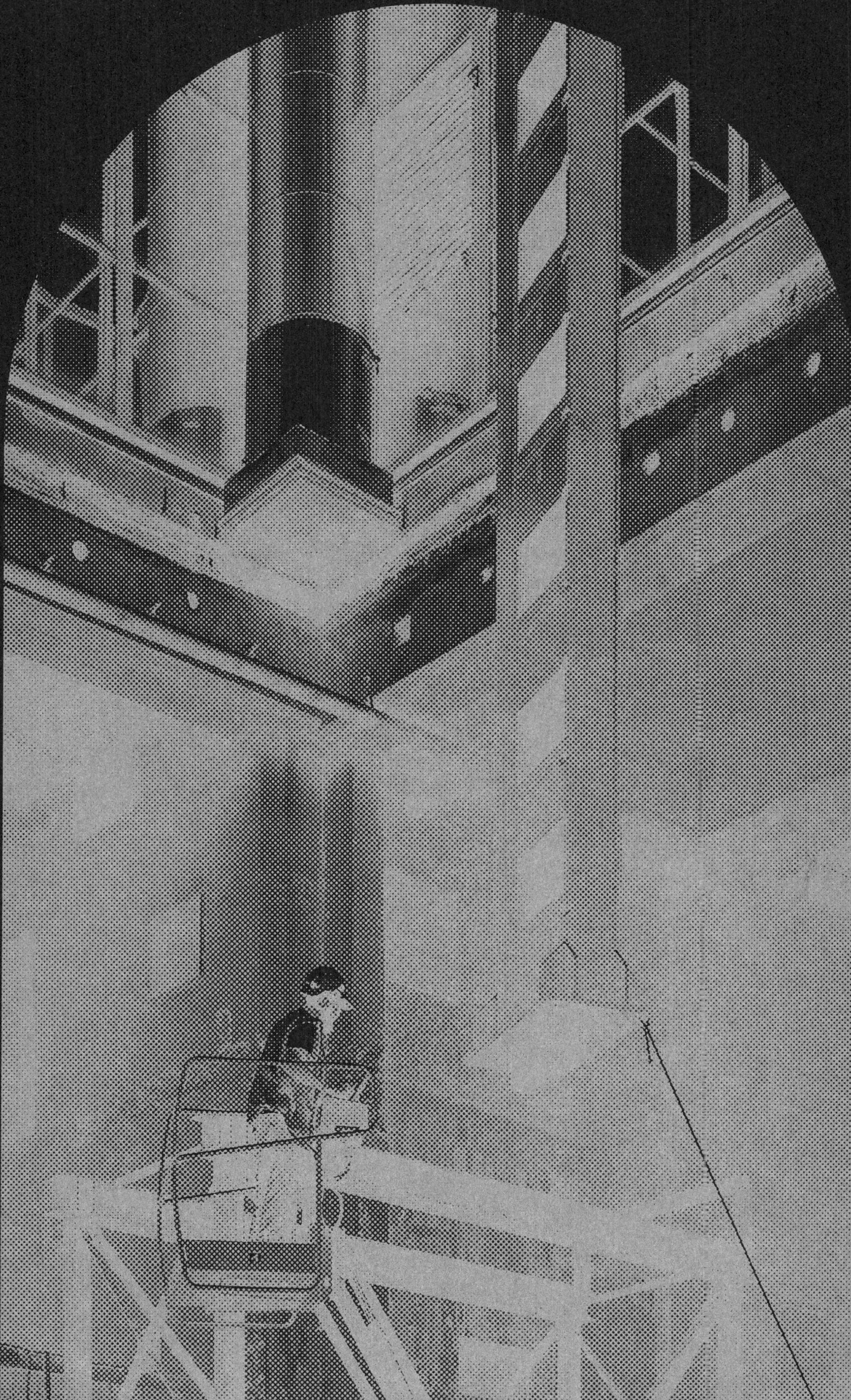